Sustainability, Green Management, and Performance of SMEs

Sustainability, Green Management, and Performance of SMEs

Edited by
Kiran Mehta and Renuka Sharma

DE GRUYTER

ISBN 978-3-11-116932-3
e-ISBN (PDF) 978-3-11-117002-2
e-ISBN (EPUB) 978-3-11-117012-1

Library of Congress Control Number: 2023948084

Bibliographic information published by the Deutsche Nationalbibliothek
The Deutsche Nationalbibliothek lists this publication in the Deutsche Nationalbibliografie; detailed bibliographic data are available on the internet at http://dnb.dnb.de.

Cover image: Sakorn Sukkasemsakorn/iStock/Getty Images Plus
Typesetting: Integra Software Services Pvt. Ltd.
Printing and binding: CPI books GmbH, Leck

www.degruyter.com

Preface

Sustainability, Green Management, and Performance of SMEs is a comprehensive book that explores the critical role of small and medium-sized enterprises (SMEs) in achieving sustainable development. In a world facing pressing environmental challenges and socio-economic inequalities, SMEs have the potential to drive positive change by integrating sustainability principles into their business practices. This book examines the relationship between sustainability, green management, and the performance of SMEs, providing valuable insights, practical strategies, and real-world case studies to inspire and guide SMEs towards a more sustainable future.

The book outlines a strong theoretical foundation, outlining the concept of sustainability and its relevance to SMEs. It explores the environmental, social, and economic dimensions of sustainability, highlighting the need for SMEs to adopt green management practices to mitigate environmental impacts, enhance social well-being, and achieve long-term economic viability.

Drawing from an extensive body of research, the book presents a comprehensive analysis of the various drivers, barriers, and motivations influencing SMEs' adoption of sustainability practices. It examines the internal and external factors that shape their decision-making processes and explores the role of stakeholders, including employees, customers, suppliers, and government agencies, in promoting sustainable business practices.

Central to the book's framework is the exploration of green management strategies and tools that enable SMEs to embed sustainability into their operations. It provides practical guidance on areas such as energy efficiency, waste reduction, sustainable supply chain management, eco-design, and responsible marketing. The book emphasizes the potential benefits of implementing these strategies, including cost savings, improved competitiveness, enhanced reputation, and access to new markets.

Furthermore, the book delves into the link between sustainability and the financial performance of SMEs. It investigates the business case for sustainability, demonstrating how environmentally and socially responsible practices can positively impact profitability, return on investment, and overall financial performance. The authors present empirical evidence and case studies that illustrate successful examples of SMEs integrating sustainability into their core business strategies and reaping financial rewards.

Recognizing the dynamic nature of the business landscape, the book also addresses the challenges SMEs face when pursuing sustainability goals. It explores resource constraints, lack of awareness, regulatory complexities, and resistance to change. Moreover, it provides practical recommendations and insights on how SMEs can overcome these challenges, offering guidance on building internal capabilities, fostering organizational learning, and leveraging external support networks.

Looking towards the future, the book examines emerging trends and opportunities for SMEs in the realm of sustainability. It explores the potential of digital technol-

https://doi.org/10.1515/9783111170022-202

ogies, circular economy approaches, clean energy transitions, and social innovation in enabling SMEs to further advance their sustainability efforts. The authors also discuss the importance of collaboration, partnerships, and knowledge sharing among SMEs, academia, and government agencies in fostering innovation and scaling up sustainable practices.

In conclusion, *Sustainability, Green Management, and Performance of SMEs* offers a comprehensive and practical guide for SMEs seeking to integrate sustainability into their business strategies. It provides a wealth of knowledge, insights, and best practices to inspire and support SMEs in their journey towards environmental stewardship, social responsibility, and long-term profitability. By embracing sustainability, SMEs can not only contribute to a more sustainable world but also unlock new business opportunities, gain a competitive edge, and secure their future in a rapidly changing global economy.

Kiran Mehta and Renuka Sharma
Chitkara Business School
Chitkara University
Punjab, India

Contents

Introduction

In recent years, the world has witnessed an increasing awareness and urgency surrounding sustainability and environmental issues. As the consequences of climate change become more evident and the demand for responsible business practices continues to grow, it is crucial for organizations, regardless of their size, to embrace sustainable practices and adopt green management strategies. The development of small and medium-sized companies (also known as SMEs) has become a global priority as a consequence of World Bank forecasts that 600 million new jobs would be needed by 2030 to handle the growing global workforce. Small and medium-sized companies account for seven out of every ten formal jobs in developing countries. Small and medium-sized firms, on the other hand, are also responsible for a significant quantity of carbon emissions and an increase in global pollution. SMEs are important players in the global climate effort not only because they are the primary agents of technology advancement, but also because they are the primary adopters of green business models and practises to decrease their environmental impact. To ensure that small businesses are able to finance their transition to a more environmentally friendly business model, however, will require the participation of a wide variety of actors operating within the financial ecosystem. These actors include financial institutions, regulators, rating firms, as well as others. Without the transformation of SMEs to more environmentally friendly practises, the ambitious climate-related goals outlined in the Paris Agreement will not be able to be met. Achieving equitable and sustainable industrial growth is a priority for the United Nations 2030 Agenda for Sustainable Development Goals (SDGs). That's why the contribution of businesses and markets to meeting the SDGs is so critical. Helping to accomplish SDGs 8, 9, and 12 (*decent work and economic growth*; *industry, innovation and Infrastructure*; *responsible consumption and production*) in particular, small and medium-sized enterprises play a crucial role in the post-2015 development framework. There is a growing amount of pressure being placed on businesses to include environmental, social, and governance (ESG) reporting into their day-to-day operations as well as their business models. The pressure comes from a wide variety of interested parties.

The significance of small and medium-sized firms cannot be ignored, particularly in developing countries. Small and medium-sized companies provide job possibilities while also contributing to the global economic growth. They are in charge of 95% of all enterprises on a worldwide basis, as well as 50% of all employment on a worldwide scale. Organized small and medium-sized firms may account for up to 40% of GDP in developing nations. The total number of SMEs goes up when informal SMEs are also counted. Recognizing the importance of sustainability for SMEs, this book delves into the intersection of sustainability, green management, and the performance of SMEs.

It might be challenging to bring about the kind of internal change and adaptability that is necessary for sustainability. It's also crucial to recognize the already difficult environment in which small firms operate. Many of the industries worst hit by

https://doi.org/10.1515/9783111170022-204

COVID-19 are dominated by small and medium-sized enterprises, which are characterized by lesser financial reserves, poorer supply chain capabilities, and lower use of digital tools and technology. This explains a recent WEF (World Economic Forum) analysis that found smaller businesses frequently have less social influence. Sixty-nine per cent of the more than 300 CEOs polled included sustainability in their mission statement, but just 51% incorporated it into their company strategy, and 21% aligned executive pay to social and environmental success. A recent survey found that 88 percent of institutional investors perceive environmental, social, and governance factors (ESG) to be on equal footing with operational and financial factors when making investment decisions; 60 percent of employees choose a place to work based on their beliefs and values, and 58 percent of consumers buy or advocate for brands based on who match their beliefs. We shouldn't ignore what's going on behind the headlines, specifically how the less-visible SME and mid-sized enterprise segment of the economy is approaching this challenge, despite the fact that a number of the world's largest corporations have recently announced their intention to modify their business procedures in order to respond to the growing amount of pressure.

Sustainability, Green Management, and Performance of SMEs explores the challenges, opportunities, and best practices that SMEs face in their pursuit of sustainable and environmentally friendly business operations. This book brings together a diverse range of perspectives, insights, and research findings from experts and scholars in the field, providing a comprehensive overview of the topic. Throughout the book, we explore the key drivers, barriers, and enablers for SMEs to adopt sustainable practices, along with the potential benefits and challenges they may encounter along the way. We analyze case studies and real-world examples to highlight successful initiatives and innovative approaches that have been implemented by SMEs across different industries and regions.

Chapter 1 titled "Enhancing SMEs' Sustainability through Innovative Practices" focuses on how the implementation of innovation practices can enhance the sustainability of small and medium-sized enterprises. Recognized as a crucial factor in driving sustainability within organizations, innovation serves as the focal point for this investigation. To achieve its objectives, the study utilizes the Technique for Order Preference by Similarity to Ideal Solution (TOPSIS) as a methodology for understanding the innovation practices that SMEs find acceptable.

Chapter 2 titled "The Approach of SMEs Towards Green Management Practices" focuses on green management practices (GMPs) that are vital for enhancing an organization's performance in the environment, economy, and society, while maintaining a competitive edge. This study explores the relationship between employee environmental behaviors and sustainable performance in small and medium-sized hospitality firms. The study influences the adoption of environmentally friendly practices in the industry and offers implications for further research, emphasizing the management practices used by SMEs.

Chapter 3 titled "Factors Influencing Financial Backers' Exit Decisions from a New Venture" explores and identifies the determinants of a profitable exit strategy from the perspective of financial backers, an area where previous studies have lacked sufficient evidence. A path model was analyzed to test the mediated and direct/indirect effects of exit triggers on the profitability of the exit. The findings of this study provide valuable insights for start-ups and factors can be utilized by financiers to facilitate successful exits from start-ups, benefiting both the financial backers and the start-up ventures themselves.

Innovation plays a crucial role in enabling the progress of new products and services that consume less energy, chemicals, and water, thus reducing waste from operations. Chapter 4 titled "Technological Advancement in Industrial Revolution 4.0 for Sustainable Development of India: Understanding Linkages in Theory and Practice" seeks to explore the potential of technological integration in promoting sustainable development within India. This simultaneous improvement in environmental sustainability and operational efficiencies can be achieved by incorporating technology into production processes, and we can proactively anticipate and prevent environmental disasters, addressing underlying causes that may initially appear harmless.

Next, Chapter 5 titled "Impact of Macroeconomic Determinants and Corporate Attributes on Firms' Financial Success in India" focuses on examining the impacts of macroeconomic determinants and corporate attributes on the financial success of certain manufacturing corporations in India. Research indicates that a company's financial performance is shaped by the interplay of micro and macro components. While management has some influence over micro variables, macro factors are beyond its control as they occur external to the organization. In India, macroeconomic factors such as interest rates, inflation, and exchange rates have undergone significant fluctuations.

"Exploring Individual Investor Intentions Towards Socially Responsible Investment" is the title of Chapter 6 that investigates the indirect impact of perceived risk, perceived return, trust, and morality through the mediating variable attitude towards intentions of Indian stock market investors. The outcomes of the study indicate that the model depicts mediation of attitude between trust, perceived risk, perceived return, and morality towards intentions of individual investors.

Chapter 7 titled "Ownership Structures and Performance of SMEs: An Empirical Analysis" uses multiple theoretical perspectives to examine whether the non-linear relationship of multiple ownership variables on the performance of Indian-listed small-cap corporates moves in the same direction or they move in the opposite direction. Panel regression indicates that an initial increase in the promoter holdings of small-cap corporates makes them more entrenched in extracting private benefits, which increases the agency cost and reduces the performance of corporates. Also, the non-institutional holdings adversely impacted Indian corporate performance. The findings result in specific implications to be addressed by the corporates, government and policymakers.

The growth of SME IPOs in the secondary market can be noticed as numerous IPOs experience a quick surge in their trading prices on the day they are listed. Newly issued stocks often conclude their first trading day at a significantly higher price than their initial offering price. Chapter 8, titled "Short-Run Pricing Performance of Selected Indian IPOs During COVID-19 for Alternative Investment Avenue" examines this increase. This study focuses on analyzing the pricing and performance of SME IPOs issued on the Indian Stock Exchanges for the Alternative Investment Market (AIM) during a two-year period encompassing the COVID-19 pandemic, specifically from January 1, 2020, to December 31, 2021. The research aims to examine the returns generated by BSE SME IPOs on their listing day, as well as the returns provided by the BSE SME IPO Index.

There is a paradigm change among SME shareholders who want to replace traditional processes with green ones and are working to remove obstacles to green innovation in an emerging economy. Studies concentrating on SMEs in developing nations are still few, even though their existence in developing areas and countries is still crucial and has been favored in economic organizations. In this background, Chapter 9, titled "Emerging Green: Exploring Strategic Factors for SMEs' Adoption of Green Technology and Innovation in India" explores various determinants supporting SMEs' adoption of green technology and innovation. The study's findings have provided a future pathway for the researcher to explore several new dimensions in helping SMEs adopt green innovation and technology.

Chapter 10 titled "Impact of Sustainability and Green Finance on SMEs to Promote Green Growth" focuses on exploring the impact of sustainability, green finance on micro, small, and medium enterprises to promote green growth. The main aim of the chapter is to explore the term "green finance" and see how it is helpful in India for micro, small, and medium enterprises. This chapter also increases academic understanding by emphasizing opportunities available to various sectors.

Chapter 11, titled "Progress Intention and Sales Revenue Growth in Micro, Small and Medium Enterprises (SMEs)" aims to examine the sales revenue growth of SMEs in the manufacturing sector and its impact on their overall development. To achieve this objective, the study uses data from their financial statements from the past three years.

Chapter 12, titled "Green Management Practices by Small and Medium Enterprises" attempts to bring together the components of green management practices, from existing literature and contemporary practices. Green management practices enable continuous improvement and sustainability. The study concludes that due to various reasons, SMEs may have been left out of the regulatory and social pressures. The time has come when ignoring environmental impacts of SMEs is no longer viable.

Chapter 13, titled "An Analysis of MSMEs' Contributions to the Promotion of SDGs in India" presents a rationale for implementing the principles of sustainable development and demonstrates how MSMEs may support it. It shows that it takes changing regulations and systemic changes in how financial markets and institutions function to fully realize the promise of MSMEs for the SDGs. The chapter concludes that all these changes would have several far-reaching effects, opening more funding sources, boosting extra economic growth, and creating more job prospects.

Chapter 14, titled "Impact of Innovation and Its Role in Small Medium Enterprises' Sustainability" is a conceptual chapter and explores innovation's role in the sustainability of small and medium enterprises. The chapter proposes strategies that SMEs can use to foster a culture of innovation, including investing in research and development, collaborating with partners, and leveraging technology. Overall, this chapter highlights the critical role that innovation plays in the sustainability of SMEs.

Government policies such as grants, subsidies, and tax incentives have been specifically crafted to foster innovation and entrepreneurship among SMEs. Chapter 15, titled "Effect of Government Policies on SME Innovation and Entrepreneurship" aims to see the effect of government policies on SME innovation and entrepreneurship. The admittance to support is essential for SME development and business. SMEs can significantly benefit from government policies that make it easier to get financing. However, a variety of factors, including the SME's size and industry, determine whether financing is available.

Chapter 16, titled "A Study on Various Aspects of SMEs' Orientation for Corporate Social Responsibility" makes a contribution by demonstrating how CSR affects various performance kinds in SMEs and how SMEs' learning orientation affects their CSR. By shedding light on the causes and effects of CSR for SMEs, the study adds to the body of knowledge on responsibility, sustainability, and SME internationalization.

Chapter 17, titled "SME and Environmental Sustenance: Digital Marketing in SMEs via Data-Driven Strategies" explores how SMEs might combine data-driven marketing tactics with environmental sustainability. The findings add to the ongoing conversation on sustainable business practises and provide useful insights for SMEs wanting to navigate the digital landscape effectively.

We feel it is beneficial to shift our perspective on this difficulty. Sustainability has the potential to foster innovation, operational efficiency, risk mitigation, and employee engagement. As a result, rather than seeing sustainability as a compliance concern, it is critical to consider it as a management strategy for long-term success. Futuristic SMEs took advantage of social and environmental sustainability's potential. This new vector provides value-creating avenues for solving SMEs' top concerns, including development and expansion, talent acquisition and retention, and capital and access to finance. The path to sustainability is difficult, but it is also rewarding. Companies/firms/businesses who do not make ESG an intrinsic part of their purpose will struggle to compete, but those that do will have a forward-thinking and resilient firm. Based on this foundation, the current book is a synthesis of all of these key concerns about SMEs' sustainability, green management and performance strategies.

We hope that this book serves as a valuable resource for researchers, academics, practitioners, and policymakers who are interested in understanding and promoting sustainable practices in SMEs. It is our belief that by empowering SMEs to adopt green management strategies, we can create a more sustainable and resilient future for both businesses and the planet. We extend our sincere gratitude to all the authors who contributed their expertise and insights to this book. Their invaluable contributions have helped shape a comprehensive and forward-thinking exploration of sustainability, green management, and the performance of SMEs.

K. Lakshminarayana, Prayag Gokhale, Basavaraj S. Tigadi,
Praveen M. Kulkarni

1 Enhancing SMEs' Sustainability Through Innovative Practices

Abstract: Contributing to economic growth, job creation, and social development, Small and Medium-sized Enterprises (SMEs) play a crucial role in many economies. However, SMEs face various challenges, including leadership, talent management, automation, and collaboration.

This study's objective is to investigate how innovation practices can boost the sustainability of SMEs, considering that innovation is widely acknowledged as a significant factor driving sustainability for enterprises. The study has adopted the Technique for Order Preference by Similarity to Ideal Solution (TOPSIS) for understanding the innovation practices acceptable to the SMES, and regression analysis is applied to understand the challenges faced by SMEs in implementing sustainable-oriented innovation in the organization. The findings suggest that SMEs that embrace innovation as a strategic approach are better positioned to address challenges, seize opportunities, and achieve long-term sustainability.

Keywords: Small and Medium-sized Enterprises, Innovation, Sustainability, Collaboration, Technology

Introduction

Small organizations are an important aspect of the economy and act as an important source of income to the economies worldwide, given their significant contributions to the economy (Mehta et al., 2017). However, SMEs encounter numerous problems that impede their development and sustainability, including a lack of resources, market competition, and evolving consumer demands. As a result, the growth of the organization is possible through sustainable innovation practices since it can aid them in overcoming challenges, staying competitive, and maintaining their operations in the long term (Han & Chen, 2021; Souto, 2022; Mehta et al., 2022a).

K. Lakshminarayana, Visvesvaraya Technological University, Dept of Management Studies, Belagavi, Karnataka, India
Prayag Gokhale, KLE Dr. M S Sheshgiri College of Engg. and Tech. Udyambag Belagavi, Karnataka, India
Basavaraj S. Tigadi, Visvesvaraya Technological University, Belagavi, Karnataka, India
Praveen M. Kulkarni, KLS Institute of Management Education and Research, Belagavi, Karnataka, India

https://doi.org/10.1515/9783111170022-001

Previous studies (Demirel & Kesidou, 2019; Schiederig, Tietze & Herstatt, 2012; Khanra et al., 2022) have identified three types of sustainability-oriented innovation: eco-innovation, social innovation, and business model innovation. Studies (Rosario et al., 2022; Jia et al., 2023; Gonzales-Gemio et al., 2020; Sharma & Sharma, 2022) also find that small organizations' motivations for engaging in sustainability-oriented innovation can vary, including regulatory compliance, stakeholder pressures, and market opportunities. Studies (Wang & Huang, 2022; DiBella et al., 2023; Inigo & Albareda, 2019) also note that organizational culture, leadership, and resources play important roles in facilitating sustainability-oriented innovation in SMEs. The consumer behavior and capital market operations can further affect the growth pattern of firms (Khanna & Sharma, 2017: Mahajan & Sharma, 2017).

Along similar lines, studies (Campos et al., 2023; Naradda et al., 2020; Chang-Muñoz et al., 2023) indicate that sustainability-oriented innovation can lead to positive outcomes for SMEs, such as increased competitiveness, improved operational efficiency, and access to new markets and funding. However, SMEs also face challenges in implementing sustainable innovation due to a lack of resources, knowledge, and measurement tools to assess the impact of innovation on sustainability. The research problems of big corporates are different from SMEs (Mehta et al., 2022a). Sustainability and governance issues in big corporates are investigated by researchers with more intensity (Sharma et al., 2022; Vyas et al. 2023).

However, the authors note (Souto, 2022; Hadjimanolis, 2019; Adams et al., 2016) that SMEs face various challenges in implementing innovation, such as limited resources, lack of awareness, and constraints of communicating the impact of sustainability-oriented innovation among the key employees.

Therefore, this study aims to comprehend the difficulties that these organizations encounter when incorporating sustainable innovation practices in the organization. The present research has applied two methods of statistical intervention; firstly, TOPSIS to comprehend the innovation practices that SMEs consider acceptable. Secondly, regression analysis is utilized to comprehend the challenges faced by SMEs in implementing sustainable-oriented innovation within their organization.

Literature Review

Two areas of literature were reviewed for the study, namely innovation and sustainable practices in small organizations.

Sustainable Development

During sustainable development, the goal is to meet the needs of both present and future generations without harming the environment. In corporate sustainability, environmental and social goals are balanced with economic objectives to minimize damage to natural environments and societies (Filser et al., 2019; Baumgartner & Rauter, 2017; Mensah, 2019). Innovation is crucial to contribute to sustainability, as it can lead to new or improved products, processes, marketing, or organizational methods. However, the successful implementation of innovations is critical to their economic impact, and they need to be novel to the market or the world (Sutton, 2004; Baumgartner, 2014; Chams & García-Blandón, 2019).

This literature assessment focuses on small organizations, which is vital to examine because of their massive contributions to the economy. SMEs possess wonderful benefits, consisting of lean organizational systems and sustainable-oriented improvements. Sustainable organizations can efficaciously diffuse these sustainable-oriented improvements, which can be critical for sustainable improvement (Herbane, 2019; Crovini et al., 2021; Ahadi & Kasraje, 2020).

SMEs innovate differently than larger companies, as demonstrated by varying degrees of innovation resulting from their strategies. Therefore, the authors suggest that deeper research on sustainable-oriented improvements of SMEs would provide a better understanding of the contribution towards sustainable development (Fenise et al., 2017; Wu, 2017; Kurpayanidi & Abdullaev, 2018).

Enhancing Sustainability Through Innovation Capabilities

Innovation capacity is critical to economic growth for both developed and developing countries worldwide (Phale et al., 2021; Chege & Wang, 2020). Innovation can transform information and ideas into new products, processes, and systems, including managing new business opportunities and merging operational business models (Battistella et al., 2017; Mendoza-Silva, 2021).

Innovation capability requires the knowledge and skills to effectively engage, lead, improve existing technologies and create innovative methods for the organization (Borah, Iqbal, & Akhtar, 2022; Migdadi, 2021).

Numerous studies (Migdadi, 2019; Azeem et al., 2021; Wamba-Taguimdje et al., 2020) have shown that there is a positive correlation between innovation and business performance, especially in the manufacturing sector. SMEs that have innovation capabilities are more competitive in both domestic and international markets, and firms that invest in their innovation potential are more likely to succeed in the future.

Empirical research (Aljuboori et al., 2021; Sahoo, 2019) have indicated that innovation and organizational performance are interrelated and can support improving the efficiency of the organization.

Research Methodology

In this section of the study profile of the respondents and the selection of statistical intervention are presented for data analysis. Further, followed by this section conceptual framework is presented in the next section of the study.

Profile of the Respondents

The selected respondents were from five small and medium-scale industries. The respondent's sample was based on the simple random sampling method, as the number of participants for the study was selected based on the application of innovative practices in the organization. The details related to the profile of the respondents are presented in Table 1.1. And questionnaire for the study is attached in Annexure 1.1.

Table 1.1: Profile of the Respondent.

Industry	N	Percentage
Foundry	10	50
Machining	2	10
Packing	3	15
Plastic	2	10
Auto Component	3	15
Total	**20**	**100**
Age (Years)	**N**	**Percentage**
30 to 35	19	38
35 to 40	13	26
40 to 45	9	18
45 to 50	5	10
50 and above	4	8
Total	**50**	**100**
Gender	**N**	**Percentage**
Male	46	92
Female	4	8
Total	**50**	**100**
Education	**N**	**Percentage**
UG	36	72
PG and Above	14	28
Total	**50**	**100**

Data Analysis Methodology

The present study has adopted multiple criteria and alternative decision-making methods. There are several methods available for application in the decision-making process of organizations, namely the Analytic Hierarchy Process (AHP), TOPSIS, Simple Additive Weighting, PROMETHEE, and ELECTRE (Teknomo,2006; Ozturk & Batuk, 2011; Afshari et al., 2010; Thakkar & Thakkar, 2021; Figueira et al., 2013; Triantaphyllou, 2000; Malczewski, 2006)

Theoretical Framework

Innovation Practices

Innovation is the pathway for sustainable business practices which can drive the organization to a new level of business and frame innovation growth plans for the organization (Aragón-Correa et al., 2008; Noci & Verganti, 1999).

Based on previous studies (Beise & Rennings, 2005; OECD, 2005; Rennings, 2000), there are three practices of innovation which can be applied in the organization, firstly, process innovation which focuses on the production, systems and practices in the organizations, this method is supportive to the small organizations by improving the production process and implementing new business practices for the growth of the organization (Huber, 2008; Rennings et al., 2006; Altham, 2007). Secondly, organizational innovations involve restructuring procedures and frameworks within a company and implementing novel management approaches, primarily "focused on individuals and work organization (Rennings et al., 2006) and thirdly, product innovations include the development of products and services which match the expectations of the customers and expand the market growth of the organization (Hart & Milstein, 2003).

Factors for Understanding SMEs' Sustainability Through Innovative Practices

Small organizations can achieve sustained innovation by leveraging their flexibility, agility, and adaptability to respond to market needs and changing trends. Here are some factors that can contribute to SMEs' sustainability through innovation:

1. Customer-centric innovation: SMEs should focus on understanding their customer's needs and preferences to develop new and innovative products, services, or business models. This can involve gathering feedback through surveys, focus groups, or social media monitoring to identify unmet needs or areas for improvement (Wechsler & Schweitzer, 2019).

2. Collaboration and networking: SMEs can collaborate with other businesses, research institutions, or government agencies to gain access to knowledge, resources, or funding. By building partnerships and networks, SMEs can share expertise, pool resources, and co-create innovative solutions (Chen et al., 2019).
3. Digitalization and automation: SMEs can leverage digital technologies to streamline their processes, reduce costs, and improve efficiency. This can involve adopting cloud-based software solutions, implementing e-commerce platforms, or automating manual tasks through robotics or artificial intelligence (Sánchez & Hartlieb, 2020).
4. Sustainable practices: SMEs can adopt sustainable practices that reduce their environmental footprint, such as using renewable energy sources, minimizing waste, or using eco-friendly materials. These practices not only benefit the environment but can also attract customers who value sustainable products and services (Cillo et al., 2019).
5. Talent development: SMEs can invest in their employees' skills and knowledge to foster a culture of innovation. This can involve providing training, coaching, or mentorship programs that enable employees to develop new skills, experiment with new ideas, and contribute to the company's innovation strategy (Tiwari et al., 2022).
6. Leadership: Strong and visionary leadership is crucial for SMEs to sustain their innovation efforts. Hence, executives need to focus on new ideas and create a culture of innovation that encourages experimentation and creativity (Afsar & Umrani, 2020).

By incorporating these factors into their operations, SMEs can increase their chances of achieving sustainability through innovation. However, innovation practices are continuous operation in organizations that requires ongoing investment, experimentation, and adaptation. SMEs that are committed to innovation and are willing to take calculated risks are more likely to succeed in the long run.

Results

The study results are presented in two phases; in the first phase, TOPSIS results are provided to understand the preference of the experts in the SMEs toward the application of innovation practices. In the second phase, regression is applied to understand the relationship between the challenges of the implementation of sustainable practices for the success of innovation in SMEs.

Result Analysis on the Application of Innovation Practices in SMEs

The data results through TOPSIS are presented in Tables 1.2, 1.3 and 1.4. Results in Table 1.4 show that organizational innovation practices are ranked 1, process innovation is ranked 2, and product innovation practice is ranked 3. The study results indicated that organizational innovation practices had supported SMEs in updating the process for introducing new ideas, workflows, processes, products, or services to improve the performance and efficiency of an organization.

Table 1.2: Weightage for the Variables for the Study.

	Non Benf.	Benf.	Benf.	Benf.	Benf.	Benf.
Weightage	**0.55**	**0.32**	**0.25**	**0.35**	**0.4**	**0.2**
Process innovations	20	12	13	13	10	15
Organizational innovations	18	10	15	10	15	10
Product innovations	21	16	11	12	14	18

Results Analysis on the Challenges of Implementation of Innovative Practices in SMEs

The study results on the challenges of implementation of innovative practices in SMEs are presented in three phases based on the innovation practices and their relationship with the challenges of implementation.

In the first phase, process innovation practices and challenges of implementation are presented in Table 1.5, where the results indicate that (A p-value of 0.421 > 0.05 level of significance for sustainable practices, which indicates that process innovation requires more understanding of the implementation of sustainable practices in SMEs for process innovation.

Results with regards to organizational innovation practices and challenges of implementation of this innovation practice shown in Table 1.6 indicate that (A p-value of 0.840 > 0.05 level of significance for customer-centric innovation, which indicates that SMEs for the success of organizational innovation needs to focus on the customer-centric innovation practices for the success of this innovation in the SMEs.

Results with regards to the product innovation and challenges of implementation of innovation practices shown in Table 1.7 (P value of 0.846 > 0.05) level of significance for customer-centric innovation, which indicates that SMEs for the success of product innovation need to focus on the customer-centric innovation practices for the success of this innovation practices in the SMEs.

Table 1.3: Weighted Normalized Matrix.

	Leadership	Talent development	Sustainable practices	Digitalization and automation	Collaboration and networking	Customer-centric innovation
Process innovations	0.586	0.537	0.573	0.640	0.438	0.589
Organizational innovations	0.527	0.447	0.661	0.492	0.657	0.393
Product innovations	0.615	0.716	0.485	0.590	0.613	0.707

Table 1.4: Ranking of the Study Variables.

	Leadership	Talent development	Sustainable practices	Digitalization and automation	Collaboration and networking	Customer-centric innovation	Si+	Si-	Pi	Rank
Process innovations	0.205	0.134	0.143	0.096	0.066	0.088	0.004	0.031	0.887	2
Organizational innovations	0.185	0.112	0.165	0.074	0.099	0.059	0.004	0.148	0.974	1
Product innovations	0.215	0.179	0.121	0.089	0.092	0.106	0.109	0.215	0.663	3
V+	0.185	0.179	0.165	0.096	0.099	0.106				
V-	0.215	0.112	0.121	0.074	0.066	0.059				

Table 1.5: Process Innovation and Challenges of Implementation.

Model	Unstandardized	Standard Error	Standardized	t	p
(Intercept)	2.48	0.188		13.2	0.0001
(Intercept)	−0.251	0.419		−0.601	0.001
Leadership	0.206	0.147	0.196	1.394	0.170
Talent development	0.213	0.16	0.213	1.326	0.002
Sustainable Practices	0.111	0.137	0.096	0.812	0.421
Digitalization and automation	0.291	0.109	0.33	2.663	0.001
Collaboration and networking	−0.095	0.141	−0.085	−0.677	0.002
Customer-centric innovation	0.188	0.127	0.212	1.475	0.147

Table 1.6: Organizational Innovation and Challenges of Implementation.

Model	Unstandardized	Standard Error	Standardized	t	p
(Intercept)	3.1	0.172		18.021	
(Intercept)	0.553	0.491		1.127	0.266
Leadership	0.241	0.173	0.251	1.394	0.27
Talent development	0.242	0.188	0.265	1.289	0.01
Sustainable Practices	0.381	0.161	0.358	2.365	0.02
Digitalization and automation	−0.1	0.128	−0.124	−0.779	0.02
Collaboration and networking	−0.033	0.165	−0.032	−0.201	0.04
Customer-centric innovation	0.014	0.149	0.017	0.095	0.84

Discussion

Process Innovations in SMEs

Process innovation in SMEs refers to the improvement of the methods and techniques used to produce goods or services. It involves creating new processes, optimizing existing ones, and adopting new technologies to enhance productivity and efficiency. Some strategies that can be employed include lean manufacturing, total quality management, and Six Sigma. The results indicated that leadership skills need more support for the organization to change and make decisions that align with the company's objectives. Further, with regards to talent development and process innovation have indicated process innovation has supported the SMEs to develop their talent by providing opportunities for employees to learn new skills, participate in job rotations, and attend training programs (Jackson, Shan, & Meek, 2022).

With regards to sustainable practices, SMEs can adopt sustainable practices by reducing their environmental footprint, using renewable energy sources, and reducing waste. SMEs can benefit from digitalization and automation by implementing software

Table 1.7: Product Innovation and Challenges of Implementation.

Model	Unstandardized	Standard Error	Standardized	t	p
(Intercept)	3.06	0.177		17.281	0.002
(Intercept)	1.517	0.496		3.06	0.002
Leadership	0.548	0.175	0.555	3.139	0.003
Talent development	0.183	0.19	0.194	0.962	0.004
Sustainable Practices	−0.073	0.162	−0.067	−0.45	0.655
Digitalization and automation	0.199	0.13	0.24	1.54	0.001
Collaboration and networking	−0.251	0.166	−0.238	−1.507	0.139
Customer-centric innovation	−0.03	0.151	−0.035	−0.196	0.846

and tools that help automate routine tasks, reduce errors, and improve productivity (Romao et al., 2019).

SMEs can collaborate with other SMEs, industry associations, and academic institutions to share knowledge, resources, and expertise. By collaborating and networking, SMEs can access new markets, share best practices, and gain new insights into their industry (Romao et al., 2019).

Innovation in the Organizations

Innovation at the organizational level is focused towards the development of new organizational structures and the development of effective management systems. It involves changing the way an organization operates to improve performance, increase efficiency, or create new opportunities. Examples of organizational innovations in SMEs include the adoption of new business models, the creation of cross-functional teams, and the implementation of agile methodologies (Chen et al., 2019).

The study outcomes indicate that leadership should encourage creativity and experimentation, foster a culture of innovation, and provide the necessary resources and support for employees to innovate and adopt sustainable practices; SMEs can create new opportunities for growth, reduce costs, and improve their brand reputation (Phale et al., 2021; Chege & Wang, 2020).

Examples of sustainable practices that can drive innovation include the use of circular economy principles, sustainable supply chains, and create customer-centric innovation; for instance, customer-centric innovation that can drive organizational innovation includes the use of customer feedback to improve products and services, the adoption of design thinking methodologies, and the creation of customer-centric cultures.

Product Innovation

Product innovation in SMEs refers to the development and improvement of products that match the demands of the customers. It involves the development of new features, functions, or designs that differentiate the product from competitors or provides added value to customers (Migdadi, 2019; Azeem et al., 2021; Wamba-Taguimdje et al., 2020). Examples of product innovations in SMEs include developing technologies for innovative services for marketing growth and development.

Sustainable practices can drive product innovation in SMEs. By adopting sustainable practices, SMEs can create new opportunities for growth, reduce costs, and improve their brand reputation. Examples of sustainable practices that can drive innovation include the use of eco–friendly materials, the development of products that reduce energy consumption, and the creation of sustainable packaging.

By working with other organizations and individuals, SMEs can gain new insights, access new resources, and create new opportunities for growth. Examples of collaboration and networking that can drive innovation include the creation of innovation ecosystems, the formation of strategic partnerships, and the participation in industry associations and networks (Sánchez & Hartlieb, 2020).

Conclusion

For the success of sustainable innovation practices, SMEs need to understand the innovation typology, which is acceptable to the SME's culture and process, and which can bring success in adopting innovative practices.

Overall, the study, the study presents the correlation between innovation and challenges faced by small organizations; further, the study also calls for understanding in a future study with regards to the innovation practices in the specific sector of SMEs and evaluates the impact on the challenges faced by the SMEs in implementing innovative practices.

References

Adams, R., Jeanrenaud, S., Bessant, J., Denyer, D., & Overy, P. (2016). "Sustainability-oriented innovation: A systematic review", *International Journal of Management Reviews*, *18*(2), 180–205.

Afsar, B., & Umrani, W. A. (2020). "Transformational leadership and innovative work behaviour: The role of motivation to learn, task complexity and innovation climate", *European Journal of Innovation Management*, *23*(3), 402–428.

Afshari, A., Mojahed, M., & Yusuff, R. M. (2010). "Simple additive weighting approach to personnel selection problem", *International journal of innovation, management and technology*, *1*(5), 511.

Ahadi, S., & Kasraie, S. (2020). "Contextual factors of entrepreneurship intention in manufacturing SMEs: the case study of Iran", *Journal of Small Business and Enterprise Development*, *27*(4), 633–657.

Aljuboori, Z. M., Singh, H., Haddad, H., Al-Ramahi, N. M., & Ali, M. A. (2021). "Intellectual capital and firm performance correlation: the mediation role of innovation capability in Malaysian manufacturing SMEs perspective", *Sustainability*, *14*(1), 154.

Altham, W. (2007). "Benchmarking to trigger cleaner production in small businesses: Dry cleaning case study", *Journal of Cleaner Production*, *15*, 798e813.

Aragón-Correa, J.A., Hurtado-Torres, N., Sharma, S., García-Morales, V.J. (2008). "Environmental strategy and performance in small firms: a resource-based perspective", Journal of Environmental Management, *86*, 88e103.

Azeem, M., Ahmed, M., Haider, S., & Sajjad, M. (2021). "Expanding competitive advantage through organizational culture, knowledge sharing and organizational innovation", *Technology in Society*, p. *66*, 101635.

Battistella, C., De Toni, A. F., De Zan, G., & Pessot, E. (2017). "Cultivating business model agility through focused capabilities: A multiple case study", *Journal of Business Research*, *73*, 65–82.

Baumgartner, R. J. (2014). "Managing corporate sustainability and CSR: A conceptual framework combining values, strategies and instruments contributing to sustainable development", *Corporate Social Responsibility and Environmental Management*, *21*(5), 258–271.

Baumgartner, R. J., & Rauter, R. (2017). "Strategic perspectives of corporate sustainability management to develop a sustainable organization", *Journal of Cleaner Production*, *140*, 81–92.

Beise, M., Rennings, K., 2005. "Lead markets and regulation: a framework for analyzing the international diffusion of environmental innovations", *Ecological Economics*, *52*, 5e17.

Borah, P. S., Iqbal, S., & Akhtar, S. (2022). "Linking social media usage and SME's sustainable performance: The role of digital leadership and innovation capabilities", *Technology in Society*, *68*, 101900.

Campos, T. L. R., Nunhes, T. V., Harney, B., & Oliveira, O. J. D. (2023). "Corporate sustainability in entrepreneurial settings: Green management and operational fairness as joint drivers of venture competitiveness", *Journal of Small Business and Enterprise Development*, *30*(2), 342–368.

Chams, N., & García-Blandón, J. (2019). "On the importance of sustainable human resource management for the adoption of sustainable development goals", *Resources, Conservation and Recycling*, *141*, 109–122.

Chang-Muñoz, E. A., Guarín-García, A. F., Charris-Sevilla, Y., Gallego-Nicholls, J. F., Santos-Rojo, C., & Ortigosa-Blanch, A. (2023). "Innovation Activities and Their Impact on Product Innovation Results: Evidence from a Sectorial Study", *Sustainability*, *15*(8), 6459.

Chege, S. M., & Wang, D. (2020). "Information technology innovation and its impact on job creation by SMEs in developing countries: an analysis of the literature review", *Technology Analysis & Strategic Management*, *32*(3), 256–271.

Chen, K., Zhang, Y., & Fu, X. (2019). "International research collaboration: An emerging domain of innovation studies?", *Research Policy*, *48*(1), 149–168.

Cillo, V., Petruzzelli, A. M., Ardito, L., & Del Giudice, M. (2019). "Understanding sustainable innovation: A systematic literature review", *Corporate Social Responsibility and Environmental Management*, *26*(5), 1012–1025.

Crovini, C., Santoro, G., & Ossola, G. (2021). "Rethinking risk management in entrepreneurial SMEs: towards the integration with the decision-making process", *Management Decision*, *59*(5), 1085–1113.

Demirel, P., & Kesidou, E. (2019). "Sustainability-oriented capabilities for eco-innovation: Meeting the regulatory, technology, and market demands", *Business Strategy and the Environment*, *28*(5), 847–857.

DiBella, J., Forrest, N., Burch, S., Rao-Williams, J., Ninomiya, S. M., Hermelingmeier, V., & Chisholm, K. (2023). "Exploring the potential of SMEs to build individual, organizational, and community resilience through sustainability-oriented business practices", *Business Strategy and the Environment*, *32(*1), 721–735.

Feniser, C., Burz, G., Mocan, M., Ivascu, L., Gherhes, V., & Otel, C. C. (2017). "The evaluation and application of the TRIZ method for increasing eco-innovative levels in SMEs", *Sustainability*, *9*(7), 1125.

Figueira, J. R., Greco, S., Roy, B., & Słowiński, R. (2013). "An overview of ELECTRE methods and their recent extensions", *Journal of Multicriteria Decision Analysis*, *20*(1–2), 61–85.

Filser, M., Kraus, S., Roig-Tierno, N., Kailer, N., & Fischer, U. (2019). "Entrepreneurship as a catalyst for sustainable development: Opening the black box", *Sustainability*, *11*(16), 4503.

Gonzales-Gemio, C., Cruz–Cázares, C., & Parmentier, M. J. (2020). "Responsible innovation in SMEs: A systematic literature review for a conceptual model", Sustainability, 12(24), 10232.

Hadjimanolis, A. (2019). "Drivers and barriers to sustainable innovation in SMEs in the context of small countries", In *Managing Sustainable Innovation* (pp. 66–86). Routledge.

Han, M. S., & Chen, W. (2021). "Determinants of eco-innovation adoption of small and medium enterprises: An empirical analysis in Myanmar", *Technological Forecasting and Social Change*, *173*, 121146.

Hart, S., Milstein, M. (2003). "Creating sustainable value", *Academy of Management Executive. 17*, 56e67.

Herbane, B. (2019). "Rethinking organizational resilience and strategic renewal in SMEs", *Entrepreneurship & Regional Development*, *31*(5–6), 476–495.

Huber, J. (2008). "Technological, environmental innovations (TEIs) in a chain analytical and life-cycle-analytical perspective", *Journal of Cleaner Production*, *16*, 1980e1986.

Hwang, C. L., Yoon, K., Hwang, C. L., & Yoon, K. (1981). "Methods for multiple attribute decision making. Multiple attribute decision making: methods and applications a state-of-the-art survey", 58–191.

Inigo, E. A., & Albareda, L. (2019). "Sustainability oriented innovation dynamics: Levels of dynamic capabilities and their path-dependent and self–reinforcing logics", *Technological Forecasting and Social Change*, *139*, 334–351.

Jackson, D., Shan, H., & Meek, S. (2022). "Enhancing graduates' enterprise capabilities through work-integrated learning in co-working spaces", *Higher Education*, *84*(1), 101–120.

Jia, J., Yuan, S., Wei, L.-Q., & Tang, G. (2023). "When firms adopt sustainable human resource management: A fuzzy-set analysis" *Human Resource Management*, *62*(3), 283–30.

Khanra, S., Kaur, P., Joseph, R. P., Malik, A., & Dhir, A. (2022). "A resource-based view of green innovation as a strategic firm resource: Present status and future directions", *Business Strategy and the Environment*, *31*(4), 1395–1413.

Khanna, Vikas and Sharma, Renuka (2017). "Customer Switching Behavior in Retail Banking in India", *International Journal of Applied Business and Economic Research*, *15*(9), 427–441.

Kurpayanidi, K. I., & Abdullaev, A. M. (2018). "Actual issues of the functioning of an innovative industrial enterprise", *ISJ Theoretical & Applied Science*, *11*(67), 74.

Mahajan, Vinay and Sharma, Renuka (2017). "Future of Depository with Introduction of Payment Bank-A Game Changer to Capital Market", *International Journal of Applied Business and Economic Research*, *15*(9), 343–356.

Malczewski, J. (2006). "GIS-based multicriteria decision analysis: a survey of the literature", *International journal of geographical information science*, *20*(7), 703–726.

Mehta Kiran and Sharma Renuka and Chugh, Aman (2017). "Management of Forex Risk Exposure: A Study of SMEs and Unlisted Non-Financial Firms in India", *International Journal of Applied Business and Economic Research*, *15*(9), 43–54.

Mehta, K., Sharma, R., Vyas, V. (2022a). "A quantile regression approach to study the impact of aluminium prices on the manufacturing sector of India during the COVID era", *Materials Today: Proceedings*, *65*(8), 3506–3511, ISSN 2214–7853, https://doi.org/10.1016/j.matpr.2022.06.087.

Mendoza–Silva, A. (2021). "Innovation capability: a systematic literature review", *European Journal of Innovation Management*, *24*(3), 707–734.

Mensah, J. (2019). "Sustainable development: Meaning, history, principles, pillars, and implications for human action: A literature review", *Cogent social sciences*, *5*(1), 1653531.

Migdadi, M. M. (2019). "Organizational learning capability, innovation and organizational performance", *European Journal of Innovation Management*.

Migdadi, M. M. (2021). "Knowledge management, customer relationship management and innovation capabilities", *Journal of Business & Industrial Marketing*, *36*(1), 111–124.

Naradda Gamage, S. K., Ekanayake, E. M. S., Abeyrathne, G. A. K. N. J., Prasanna, R. P. I. R., Jayasundara, J. M. S. B., & Rajapakshe, P. S. K. (2020). "A review of global challenges and survival strategies of small and medium enterprises (SMEs)", *Economies*, *8*(4), 79.

Noci, G., Verganti, R., 1999. "Managing 'green' product innovation in small firms", R&D Manag. 29, 3e15.

Organization for Economic Co-Operation and Development (OECD), 2005. Oslo Manual. Guidelines for Collecting and Interpreting Innovation Data, third ed. OECD Publishing, Paris.

Ozturk, D., & Batuk, F. (2011, May). "Technique for order preference by similarity to ideal solution (TOPSIS) for spatial decision problems", In *Proceedings ISPRS* (Vol. 1, No. 4).

Phale, K., Li, F., Adjei Mensah, I., Omari-Sasu, A. Y., & Musah, M. (2021). "Knowledge-based economy capacity building for developing countries: a panel analysis in Southern African Development Community", *Sustainability*, *13*(5), 2890.

Rennings, K. (2000). "Redefining innovation e eco-innovation research and the contribution from ecological economics", *Ecological Economics*, *32*, 319e332.

Rennings, K., Ziegler, A., Ankele, K., & Hoffmann, E. (2006). "The influence of different characteristics of the EU environmental management and auditing scheme on technical environmental innovations and economic performance," *Ecological Economics*, *57*(1), 45–45.

Romao, M., Costa, J., & Costa, C. J. (2019, June). "Robotic process automation: A case study in the banking industry", In 2019 14th Iberian Conference on information systems and Technologies (CISTI) (pp. 1–6). IEEE.

Rosário, A. T., Raimundo, R. J., & Cruz, S. P. (2022). "Sustainable Entrepreneurship: A literature review", *Sustainability*, *14*(9), 5556.

Sahoo, S. (2019). "Quality management, innovation capability and firm performance: Empirical insights from Indian manufacturing SMEs", *The TQM Journal*, *31*(6), 1003–1027.

Sánchez, F., & Hartlieb, P. (2020). "Innovation in the mining industry: Technological trends and a case study of the challenges of disruptive innovation", *Mining, Metallurgy & Exploration*, *37*(5), 1385–1399.

Schiederig, T., Tietze, F., & Herstatt, C. (2012). "Green innovation in technology and innovation management–an exploratory literature review", *R&d Management*, *42*(2), 180–192.

Sharma, A. & Sharma, R. (2022). Exploring Tax Decision Factors: A Perspective from North Indian Tax Practitioners, *Journal of Tax Reform*, *8*(3): 285–297. https://doi.org/10.15826/jtr.2022.8.3.122.

Sharma, R., Mehta, K. & Goel, A. (2022). "Non-linear relationship between board size and performance of Indian companies", *Journal of Management and Governance* (2022). https://doi.org/10.1007/s10997-022-09651-8.

Souto, J. E. (2022). "Organizational creativity and sustainability-oriented innovation as drivers of sustainable development: overcoming firms' economic, environmental and social sustainability challenges", *Journal of Manufacturing Technology Management*, *33*(4), 805–826.

Sutton, P. (2004). "A perspective on environmental sustainability", Paper on the Victorian Commissioner for Environmental Sustainability, 1, 32.

Teknomo, K. (2006). "Analytic hierarchy process (AHP) tutorial", *Revoledu. com*, *6*(4), 1–20.

Thakkar, J. J., & Thakkar, J. J. (2021). "Preference Ranking Organization Method for Enrichment Evaluations (PROMETHEE)", *Multicriteria Decision Making*, 119–127.

Tiwari, B., Mishra, I., & Thakur, V. (2022). "Talent Development: A Thematic Categorization Using Systematic Literature Review", *FIIB Business Review*, 23197145221104189.

Triantaphyllou, E., & Triantaphyllou, E. (2000). "Multicriteria decision-making methods" (pp. 5–21). Springer US.

Vyas, V., Mehta, K., Sharma, R. (2023). "The nexus between toxic-air pollution, health expenditure, and economic growth: An empirical study using ARDL", *International Review of Economics and Finance, 84*, 154–166 https://doi.org/10.1016/j.iref.2022.11.017.

Wamba-Taguimdje, S. L., Fosso Wamba, S., Kala Kamdjoug, J. R., & Tchatchouang Wanko, C. E. (2020). "Influence of artificial intelligence (AI) on firm performance: the business value of AI-based transformation projects", *Business Process Management Journal*, *26*(7), 1893–1924.

Wang, S., & Huang, L. (2022). "A Study of the Relationship between Corporate Culture and Corporate Sustainable Performance: Evidence from Chinese SMEs", *Sustainability*, *14*(13), 7527.

Wechsler, J., & Schweitzer, J. (2019). "Creating customer-centric organizations: the value of design artefacts", *The Design Journal*, *22*(4), 505–527.

Wu, G. C. (2017). "Effects of socially responsible supplier development and sustainability-oriented innovation on sustainable development: Empirical evidence from SMEs", *Corporate Social Responsibility and Environmental Management*, *24*(6), 661–675.

Priyanka Singh* and Chaman Pal

2 The Approach of SMEs Towards Green Management Practices

Abstract: Everyone should be concerned about a sustainable future because we all want to leave a good world for future generations. Achieving sustainability requires significant financial investments in tangible assets, conservation efforts, institutions, and human resources and cannot be accomplished using business-as-usual methods. Additionally, we must cultivate a culture that can balance the competing interests of participating communities with those of the environment. Our understanding of the effects of climate change, such as global warming, and its implications for food security and human existence has grown over the past few decades as more information becomes available.

Green management practices (GMPs) are vital in improving an organization's performance across three critical aspects: the environment, the economy, and society. Furthermore, they can contribute to maintaining a competitive edge for organizations. Given that the tourism and hospitality sectors face environmental expectations from customers, governments, and the community, it becomes imperative to comprehend the driving factors behind GMPs. By doing so, organizations can effectively address environmental concerns, meet established standards, and satisfy stakeholders.

This study clarifies the relationship between employee environmental behaviors and sustainable performance in small and medium-sized hospitality firms. It is significant because it has the potential to influence the industry's adoption of more environmentally friendly practices. The chapter offers implications for further research, both theoretical and practical. It emphasizes the management practices that small and medium-sized businesses (SMEs) use in various ways.

Keywords: Environmental performance, Sustainable practices, Economic performance, Social performance, CSR activity

Introduction

The environmental movement gained momentum during the 1960s as a response to the excessive utilization and depletion of non-renewable resources, coupled with the alarming increase in consumption, waste generation, and environmental pollution (Vyas

Note: We have no conflicts of interest to disclose.

***Corresponding author: Priyanka Singh**, Department of Mathematics, Govt. Naveen Girls College Nawapara Raipur (C.G), email: singhpriyanka2107@gmail.com
Chaman Pal, Department of Mechanical Engineering, NIT Raipur (C.G)

https://doi.org/10.1515/9783111170022-002

et al., 2023). This movement has gathered strength and influence over the following decades, driven by growing concerns about sustainability and the need to address these pressing environmental challenges. The public began to hold businesses responsible for addressing many of the world's environmental issues (Roh & Yang, 2021), businesses were forced to incorporate their operating procedures to incorporate green management practices. In the early 2000s, the phrase "green management" gained prominence across the globe, and managerial leaders realized that environmental and business goals should be aligned (Banerjee, 2001). Adopting environmentally conscious strategies helps businesses maintain them over time by staying competitive in their markets, enhancing their financial results, company value, and product innovation (Li & Albita et al., 2020). It also allows businesses to uphold social responsibility and act morally towards the environment (Nattrass, 1999; Wu & Liu, 2022; Sharma, 2020). According to institutional theory and stakeholder theory, businesses usually employ green practices and innovation to minimize financial expenses and political pressure (Li & Zhuang, 2021; Almaqtari et al., 2022), meet the expectations of various stakeholders by abiding by social and moral norms (Ortiz & Aragon-Correa, 2019), and escape the pressure of imitative competitors (Suk & Liu, 2012). Consequently, businesses believe that good green management can help them achieve the three sustainability principles of social equality, environmental integrity, and economic success (Berry & Rondinelli, 1998; Lee, 2009). Green management practices aim to improve the long-term viability of a company by effectively converting inputs, such as natural materials and resources, into valuable products or outputs, which encompass goods and services. These practices prioritize achieving a harmonious and interdependent balance among the benefits provided to the economy, society, and the environment. By focusing on this holistic approach, organizations can foster sustainable growth and contribute positively to multiple stakeholders (Raharjo, 2019). Additionally, staff members who are cognizant of the relevance and gravity of environmental issues can satisfactorily address them by taking part in pro-environmental actions that cut down on resource waste and lower operational expenses (Farrukh &Wang, 2022). Previous studies showed the value of employees' pro-environmental behaviors in aiding green management's attempts to improve business sustainability (Li, Chen & Wang, 2020).

Small and medium-sized enterprises (SMEs) are crucial in promoting sustainable and environmentally responsible business practices. Using green management practices entails incorporating environmental factors into decision-making and business operations. SMEs, which typically have fewer than 500 employees and generate less than a certain amount of revenue per year, depending on the country and industry, are often considered the backbone of the economy, as they make up a significant proportion of businesses and provide jobs for a vast number of individuals. SMEs can adopt various green management practices, including energy efficiency, waste reduction and recycling, sustainable sourcing, and employee engagement. By adopting these practices, SMEs can reduce their environmental footprint, enhance their reputation and brand image, and potentially increase their competitiveness and profitabil-

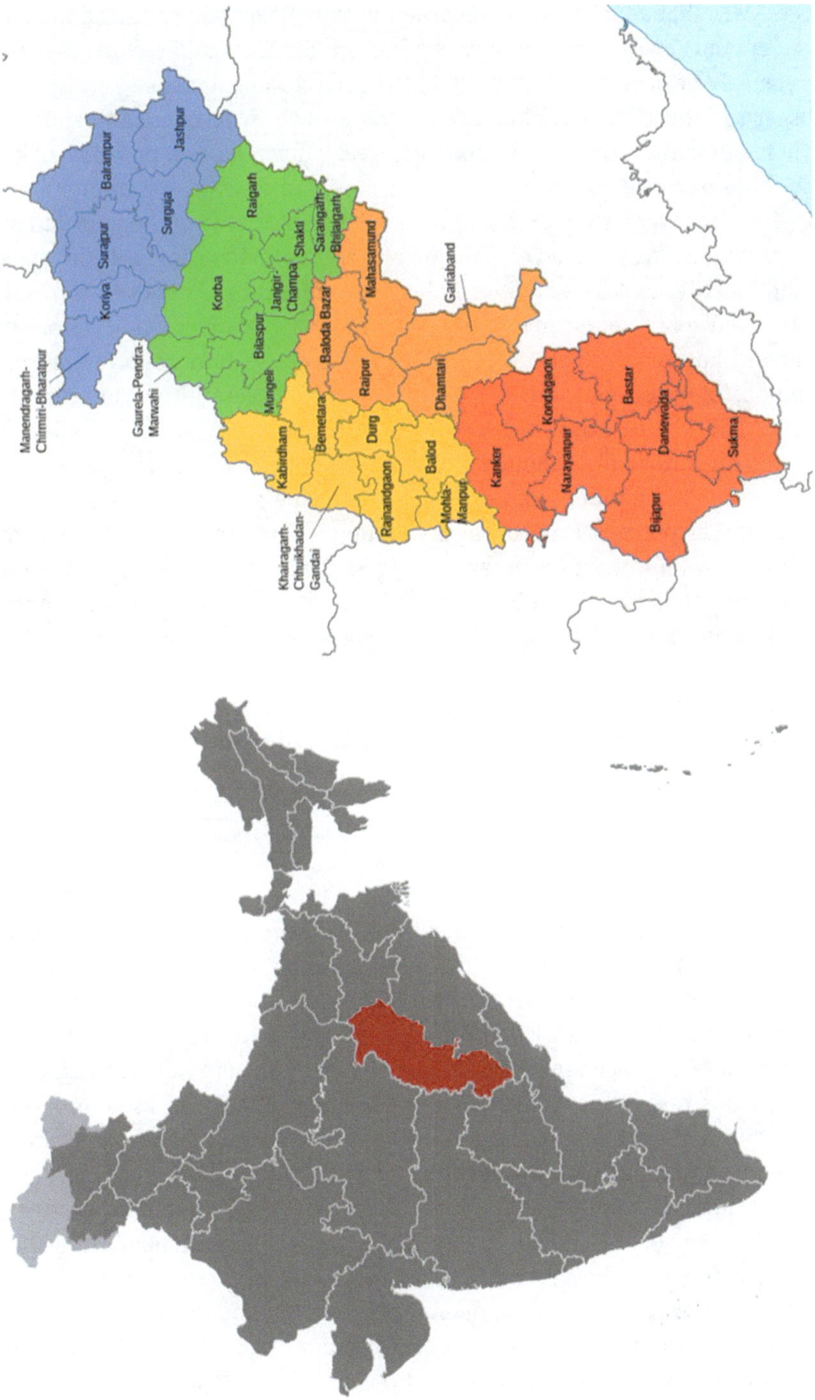

Figure 2.1: Districts of Chhattisgarh (Study Area).

ity. Moreover, SMEs that adopt sustainable practices may be better positioned to meet the growing demand for environmentally responsible products and services as consumers increasingly prioritize sustainability in their purchasing decisions.

Chhattisgarh's industrial sector has seen rapid growth in recent years, with the state being home to various industries, including steel, power, aluminum, and cement production. Chhattisgarh is one of India's largest steel producers and accounts for nearly 20% of the country's steel production (see Figure 2.1). It is also one of India's largest cement producers, with several major cement plants operating in the state. Iron ore, coal, bauxite, and limestone are abundant mineral resources in the state that have attracted much investment in the mining and metallurgical sectors. The state government has taken several initiatives to promote sustainable and environmentally responsible business practices in the industrial sector. The Chhattisgarh State Industrial Policy 2019–24 aims to promote environmentally sustainable industrial growth and encourage the adoption of green technologies by offering incentives for establishing eco-friendly industrial parks, green energy projects, and waste management facilities. The policy also encourages the adoption of clean production techniques and using renewable energy sources to mitigate the adverse effects of industrial activity on the environment. The state government has also set up a Pollution Control Board to monitor and regulate industrial emissions and waste management. By promoting sustainable and environmentally responsible business practices, Chhattisgarh's industrial sector can contribute to the state's economic growth while protecting the environment and preserving natural resources for future generations.

Literature Review

Research on the ways in which small and medium-sized enterprises (SMEs) engage in green management (GM) practices has attracted increasing attention. Several trends common to most SMEs have been identified in studies conducted in various nations, including Europe, Australia, the UK, and the United States (Hutchinson & Chaston, 1994). However, there are becoming more concerns around the environmental impact of SMEs as previous research on business and GM has primarily focused on larger firms. Despite this, SMEs are less likely to follow environmental management practices or have environmental strategies than their larger counterparts, often due to a belief that environmental management incurs an expense with no immediate financial advantages (Mckeiver & Gadenne, 2005). While various environmental practices have been implemented, Studies have attempted to explain why certain practices are chosen and the justification for environmental practices (Leopoutre & Heene, 2006). The features of SMEs, the availability of resources, and individual interest in and expertise in environmental management are the three key obstacles standing in the way of SMEs implementing good environmental practices (Suk & Shishime et al., 2012). Several SMEs do not view environmental concerns or the requirement to do business in an ecologically responsible manner as being important for their firm (Revell & Blackburn, 2007).

Green Human Resource Management (HRM) combines environmental activities and procedures for sustainable HR resource utilization, which leads to increased efficiency, less waste, and a better work attitude (Margaretha & Saragih, 2013). Green HRM is defined by (Rashid & Saad, 2006; Margaretha & Saragih, 2013), as the application of Sustainable HRM policies and practices. Sustainable HRM policies and practices es resource consumption within business organizations, which typically advances environmental causes. According to (Opatha, Arulrajah, & Nawaratne, 2016), in the process of educating employees about the application of green human resources, Individuals, society, the community, and the earth all gain from policies and practices. By implementing its green HRM policies and practices with the goal of an Environmental Performance Framework (EPF), the HRM function serves as a driver of sustainability. The idea of green HRM is currently generating more concern among businesses, both public and private, who try to downplay the role that green HRM activities play in supporting and possibly undermining EPF.

The importance of incorporating green initiatives in organizations cannot be understated, as it helps to reduce environmental degradation and ensures a sustainable future for generations to come (Jackson et al., 2011). To promote green HRM, crucial factors such as green training and development (GTD), energy-efficient workspaces (EEW), and rewards and recognition must be implemented (Daily & Govindarajulu, 2008). Studies have shown that efficient green training is necessary for effective EPF, and HRM plays a significant role in promoting green practices. Human factors like employee motivation and training are critical for an employee's ability to implement green practices. Integrating green practices with training and development can help ensure the effective execution of green practices (Fernandez, Junquera & Ordiz, 2003).

Public and private organizations across the globe are actively pursuing green initiatives as a means to address the root causes of environmental degradation and strengthen their Environmental Performance Framework (EPF). It is imperative for organizations to proactively establish a robust green program right from the beginning to ensure their long-term sustainability, success, and corporate reputation. Many organizations provide incentives, such as monetary rewards, to encourage employees to enhance their EPF. However, there is a dearth of research exploring the individual benefits of a green workplace on employees' EPF, health, and overall well-being.

Research Methods

To accomplish our research goal regarding the significance of green innovation in SMEs, exploratory qualitative research (case study method) was used in this study. The characteristics of qualitative research include

1) Using direct sources of data, where the researcher is the primary data collector;
2) The information gathered is descriptive;
3) The inductive approach is used to analyze data.
4) Understanding the significance of the data is the researcher's goal.

To get around the method's poor external validity, data were also triangulated using the studied literature. Numerous case studies, which are ideal for exploring a phenomenon immersed in its real surroundings, as is the case with the subject under study, were used to operationalize the method that was chosen. The phenomenon under study is examined where it occurs, allowing for the determination of its true meaning, contrary to Yin's contention that research subjects are merely variables. Since "the case study deals with the processes that take place and their interrelationship," Having the data already allows for the identification of explanatory variables for the behavioral patterns of a certain unit of analysis as a whole.

In qualitative research, the sample selection aims to gather as much data as possible to provide a foundation for the project and develop theories based on both theoretical and practical criteria. For a small geographic area and a limited sample size, the case study method is appropriate. As a result, we selected three SMEs/case studies from Chhattisgarh, India, that operate in various sectors. We considered the following criteria when selecting these three cases/SMEs:

1. Prior experience with businesses that employ green innovation techniques.
2. Geographical proximity and easy information access for the researchers.

We used a convenience sample to be more precise. Using the non-probability sampling strategy of a convenience sample, researchers can choose individuals based on their accessibility and interest in participating in the study. In social science research, convenience sampling is widely utilized, particularly when it's required to collect data quickly, cheaply, or in challenging regions.

We selected to interview the top management of the three SMEs (Manager I1, Manager I2, and Manager I3), including owner-managers, as our method of gathering data. The case study approach minimizes biased data because it enables data to be collected from a variety of key informants.

Discussion and Finding

Case Study

National Mineral Development Corporation (NMDC)

National Mineral Development Corporation (NMDC) in Chhattisgarh has made considerable efforts to incorporate green management practices into its operations. One area of focus is waste management, which involves the implementation of waste management systems to ensure proper disposal and recycling of waste. Furthermore, NMDC has also implemented measures to reduce waste generation in the first place. In terms of water conservation, NMDC has undertaken several measures, including rainwater harvesting, wastewater treatment and reuse, and the use of recycled water for various processes. Additionally, NMDC has implemented measures to conserve energy, such as the utilization of energy-efficient lighting and equipment and the implementation of energy management systems.

NMDC has also made significant efforts to develop green cover in the areas surrounding their mines and plants through tree plantation and afforestation programs. To minimize their environmental impact, NMDC conducts regular environmental monitoring and reporting to ensure compliance with local regulations (for detail, see Table 2.1). Overall, these green management practices demonstrate NMDC's commitment to environmental sustainability and contribute to the long-term sustainability of their business.

Table 2.1: List of Minerals Mining in NMDC.

NMDC participates in examination of											
Iron	Copper	Rock Phospate	Limestone	Dolomite	Gypsom	Bentonite	Magnesite	Diamond	Tin	Tungsten	Graphite

National Mineral Development Corporation (NMDC) has undertaken several Corporate Social Responsibility (CSR) activities in Chhattisgarh to support the communities in which they operate (see Figure 2.2). Some of these CSR activities include:

A. Education

One of the main areas of our CSR programs is education. NMDC has built residential schools for Native American children, including those with special needs. To encourage individuals from low socio-economic backgrounds to pursue higher education, the corporation offers scholarships. In addition, NMDC runs two industrial training institutes and one polytechnic to provide technical education in rural areas of the country. Through these educational initiatives, over 30,000 students have benefited.

B. Health and Hygiene

At its hospitals close to the mines, NMDC offers free medical care to about 10,000 in-patients and 100,000 out-patients each year. It also organizes regular medical camps and sends mobile hospitals into the most distant areas to provide basic healthcare services. Chhattisgarh and Karnataka's 165 villages are serviced by Hospital on Wheels. NMDC has distinguished itself as a leader in health management thanks to its initiatives on menstrual hygiene and cleanliness drives.

C. Skill Development

By implementing Skill Development programmes for the tribal young, NMDC has transformed into a willing participant in the National Skill Mission. 1600 local youth have received training from NMDC in trades related to mining and steel. The business has run training programmes in the tribal community's traditional trades of bell metal, bamboo, and tumba art. More than 100 indigenous youth who were unemployed were included in the campaign.

Figure 2.2: CSR Activities in NMDC.

Bhilai Steel Plant (BSP)

Bhilai Steel Plant (BSP), one of the largest steel plants in India located in Chhattisgarh, has implemented several Green Human Resource Management (GHRM) practices in its operations. One of the primary GHRM practices at BSP is promoting environmental awareness among its employees. The plant conducts regular training programs to educate employees on environmental issues and sustainability. Employees are also encouraged to suggest ideas for improving the plant's environmental performance. Another key practice implemented by BSP is reducing its carbon footprint. The plant has adopted energy-efficient technologies and practices, such as lowering greenhouse gas emissions through the utilization of renewable energy sources. Additionally, BSP has put in place a waste management system that encourages recycling and lowers trash production.

In addition, BSP has implemented sustainable transportation practices to reduce air pollution. The plant provides shuttle services for its employees, reducing the number of vehicles on the road. BSP also encourages the use of public transportation among its employees and provides incentives to those who use eco-friendly modes of transportation, such as bicycles.

Furthermore, BSP has implemented a green procurement policy. The plant sources environmentally sustainable products and services such as recycled paper and eco-friendly cleaning products to reduce its environmental impact.

BSP's implementation of GHRM practices demonstrates its commitment to environmental sustainability. By integrating environmental concerns into its human resource management practices, BSP not only contributes to a healthier environment but also creates a culture of sustainability among its employees.

Bhilai Steel Plant (BSP) in Chhattisgarh is committed to corporate social responsibility (CSR) and has undertaken several initiatives in this regard. One of the main focus areas of BSP's CSR activities is education. The plant provides scholarships to students from economically disadvantaged backgrounds to help them pursue their education. BSP also runs a number of vocational training programs to help young people gain employable skills. The plant's skill development programs focus on areas such as welding, carpentry, and electrical work. In addition, BSP has undertaken several initiatives to promote health and wellness in the surrounding communities. The plant has set up medical camps in nearby villages to provide free medical check-ups and treatment. BSP also runs health and hygiene awareness programs to educate people on the importance of maintaining good health and hygiene. BSP has also implemented various environmental initiatives as part of its CSR activities. The plant has undertaken afforestation programs to increase green cover in the surrounding areas. BSP has also set up rainwater harvesting systems to conserve water and reduce the plant's impact on the environment. Overall, BSP's CSR activities have helped to improve the lives of people in the surrounding communities and contribute to sustainable development. The plant's focus on education, vocational training, health, and the environment has made a positive impact on the lives of many people in the region.

Jindal Steel Plant

It is India's sole privately held rail manufacturer and ranks third in terms of tonnage among private steel producers. Jindal Steel Plant, located in Chhattisgarh, has implemented several Green Human Resource Management (GHRM) practices to encourage sustainable environmental practices. The company conducts regular training programs and awareness campaigns to educate employees on environmental issues and sustainability, encouraging them to come up with innovative ideas for improving the plant's environmental performance. Additionally, the plant has adopted energy-efficient technologies and practices, such as the use of renewable energy sources to reduce its greenhouse gas emissions and implemented a waste management system to promote recycling. Sustainable transportation practices have also been implemented, including shuttle services for employees, promotion of public transportation use, and incentives for eco-friendly transportation such as bicycles. Jindal Steel Plant's commitment to GHRM practices demonstrates its contribution to a healthier environment and a culture of sustainability among its employees.

Jindal Steel Plant in Chhattisgarh has also undertaken several Corporate Social Responsibility (CSR) activities to give back to the community and promote sustainable development. The company has established Jindal Vidya Mandir, a school that provides education to children from nearby villages. Jindal Steel Plant also offers scholarships to students from economically disadvantaged backgrounds to help them pursue their education.

The company has also set up healthcare centers in nearby villages to provide free medical treatment to those who cannot afford it. In addition, Jindal Steel Plant has undertaken various initiatives to promote sustainable agriculture and improve the livelihoods of farmers in the surrounding areas. The company provides training to farmers on modern farming techniques, distributes high-yield seeds, and sets up water harvesting structures to improve irrigation.

Moreover, Jindal Steel Plant has taken steps to conserve the environment and mitigate its impact on the surroundings. The company has undertaken afforestation drives to increase green cover in the surrounding areas and has set up rainwater harvesting systems to conserve water.

Overall, Jindal Steel Plant's CSR activities have made a positive impact on the lives of people in the surrounding communities and contributed to sustainable development. The company's focus on education, healthcare, agriculture, and the environment has helped to improve the socio-economic conditions of the region. Table 2.2 shows the list of products produced in JSP.

Table 2.2: List of Products Produced in JSP.

JSP Participates in Production of										
Rails	Parallel Flange Beams and Columns	Plates and Coils	Jindal Panther Cement	Speedfloors	Angles and Channels	Wire Rods	Round Bars	Jindal Panther TMT Rebars	Semi Finished	Fabricated Sections

Significant Sustainable Development Initiative

To establish the ore body boundary, a systematic preliminary process is carried out inside the rented space in a grid pattern. Conceptual pit limits are then created to minimize the handling or movement of dumps and infrastructure.

i. Mine Planning:
   - within the roads and ramps, operating mines are designed to maintain command distances between ore and the CP and waste and the dump as short as possible.
   - In order to balance the up- and down-hauling of fully loaded dumpers, pits were created.
   - To stop the degradation of the forest area under the lease, systematic production planning is done.

ii. At the mine level, combining low-grade and high-grade ore to produce a marketable product aids in reducing rejects and extending mine life.

iii. Comprehensive healthcare facilities, such as workplace check-ups and treatment centres, are provided to employees.

iv. NMDC has taken steps to offer safe drinking water to the people near its Projects under the flagship CSR program “Payjal”.

v. Energy audits are carried out to locate and rank energy-saving technical solutions and opportunities.

vi. Solar power initiatives are implemented at NMDC’s office locations, including a 30 KW rooftop solar power generating system at the head office.

vii. The CSR programme “Niramaya – Towards Healthy Life” provides community healthcare that is both preventive and curative.

viii. Examples of water conservation practices include water audits, physical groundwater quality and level monitoring, checking dams, and sewage treatment facilities, improving the efficiency of motors and pumps, etc.

ix. All NMDC projects underwent a water audit, and the recommendations are being implemented to conserve water.

x. NMDC production facilities are implementing a 1 MW rooftop solar power generation system.

xi. The UNFCCC has registered a 10.5 MW wind project.

xii. Both NMDC and BSP are committed to reducing outputs of trash, effluent, and emissions as well as inputs of water, energy, land, chemicals, and other elements. BSP is dedicated to sustainable development that reduces pollution and waste.

xiii. NMDC and BSP are gradually incorporating environmental and social considerations into procurement processes with the implementation of systems like ISO 14001 and SA-8000 Standard. In an effort to promote sustainability, both companies are constantly pursuing green practices.

2.4.1 Recommendation

The following recommendations are made for the industries:

i. Businesses should adopt numerous green HRM practices, which should boost their return on investment. As a result, less money should be spent on pointless training initiatives. In order to lower the cost of HR recruitment, the HRP system must be correctly applied.
ii. The concept of digitization should be widely applied so that everything is simple and paperless.
iii. Artificial intelligence should be used since it helps the company function more effectively.
iv. By using electronic filing, you may lessen the carbon footprint of your employees. Green HR entails lowering carbon footprint through fewer paper printing, video conferencing, and interviewing, among other things.
v. Office spaces that are energy efficient should be created, such as green buildings.
vi. Techniques for Green Payroll should be used.
vii. To reduce pollution, more people should use public transport.
viii. Staff ID card disposal and green manufacturing are two options.
ix. Job sharing, or having two people share one full-time position, facilitates flexible work.
x. Virtual and telephonic interviews ought to be promoted more.
xi. Recycling needs to be done in order for items to be reused.
xii. To reduce paperwork, online training should be used.
xiii. To reduce waste and paperless work should be encouraged.
xiv. Data maintenance and retrieval should be carried out to consolidate all information into a single database.
xv. Green Sigma best practices ought to be applied.
xvi. The organization should adopt green printing.

Conclusion

The findings of this study suggest that SMEs in Chhattisgarh have started to adopt Green Management Practices (GMP) and Corporate Social Responsibility (CSR) initiatives to reduce their environmental impact. Although only three SMEs were examined in this study, the results suggest that SMEs can implement GMP and CSR practices in a cost-effective manner while contributing to the sustainable development of their communities. However, further research is needed to explore the impact of these practices on the long-term environmental, social, and economic sustainability of SMEs.

The study also emphasizes the significance of Green HRM practices in promoting environmental sustainability. The HR department of companies has a crucial role in managing employees and should have an environmentally conscious approach in addition to their HR policies. By promoting green people management, organizations can address the root causes of environmental degradation and raise awareness among employees through green movements, programs, and resource-saving practices. Green HR initiatives can lead to better employee performance and retention, increased efficiency, sustainable resource use, reduced waste, better work-related attitudes, improved work/life balance, and lower expenses.

In conclusion, this study highlights the importance of SMEs adopting GMP and CSR practices to mitigate their environmental impact. By implementing these practices, SMEs can contribute to the long-term sustainability of their businesses, communities, and the environment. Further research is needed to explore the impact of these practices on the financial performance and long-term sustainability of SMEs. The study also underscores the significance of Green HRM practices in promoting environmental sustainability and highlights the HR department's responsibility in managing employees with an environmentally conscious approach.

References

A. Almaqtari, F., Elsheikh, T., Tawfik, O. I., & Youssef, M. A. E. A. (2022). "Exploring the Impact of Sustainability, Board Characteristics, and Firm–Specifics on Firm Value: A Comparative Study of the United Kingdom and Turkey", *Sustainability*, *14*(24), 16395. https://doi.org/10.3390/su142416395

Banerjee, S. B. (2001). "Managerial perceptions of corporate environmentalism: Interpretations from industry and strategic implications for organizations", *Journal of management studies*, *38*(4), 489–513. https://doi.org/10.1111/1467-6486.0024

Berry, M. A., & Rondinelli, D. A. (1998). "Proactive corporate environmental management: A new industrial revolution", *Academy of Management Perspectives*, *12*(2), 38–50. https://doi.org/10.5465/ame.1998.650515

Daily, B. F., Bishop, J. W., & Govindarajulu, N. (2009). "A conceptual model for organizational citizenship behavior directed toward the environment", *Business & Society*, *48*(2), 243–256. https://doi.org/10.1177/0007650308315439

Esteban Fernández, Beatriz Junquera & Mónica Ordiz (2003). "Organizational culture and human resources in the environmental issue: a review of the literature", *The International Journal of Human Resource Management*, *14*(4), 634–656, https://doi.org/10.1080/0958519032000057628.

Farrukh, M., Ansari, N., Raza, A., Wu, Y., & Wang, H. (2022). "Fostering employee's pro–environmental behavior through green transformational leadership, green human resource management and environmental knowledge", *Technological Forecasting and Social Change*, *179*, 121643. https://doi.org/10.1016/j.techfore.2022.121643

Hutchinson, A., & Chaston, I. (1994). "Environmental management in Devon and Cornwall's small and medium sized enterprise sector", *Business Strategy and the Environment*, *3*(1), 15–22. https://doi.org/10.1002/bse.3280030102

Jackson, S. E., Renwick, D. W., Jabbour, C. J., & Muller-Camen, M. (2011). "State-of-the-art and future directions for green human resource management: Introduction to the special issue", *German Journal of Human Resource Management*, *25*(2), 99–116. https://doi.org/10.1177/239700221102500203

Lee, K. H. (2009). "Why and how to adopt green management into business organizations? The case study of Korean SMEs in manufacturing industry", *Management Decision*, *47*(7), 1101–1121. https://doi.org/10.1108/00251740910978322

Lepoutre, J., & Heene, A. (2006). "Investigating the impact of firm size on small business social responsibility: A critical review", *Journal of Business Ethics*, *67*, 257–273. https://doi.org/10.1007/s10551-006-9183-5

Li, X., Yang, J., Liu, H., & Zhuang, X. (2021). "Entrepreneurial orientation and green management in an emerging economy: The moderating effects of social legitimacy and ownership type", *Journal of Cleaner Production*, *316*, 128293. https://doi.org/10.1016/j.jclepro.2021.128293

Li, Z., Liao, G., & Albitar, K. (2020). "Does corporate environmental responsibility engagement affect firm value? The mediating role of corporate innovation", *Business Strategy and the Environment*, *29*(3), 1045–1055. https://doi.org/10.1002/bse.2416

Li, Z., Xue, J., Li, R., Chen, H., & Wang, T. (2020). "Environmentally specific transformational leadership and employee's pro-environmental behavior: The mediating roles of environmental passion and autonomous motivation", *Frontiers in Psychology*, *11*, 1408. https://doi.org/10.3389/fpsyg.2020.01408

Liao, Z. (2020). "Is environmental innovation conducive to corporate financing? The moderating role of advertising expenditures", *Business Strategy and the Environment*, *29*(3), 954–961. https://doi.org/10.1002/bse.2409

Margaretha, M., & Saragih, S. (2013, March). "Developing new corporate culture through green human resource practice", *In International Conference on Business, Economics, and Accounting*, 1(10). 20–23. http://repository.maranatha.edu/id/eprint/4061

McKeiver, C., & Gadenne, D. (2005). "Environmental management systems in small and medium businesses", *International Small Business Journal*, *23*(5), 513–537. https://doi.org/10.1177/0266242605055910

Mehta, K., Sharma, R., Vyas, V. and Kuckreja, J.S. (2022), "Exit strategy decision by venture capital firms in India using fuzzy AHP", *Journal of Entrepreneurship in Emerging Economies*, *14*(4), 643–669. https://doi.org/10.1108/JEEE-05-2020–0146

Menguc, B., Auh, S., & Ozanne, L. (2010). "The interactive effect of internal and external factors on a proactive environmental strategy and its influence on a firm's performance", *Journal of Business Ethics*, *94*, 279–298. https://doi.org/10.1007/s10551-009-0264–0

Nattrass, B., & Altomare, M. (1999). "The natural step for business: Wealth, ecology and the evolutionary corporation", New Society Publishers. https://play.google.com/store/books

Opatha, H. H. D. N. P., Arulrajah, A. A., & Nawaratne, N. N. J. (2016). "Employee green performance of job: a systematic attempt towards measurement", *Sri Lankan Journal of Human Resource Management*, *6*(1). http://journals.sjp.ac.lk/index.php/sljhrm/article/view/2785

Ortiz-de-Mandojana, N., Bansal, P., & Aragón-Correa, J. A. (2019). "Older and wiser: How CEOs' time perspective influences long-term investments in environmentally responsible technologies", *British Journal of Management*, *30*(1), 134–150. https://doi.org/10.1111/1467-8551.12287

Pane Haden, S. S., Oyler, J. D., & Humphreys, J. H. (2009). "Historical, practical, and theoretical perspectives on green management: An exploratory analysis", *Management Decision*, *47*(7), 1041–1055. https://doi.org/10.1108/00251740910978287

Porter, M., & Van der Linde, C. (1995). "Green and competitive: ending the stalemate. The Dynamics of the eco–efficient economy", *Environmental Regulation and Competitive Advantage*, *33*, 120–134. https://play.google.com/store/books

Raharjo, K. (2019). "The role of green management in creating sustainable performance for small and medium enterprises", *Management of Environmental Quality: An International Journal*, *30*(3), 557–577. https://doi.org/10.1108/MEQ-03-2018–0053

Rashid, N. R. N. A., Wahid, N. A., & Saad, N. M. (2006, November). "Employees' involvement in EMS, ISO 14001 and its spillover effects in consumer environmentally responsible behaviour", *In International Conference on Environment Proceedings*, *3*(5), pp. 57–62).

Revell, A., & Blackburn, R. (2007). "The business case for sustainability? An examination of small firms in the UK's construction and restaurant sectors", *Business Strategy and the Environment*, *16*(6), 404–420. https://doi.org/10.1002/bse.499

Roh, T., Lee, K., & Yang, J. Y. (2021). "How do intellectual property rights and government support drive a firm's green innovation? The mediating role of open innovation", *Journal of Cleaner Production*, *317*, 128422. https://doi.org/10.1016/j.jclepro.2021.128422

Sharma, R., Mehta, K., & Vyas, V. (2020). "Responsible Investing: A Study on Non–Economic Goals and Investors' Characteristics", *Applied Finance Letters*, *9*(SI), 63–78. https://doi.org/10.24135/afl.v9i2.245.

Suk, S., Liu, X., Niu, D., Bao, C., & Shishime, T. (2012). "A survey study of energy saving activities of industrial companies in Taicang, China", *Journal of Cleaner Production*, *26*, 79–89. https://doi.org/10.1016/j.jclepro.2011.12.030

Vyas, V., Mehta, K., Sharma, R. (2023). "The nexus between toxic–air pollution, health expenditure, and economic growth: An empirical study using ARDL", *International Review of Economics and Finance*, *84*, 154–166 https://doi.org/10.1016/j.iref.2022.11.017.

Wu, L., & Liu, H. (2022). "How bricolage influences green management in high-polluting manufacturing firms: The role of stakeholder engagement", *Business Strategy and the Environment*, *31*(7), 3616–3634. https://doi.org/10.1002/bse.3111

Yacob, P., Moorthy, M. K., Chelliah, M. K., & Arokiasamy, L. (2012). "Drivers for Malaysian SMEs to go green", *International Journal of Academic Research in Business and Social Sciences*, *2*(9), 74–86. https://hrmars.com/index.php/pages/detail/all-journals

Renuka Sharma and Kiran Mehta

3 Factors Influencing Financial Backers' Exit Decisions from a New Venture

Abstract: The extant literature is more vocal about the exit routes, the success of specific exit route and impacts various variables on the choice and success of exit routes. The current research has made an attempt to identify the determinants of a profitable exit strategy from the perspective of financial backers for which the previous research has not provided sufficient evidence. A structured questionnaire was developed after a critical review of extant literature. The researchers applied exploratory factor analysis (EFA) based on 306 respondents to determine the latent factors or determinants of an exit strategy. Once the factors are explored and labelled, a fresh sample (339 respondents) was used to validate the scale developed through EFA. And thus, a path model was developed to study the causal relationship between determinants of exit strategy and its profitability. The path model was further tested for mediated and direct/indirect effect of triggers of an exit strategy on the profitability of exit was tested. The findings of the study are useful for financial backers and startups both as suggested factors that could be used by these financiers for the successful exit from the startups. The constituents of the exit strategy of outsized funding organisations like VC, PE firms, and banks/financial institutions/NBFCs, might not befit other financial backers addressed in the present study. It is the major contribution of study under consideration as it has divulged that the financial backers of new ventures consider six determinants explored by the current study.

Keywords: Exit strategies, Moderation and mediation effect, Startups, Angel investors, Financial backers, New venture

Background and Introduction

The surge in the number of new businesses opening in India, along with the increase in capital invested in innovative enterprise concepts, has aided the country in meeting its employment needs. However, developing successful ventures from unique company concepts is challenging, and aspiring business owners carefully examine various factors before launching. Among the most critical factors for establishing a new business are the availability of potential customers, the level of technical innovation, the story of rivalry, and the existing market circumstances (Kirkley, 2016). Startups, founded on novel concepts and driven by technological advancements (Ghazy

Renuka Sharma, Kiran Mehta, Chitkara Business School, Chitkara University, Punjab, India

https://doi.org/10.1515/9783111170022-003

et al., 2022), operate in an unpredictable business ecosystem that often results in loss (Mason and Harrison, 2002; Nahata, 2008, Mueller and Reize, 2013; Cochrane, 2005).

The overall state of the economy affects investors' willingness to fund new companies, and startups face an increased risk due to macroeconomic fluctuations (Mahajan & Sharma, 2017). Investment plan, growth rate and risk is a significant factor in the value of new initiatives and startups, making investors eager to provide them with funding in any form (Hidayat et al., 2022; Hellmann & Puri, 2002; Dimov & DeClerq, 2006; Gorman & Sahlman, 1989; Streletzki & Schulte, 2013). In ventures that involve high-tech-based services and innovative products or processes, the background of founder members becomes a key indicator for success and affects the startup's ability to raise funds (MacMillan et al. 1985; Zacharakis & Meyer, 2000; Knockaert & Vanacker, 2013). Similarly the increasing concern for responsible behavior and environment also affect the investors' behavior (Vyas et al., 2020; Vyas et al., 2023). The behavior of consumer also affect the overall revenue of the business and hence the interest of investors shifts from one company to another (Khanna & Sharma, 2017).

Venture capitalists, banks, angel investors, and private equity companies are the primary funding sources for startups, but there are other types of financial backers for aspiring business owners, such as individual investors, business entrepreneurs, business incubators, angel forums, high-net-worth individuals (HNI), competitions happening across geographical areas to provide a stage for startups to pitch their ideas and raise funds, and various government funding platforms. Each individual investor thoroughly analyses multiple criteria before investing in startups. The risk is usually high while investing in startups; therefore, identifying the prime stage of investment in these ventures is crucial (Hidayat et al., 2022; Hoffman, 1972; Tyebjee & Bruno, 1984). Financial supporters, including individuals, angel investors, and venture capital (VC) organizations, are increasingly concerned about the funding of startups. During different stages of development, a startup frequently encounters distinct challenges that can influence investment decisions. These decisions may also be affected by how venture capitalists perceive the startup's competitors in the industry (Gompers & Lerner, 2000). When more money is available in the venture capital market, there are higher possibilities of completing a transaction at a discount. In addition, the venture capital firm's vast syndicate of partners boosts its ability to provide funding to startups (Dimov & DeClercq, 2006).

Investors are interested in investing in startups because of their potential for explosive growth. There is a long-term aim of exit for venture capitalists and angel investors when they invest in startups. For a financial backer, return on investment can only be assessed when the financial backer chooses an exit route. The success of an exit defines a venture capital firm's success rate and, therefore, it's standing (Berlin, 1998). Venture capital providers do consider the success of a business's exit when making investment decisions (Black & Gilson 1998). There are several tactical options for these investors, such as an initial public offering (IPO), a mezzanine stage of a startup, an upcoming merger, or a strategic sale. Capital gains prompt investors to leave their investments (Cumming et al. 2006). It's impossible to define a "successful exit" for every form of departure.

A disagreement between an entrepreneur and an investor might lead to an exit or vice versa (Aghion et al., 2004; Bascha & Walz, 2001; Berglof, 1994). Although the exit stage of venture capital investment hasn't been spoken about much, it's an integral part of the process (Bygrave & Timmons 1992). The investors supporting the enterprises also seek to recoup their investment capital, making a departure inevitable (Black & Gilson, 1998), despite the enterprise thriving (Haveman & Khaire, 2004). Therefore, financial supporters must recycle their investments for their continued existence, and harvesting is part of the venture capital business model (Mason and Harrison, 2006). Research on startups and their financing has touched on many subjects, including how to raise money at various stages, how to value them, what variables influence their development, how founder traits affect new venture performance, and how to exit as an entrepreneur. Scholars have not extensively researched the departure plans of financial supporters other than financial institutions, venture capitalists, and private equity companies. It is equally important to consider exit strategy triggers as it is to consider investment strategy triggers. Due to its focus on investors other than banks, venture capital companies, and private equity firms as exit strategies, this study stands out from others in that it is the first of its kind. This study aims to fill this research gap and is unique in its focus on investors other than banks, venture capital companies, and private equity firms as exit strategies. A scale can be developed for future practitioners and researchers with a list of triggers and factors. In summary, this section has discussed the prime focus of existing literature on the related field, identified the research gap, and justified the need for current research.

Literature Review

The current body of literature on startups predominantly discusses entry points, the impact of founders and human capital on success and fundraising, financing, factors influencing growth, founder and venture capitalist exit intentions and timing, and entrepreneurial exit. However, very few studies have delved into the triggers and drivers of departure strategies for financial supporters. Previous research has also identified inconsistencies in departure strategy factors across nations, such as the availability of buyers and sellers, predicted investment profitability, information asymmetry, and ambiguity. This section highlights key findings and observations from past studies, which reveal a research gap and the need for current research. The authors have categorized the related research under various sub-headings to better understand the variables for further exploration in this area. In summary, these reviews have provided valuable insights for identifying gaps in the research and justifying the need for further investigation.

Role of Human Capital, the Experience of the Founder and Traits of the Founder

The value of human capital within an organization is widely acknowledged (Beckman et al., 2007). When investing in startups, venture capital firms place considerable importance on the experience of the business's managers and leaders (MacMillan et al., 1987; Teece & Pisano, 1994; Zacharakis & Shepherd, 2005). Unger et al. (2011) conducted a meta-analysis that documented the role of human capital in entrepreneurial success, finding a positive relationship between the two. However, this relationship's effect size was smaller than those found in studies examining entrepreneurial orientation and personality. A study of 439 Italian firms focused on new technology-based firms and found that the founder's human capital had a positive impact on the business's growth and its ability to attract investment from venture capitalists. The study confirmed that a startup's founder and their human capital were critical to its future growth (Colombo & Grilli, 2010). The knowledge and experience of the founder are crucial in determining the profitability of investment (Casson, 2005). For technology-based ventures, the founder's traits also contribute to attracting more investments (Gimmon & Levie, 2010). In this study, the researchers evaluated the characteristics of 193 founders of Israel-based startups, such as their academic status, technological expertise, and business management skills to attract external investment. The entrepreneur's experience is also significantly related to the survival prospects of new ventures and venture capitalists' performance forecasts (Sine et al., 2006; Soriano & Castrogiovanni, 2012). Experienced entrepreneurs possess more precise information about the industry, including the required skills and knowledge, pricing of goods and services, cost structure, risk and uncertainty, processes involved, profit possibilities, and industry trends (Landier & Thesmar, 2009; Dimov, 2010; Ronstadt, 1986; Chandler, 1996; Brudel et al., 1992; Eesley & Roberts, 2012). Venture capital firms consider the entrepreneur's experience as an essential characteristic when financing the venture (Hall & Hofer, 1993; Kaplan & Stromberg, 2004). Their selection criteria, as stated by Knockaert and Vanacker (2013), primarily consist of success predictors related to the founder. Additionally, the type of human capital is also relevant for venture capital firms, as it affects the overall fund performance (Zarutskie, 2010).

Innovation and Risk in Startups

Innovation is an important factor that increases the likelihood of a startup's success. Many studies have found evidence supporting the positive impact of innovation on startups' survival rates. This is because innovation can enhance production capacity, improve competitiveness in the market, and strengthen businesses in a rapidly changing environment (Cohen & Clapper, 1996 a & b; Schumpeter, 1936; Porter, 1980). However, innovation also entails risks that startups must commit to continuously practicing in their industry. This may result in longer payback periods on investments and reduced ability to raise funds due to the lack of collateralized assets (Amason et al., 2006; Brown et al., 2012; Sharma et al. 2022). According to a study conducted by Hyytinen et al. (2014), there is a negative correlation between innovativeness and startup survival rates. The research suggests that as a new venture incorporates more innovative practices, the risk factor for survival also increases. Apart from innovativeness, other parameters can be used to measure risk in a unique experience. Researchers have identified various key-performance benchmarks that should be monitored to maximize return on investment during exit events in Investee Companies (Petty & Gruber, 2011; Zacharakis & Meyer, 2000; Schulte, 2015).

Alternative Exit Routes and Existing Market Scenario

Backing a startup is intriguing because investors do not view it as a typical equity investment, but rather as a chance to exit the startup at some point. Exit routes from a startup include IPO, merger, acquisition, strategic alliance, LBO, and more, and the preferred route varies depending on the company and the investor (Gompers & Lerner, 2005). For example, going public through an IPO is a common exit route for family-owned startups (Petty et al., 1994; Black & Gilson, 1998). Research has been carried out on the factors that affect the decision of Italian and US manufacturing firms to go public (Chemmanur et al., 2010; Pagano et al. 1998).

Entrepreneurs and venture capital firms can benefit from IPOs, as they increase the market value of owners' equity (Black & Gilson, 1998; Holmberg, 1991). Wang and Sim (2001) conducted a study on the preferred exit route for venture capital firms in Singapore. According to their research results, high technology and family-owned enterprises exhibit a greater preference for IPOs. The study also suggests that older VCs tend to have a greater preference for IPOs than younger VCs. A trade sale is also a preferred exit route since, in the case of a private sale, the acquirer is more familiar with the acquiring firm, resulting in higher value for both the acquiring firm and its investors (Schilit, 1991; Wright et al., 1990; Sharma et al., 2022). However, determining the optimal exit route is complex, and several factors influence the decision.

Cumming and MacIntosh (2003) identified five key methods/routes for exit events, including partial and complete exit, and itemized IPO, secondary sale, acquisition, write-off, and buyback as principle exit routes. A sample of 223 firms financed by 35 VC funds was analyzed in a study that examined the correlation between VC contracts and their exits. The study focused on eleven European VCs and observed that the VC funds exited through various means such as buybacks, IPOs, acquisitions, and write-offs. The study found that whenever VCs have weak control rights, there is a higher probability of IPO exits, as well as a greater likelihood of write-off exits.

Researchers have observed differences in exit strategy choices and the effect of these choices on future financing between VC firms in the United States and Canada (Cumming, 2008; Cumming et al., 2007). Ewelt-Knauer et al. (2014) analyzed a sample of 1,435 European–based exits during the period 1992–2010 and identified factors influencing the selection of a particular exit route. A robust correlation was discovered between the exit mechanism preferred by venture capitalists and variables such as the size of the syndicate, the reputation of the selling investment firm, the quality of the transaction, and partial exit. The findings of this study indicate that the economic environment and the state of the capital markets have a significant impact on the selection of the exit strategy. Ozmel et al. (2012) conducted research on the interaction between venture capital and funding from strategic alliances in the private capital market, and how this affects exit outcomes. The study found that venture capital firms with superior networks have a higher likelihood of successfully exiting from startups, as they have access to more information channels and private information. This leads to a higher value for their portfolio companies (Hochberg et al., 2007; Sorensen & Stuart, 2000). Another study conducted by Wang and Sim (2001) investigated the exit route mechanism of startups supported by Venture Capitalists based in Singapore.

Financial Performance of Startups and Reputation of the Investor

Past studies have investigated various other variables to ensure successful investment in an Investee Company. Some researchers have focused on quantitative and analytical models to maximize returns from investments in startups. These models include analytical and econometrics-based models to determine the best time to exit and obtain maximum returns (Shiryaev et al., 2008; Li et al., 2013). Streletzki and Schulte (2013) examined the success factors of venture capitalists' exits, focusing on 64 exits primarily associated with information technology, telecommunication, biotechnology, and microsystem technology segments. They identified educational background, functional parameters, and experience as the three main success factors influencing VCs' exit decisions. Valuable insights for the study can also be obtained from research on exit decisions by angel investors, corporate investors, and angel syndicates.

Mahapatra (2014) conducted an interview with 19 angel investors, categorized as individual investors, syndicate angels, and corporate investors, to examine the impact of investor category on their exit decisions. The study found that the category of investors did not significantly affect their exit phase. However, exit decisions have a significant impact on the reputation of venture capital firms, and vice versa. Another research on US venture exits compared the merger and acquisition and IPO routes and their impact on the reputation of VC. The experience and reputation of venture capitalists also have an impact on the pricing and selection of exit strategies for IPOs (Amor and Kooli, 2020). Additionally, existing market conditions play a substantial role in any exit event (Guillaume & Groh, 2020; Sharma et al., 2022).

The liquidity of the venture capital market in India is not favorable, which reduces the success of exits. The VCs often cannot execute an exit decision due to general illiquidity in the VC industry (Dominic & Gopalswamy, 2019). The features of venture capital firms and other situational factors of funds significantly impact the extent of exit (Schmidt & Bock, 2015).

The *factors* like the attitude of investors towards risk and return, issues related to tax exemption, nature of the business model, a realization of the product's success, the possibility of conflict with the entrepreneur, and supposition regarding the success of the business etc. were found, to contribute to the exit phase (Sharma et al., 2021). The existing research has unfolded many aspects and issues related to startups, their growth, funding, VCs' role, human capital, the impact of innovation on growth and risk factor, performance indicators, etc. Research on the exit of financial backers of startups is limited. However, the researchers have investigated several alternative exit options chosen by entrepreneurs and the exit strategies favored by VC firms. Moreover, such types of studies have done an in-depth analysis of the relationship between experience and reputation of both entrepreneur and VC on the valuation and success of exit. The extant literature is vocal about factors affecting the funding capability of startups, their success factors, and factors affecting the valuation of startups at different stages. However, there is no research articulating the factors or determinants of exit exclusively. Moreover, there is no fully established theory talking about determinants of exits.

Above all, there are other financial backers of startups than VCs, PEs and financial institutions who are the major fund providers. These include angel investors, individual investors and high net worth investors who decide to invest in startups. How do these investors determine their exit strategies? The triggers or determinants of exit strategy have not been addressed distinctly in past studies and are yet to be researched satisfactorily. Exit is an important and last step of any investment process, and current research fills this research gap by exploring the determinants of exit strategies of financial backers providing funds to startups. These financial backers are investors other than VCs, PE firms and financial institutions. The study findings will provide determinants of the profitable exit strategy by financial backers and have managerial implications for startups and financial backers of different categories.

Research Objectives

In lieu of the above research questions, the current study is intended to examine the determinants of the profitable exit strategy by financial backers of startups. In addition to this, the impact of *three characteristics* of startup financial backers, i.e., category or type of investor, the experience of investor and amount of investment, has been used as *moderating variables* to elaborate the causal relationship. Finally, the mediating effect of the impact of the existing market structure was examined to study the causal relationship between the profitability of exit strategy and its determinants.

Research Instrument, Data Inputs and Research Methods

The study is principally based on primary data. A structured questionnaire was developed after a critical review of extant literature. The statements of the questionnaire were developed through a literature survey. Initially, the statements allied to *human capital* (Unger et al., 2011; Zacharakis & Shepherd, 2005), *the experience of the founder and entrepreneur* (Colombo & Grilli, 2010; Casson, 2005; Soriano & Castrogiovanni, 2012; Landier & Thesmar, 2009; Dimov, 2010;), *innovation, technology related aspects* (Gimmon & Levie, 2010; Cohen & Clapper, 1996a&b; Schumpeter, 1936; Amason et al., 2006, Brown et al., 2012), *risk related parameters* (Hyytinen et al. 2014), *the financial performance of startups* (Sine et al., 2006), *financial backer related parameters* (Knockaert & Vanacker, 2013; Petty & Gruber, 2011; Schulte, 2013; Zarutskie, 2010; Zacharakis & Meyer, 2000; Mehta et al., 2023) and *market conditions and startup ecosystem* (Cumming et al., 2007; Knauer et al., 2014; Chemmanur et al., 2010; Dominic & Gopalswamy, 2019; Schmidt & Bock, 2015; Mehta et al., 2022) etc. were included to develop statements of the instrument. The opinion of industry experts was also taken to improve the statement of the research instrument. Further, to ensure face validity and content validity of the research instrument, the expert opinion from industry and academia was both taken (five from industry and four from academia). The questionnaire started with basic questions like characteristics of investors, their experience, the preferred route of exit and amount of investment in startups etc. There were 30 items related to determinants/triggers of exit stratagem by various categories of financial backers, and two items were related to the profitability of exit strategy. The sampling frame of the study includes all individual investors, High Networth Individuals, Angel Investors, Angel forums, Startups, entrepreneurs and any other investor (excluding VCs, PE firms and Banks/Financial institutions/NBFCs (Non-banking financial companies)) investing money in startups. It has executed an exit event in the last ten years. The exclusion of VCs, PE firms and banks/financial institutions/NBFCs is non-availability of data as most of these units approached by researchers were not ready to share the information as their business strategy.

To attain the study's objective, the researchers applied exploratory factor analysis (EFA) based on *306* respondents to determine the latent factors/determinants of an exit strategy. Once the factors were explored and labelled, a fresh sample was used to validate the scale developed through EFA. Data was collected from *339* respondents (please refer to Table 3.5). All required data was collected through references or the snowball method of sampling, wherein the researchers took the utmost care to keep the sample free from researchers' biasness. Through confirmatory factor analysis, the convergent and discriminant validity of the data was investigated. And thus, the final path model was developed to study the causal relationship between determinants of exit strategy and its profitability. Three characteristics of financial backers, i.e., investor category, investor experience and annual investment in a startup, were used as moderators. The path model was further tested for the mediated, direct and indirect effect of triggers of an exit strategy on the profitability of exit.

Results and Discussion

Extraction of Factors/Determinants by Using EFA

The EFA results were obtained using the principal component method of extraction and varimax rotation. To begin with, the KMO value was assessed to ensure reliability, and the obtained value of 0.870 (see Table 3.1) exceeded the threshold limit of 0.6. Furthermore, Bartlett's test of sphericity indicated that the correlation among statements was significant enough for principal component analysis, validating the suitability of the data for factor analysis. An initial assessment of eigenvalues was performed to determine the value for each component in the dataset. Statements with factor loadings below 0.4 were removed (Hair et al., 2005).

Consequently, two statements were removed from the analysis owing to low factor loading (less than 0.4). To check the appropriateness of the data for applying factor analysis, the communalities calculated from the EFA were also examined (please refer to Table 3.2). Six factors had eigenvalues above Kaiser's criterion 1; collectively, these factors explained 79.477 per cent of the total variance (please refer to Table 3.3). These six constructs/factors/determinants were named under (please refer to Table 3.4)

1. Investors'/Financiers' Related Parameters (IRP) (items included=05)
2. Easiness in Execution of Exit Strategy (EEES) (items included=05)
3. Risk Related Parameters (RRP) (items included=03)
4. Startup Related Parameters (SRP) (items included=06)
5. Finance Related Parameters (FRP) (items included=05)
6. Existing Market Set-up and Arrangements (EMSA) (items included=04)

Table 3.1: KMO and Bartlett's Test.

Kaiser-Meyer-Olkin Measure of Sampling Adequacy.		0.870
Bartlett's Test of Sphericity	Approx. Chi-Square	7418.396
	df	378
	Sig.	.000

Table 3.2: Communalities.

	Initial	Extraction
IRP1	1.000	0.825
IRP2	1.000	0.812
IRP3	1.000	0.780
IRP4	1.000	0.835
IRP5	1.000	0.861
FRP1	1.000	0.892
FRP2	1.000	0.902
FRP3	1.000	0.845
FRP4	1.000	0.862
FRP5	1.000	0.836
SRP1	1.000	0.767
SRP2	1.000	0.767
SRP3	1.000	0.787
SRP4	1.000	0.912
SRP5	1.000	0.857
SRP6	1.000	0.825
RRP1	1.000	0.777
RRP2	1.000	0.815
RRP3	1.000	0.792
EMSA1	1.000	0.799
EMSA2	1.000	0.903
EMSA3	1.000	0.843
EMSA4	1.000	0.828
EEES1	1.000	0.644
EEES2	1.000	0.638
EEES3	1.000	0.573
EEES4	1.000	0.610
EEES5	1.000	0.665

Extraction Method: Principal Component Analysis.

Scale Validation (Convergent and Discriminant Validity Using CFA)

As mentioned above, for the validation of the scale developed through EFA, a fresh sample of 339 financial backers was collected. Table 3.5 summarizes the profile of these financial backers. The most significant number of respondents were angel investors and angel forums. These angel forums are informal groups made by angel investors in local areas who collectively invest in startups as a forum, not as an individual angel investor. Out of 339 financial backers of the study, 128 financial backers (67 individual angel investors and 61 angel forums) were in the category of angel investors. Even startups were also putting their own money (popularly called bootstrapping) to exit at a strategic time. There were 58 financial backers in this category.

Table 3.3: Total Variance Explained.

Component	Initial Eigenvalues			Extraction Sums of Squared Loadings			Rotation Sums of Squared Loadings		
	Total	**% of Variance**	**Cumulative %**	**Total**	**% of Variance**	**Cumulative %**	**Total**	**% of Variance**	**Cumulative %**
1	6.454	23.051	23.051	6.454	23.051	23.051	4.925	17.588	17.588
2	4.033	14.403	37.454	4.033	14.403	37.454	4.348	15.529	33.117
3	3.758	13.421	50.875	3.758	13.421	50.875	4.137	14.773	47.890
4	3.264	11.658	62.534	3.264	11.658	62.534	3.386	12.091	59.981
5	2.767	9.884	72.417	2.767	9.884	72.417	3.070	10.965	70.946
6	1.977	7.060	79.477	1.977	7.060	**79.477**	2.389	8.531	**79.477**

Extraction Method: Principal Component Analysis.

Table 3.4: Rotated Component Matrix.

Statements	Component					
	1	2	3	4	5	6
IRP1			0.900			
IRP2			0.888			
IRP3			0.872			
IRP4			0.902			
IRP5			0.922			
FRP1		0.933				
FRP2		0.938				
FRP3		0.912				
FRP4		0.925				
FRP5		0.903				
SRP1	0.869					
SRP2	0.846					
SRP3	0.866					
SRP4	0.945					
SRP5	0.916					
SRP6	0.902					
RRP1						0.863
RRP2						0.871
RRP3						0.864
EMSA1				0.888		
EMSA2				0.949		
EMSA3				0.914		
EMSA4				0.904		
EEES1					0.776	
EEES2					0.794	
EEES3					0.742	
EEES4					0.769	
EEES5					0.807	

Further, the majority (116) of financial backers had 5–8 years of experience investing in startups, and only 77 out of 339 respondents had more than eight years of investment experience with startups. After that, 83 financial backers said that they had invested less than INR 5 lakh (per annum) in startups, while a maximum (111) investors said that they had invested INR 10–15 lakh (per annum) in startups. Only 37 financial backers invested more than 20 lakhs in startups annually (please refer to Table 3.5).

Results of CFA

As mentioned earlier, a confirmatory factor analysis (CFA) was applied to examine the hypothesis that exit strategy is a six-factor structure comprising of Investors'/Financiers' Related Parameters (IRP), Easiness in Execution of Exit Strategy (EEES), Risk Related Pa-

Table 3.5: Profile of the Respondents.

	Type of Investors	No.
1	Individual investor	40
2	Angel Investor	67
3	HNI	42
4	Startup (Bootstrapping)	58
5	Angel Forum	61
6	Others except VCs/PEs/Banks/NBFCs/ Financial Institutions (Business Incubators, Accelerators, Private Educational Institutes, Government funding and Winning from Contests etc.)	71
	Total	339
	Experience of Investing in Startups	
1	Less than 2 years	49
2	2–5 years	97
3	5–8 years	116
4	More than 8 years	77
	Total	339
	Annual Investment (INR Lakhs)	
1	Less than 5	83
2	5–10 lakh	38
3	10–15 lakh	111
4	15–20 lakh	70
5	Above 20 lakh	37
	Total	339

rameters (RRP), Startup Related Parameters (SRP), Finance Related Parameters (FRP), and Existing Market Set-up and Arrangements (EMSA). The study's model fit summary shows that all excellent model indicators were above the predicted level or benchmark. CMIN/Df, GFI, AGFI, RMSEA, NFI, CFI, and TLI are analyzed to determine model fit. All these indicators met the researchers' threshold criteria. Figure 3.1 shows the model fit summary that the measurement model meets all standard criteria for a successful model.

Results of Default Model is, Chi-square = 586.969, Degrees of freedom = 398 and Probability level = 0.000. Both convergent and discriminant construct validity were investigated (see Table 3.6). The convergent validity was examined using both CCR and AVE. Composite reliability tells whether items measure latent components consistently. Table 3.6 shows that the CCR score of all constructs is above 0.7, indicating that observable factors or items explain a substantial share of latent construct variance. The AVE index of Exit strategy is found to be 0.311, 0.8 for Existing Market setup and Arrangements AVE and 0.519 for Profit/Loss of Exit strategy. The AVE of all constructs

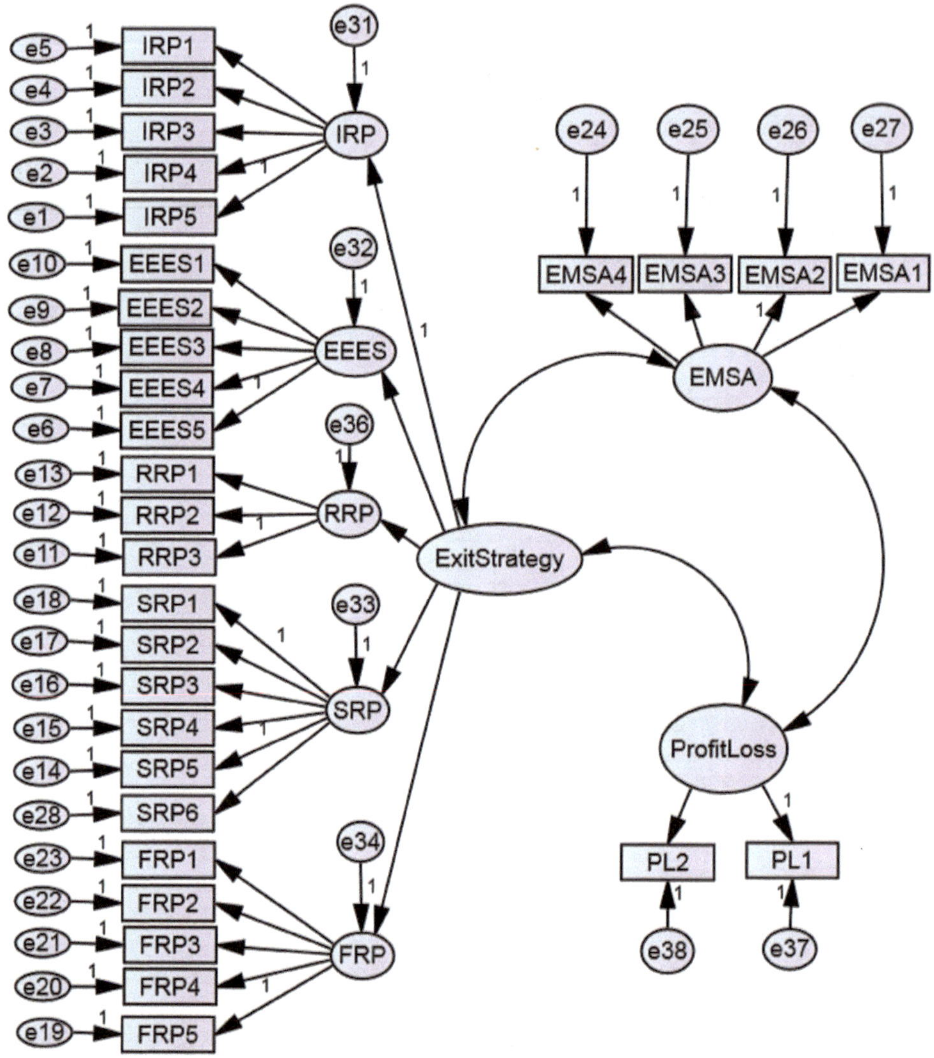

Figure 3.1: Measurement Model of Determinants of Profitable Exit Strategy CMIN/df = 1.475, df = 398, RMSEA = 0.028, GFI = 0.901, AGFI = 0.884, CFI =0.979, TLI = 0.977, NFI = 0.939.

of the measurement model except exit strategy (0.311) is found above 0.5, which further confirms good convergent validity (Fornell & Larcker, 1981, Bagozzi & Yi, 1988).

Discriminant validity describes how one concept differs from another. Table 3.7 shows the discriminant validity findings, indicating that the study's constructs have appropriate discriminant validity. It signifies separate constructions. It says that a specific latent construct may be interpreted for higher item variance than other measurement model constructs.

Table 3.6: Composite Construct Reliability and Average Variance Extracted.

Factors↓	Variables↓	SRW	Composite Construct Reliability	Average Variance Extracted
IRP	IRP1	0.882	0.893	0.786
	IRP2	0.894		
	IRP3	0.853		
	IRP4	0.901		
	IRP5	0.903		
EEES	EEES1	0.753	0.793	0.581
	EEES2	0.794		
	EEES3	0.692		
	EEES4	0.781		
	EEES5	0.788		
RRP	RRP1	0.852	0.809	0.725
	RRP2	0.882		
	RRP3	0.820		
SRP	SRP1	0.885	0.922	0.796
	SRP2	0.838		
	SRP3	0.884		
	SRP4	0.938		
	SRP5	0.925		
	SRP6	0.881		
FRP	FRP1	0.940	0.950	0.868
	FRP2	0.961		
	FRP3	0.922		
	FRP4	0.924		
	FRP5	0.910		
EMSA	EMSA1	0.848	0.890	0.800
	EMSA2	0.963		
	EMSA3	0.889		
	EMSA4	0.874		
PROFIT/LOSS			0.547	0.519
Exit Strategy			0.606	0.311

Path Model and Mediation Effect

Figure 3.2 shows the path model of the study. The determinants of exit strategy were found significantly affect the profit of exit strategy, as the regression coefficient was found to be significant (please refer to Table 3.8). The direct path's significance permits examining it further for mediation effect. The existing market setup and arrangements

Table 3.7: Discriminant Validity.

Method 1	**Exit strategy**	**EMSA**	**Profit Loss**
Exit strategy	1.000		
EMSA	0.377	1.000	
Profit/Loss	0.349	0.403	1.000
	Exit strategy	**EMSA**	**ProfitLoss**
Exit strategy	0.557		
EMSA	0.377	0.895	
ProfitLoss	0.349	0.403	0.721
Method 2	**Exit strategy**	**EMSA**	**ProfitLoss**
Exit strategy	0.311		
EMSA	0.142	0.800	
ProfitLoss	0.122	0.162	0.519

(EMSA) for startups also affect the profit or loss (ProfitLoss) of an exit strategy. Also, it is affected by other determinants of exit strategy (ExitStrategy). Hence, it is used as a mediator. Figure 3.3 and Table 3.8 explain the results of the path model before and after the mediation effect. The direct path model has shown that the determinants of exit routes significantly impact the profit/loss strategy of exit as β (ExitStrategy) = 0.861 and significant at 5 per cent significance. After the incorporation of the existing market structure and agreement (EMSA) as a mediating variable in the direct path, the β (ExitStrategy) is reduced to 0.573 and β (EMSA) is 0.441. Both of these parameters were found significant; hence, it is a case of partial mediation. There is also some improvement in the r-square value obtained after the mediation effect.

Table 3.8: Results of Regression Analysis.

			SRW	**S.E.**	**C.R.**	**p-value**	**R-Square**
Before Mediation							0.742
ProfitLoss	<---	ExitStrategy	0.861	0.075	10.633	0.000	
After Mediation							
ProfitLoss	<---	ExitStrategy	0.573	0.03	18.853	0.000	0.752
EMSA	<---	ExitStrategy	0.454	0.105	9.376	0.000	
ProfitLoss	<---	EMSA	0.441	0.014	14.492	0.000	

The current research has discovered six exit route/strategy determinants. These are, Investors'/Financiers' Related Parameters (IRP) (items included=05), Easiness in Execution of Exit Strategy (EEES) (items included=05), Risk Related Parameters (RRP)

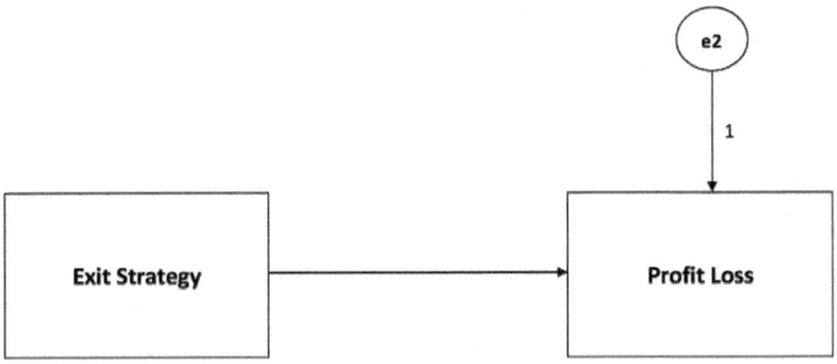

Figure 3.2: Path Model.

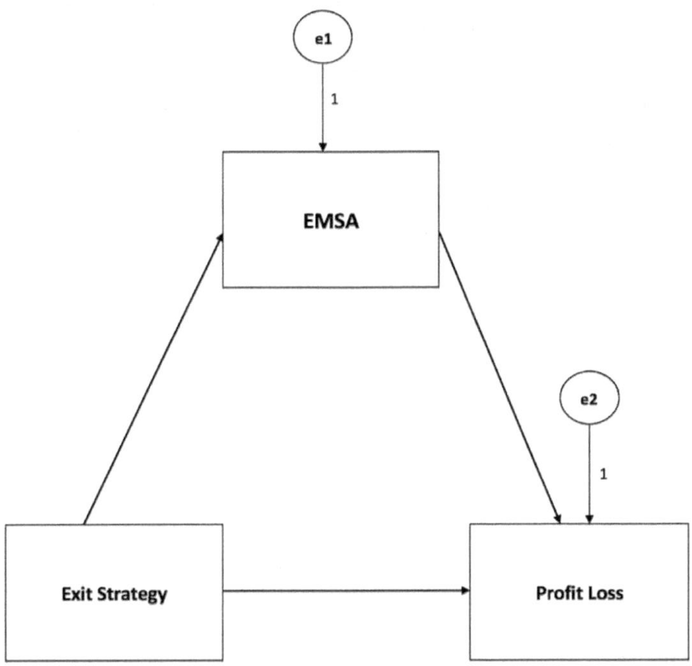

Figure 3.3: Mediation Effect.

(items included=03), Startup Related Parameters (SRP) (items included=06), Finance Related Parameters (FRP) (items included=05), and Existing Market Set-up and Arrangements (EMSA) (items included=04). The investors'/financiers' related parameters include their corpus size, ability to anatomize the deal, the practice of taking exit decision and their reputation etc.

The findings of research stipulated by Wang & Sim (2001), Ozmel et al. (2012), and Knauer et al. (2014) established that the existing exit routes, the preference for an exit route and the market scenario affect the selection of exit alternative by the investor-investee. Similarly, the next factor of the study has also captured these components. The variables like an easement in executing a specific exit route, the engagement of startup managers in executing exit, and the availability of exit options, etc., characterize easiness in executing exit strategy (EEES). Similarly, the variables like the risk involved in technology used by startups and the threat of entry of new competitors culminate in the risk-related parameters (RRP). In one of the previous research by Hyytinen et al. (2014) significance of the risk element due to innovative practices by startups is addressed. The background and experience of founder members, their human capital, the commitment of the managerial team in the operation of the startup and the monitoring capability of startups to better utilize their funds etc., are among the startup-related parameters (SRP). Previous research (Colombo & Grilli, 2010; Casson, 2005; Soriano & Castrogiovanni, 2012; Landier & Thesmar, 2009; Dimov, 2010) have emphasized the characteristics and experience of founder members and human capital in startups.

The research findings reported by MacIntosh (2003), Cumming et al. (2007), Chemmanur et al. (2010), Knauer et al. (2014) and Schmidt & Bock (2015) have sturdily postulated the role startup related parameters. The finance-related parameters include the target profit or capital appreciation expected by investors or financial backers, the expected rate of return on investment and the profitability of the startups. Sine et al. (2006) has also highlighted the relevance of financial performance. And at the end, the regulatory framework of the country, the overall market structure, and the echo system for startup funding represent the existing market setup and arrangements (EMSA). It conforms with the results of Dominic and Gopalswamy, 2019 that pinpointed the liquidity position of the market as an essential factor in a deal with startups.

Moderation Effect

In the end, the path model of the study was moderated by three characteristics of financial backers, i.e., type, experience and investment size of financial backers. Table 3.9

Table 3.9: Results based on Type, Experience and Annual Investment of Financial Backers.

	Type of Financial Backers	Estimate	SRW	S.E.	C.R.	p-value
1	Individual investor	0.802	0.861	0.075	10.633	0.000
2	Angel Investor	0.257	0.311	0.097	2.652	0.008
3	HNI	0.45	0.531	0.112	4.021	0.000
4	Startup (Bootstrapping)	0.652	0.764	0.073	8.942	0.000
5	Angel Forum	0.738	0.794	0.073	10.107	0.000
6	Others except VCs/Pes/Banks/NBFCs/Financial Institutions (Angel Forums, Business Incubators, Accelerators, Government funding and Winning from Contests)	0.192	0.311	0.07	2.734	0.006

Table 3.9 (continued)

	Type of Financial Backers	Estimate	SRW	S.E.	C.R.	p-value
	Experience					
1	Less than 2 years	0.6	0.695	0.089	6.726	0.000
2	2–5 years	0.624	0.739	0.058	10.732	0.000
3	5–8 years	0.673	0.752	0.055	12.227	0.000
4	More than 8 years	0.69	0.77	0.065	10.541	0.000
	Annual Investment (INR Lakhs)					
1	less than 5	0.739	0.748	0.072	10.201	0.000
2	5–10 lakh	0.78	0.703	0.129	6.052	0.000
3	10–15 lakh	0.768	0.808	0.054	14.35	0.000
4	15–20 lakh	733	0.762	0.075	9.781	0.000
5	Above 20 lakh	0.786	0.783	0.103	7.604	0.000

has clearly shown that the determinants of exit strategy have a significant impact on the profit/loss of an exit decision. Furthermore, the p-value for determinants of exit strategy is found to be significant at a 5 per cent level of significance across all moderating variables.

Conclusion and Implications

Exit decisions are a matter of contention for investors, as they aim to obtain the highest returns from their investments in companies. Venture capital firms, private equity firms, and banks/financial institutions/non-banking financial companies, being large funding organizations, have well-equipped professional teams that perform cost-benefit analyses to determine the appropriate exit time and customized exit routes. These experts help to devise a suitable mechanism to exit investments profitably. However, the exit strategy components employed by these significant investors may or may not be suitable for other financial backers analyzed in the current study.

The study provides a noteworthy contribution as it uncovers that financial backers of startups consider six factors, namely, Investors/Financiers related parameters (IRP), Easiness in Execution of Exit Strategy (EEES), Risk related parameters (RRP), Startups related Parameters (SRP), Finance related parameters (FRP), and Existing Market Set-up and Arrangements (EMSA), while making exit decisions. These determinants are collectively referred to as determinants of exit strategy, and they significantly impact the success or failure of an exit decision. Furthermore, these determinants are crucial for financial backers across different categories, including the type of financial backer, experience, and annual investment amount.

The study has significant implications for both theoretical and managerial aspects. The researchers' findings have contributed to the current literature and provided valuable insights into the determinants of exit strategies by investors. The study's uniqueness lies in the development of a scale to examine the factors influencing exit strategies, which was previously lacking in meticulous research. The identified determinants need to be continuously studied to build upon existing theories of exit strategies. With an increasing number of startups exits globally, the significance of the issue highlighted in this study cannot be overstated, and researchers will continue to benefit from further exploration in this area.

Additionally, the study has important managerial implications. It offers valuable insights for both investors and financial backers of startups. These stakeholders often concentrate on valuation and fundraising to ensure the success of their businesses. However, the true return on investment can only be ascertained when financial backers withdraw their investment. Thus, identifying the factors that contribute to successful exits can offer useful information for managerial applications. Investments in startups are made for both financial gain and strategic advantage.

Investing in startups generally carries a higher expectation of a premium compared to investing in traditional businesses. As a result, the research results can assist various stakeholders such as individual investors, high-net-worth individuals (HNIs), angel investors and forums, business incubators, accelerators, startups, and entrepreneurs in considering crucial factors when devising their exit strategy.

Limitation and Scope for Future Research

The study excluded venture capitalists (VCs), private equity (PE) firms, and banks/financial institutions/non-banking financial companies (NBFCs) that invest in startups due to data collection challenges. Nevertheless, these financial backers possess valuable expertise about startup backers. Thus, future researchers could investigate the insights shared by these financial backers to advance the understanding of exit strategies for startup investments.

References

Aghion, P., Bolton, P. & Tirole, J. (2004). "Exit Options in Corporate Finance: Liquidity versus Incentives", *Review of Finance*, *8*, 327–353.

Amason, A.C., Shrader R.C. & Tompson, G. H. (2006). "Newness and novelty: relating top management team composition to new venture performance", *Journal of Business Venture*, *21*, 125–148.

Amor, S. B., & Kooli, M. (2020). "Do M&A exits have the same effect on venture capital reputation than IPO exits?", *Journal of Banking & Finance*, *111*, *105704*. doi:10.1016/j.jbankfin.2019.105704.

Bagozzi, R. & Yi, Y. (1988). "On the Evaluation of Structural Equation Models", *Journal of the Academy of Marketing Sciences*, *16*, 74–94.

Bascha, A. & Walz, U. (2001). "Convertible Securities and Optimal Exit Decisions in Venture Capital Finance", *Journal of corporate Finance*, *7*(3), 285–306.

Beckman, C.M., Burton, M.D. & O'Reilly, C. (2007). "Early teams: The impact of team demography on VC financing and going public", *Journal of Business Venturing*, *22*, 147–173.

Berglof, E. (1994). "A Control Theory of Venture Capital Finance", *Journal of Law, Economics & Organisation*, *10*, 247–267.

Berlin, M. (1998). "That thing venture capitalists do", *Business Review–Federal Reserve Bank of Philadelphia*, Jan/Feb, 15–26.

Black, B. S. & Gilson, R. J. (1998). "Venture capital and the structure of capital markets: Bank versus stock markets", *Journal of Financial Economics*, *47*, 243–277.

Brown, J.R., Martinsson, G., & Petersen, B.C. (2012). "Do financing constraints matter for R&D?', *European Economic Review*, *56*(8), 1512–1529.

Brüderl, J., Preisendörfer, P., and Ziegler, R. (1992). "Survival chances of newly founded business organizations", *American Sociological Review*, *57*, 227–242.

Bygrave, W. D. & Timmons, J. A. (1992). "Venture Capital at the Crossroads" (Boston: Harvard Business School Press).

Casson, M. (2005). "Entrepreneurship and the Theory of the Firm", *Journal of Economic Behavior and Organization*, *58*(2), 327–348.

Chandler, G. (1996). "Business similarity as a moderator of the relationship between pre-ownership experience and venture performance", *Entrepreneurship Theory and Practice*, *20*, 51–65.

Chemmanur, T. J., He, S., & Nandy, D.K. (2010). "The Going-Public Decision and the Product Market: Empirical Evidence", *Review of Financial Studies*, *23*, 1855–1908.

Clement, K. W. & Valerie Y.L. S. (2001). "Exit strategies of venture capital-backed companies in Singapore", *Venture Capital: An International Journal of Entrepreneurial Finance*, *3(*4), 337–358

Cochrane, J. H. (2005). "The Risk and Return of Venture Capital", *Journal of Financial Economics*, *75*(1), 3–52.

Cohen, W.M., & Klepper S. (1996a). "Firm size and the nature of innovation within industries: the case of process and product R&D", *The Review of Economics and Statistics*, *78*(2), 232–243.

Cohen, W.M., & Klepper S. (1996b). "A reprise of size and R&D", *The Economic Journal*, *106*(437), 925–951.

Colombo, M. G., & Grilli, L. (2005). "Founders' Human Capital and the Growth of New Technology Based Firms: A Competence-Based View", *Research Policy*, *34*, 795–816.

Colombo, M. G., & Grilli, L. (2010). "On Growth Drivers of High-Tech Start-Ups: Exploring the Role of Founders' Human Capital and Venture Capital", *Journal of Business Venturing*, *25*(6), 610–626.

Cooper, A. C., Gimeno-Gascon, F. J. & Woo, C. Y. (1994). "Initial Human and Financial Capital as Predictors of New Venture Performance", *Journal of Business Venturing*, *9*, 371–395.

Cumming, D. & Macintosh, J. G. (2003). "A cross-country comparison of full and partial venture capital exits", *Journal of Banking & Finance*, *27*, 511–548.

Cumming, D., Grant, F. & Schwienbacher, A. (2006). "Legality and Venture Capital Exits", *Journal of Corporate Finance*, *12*, 214–245.

Cumming, D.J. (2008). "Contracts and exits in venture capital finance", *Review of Financial Studies*, *21*(5), 1947–1982.

Cumming, D.J., Siegel, D.S. & Wright, M. (2007). "Private equity, leveraged buyouts and governance", *Journal of Corporate Finance*, *13*(4), 439–460.

Dimov, D. (2010). "Nascent Entrepreneurs and Venture Emergence: Opportunity Confidence, Human Capital, and Early Planning", *Journal of Management Studies*, *47*, 1123–1153. 10.1111/j.1467-6486.2009.00874.x.

Dimov, D., & DeClercq, D. (2006). "Venture Capital Investment Strategy and Portfolio Failure Rate: A Longitudinal Study", *Entrepreneurship Theory and Practice*, *30*, 207–223.

Dominic, J., & Gopalaswamy, A. K. (2019). "Is the venture capital market liquid? Evidence from India", *Global Finance Journal*. doi:10.1016/j.gfj.2019.04.002

Eesley, C. E., & Roberts, E.B. (2012). "Are You Experienced or Are You Talented? When Does Innate Talent Versus Experience Explain Entrepreneurial Performance?", *Strategic Entrepreneurship Journal*, *6*(3), 207–219.

Ewelt-Knauer, C., Knauer, T. & Thielemann, M. (2014). "Exit behaviour of investment companies: the choice of exit channel", *Journal of Business Economics*, *84*. 10.1007/s11573-013-0699-8.

Fornell, C. & Larcker, D. (1981). "Evaluating Structural Equation Models with Unobservable Variables and Measurement Error", *Journal of Marketing Research*, *18*(1), 39–50. doi:10.2307/3151312

Ghazy, N., Ghoneim, H. & Lang, G. (2022). "Entrepreneurship, productivity and digitalization: Evidence from the EU", *Technology in Society*, *70*, 102052, ISSN 0160–791X, https://doi.org/10.1016/j.techsoc.2022.102052.

Gimmon, E. & Levie, J. (2010). "Founder's human capital, external investment, and the survival of new high-technology ventures", *Research Policy*, *Elsevier*, *39*(9), 1214–1226, November.

Gompers, P. A. & Lerner, J. (2005). "Venture Capital Investment Cycles: The Impact of Public Markets", National Bureau of Economic Research.

Gompers, P. A. & Lerner. J. (2000). "Money Chasing Deals? The Impact of Fund Inflows on the Valuation of Private Equity Investments", *Journal of Financial Economics*, *55*, 281–325.

Gorman, M. & Sahlman, W. A. (1989). "What Do Venture Capitalists Do?", *Journal of Business Venturing*, *4*(4), 231–248.

Guillaume, A. & Groh, A.P. (2020). "Strategic exits in secondary venture capital markets. *Journal of Business Venturing*, 105999–. doi:10.1016/j.jbusvent.2019.105999.

Hair, J. F., Black, W. C., Babin, B. J., Anderson, R. E. & Tatham, R. L. (2006). "Multivariate Data Analysis', 6th ed. Upper Saddle River, NJ: Prentice Hall.

Hair, J. F., Anderson, R. E., Tatham, R. L., & Black, W. C. (2005). Multivariate Data Analysis (5th ed.). Prentice Hall.

Hall, J. & Hofer, C.W. (1993). "Venture capitalists' decision criteria in new venture evaluation", *Journal of Business Venturing*, *8*, 25–42.

Haveman, H.A. & Khaire, M.V. (2004). "Survival beyond Succession? The contingent impact of founder succession on organizational failure", *Journal of Business Venturing*, *19*(3), pp. 437–63.

Hellmann, T. & Puri. M. (2002). "Venture Capital and the Professionalization of Startup Firms: Empirical Evidence", *Journal of Finance*, *57*, 169–197.

Hidayat, S. E., Bamahriz, O., Hidayati, N., Sari, C. A. & Dewandaru, G. (2022). "Value drivers of startup valuation from venture capital equity-based investing: A global analysis with a focus on technological factors", *Borsa Istanbul Review*, *22*(4), 653–667, https://doi.org/10.1016/j.bir.2021.10.001.

Hochberg, Y. & Ljungqvist, A., Lu, Y. (2007). "Whom you know matters: venture capital networks and investment performance", *Journal of Finance*, *62*, 251–301.

Hoffman, C.A. (1972). "The venture capital investment process. A particular aspect of regional economic development. Un unpublished doctoral dissertation. The University of Texas at Austin.

Holmberg, S. R. (1991). "Value creation and capture: entrepreneurship harvest and IPO strategies. In *Frontiers of Entrepreneurial Research*, proceedings of the annual Babson College Entrepreneur- ship Research Conference (Wellesley, MA: Centre for Entrepreneurial Studies, Babson College).

Hyytinen, A., Pajarinen, M. & Rouvinen, P. (2014). "Does innovativeness reduce startup survival rates?", *Journal of Business Venturing*, *30*(4), 564–581.

Kaplan, S.N. & Strömberg, P. (2004). "Characteristics, contracts and actions: evidence from venture capitalist analyses", *The Journal of Finance*, *59*(5), 2177–2210.

Khanna, V. & Sharma, R. (2017). "Customer Switching Behavior in Retail Banking in India", International Journal of Applied Business and Economic Research (SCOPUS), *15*(9), 427–441.

Kirkley, W.W. (2016). "Entrepreneurial Behaviour: The Role of Values." *International Journal of Entrepreneurial Behavior & Research*, 22(3), 290–328.

Knockaert, M. & Vanacker, T. (2013). "The Association Between Venture Capitalists' Selection and Value Adding Behavior: Evidence from Early Stage High Tech Venture Capitalists', *Small Business Economics, 40*(3), 493–509.

Landier, A. & Thesmar, D. (2009). "Financial Contracting with Optimistic Entrepreneurs", *The Review of Financial Studies, 22*(1), 117–150.

Li, Y. & Chi, T. (2013). "Venture Capitalists' Decision to Withdraw: The Role of Portfolio Configuration from a Real Options Lens." *Strategic Management Journal* 34, 1351–1366.

MacMillan, I. C., Siegel, R. & SubbaNarasimha, P. N. (1985). "Criteria Used by Venture Capitalists to Evaluate New Venture Proposals", *Journal of Business Venturing, 1*, 119–128.

MacMillan, I.C., Zemann, L., & Subbanarasimha, P.N. (1987). "Criteria distinguishing successful from unsuccessful ventures in the venture screening process", *Journal of Business Venturing, 2*, 123–137.

Mahajan, V. & Sharma, R. (2017). "Future of Depository with Introduction of Payment Bank- A Game Changer to Capital Market", International Journal of Applied Business and Economic Research (SCOPUS), *15*(9), 343–356.

Mahapatra T. (2014). "The Exit Phase of Individual Angels, Angel Syndicates and Corporate Angels", *Journal of Management Research, 14*(2),

Mason, C. M. & Harrison, R. T. (2006). "After the exit: Acquisitions, entrepreneurial recycling and regional economic development", *Regional Studies, 40*(1), 55–73.

Mason, M. C. & Harrison T. R. (2002). "Is it worth it? The rates of return from informal venture capital investments", *Journal of Business Venturing, 17(*3), 211–236.

Mehta, K., Sharma, R. & Khanna, V. (2023). "Customer switching behaviour in Indian retail banking using logit regression", *International Journal of Business Excellence*, Article in Press.

Mehta, K., Sharma, R., Vyas, V. & Kuckreja, J.S. (2022). "Exit strategy decision by venture capital firms in India using fuzzy AHP", *Journal of Entrepreneurship in Emerging Economies, 14*(4), 643–669. https://doi.org/10.1108/JEEE-05-2020-0146.

Mueller, E. & Reize, F. (2013). "Loan availability and investment: can innovative companies better cope with loan denials?", *Applied Economics, Taylor & Francis Journals, 45*(36), 5001–5011.

Nahata, R. (2008). "Venture Capital Reputation and Investment Performance", *Journal of Financial Economics, 90*(2), pp.127–151.

Ozmel, U., Robinson, S.T. & Stuart, T.E. (2012). "Strategic alliances, venture capital, and exit decisions in early stage high–tech firms", *Journal of Financial Economics, 107*, 655–670.

Pagano, M., Panetta, F. & Zingales, L. (1998). "Why do companies go public? An empirical analysis", *Journal of Finance, 53*(1), 27–64.

Petty, J. S., & Gruber, M. (2011). "In Pursuit of the Real Deal': A Longitudinal Study of VC Decision Making", *Journal of Business Venturing, 26*(2), 172–188.

Petty, W. J., Bygrave, W. D. & Shulman, J. M. (1994). "Harvesting the entrepreneurial venture: a time for creating value", *Journal of Applied Corporate Finance, 7*(1), 48–58.

Porter, M.E. (1980). "Competitive Strategy: Techniques for Analyzing Industries and Competitors. The Free Press, New York.

Ronstadt, R. (1986). "Exit, stage left: why entrepreneurs end their entrepreneurial careers before retirement", *Journal of Business Venturing, 1*(3), 323–338.

Schilit, W. K. (1991). "Dream makers and deal breakers: Inside the venture capital industry. Englewood Cliffs, N.J.; London; Toronto and Sydney: Prentice Hall, p xxiv, 215.

Schmidt, M. & Bock, C. (2015). "Should I stay, or should I go? How fund dynamics influence Venture Capital exit decisions", *Review of Financial Economics*. 27(C), 68–82

Schulte, P. (2015). "Does skill-biased technical change diffuse internationally?', ZEW Discussion Papers 15–088, ZEW – Leibniz Centre for European Economic Research.

Schumpeter, J. A. (1936). "The theory of economic development, Harvard University Press, Cambridge, 1936.

Sharma, A. & Sharma, R. (2022). "Exploring Tax Decision Factors: A Perspective from North Indian Tax Practitioners", *Journal of Tax Reform*, *8*(3): 285–297. https://doi.org/10.15826/jtr.2022.8.3.122

Sharma, R., Mehta, K. & Goel, A. (2022). "Non-linear relationship between board size and performance of Indian companies", *Journal of Management and Governance* (2022). https://doi.org/10.1007/s10997-022-09651-8.

Sharma, R., Mehta, K. & Sharma, O. (2021). "Exploring Deep Learning to Determine the Optimal Environment for Stock Prediction Analysis", 2021 International Conference on Computational Performance Evaluation, ComPE 2021, 2021, pp. 148–152

Sharma, R., Mehta, K., & Vyas, V. (2020). "Responsible Investing: A Study on Non–Economic Goals and Investors' Characteristics", *Applied Finance Letters*, *9(SI)*, 63–78. https://doi.org/10.24135/afl.v9i2.245

Shiryaev, A., Xu, Z.Q. & Zhou, X.Y. (2008). "Thou shalt buy and hold", *Quantitative Finance*, *8*(8), 765–776.

Sine, W. D., Mitsuhashi, H. & Kirsch, D. A. (2006). "Revisiting Burns and Stalker: Formal Structure and New Venture Performance in Emerging Economic Sectors", *Academy of Management Journal*, *49*(1), 121–132.

Sørensen, B. J. & Stuart, E. T. (2000). "Aging, Obsolescence, and Organizational Innovation", *Administrative Science Quarterly*, *45*, 81–112. 10.2307/2666980.

Soriano, D. R. & Castrogiovanni, G. J. (2012). "The Impact of Education, Experience and Inner Circle Advisors on SME Performance: Insights from a Study of Public Development Centers", *Small Business Economics*, *38*(3), 333–349.

Streletzki, J. G. & Schulte, R. (2013). "Which Venture Capital Selection Criteria Distinguish High– Flyer Investments?", *Venture Capital: An International Journal of Entrepreneurial Finance*, 15(1), 29–52.

Stuart, R. W. & Abetti, P. A. (1990). "Impact of Entrepreneurial and Management Experience on Early Performance", *Journal of Business Venturing*, *5*, 151–162.

Teece, D. & Pisano, G. (1994). "The Dynamic Capabilities of Firms: An Introduction", *Industrial and Corporate Change*, *3*(3), 537–556.

Tyebjee, T. T. and Bruno, A. V. (1984). "A Model of Venture Capitalist Investment Activity", *Management Science*, *30*, 1051–1066.

Unger, J.A., Rauch,A., Frese, M. & Rosenbusch, N. (2011). "Human Capital and Entrepreneurial Success: A Meta–Analytical Review", *Journal of Business Venturing*, 26(3), 341–358.

Wang, C.K. & Sim, V. (2001). "Exit Strategies of Venture–backed Companies in Singapore", *Venture Capital*, *3*, 337–358.

William W. K. (2016). "Creating ventures: decision factors in new venture creation", *Asia Pacific Journal of Innovation and Entrepreneurship*, *10*(1), 151–167.

Wright, M., Chiplin, B., Thompson, S. & Robbie, K. (1990). "Realizations of venture capital investments: the case of management buy–outs in the UK", *Service Industries Journal*, *10*, 499–520.

Xun L., Tan, H. H., Wilson, C., & Wu, Z. (2013). "When should venture capitalists exit their investee companies?", *International Journal of Managerial Finance*, *9*(4), 351–364.

Vyas, V., Mehta, K. & Sharma, R. (2020). "Investigating socially responsible investing behaviour of Indian investors using structural equation modelling", *Journal of Sustainable Finance & Investment*, 1–23 DOI: 10.1080/20430795.2020.1790958

Vyas, V., Mehta, K., Sharma, R. (2023). "The nexus between toxic-air pollution, health expenditure, and economic growth: An empirical study using ARDL", *International Review of Economics and Finance, 84*, 154–166 https://doi.org/10.1016/j.iref.2022.11.017

Zacharakis, A. L., & G. D. Meyer. (2000). "The Potential of Actuarial Decision Models: Can They Improve the Venture Capital Investment Decision?", *Journal of Business Venturing*, 15(4), 323–346.

Zacharakis, A.L. & Shepherd, D.A. (2005). "A non-additive decision-aid for venture capitalists' investment decisions", *European Journal of Operational Research*, *162*, 673–689.

Zarutskie, R. (2010). "The Role of Top Management Team Human Capital in Venture Capital Markets: Evidence from First-Time Funds", *Journal of Business Venturing*, *25*(1), 155–172.

Ram Singh and Vyomkesh Bhatt

4 Technological Advancement in Industrial Revolution 4.0 for Sustainable Development of India: Understanding Linkages in Theory and Practice

Abstract: Human progress has been fueled by technological advancement throughout history. The innovation of apparatuses for developing, reaping, and handling crops added to the beginning of the rural age and the arrangement of the principal civilizations approximately a long time ago. The modern era of information technology is another chapter in human history that has been transformed by technology. In more recent history, the discovery and application of the scientific principles of mechanics and physics led to the invention of the machines that pushed humanity into the industrial revolution. Sustainable development aims to achieve human development goals while preserving the natural systems' capacity to provide resources and ecosystem services that the economy and society rely on. This study aims to investigate whether technological integration can be used to promote sustainable development in India. The data for the study is collected from various secondary sources. Innovation empowers the advancement of new items and administrations that utilize less energy, synthetics, and water and diminishes squandering from tasks, which can, at the same time, work on both natural maintainability and functional efficiencies. By coordinating innovation into creation processes, we can anticipate and forestall environmental calamities and tackle the causes that frequently appear innocuous.

Keywords: Industrial Revolution, Sustainability, Artificial Intelligence, Machine Learning, IBM Environmental Intelligence Suite

Introduction

Human progress has been fueled by technological advancement throughout history. The innovation of apparatuses for developing, reaping, and handling crops added to the beginning of the rural age and the arrangement of the principal civilizations approximately a long time ago. The modern era of information technology is another chapter in human history that has been transformed by technology. In more recent

Ram Singh, MM Institute of Management, Maharishi Markandeshwar (Deemed to be University), Mullana-Ambala, Haryana, India
Vyomkesh Bhatt, Department of Management Studies, G L Bajaj Institute of Technology and Management, Greater Noida, India

https://doi.org/10.1515/9783111170022-004

history, the discovery and application of the scientific principles of mechanics and physics led to the invention of the machines that pushed humanity into the industrial revolution. Sustainable development aims to achieve human development goals while preserving the natural systems' capacity to provide resources and ecosystem services that the economy and society rely on. Industrial 4.0 gives that ideal ground and climate for such arising innovations to develop and convey arrangements equipped for conveying a customized client experience to the majority across the planet. For example, each client has a particular solace list and spending plan section, while thinking about purchasing an item/administration and satisfying those perquisites genuinely conveys worth to the client and, in the end, one's business.

Technological Innovation

Innovations in technology have been crucial to the progress of humanity, civilization, and sovereign nations. It has been argued that technology, at least in certain forms, is a key component of what sets humans apart from other species and determines our advancement. Artificial Intelligence (AI), Machine Learning (ML), Big Data Analytics (BDA), the Internet of Things (IoT), etc., have replaced the technology of the Stone Age, which consisted of making tools out of stone, growing crops, and sewing clothes out of animal hides. Inventions in technology were spurred by growing scientific understanding, which in turn fueled the growth of the industrial revolution. The term "industrial revolution" describes the period in which individuals were able to use new technologies to make manufacturing more efficient (see Figure 4.1). Because of these changes, business operations are now more efficient, the amount of resources used has gone down, company sizes have grown, and the economy as a whole has grown.

The industrial revolution advances, wherein each phase led to technological innovations, are significantly responsible for the current prosperous state of the economy. When dependent on resource cultivation and distinctive creation, the Modern Transformation introduced another period of large-scale manufacturing, computerized processing plants, and mass utilization. New machinery, power sources, and organizational strategies enabled existing industries to boost output and efficiency. Additionally, it contributed to the growth of the middle class by creating wealth that was more evenly distributed than in previous centuries. In addition to scientific advancements, the Industrial Revolution also impacted society and culture. The creation of new machines like the spinning Jenny and the power loom that allowed for more output with less labor input and the introduction of new energy sources like coal, electricity, petroleum, the internal combustion engine, and new materials like iron and steel all contributed to the rise of industrialization. These innovations made the massive industrialization of industry and the expanding utilization of the world's natural resources possible.

Industry Revolution Phases

Industry 1.0

The use of water and steam in production was revolutionized during the First Industrial Revolution, which began around 1760. As a result, more commodities of different types may be produced, raising living standards for certain people. Industrialization had a profound impact on the textile industry and on the development of the transportation sector. Machine usage became more practical with the advent of cheap, readily available fuels like steam and coal, and the concept of producing with machines caught on swiftly. Modern machinery has facilitated increased production efficiency and opened the door to several new scientific discoveries and technological advancements.

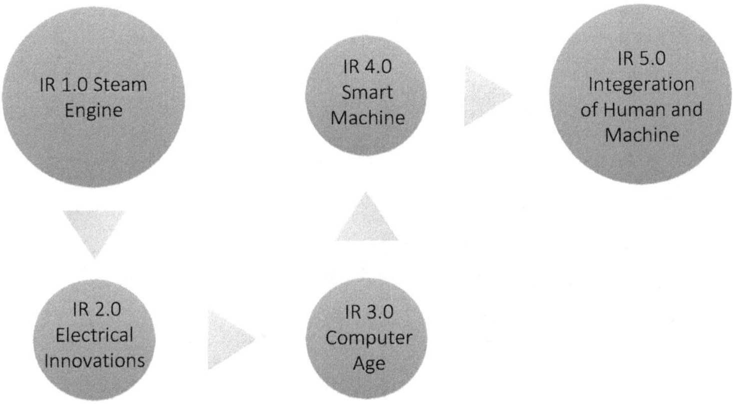

Figure 4.1: Technological Innovation- Industrial Revolution Phases.
Source: Authors' Compilation.

Industry 2.0

From around the 1760s until the 1840s, this time frame encompassed the Second Industrial Revolution (Editors of Encyclopedia Britannica 2022). The beginning of the second wave of the industrial revolution may be traced herein. The term "the Technological Revolution" describes the period of rapid technological advancement that occurred mostly in the U.K., Germany, and the U.S.A. This period also saw the introduction of cutting-edge technical systems, such as improved electrical innovation that enabled higher manufacturing rates and more complex machinery.

Industry 3.0

The first computer age marked the beginning. Even though early computers were sometimes cumbersome, big, and inefficient, they laid the framework for a world where the absence of computers is difficult to conceive of today (Editors of Encyclopedia Britannica 2022). Electronics and IT (Information Technology) were utilized to further automate manufacturing during the Third Industrial Revolution, which began about 1970. The proliferation of the Internet, widespread connection, and using renewable energy have all contributed to significant developments in manufacturing and automation. Assembly lines in Industry 3.0 were outfitted with more automated systems, such as those controlled by programmable logic controllers (PLC), to formerly perform human-only responsibilities (PLC). Despite automated systems, regular human oversight and participation were required.

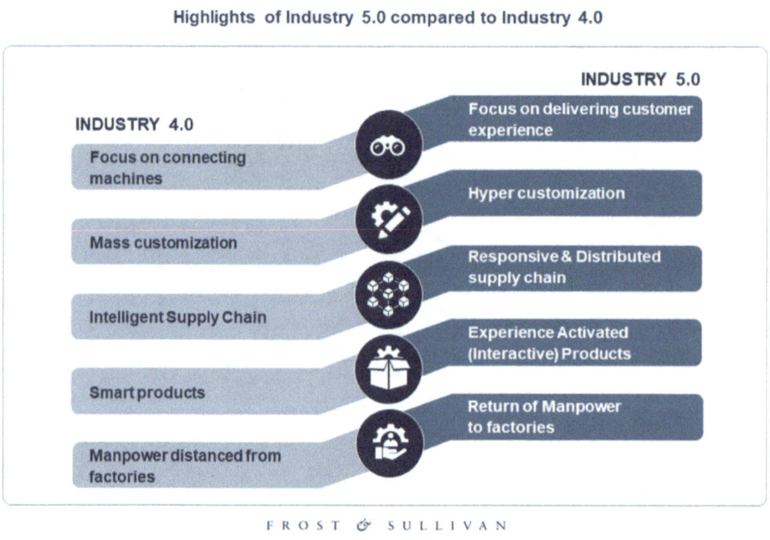

Figure 4.2: Industry 4.0 and 5.0.
Source: Frost Sullivan.

Industry 4.0

This new era, called the Fourth Industrial Revolution, is characterized by smart machines, databases, and factories that can coordinate their operations independently of human intervention. G. Beier et al. al. 2021). This information exchange is made possible by the Industrial Internet of Things (IIoT), as it currently exists in its current form. The following are the fundamentals of Industry 4.0 (see Figure 4.2):

- Cyber-physical system: a machine controlled by computer-based algorithms and mechanized.
- The Internet of Things, or the IoT, is a network of machines, gadgets, and vehicles equipped with digital capabilities for sensing, scanning, and monitoring.
- Cloud computing, which is the seaward facilitation of organizations and reinforcement of information.
- Several technology platforms that use some kind of artificial intelligence are called "cognitive computing."

Industry 5.0

Industry 4.0 has been discussed in the industrial sector for less than a decade, but futurists are already looking ahead to the next revolution, which they call "Industry 5.0" (Beier, G. et al., 2021). In contrast to the current revolution, which focuses on retrofitting manufacturing facilities with Internet of Things (IoT) technology to function as smart, cognitive, cloud-based, interconnected facilities, Industry 5.0 will focus on integrating computing technologies with human hands and brains into manufacturing. The integration of humans and machines in order to improve manufacturing procedures is known as Industry 5.0, or the fifth industrial revolution (see Figure 4.2). Strangely, businesses that have just begun implementing Industry 4.0 concepts may already be in the midst of the fifth revolution. The reception of innovation by assembling doesn't guarantee the end of occupations and the progress towards mechanization.

Software for manufacturing costing can be used to estimate how much it will cost to produce a new product. The benefits of automating the costing procedures outweigh the time saved in bringing a new product to market. Numerous Southeast Asian countries, including Vietnam, are now carrying out Industry 4.0 to a limited extent because of the organization stages' help overseeing plant tasks to make "brilliant production lines" (Ooi et al., 2018). This original thought was portrayed as the formation of a constant coordinated stream and information sharing utilizing the Web of Things (IoT), cloud-based administrations, and actual digital foundation to work-savvy manufacturing plants (Peruzzini et al., 2017) (Ng et al., 2022). As indicated by (Tupa et al. 2017), it is anticipated that the company will become more digitally advanced due to developments in the digital realm and can collaborate with customers and suppliers in that environment.

Impression of Industrial Revolutions on Sustainable Development

According to (Longoni et al., 2018), a requirement for sustainable business transformation is the organization's strategic positioning in the economic environment while considering opportunities and challenges in sociological, ecological, and financial terms. According to (Tiwari, 2020), the digital transformation of Industry 4.0 has a far-reaching impact beyond specific businesses, necessitating partner integration across the entire value chain. Industry 4.0, in some cases, alluded to as "modern computerized progress, is remembered for its promising potential for handling modern tasks' manageability issues (Luthra et al., 2020). According to Ardito et al., Industry 4.0 envisions integrating intelligent physical objects, decentralized subsystems, and even human components into a hyper-connected, decentralized, interoperable production system that can respond autonomously and in real-time to external stimuli. 2019). Environmental pollution is an undesirable side effect of industrialization that negatively impacts people's health and standard of living (Vyas et al., 2023). A negative externality happens when firms are not required to compensate for the environmental damage they do or when this cost is not accounted for in consumer pricing. A monetary cost is associated with environmental deterioration caused by deforestation, wildlife extinction, widespread pollution, and garbage accumulation. It is abundantly clear that air pollution, caused by the combustion of fossil fuels and other potential sources of smoke and toxins, is the most significant problem. The Environmental Protection Agency of the United States is responsible for regulating more than eighty separate toxins, including asbestos, dioxin, lead, and chromium, among others (EPA). Despite these rules, industrial facilities are among the most significant causes of air pollution worldwide.

Furthermore, water pollution can be a concern in some regions, particularly when businesses are located close to potable water sources. All these contaminants, whether solid, liquid, or gas, have the potential to contaminate water supplies. For example, the Nile's pollution shows that even landfills and other garbage dumping areas may taint potable water. Soil contamination is another problem that has emerged because of industrialization. Although lead poisoning is the most prevalent form of soil contamination, other heavy metals and toxic compounds can also seep into the soil and harm crops that are grown there.

In conclusion, industrialization has led to the destruction of a significant amount of habitat. The destruction of ecosystems is caused by the extraction of raw resources like trees for construction and the excavation of land for things like roads, mines, and gravel pits. Plant and animal species that cannot relocate or adapt to a new ecology may become extinct due to human interference. Common outcomes of industrialization include people migrating to cities for employment, working in automated industries, and performing ordinary household tasks. As a result, many people who work in the industrial sector struggle with feelings of alienation, dissatisfaction with their jobs, and identity crises. Noise and dust are only two examples of environmental and occupational risks that can negatively impact workers' health. Among the many societal problems that worsen due to fast urbanization by industry are increased crime, stress, and mental health difficulties. Long work hours can result in a loss of sleep and the practice of eating while on the go. This, in turn, can increase the likelihood of acquiring diseases such as diabetes, cardiovascular disease, and stroke.

Industrial Revolution 4.0 and Sustainable Development

The enormous potential of technologies emerging from the Fourth Industrial Revolution to address fundamental issues confronting the world today, such as poverty, climate change, the disappearance of natural habitats, and inequality, has not even come close to being realized. As a result, insufficient progress towards achieving the UN Global Goals for sustainable development by 2030 has been made. Progress has been made on several goals since 2015, but the global response has not been as bold as needed, and progress has been delayed or even reversed on some of the goals. (UN General Assembly, 2015). According to the latest Sustainable Development Progress Report, we are not on track to reach economic and inclusive development objectives for developing nations, industrialization in these countries is too sluggish to meet the 2030 agenda target, especially in technology-related industries, and the world is not on track to eradicate poverty by 2030. In order to unleash the environmental, economic, and social transformation needed to combat climate change and achieve Global Goals by 2030, we must implement radical change and innovative solutions across all sectors of our economy.

The result of Industry 4.0 is industrial value creation that is sustainable in terms of the three sustainability dimensions of economic, social, and environmental sustainability, which holds enormous promise for the future. (Stock et al. 2016) New advancements like actual digital frameworks (CPSs), the Web of Things (IoT), and others make entryways for modern development that empower expanded efficiency and proficiency in assorted organizations. New technologies that maximize output while effectively utilizing resources have been introduced by I4.0 in manufacturing (Kamble et al., 2018). As a result, 4.0 has tremendous potential to improve resource efficiency and sustainably generate commercial value across all social, economic, and environmental spheres (Sharma et al., 2020; Mehta et al., 2019; Mehta et al., 2022). Amid significant global issues, the Fourth Industrial Revolution is transforming businesses and supply networks, scientific advancement, human involvement, and even national economic power at an unprecedented rate and scale (Olah et al. 2020). Society is already being reshaped by artificial intelligence (AI), robots, blockchain, the Internet of Things, 5G connections, improved materials, and biotechnology. According to PwC and Microsoft's research, the digital readiness, and levels of tech adoption in Europe, East Asia, and North America would allow those regions to mostly reap the economic and environmental benefits of deploying AI to handle environmental concerns. (Chen et al. 2021) looked at Middle Eastern and North African countries. Exhibited how the Business 4.0 worldview's innovative steps increment energy productivity. Furthermore, Ghobakhloo et al. (2021) offered comparable viewpoints regarding the significance of the technical advancements made by Industry 4.0 for energy sustainability.

Big Data Role in Sustainability

Data on natural phenomena (such as fires, droughts, floods, and earthquakes) and human activities (such as social interactions) are collected, cross-referenced, and related as part of big data's application to sustainable development. Collaborating across the public and commercial sectors is necessary since the data is mostly extracted from publicly available sources like satellite images and databases. Moreover, insights gained from combining these datasets have the potential to mitigate geopolitical tensions, improve response to natural disasters and humanitarian crises, and deepen our comprehension of the factors that make people susceptible to harm (World Economic Forum 2018).

Management and policy may be drastically altered, and lives can be improved thanks to the availability of evidence. Big data from several sources allows for consideration of sustainability aspects that cut beyond conventional economic, social, and environmental silos in a manner that previous and static data-gathering techniques could not. This is due to the data's sheer amount, diversity, and velocity and the technology available to consolidate and analyze it. Insights into behaviors and trends may be gained in real-time and at either the macro or micro scales using big data, allowing experts to examine indications, measures, and their interrelationships from novel, multi-dimensional perspectives. In Indonesia, for instance, where the Ministry of National Development Planning (BAPPENAS) worked with the Global Pulse Lab project of the United Nations Secretary-General to develop the Global Pulse Lab Journal (GPLJ), prospects for big data usage include generating real-time situational awareness at local and central government levels, upgrading early warning systems, and conducting quick evaluations of the effects of proposed and implemented policies. Experimental research methods, including integrating social media and geo-location and collaboration with national mobile operators, have been used to examine the efficacy of using big data. However, it is essential to remember that the theory, the design of indicators, and the monitoring and evaluation feedback loops that are the bedrock of the policy-making process must serve as the basis for interventions if big data is to be employed in policy making.

The Republic of Korea is widely regarded as a pioneer in public big data applications, particularly about planning transportation at the municipal level, monitoring infectious illness, analysing industrial processes, and corporate engagement. China's government has implemented the "Internet+" program to promote economic growth by analysing large amounts of data. The goal of Internet+ is to facilitate the development of a centrally planned economy by increasing market efficiency. The Chinasti Steel Online Monitoring Platform could be exhibited as a case study, and the effective combination of big data with information about trade and finance conducting business using big data (The Alliance between Artificial Intelligence and Sustainable Development 2021). There are many ways in which big data may be used to help achieve Sustainable Development Goals (SDGs) since it allows professionals to go beyond the limitations of traditional statistics, supplement evidence-based policy and decision-making, and provide a more comprehensive, linked picture of how many aspects of sustainable development function together.

Artificial Intelligence (AI) Role in Sustainability

Artificial intelligence is the accomplice that economic improvement expects to make, execute, and exhort on tentative arrangements for our planet and its progress with practicality more really. Artificial intelligence (AI) technology will aid humanity in numerous ways, including improved construction methods, sustainable resource utilization, and waste minimization and management. When AI is used with sustainable development, businesses of all kinds may create a better world that meets people's needs today without putting future generations at risk from climate change or resource depletion. According to research that was published in Nature, artificial intelligence has the potential to help achieve 79% of the Sustainable Development Goals (SDGs). It also has the potential to become a key tool in promoting a circular economy and constructing smart cities that make efficient use of their resources (The Alliance between Artificial Intelligence and Sustainable Development 2021). How AI has helped with traffic management is a prime illustration of its positive environmental impact. When AI improves urban transportation, congestion may be anticipated, and alternate routes can be recommended. This innovation estimates the need for cars at certain times and locations as part of a shared mobility strategy. That implies businesses may better meet the demands of their customers by allocating cars to them by their requirements. In addition to improving accessibility, this method reduces harmful effects on the natural world (Prakash 2022).

The Alliance Between Artificial Intelligence and a Sustainable Economy

The efficiency enhancements that AI makes possible can also benefit alternative energy sources. Businesses are already using this technology to determine the daily availability of energy-generating facilities like wind turbines, hydroelectric plants, biomass plants, and others (Sharma et al., 2021). To anticipate the required amount of energy over the next few days and, ultimately, to avoid and diagnose failures (The Alliance between Artificial Intelligence and Sustainable Development 2021). AI has the potential to enhance a wide range of sectors and enterprises beyond only the energy industry, all while contributing to environmental improvement. For example, it's utilized to improve the efficacy of agricultural practices, including irrigation and fertilization. By monitoring environmental conditions such as humidity, temperature, and fertilizer, artificial intelligence can anticipate what is needed to sustain plant growth. Farmer-assisted drone monitoring and hyperspectral image analysis for total pest management are two of the most cutting-edge innovations in sustainable agriculture today.

Artificial Intelligence in Error Prediction

Furthermore, in the manufacturing sector, artificial vision systems allow for the detection of flaws in assembly lines that are not visible to the naked eye, as well as safety issues or potential disasters. Researchers have examined various fields of research related to the manufacturing sector (Mehta et al., 2022). This is paramount in fields like construction, where worker safety is paramount. Advanced technology in tunnel boring equipment is a good illustration of how artificial intelligence is being used to improve sustainability. It is possible for a breakdown to halt all or a large portion of underground activity for an extended period. In this endeavor, artificial intelligence plays the role of an oracle and takes center stage. It analyzes data from 3,000 variables in real time to foresee when a malfunction can occur. This method allows massive tunnels to be drilled with unparalleled efficiency and cost savings. Consequently, AI plays a crucial role in identifying potential issues with sustainable growth and providing solutions to them before they become serious (The Alliance between Artificial Intelligence and Sustainable Development 2021).

Technological Status Quo in India During Industrial Revolution 4.0

India is at the forefront of adopting Industrial Revolution 4.0, which is crucial in becoming the prominent economy of tomorrow. In terms of Big Data, AI, and IoT, India has seen an encouraging start (see Figure 4.3), thus ensuring that the development of today is not at the cost of future generations.

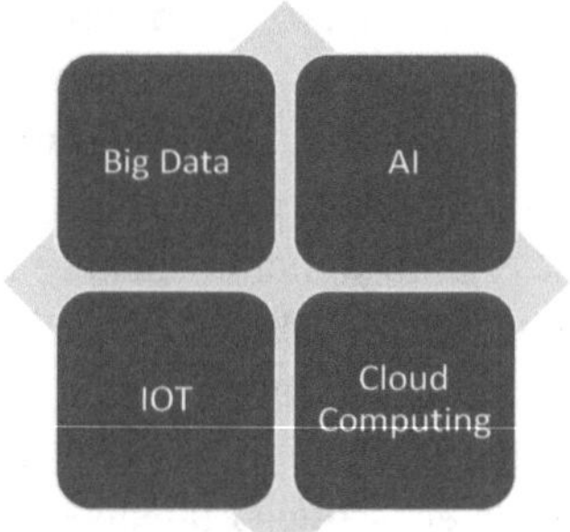

Figure 4.3: IR 4.0 Emergence in India.
Source: Authors' Compilation.

Big Data

The number of internet users in India is expected to double from 658 million by 2025. The data analytics market was worth $45.4 billion in 2021, or a 26.5 per cent CAGR. By the end of 2022, it is anticipated that India's IT industry, which controls 43% of the data analytics industry, will employ 4.5 lakh people. The fintech company BharatPay, which uses it to fund SMEs and boasts a 96% payback record with a goal of disbursing $1.86 billion by 2023, is one example of the BFSI industry in India that has made extensive use of data analytics and artificial intelligence (AI). In addition, data analytics have proven essential in the e-commerce industry to simplify warehouse operations, with a market share of 5.9% and approximately 1.2 million transactions per day in India alone.

Cloud Computing

India's Industry 4.0 is significantly made possible by cloud computing. By 2025, its anticipated value will reach $10.8 billion, making it an essential component of digital transformation and innovation. In light of the numerous positive effects of cloud computing on the service industry, the government has initiated the project "Meghraj" to speed up the supply of electronic services by optimizing expenditures on information and communication technologies. Platform as a Service (PaaS), Infrastructure as a Service (IaaS), and Software as a Service (SaaS) are among the many variants of the service currently available. A significant portion of the market for public cloud services is software as a service (SaaS). IaaS stands for Infrastructure as a Service, and PaaS is an abbreviation for Platform as a Service. Thanks to initiatives like the Bharat Interface for Money (BHIM) and the Unified Payments Interface (UPI), cloud computing has also been extremely successful in India's banking, financial services, and insurance (BFSI) industry. In January 2022 alone, transactions totalled INR 461 crore.

Internet of Things (IoT)

India's IOT market is expected to grow from $4.98 billion in 2020 to $9.28 billion in 2025. Sensors and RFID tags are used in IOT to collect data and provide operational and environmental metrics in real-time. In India, Internet of Things (IoT) applications are most readily apparent in agriculture. By installing GPS receivers in farm tractors, agriculture has become more connected, speeding up harvesting and reducing the time spent treating crops. Precision agriculture, which includes drones and other tools, has been a big change in the industry because it allows for more careful crop monitoring and targeted agricultural interventions, both increasing crop yields.

IBM Environmental Intelligence Suite's Role in Sustainability in India

Based on the most solid meteorological information on the planet, IBM's Natural Knowledge Suite is an artificial intelligence-controlled SaaS arrangement that conveys convenient and reality-based noteworthy insight for proactively arranging and dealing with the monetary effects of extreme climate and environmental change events. As of late uncovered, IBM's Environmental Knowledge Suite is intended to help organizations operationalize basic cycles, for example, carbon bookkeeping and decrease, to oversee ecological dangers and accomplish ecological objectives (IBM, 2021). *"Above all, becoming more sustainable is an opportunity to innovate", Kareem Yusuf, PhD, General Manager of IBM Sustainability Software.*

The core of this package is brand-new discoveries from IBM Research, advanced geospatial analytics utilized by businesses worldwide, and IBM's current meteorological data, which is the most accurate of any source in the world. Since this help is the first to unite simulated intelligence, meteorological information, environmental risk investigation, and carbon bookkeeping, organizations will never again need to invest as much in assembling this convoluted information. On the other hand, they can spend more time and effort analyzing it for clues and making changes to their operations. The Environmental Intelligence Suite from IBM is a software as a service (SaaS) product intended to aid businesses in a variety of ways (IBM, 2021), including:

- Keep an eye out for potentially dangerous environmental phenomena, including storms, fires, floods, and poor air quality, and provide warnings if any are identified;
- Use climate risk analytics to predict how climate change and weather might affect the company as a whole;
- identify possible disturbances in operations and determine which ones warrant the most attention for mitigation and reaction;
- Implement carbon accounting and require the procurement and operations departments to measure, report on, and reduce their workload.

Through application programming interfaces (APIs), dashboards, maps, and alarms, the suite provides environmental insights that can help businesses with both day-to-day operations and the creation of long-term strategies. For example, retailers could use the suite to plan for severe weather-related delays in shipping and inventory or to include environmental risks in future warehouse locations.

The suite could be used by energy and utility companies to determine which of their essential assets may soon be more vulnerable to wildfires as a result of climate change or where to cut vegetation along power lines. Additionally, grocery stores might be able to use the suite to see how their refrigeration systems affect their overall GHG emissions, allowing them to better prioritize where to make adjustments.

Businesses worldwide already use many fundamental AI and meteorological technologies in IBM's Environmental Intelligence Suite. For example, Brazilian ethanol, bioelectricity, and sugar giant BP Bunge Bioenergia are using IBM environmental data and geospatial analytics to better understand its agricultural sugarcane output and improve its market intelligence estimates of global sugar production. Spanish agribusiness leader Cajamar uses IBM's digital platform Tierra to help farmers improve yields and reduce their environmental impact (IBM, 2021). The EIS can be used by a corporation with a sizable fleet of vehicles, such as a logistics provider, to collect data on individual vehicles' fuel use. After that, carbon accounting application programming interfaces might convert a mobile device's emissions to carbon equivalents. After collecting this information, an operational view may be created to account for the gasoline a whole truck fleet uses. As a result of combining the operating fleet data with other aspects of carbon emissions accounting, an enterprise-wide perspective may be obtained. In a similar vein, EIS's insights might be useful for:

- Stores plan ahead for shipping and inventory interruptions due to extreme weather or consider the possibility of flooding when choosing a site for a new distribution center.
- Energy and utility providers may use this information to determine which of their vital assets are most at risk from future wildfires and where to cut vegetation near power lines.
- Supermarkets can better understand their refrigeration systems' role in their GHG emissions and allocate resources accordingly.

Conclusion

It has been resolved that the worldwide economy consumes around two times as much as the world can reestablish yearly as far as its asset use, which is inconsistent with our environmental change relief objectives and the restricted idea of the world's assets. Social externalities occur when many people lose their jobs or have to move, and new ones take too long to appear in several industries. The distribution of wealth and the future of economic growth may be significantly altered by the Fourth Industrial Revolution (World Economic Forum 2018). As a result of advancements in technology, efficiency and output enhancements are increasingly becoming the norm. It is essential to assist SMEs in initiating the transformation process and integrating small and medium technology providers to unlock the industrial sector's full potential. At the same time, addressing the issue of a lack of digital competence is one of the most significant obstacles. Thus, the public and global policymakers should guarantee that all share the upsides of this memorable change.

Countries like India, Thailand, and Vietnam, among the Asia-Pacific region's focal economies, are large markets with access to substantial capital and important production centers. Due to their extensive trading networks, these countries can easily import cutting-edge technologies used in the regionally major automobile and electronics sectors. Significant gains can also be made in traditionally low-tech industries like the textile, garment, and agricultural food processing sectors. Therefore, workers must be familiar with cutting-edge technology, and exposure to these tools begins in elementary school.

The government may play a pivotal role by instituting training and education programs, such as the Pradhan Mantri Kaushal Vikas Yojana introduced by the Government of India. The program's goal is to help young people acquire marketable skills to improve their employment and living prospects. Historically, the globe has had a poor performance record, with the profits from environmental destruction being privatized and the costs of fixing the harm the public sector bears. It is possible to alter this trend at this point. Utilizing technologies from Industrial Revolution 4.0, such as artificial intelligence (AI), IBM Environmental Intelligence Suite, Big Data (BD), the Internet of Things (IoT), and so on, a more enlightened approach to sustainability concerns In order to implement the United Nations 2030 Agenda for Sustainable Development's shared commitment, government and business must work together more closely. Manageability has been viewed as a cost far too often. It is essential to the success of any modern organization to take advantage of the numerous opportunities it presents to dispel this misconception.

Clashes and ambiguities between the natural, financial, and social parts of manageability are expected to emerge through the advanced change of the modern area, requiring serious compromises and splitting the difference. However, suppose all parties involved participate in mutually co-designing goals, regulations, and rules for a system of governance that aligns with the societal goals of sustainability. In that case, many of these conflicts can be effectively resolved.

References

Ardito, L., Petruzzelli, A. M., Panniello, U., & Garavelli, A. C. (2019). "Towards Industry 4.0: Mapping digital technologies for supply chain management–marketing integration", *Business Process Management Journal*, *25*(2), 323–346.

Beier,G., Niehof, S. & Hofmann, M. (2021). "Industry 4.0: A step towards achieving the SDGs? A critical literature review", *Discover Sustainability*, 2(22).

Bogojeska, J., Giurgiu, I., Stark, G., & Wiesmann, D. (2021). "IBM Predictive Analytics Reduces Server Downtime", *INFORMS Journal on Applied Analytics*, *51*(1), 63–75.

Chen, M., Sinha, A., Hu, K., & Shah, M. I. (2021). "Impact of technological innovation on energy efficiency in Industry 4.0 era: Moderation of shadow economy in sustainable development", *Technological Forecasting and Social Change*, *164*, 120521.

Editors of Encyclopedia Britannica (2022, Oct 27). "*Industrial Revolution*". Britannica. https://www.britannica.com/event/IndustrialRevolution#:~:text=Industrial%20Revolution%2C%20in%20modern%20history,living%20and%20fundamentally%20transformed%20society

Ghobakhloo, M., & Fathi, M. (2021). "Industry 4.0 and opportunities for energy sustainability", *Journal of Cleaner Production*, p. *295*, 126427. https://www3.weforum.org/docs/WEF_39558_White_Paper_Driving_the_Sustainability_of_Production_Systems_4IR.pdf

Kamble, S. S., Gunasekaran, A., & Gawankar, S. A. (2018). "Sustainable Industry 4.0 framework: A systematic literature review identifying the current trends and future perspectives", *Process safety and environmental protection*, *117*, 408–425.

Longoni, A., & Cagliano, R. (2018). "Sustainable innovativeness and the triple bottom line: The role of organizational time perspective", *Journal of Business Ethics*, *151*(4), 1097–1120

Luthra, S., Kumar, A., Zavadskas, E. K., Mangla, S. K., & Garza-Reyes, J. A. (2020). "Industry 4.0 as an enabler of sustainability diffusion in the supply chain: an analysis of influential strength of drivers in an emerging economy", *International Journal of Production Research*, *58*(5), 1505–1521

Mehta, K., Sharma, R., & Vyas, V. (2022). "A quantile regression approach to study the impact of aluminium prices on the manufacturing sector of India during the COVID era", *Materials Today: Proceedings*, *65*(8), 3506–3511, ISSN 2214-7853, https://doi.org/10.1016/j.matpr.2022.06.087.

Mehta, K., Sharma, R., & Vyas, V. (2019). "Efficiency and ranking of sustainability index of India using DEA-TOPSIS", *Journal of Indian Business Research*, *11*(2), 179–199. https://doi.org/10.1108/JIBR-02-2018-0057.

Mehta, K., Sharma, R., Vyas, V. and Kuckreja, J.S. (2022). Exit strategy decision by venture capital firms in India using fuzzy AHP. Journal of Entrepreneurship in Emerging Economies, 14 (4), 643–669. https://doi.org/10.1108/JEEE-05-2020-0146.

Ng, T. C., Lau, S. Y., Ghobakhloo, M., Fathi, M., & Liang, M. S. (2022). "The application of industry 4.0 technological constituents for sustainable manufacturing: A content-centric review", *Sustainability, 14* (7), 4327.

Oláh, J., Aburumman, N., Popp, J., Khan, M. A., Haddad, H., & Kitukutha, N. (2020). "Impact of Industry 4.0 on environmental sustainability", *Sustainability*, *12*(11), 4674.

Ooi, K. B., Lee, V. H., Tan, G. W. H., Hew, T. S., & Hew, J. J. (2018). "Cloud computing in manufacturing: The next industrial revolution in Malaysia?", *Expert Systems with Applications*, *93*, 376–394.

Peruzzini, M.; Grandi, F.; Pellicciari, M. (2017). "Benchmarking of Tools for User Experience Analysis in Industry 4.0", *Procedia Manuf.*, *11*, 806–813.

Prakash N. (2022). "*AI will help businesses face challenges related to sustainability, resiliency, and supply chain*". CRN. https://www.crn.in/interviews/ai-will-help-businesses-face-challenges-related-to-sustainability-resiliency-and-supply-chain/

Sharma, A. & Sharma, R. (2022). "Exploring Tax Decision Factors: A Perspective from North Indian Tax Practitioners", *Journal of Tax Reform*, *8*(3): 285–297. https://doi.org/10.15826/jtr.2022.8.3.122

Sharma, R., Mehta, K. & Sharma, O. (2021). "Exploring Deep Learning to Determine the Optimal Environment for Stock Prediction Analysis", *2021 International Conference on Computational Performance Evaluation, ComPE 2021*, 148–152.

Sharma, R., Jabbour, C.J.C., & de Sousa Jabbour, A.B.L.(2020). "Sustainable manufacturing and industry 4.0: what we know and what we don't", *Journal of Enterprise Information Management*, *34*(1), 230–266.

Stock, T., Seliger, G.(2016). "Opportunities of sustainable manufacturing in industry 4.0". *Procedia CIRP*, *40*, 536–541.

The Alliance between Artificial Intelligence and Sustainable Development. (2021).Active Sustainability. https://www.activesustainability.com/sustainable-development/the-alliance-between-artificial-intelligence-and-sustainable-development/?_adin=02021864894

Tiwari, S. (2020). "Supply chain integration and Industry 4.0: A systematic literature review". *Benchmarking: An International Journal*, *28*(3), 990–1030.

Tupa, J.; Simota, J.; Steiner, F. (2017). "Aspects of Risk Management Implementation for Industry 4.0." *Procedia Manufacturing, 11,* 1223–1230.
UN General Assembly (UNGA). (2015). "Transforming our world: the 2030 Agenda for Sustainable Development", *Resolut. A/RES/70/1, 25* 1–35.
Vyas, V., Mehta, K., & Sharma, R. (2023). "The nexus between toxic-air pollution, health expenditure, and economic growth: An empirical study using ARDL", *International Review of Economics and Finance, 84,* 154–166 https://doi.org/10.1016/j.iref.2022.11.017
World Economic Forum (2018). "Driving the Sustainability of Production Systems with Fourth Industrial Revolution Innovation".

Neha Kamboj, Vinita Choudhary, and Sonal Trivedi

5 Impact of Macroeconomic Determinants and Corporate Attributes on Firms' Financial Success in India

Abstract: Both macro and microeconomic dynamics affect the financial results of a firm. To reduce their impact on future cash flows and profitability, it is critical that businesses are aware of these issues. Microeconomic elements include organizational culture, leadership, demand, quality of product, constituents in production and the effect of which could be executed and controllable by the management. However, macroeconomic factors such as government regulations and policies, unemployment rates, socio-political and environmental conditions, corporation tax rates, suppliers, and competitors exist outside the business organization and are out of management's control. Hence, this is necessary for firms to prognosis the varied impact of important variables on the firms' imminent performance. There are various studies which have analyzed the effect of general macroeconomic determinants on the enactment of corporations in established countries. Conversely, there is very diminutive literature available on the impact of general macroeconomic variables and features of firms on the enactment of firms in a developing country like India. In India, chief general macroeconomic variables have shown significant fluctuations in the time period from 2018 to 2021, more especially as the country and firms emerge from lockdown post-Covid. Therefore, the current study focuses on examining macroeconomic determinants and corporate attributes on a firm's financial success of certain manufacturing corporations in India.

Studies show that a firm's financial success is influenced by the interaction of micro and macro elements. Although it has some control over micro variables, management has no comparable power over macro factors because they happen outside of the company. The interest rate, inflation, and exchange rate are only a few macroeconomic factors that have drastically changed in India. Over the period, these had not hampered a firm's performance, but a firm's performance also depended on how these elements combined with a firm's unique qualities. Because choices about funding and liquidity are solely the manager's domain

Keywords: Financial performance, Firms' characteristics, India, Macroeconomics, Manufacturing industries

Neha Kamboj, IILM School of Management, IILM University Gurugram, Haryana, India
Vinita Choudhary, School of Management & Commerce, K. R. Mangalam University, Gurugram, Haryana, India
Sonal Trivedi, School of Management, Birla Global University, Orissa, India

https://doi.org/10.1515/9783111170022-005

Introduction

Both macro and microeconomic dynamics affect the financial results of a firm. To reduce their impact on future cash flows and profitability, it is critical that businesses are aware of these issues. Microeconomic elements include organizational culture, leadership, demand, quality of product, constituents in production and the effect of which could simply be executed and controllable by the management. However, macroeconomic factors such as government regulations and policies, unemployment rates, socio-political and environmental conditions, corporation tax rates, suppliers, and competitors exist outside the business organization and are out of management's control. Hence, this is necessary for firms to prognosis the varied impact of important variables on the firms' imminent performance (Broadstock et al., 2011; Abeyrathna & Priyadarshana, 2019). In order to at least comprehend how economic factors, affect enterprises' financial performance over time, economists and finance experts around the world have produced a variety of models and theories. However, as the crunches in America, Russia, some parts of Asia, and the worldwide monetary crunch in 2007 show, these models and theories have not been very successful (Issah & Antwi, 2017).

Recently, the Indian economy has been experiencing a growth slowdown, with the annual GDP growth rate touching 4.5 per cent in the latest updated third quarter of the financial year 2019–20. This slowdown has witnessed to lead India's unemployment rate hit 45 years high in 2017–18 and was an overall unemployment rate of 6.1 per cent (NSSO, 2018). Many firms have shut down their doors with decreasing demand for their products. In spite of this, due to a decrease in confidence both in consumers and businesses along with the infamous bad loans in the public sector banks' balance sheet and a number of corporate governance issues that have come into the limelight, the transmission of the interest rate cuts has not been effective, thus leading the Reserve Bank to engage in Operation Twist by trying to 'twist' the yield curve so as to transmit the lower interest rates in the market by carrying out open market operations. The central bank's goals of managing price stability and managing economic growth appear to be the right approach in this current Indian context (Akadiri & Adebayo, 2022). For illustration, a nation's monetary policy has an impact on every sector of the economy through the interest rate on loans and the accessibility of loan facilities, which may limit a corporation's capacity to get outer ways of funding. In most developing countries like India, macroeconomic variables, for instance, increase in currency rates and hyperinflation, are the imperative dynamics influencing how well manufacturing companies' function. Therefore, several researchers have concentrated on the connection between macroeconomic variables and a firm financial position (Akben-Selcuk, 2019; Sharma & Sharma, 2022; Velte, 2020; Broadstock et al., 2011; Vyas et al., 2023). A company's operations are run by its board of directors (Sharma et al., 2022). Therefore, the orientation of board of directors towards macroeconomic indicators determines the strategic action plan of the company.

Problem Statement

There are various studies which have analyzed the impact of general macroeconomic variables on the enactment of firms in established countries (Broadstock et al., 2011; Abeyrathna & Priyadarshana, 2019). Conversely, there is very diminutive literature available on the impact of general macroeconomic variables and features of firms on the enactment of firms in a developing country like India. In India, chief general macroeconomic variables have shown significant fluctuations in the period from 2018 to 2021, more especially as the country and firms emerge from lockdown post-Covid. Therefore, the current study focuses on examining macroeconomic factors, corporate attributes, and monetary enactment of certain manufacturing corporations in India.

Objective of Study

- To examine the correlation between macroeconomic determinants, corporate attributes and monetary enactment of certain manufacturing corporations in India.
- To examine the comparison between the performance of a selection of manufacturing corporations in India before the outbreak of COVID (2018 & 2019), During COVID (2020) and post-COVID period (2021).

Review of Literature

Econ big picture(s) Macroeconomics is a discipline of economics that examines the structure, behaviour, performance, and decision-making of the economy as a whole. The phrase "macroeconomics" is resultant of the Greek word prefix "macro," connotation "big," and connate economics finances (Ibrahim & Aziz, 2003; Liu, 2021). The external surroundings of a corporation that have the capacity to affect its operational activities are included in the macro conditions. The term "macro environment" refers to those elements or circumstances that affect the business rather than just a single business unit (Itani & Mason, 2014). According to Tymon et al. (1998), the term "external environmental factors" refers to all of the variables that are present outside of a corporate organization and that the management takes into account when making decisions. These elements mainly focused on the dynamism and complexity of the outside atmosphere (Henry, 2022).

Macroeconomic Factors

It is confirmed by several pragmatic studies that the financial performance of firms can be influenced by microeconomic factors. There are many other factors, viz macroeconomic factors and characteristics of the firm, that have or have not a direct impact on the monetary enactment of certain manufacturing corporations in factors, the globe, various empirical types of research have been conducted to examine the correlation between macroeconomic determinants, corporate attributes and monetary enactment of chosen manufacturing corporations in India. Most studies concluded that macroeconomic factors and characteristics of the firm significantly influence the firm's financial performance. Yet, the specific relationship among the three factors varied according to countries and markets. The impact of macroeconomic factors and characteristics of the firm on a firm's financial performance was positive in several studies, while in some studies, it has a mixed mark, which means some variables affect the monetary enactment of the firms and some variables do not affect the on monetary enactment of the companies. One of them is Kandir (2008) in Turkey, an empirical study which was built upon the data from Turkish firms. He has employed a multiple regression model. The author used the exchange rate, return on the World equity index, the progression rate of industrial production index money supply, industrial production, oil prices and interest rate as macroeconomic variables. The researcher found that world market return, lending rate, and Forex rate distress the assets yields. Conversely, the amount of money in circulation, the price of oil, and industrial production do not significantly influence returns.

The corporation makes plentiful strategic and operational pronouncements that are generally affected by influenced by macro conditions; these comprise investing assessment, financing assessment and operational assessment (Hitt & Collins, 2007). As a result, performance is usually judged from the macroeconomy's stability viz lending rates, foreign exchange rate, and inflation rate fluctuations etc., though; Compared to developed countries, developing countries have significantly more macroeconomic instability (Khan et al., 2014). For illustration, the Indian economy has presented instability in lending rate, exchange rate, and money supply rate, among several others (Pal & Mittal, 2011; Giri & Joshi, 2017). Investigators orate that development in the industrial segment is curbed pessimistically from great advancing rates, which consistently is accountable in lieu of increased rate of manufacture (Damani & Vora, 2018; Ngene et al., 2016). In advanced economies, the impact of macroeconomic conditions on corporate performance has been thoroughly studied (D'Souza et al., 2005; Stock & Watson, 2009; Broadstock et al., 2011). However, firms' enactment also be determined by relations between macroeconomic aspects and firm characteristics (Dang & Yang, 2018). On the impact of firm characteristics on the calibre of financial reporting, Ghareli & Mohammadi (2016) presented a variety of findings. The impact of firm attributes on a firm's success has also been demonstrated by the studies. The firm's attributes, such as its age (Coad et al., 2013), firm size (Ghareli & Mohammadi, 2016), liquidity and leverage, have been associated with profitability (Das & Barai, 2016). According to a study by Shergill and Sarkaria (1999), there is a substantial positive correlation between firm characteristics and financial performance for a sample of 171 Indian companies from 21 different business sectors. Henceforth, it is a requisite for additional support on the mutual link between firm characteristics, macroeconomic determinants, and financial enactment in embryonic nations (Adeoye & Elegunde, 2012). Furthermore, Fifield et al. (2002) noted that the impact of macroeconomic attributes differed by segment. So, it is necessary to investigate using such manufacturing-related companies.

It has been evident from the extant literature that the change in the worth of economic resources is totally responsible for macroeconomic elements such as exchange rate, gross domestic product, lending rate, money supply rate, unemployment rate, dividends yield etc. (Gay, 2016). Further, researchers such as (Nisha, 2015; Barakat et al., 2016) put forward that the macroeconomic environs have a strongly significant wave on the corporations' financial performance. Contrary, McNamara & Duncan (1995) condemned the abovementioned study and contended to forecast an amendment in the way of future retributions rather than predicting the complete value of future retributions. The present study focuses on the following selective macroeconomic variables: inflation rate (INF_Rate), exchange rate EXE_Rate) interest rate (INT_Rate), money supply (M&S), and gross domestic product (GDP).

Interest Rate (INT_Rate)

The interest rate may be defined as the price which is rewarded by the borrowers for the usage of funds they lend from a lender. To put it another way, the fee paid on borrowed assets is known as the interest rate. However, economists argue that the interest rate is the rate charged on funds distribution over time. Anarchic capitalists consider it as an imperative macroeconomic gizmo to attract savings of investors, while the reduction in interest rate would inspire them to find other alternative ventures available in the market and also generate more return. Interest rate plays a vital and substantial role in any economy because it controls the flow of money in the economic system. On the one hand, High mortgage rates prevent price rises, conversely, decelerate the nation. Khan et al. (2019) concluded that both lending rates and financial reform had a significant impact on economic growth. Khan et al. (2014) articulated that an industry firm's financial structure makes it more vulnerable to lending rate instabilities than others in that industry. The economic performance of corporations in Kenya was significantly correlated with interest rates (Mnang'at et al., 2016). On the other hand, Awadzie & Garr (2020) discovered a considerable adverse influence of interest rates on the stock market returns of Ghanaian companies that are listed.

Inflation Rate

There are several ways to assess inflation. However, the Gross Domestic Product Deflator and a Consumer Price Index indicator are the two most frequently applied metrics. The Consumer Price Index calculates typical retail prices that customers spend.

Inflation is present when the CPI is high or rising. While price rises are not depraved, quick mounting rates of inflation signal feeble macroeconomic conditions. Higher prices tend to diminish overall consumer expenditure. As a result, causing a fall in GDP (Dunn et al., 2018). Hence, customer behaviour also play an important role in determining the revenues of the firm (Khanna & Sharma, 2017).

The key gauge of inflation in Nigeria is the CPI, which also contains the food and core indices. The CPI calculates the value of products and amenities like food, alcohol, drinks, electricity, transportation, housing, clothing, transportation, health, and other related services (Bala-Keffi et al., 2020).

Several research have shown that inflation has a negative effect on economic expansion.

Okorie & Ohakwe (2018) studied the Market share index, market size, and GDP were found to be negatively correlated with inflation in Nigeria. In a similar case, the study has been conducted by Sahu (2021) which had shown that a negative impact of price rises on economic progress, a comprehensive description of funds as a share of Gross domestic product, semi as a portion of Economic output, and the private sector's credit as a fraction of GDP are all examples of proxy measures.

Exchange Rate

The value of two currencies relative to one another, as determined by the exchange rate, is how Bahmani-Oskooee et al. (2012) defined the forex rate. It is the rate used to translate the value of one currency into another (Greenstone et al., 2020).

Yang (2017) exhibited that for the purposes of corporate valuation and peril management, knowing the foreign exchange risk's effect is a crucial component. Awadzie & Garr (2020) studied listed firms in Ghana, and exchange rates ought to have a robust favourable influence on script market enactment.

Gross Domestic Product

A country's GDP represents the entire marketplace worth of the commodities and services produced within its economy over a specific time frame. It contains entire finished commodities and services, which are shaped by business based in that motherland, irrespective of proprietorship and not being sold again in any way (Mwangi & Jserotich, 2013). This is a macroeconomic indicator that is most often used; its growth rate indicates where the economy is in the financial cycle. It is acted as the main global indicator of productivity and fiscal activity. In finances, three main types of end customers are households, corporations, and the government. By adding together, the money spent by these three user groups or the expenditure approach, one-way GDP is computed (Menegaki, 2014).

Firm Characteristics

Firm characteristics were defined by Sari & Rahmantika (2021) as the managerial and demographic factors that make up a business's inner environment. Firm features contain business magnitude, leverage, liquidity, sales progress, asset progress, and gross revenue, according to Khatib & Nour (2021). Additional factors include the firm's age, dividend payout, profitability, access to capital markets, ownership structure, board qualities, and growth potential (Sari & Rahmantika, 2021; Mehta et al., 2022; Khatib & Nour, 2021).

Firm Size

Firm Size has increasingly taken the lead in experimental business finance works and is largely acknowledged as one of the most important variables (Hu et al., 2021). However, studies show conflicting findings on the impact of size, with some confirming it and others finding little to no impact. Size and profitability have a considerable positive association. He found that debt negatively mediates the connotation amid the company's magnitude and financial enactment (Drempetic et al., 2020).

Leverage

Leverage is the ratio of debt to equity in a company's capital structure. It aims to determine how much of the entire properties are backed by advances. Using leverage ratios, one can assess a company's commercial and financial risks. Leverage and firm size have a positive, statistically significant relationship, according to studies. Leverage is the extent of debenture utilized to fund additional funds investments that could boost a company's financial performance (Mbonu & Amahalu, 2021).

Liquidity

The term "liquidity" denotes a company's capacity to transform brief assets into cash for use in day-to-day operations. The ability of a company to pay its current impending liabilities is measured by its liquidity. He said that companies might be using liquid assets to fund their operations and investments if outside financing is not available. A company's ability to pay down its short-term financial obligations is measured by liquidity ratios. The current ratio and quick ratio are a couple of examples of measures used to evaluate a company's immediate health (Štangová & Víghová, 2021).

Sales

Market growth is the term used to describe an increase in sales over a given time frame. A growing economy is the annual percentage rise in sales that is acceptable to the company's financial plans. The difference between present-year sales and preceding-year sales divided by past-year sales is the way many researchers define sales growth (Baker et al., 2021; Mehta et al., 2022; Yadav et al., 2022).

Financial Performance

ROA (Return on Assets)

Performance has many facets, and the best way to evaluate corporate performance will depend on the sort of business being assessed as well as the goals the evaluation would seek to accomplish. Three distinct facets of a firm's earnings are its financial (returns, Return on Assets, etc.), merchandise market (rate of sales, market share, etc.), and investors (total shareholder return, market value added) returns (Yadav et al., 2022).

As a result, the focus of financial enactment is on factors that are positively related to the fiscal report. Activity, Profitability, Debt, Liquidity and Market are some of the categories of ratios.

- Activity ratios, on the other hand, gauge how rapidly a company turns over non-cash assets into cash.
- Market ratios: gauge how investors feel about owning shares in a company and the price of scripts. They are worried about the stockholders' ROI.
- Profitability ratios: This gauge how effectively a company uses its resources to provide a reasonable rate of return.
- Debt ratios gauge a company's capacity to service its long-term debt.
- Liquidity ratios evaluate the amount of money available to settle debenture (Devi et al., 2020).

Research Approaches

Data

The data set comprises all the listed firms of the BSE 500 Index for the period of provide (2018, 2019), during covid (2020) and post covid (2021) in India. The accounting variables must not have any omitted figures for the first to be encompassed in the sample and used in the regression.

Table 5.1: Industry Sector Category.

1	Primary sector, Fertilizers, Agriculture/Horticulture/Lives, yard goods
2	Equipment, Tools, Fixtures, Reprocessing, Manufacture, Engineering
3	Trade in Wholesale, Consumer Durables, Retail
4	Lodging house, Cafeterias, Estate activities, Broadcastings
5	Teaching, Fitness, Computing, Computer Science Services
6	Banks, Finance, Additional Services
7	Prime sector, Chemical Substances, Quasi goods,

Source: https://www.zeebiz.com/market/sectors-bse accessed on 5/9/2022.

Table 5.1 expresses the manufacturing classification taken in this chapter. The study excludes 12 firms having either missing values or that have been delisted. Hence, 488 firms have been taken for further analysis.

Variables Were Chosen as Predictors

The macro-economic elements and Characteristics of the firm were taken as independent variables, and the firm's performance was chosen as the dependent variable (see Table 5.2).

Table 5.2: Predictor Variables.

Independent variables		**Dependent variable**
Macroeconomic Variables	**Corporate Attributes**	**Firm's Financial Success**
Exchange rate	Size of Company	ROA
Lending Interest rate	Profit After Tax (PAT)	
GDP	Total asset	
Inflation	Total expenses	

Source: Compiled by Author.

Dependent Variables: The return on assets (ROA) is the proportion of net revenue to the total assets in period t.

Independent Variables

(IntR)t: calculated as annualized lending rate.

(Profit after Tax)it: calculated as a company's earnings for the time period t.

(InfR)t: calculated as the CPI's yearly change.

(ExcR)t: the official Exchange rate throughout the course of a year.

(Sales)it: the percentage of sales during the specified time period.

(GDPR): Economic growth is a variable that is quantified by the annual change in GDP.

(Expenses)it is the percentage of costs that firms incur to operate during the period t.

(Company Size): It is expressed as a logarithm of the total assets throughout the time t.

Hypothesis

H_1: Lending interest rates have an impact on the return on assets (ROA) of particular companies;
H_2: Selective firms' ROA is impacted by the inflation rate;
H_3: Selective firms' ROA is impacted by the exchange rate;
H_4: Selective firms' ROA is impacted by the GDP growth rate;
H_5: Selective firms' ROA is impacted by the firm size;
H_6: Selective firms' ROA is impacted by PAT;
H_7: Selective firms' ROA is impacted by total assets; and
H_8: There is an effect of total expenses on the ROA of selected firms

Models

This chapter uses the Panel Autoregressive Distributed Lag (ARDL) Model and the Correlation Model as its two major models.

Autoregressive Distributed Lag Model

The most popular techniques for examining the long-run equilibrium connection amid variables are Engle and Granger test from 1987, the Maximum Likelihood (ML) test from 1988 and 1991, and the Johansen test from 1990. All of the model's variables must be stationary at the first difference, according to the method's premise. The poor performance of a lesser sample size is another restriction.

The aforementioned restrictions are avoided by the autoregressive distributed lag model. This strategy was developed by Pesaran and Shin (1996), and Pesaran et al. (1999), and it was further modified by Pesaran et al. (2001). Unlike previous models, with this one, it is not necessary for the constituents to be stationary. This technique is correspondingly as good if every variable is I(1), I(0), or even a combination.

The most popular techniques for examining the long-run equilibrium connection between variables are the Engle and Granger test from 1987, the Maximum Likelihood (ML) test from 1988 and 1991, and the Johansen test from 1990. All of the model's variables must be stationary at the first difference, according to the method's premise. The poor performance of a lesser sample mass is another restriction.

The aforementioned restrictions are avoided by the autoregressive distributed lag model. This strategy was established by Pesaran and Shin (1996), and Pesaran et al. (1999), and it was further modified by Pesaran et al. (2001). Unlike previous models, this one does not necessitate that all of the elements be stationary in the same order. This approach is equally as good if every variable is I(1), I(0), or even a combination.

Model Specification

Return_On_Assets = C(1)*Return_On_Assets(−1) + C(2)*Return_On_Assets(−2) + C(3)-*Return_On_Assets(−3) + C(4)*Exchange_Rate + C(5)*Gdp + C(6)*Inflation_Ratebase_Year_ + C(7)*Lending_Interest_Rate + C(8)*Profit_After_Tax + C(9)*Profit_After_Tax(−1) + C(10)*Size + C(11)*Total_Assets + C(12)*Total_Expenses + C(13)*Total_Expenses(−1) + C(14)-*Total_Expenses(−2) + C(15)*Total_Expenses(−3) + C(16)*Total_Expenses(−4) + C(17)

Correlation Model

Correlation is a technique that shows the potency and direction of a relationship among variables. The variables can be either two variables or more than two variables used for the study. A low correlation coefficient value marks that the two or more variables are hardly related, while a high correlation coefficient value means that constituents have a very sturdy relationship with one another. Correlation coefficients range from −1 to +1, and if the value is zero, there is no indication that the variables are related. The formula is as below:

$$r = \frac{n(\sum xy) - (\sum x)(\sum y)}{\sqrt{\left(\pi \sum x^2 - (\sum x)^2\right)\left(\pi \sum y^2 - (\sum y)^2\right)}}$$

Where x and y are variables, and n is the number of sets of data taken for the study;

Data Analysis

Total firms of the BSE 500 Index have been taken for the period of provide (2018, 2019), during covid (2020) and post covid (2021). Analyses of data are broken down into three categories: descriptive, correlational, and empirical.

Descriptive Assessment

The descriptive assessment is shown in Table 5.3. The total size of observations was 2438. It represents values of Mean, Maximum, Medium, Minimum, Std. Deviation, Kurtosis, Skewness, etc., whereas the p-value for the Jarque-Bera statistics indicated that none of the variables was distributed regularly.

Table 5.3: Descriptive Analysis.

	ROA	EXCHANGE_RATE	GDP	INFLATION	LENDING RATE	PAT	SIZE	TOTAL_ASSETS	TOTAL_EXPENSES
Mean	0.778525	70.39432	3.857588	146.2304	9.279820	8818.716	271491.5	473103.9	115940.0
Median	0.688973	70.42000	6.500000	143.9000	9.500000	2460.000	37502.35	46299.80	27800.25
Maximum	5.660891	74.10000	8.900000	161.4000	9.500000	351630.0	21786604	45438309	6073365.
Minimum	8.32E-05	65.12000	−6.60	133.5000	8.700000	−731,315.00	0.400000	0.900000	2.700000
Std. Dev.	0.614002	3.404589	5.488200	10.05610	0.312539	39253.56	1050839.	2127384.	378742.3
Skewness	1.664795	−0.30	−1.18	0.275211	−1.07	−0.87	11.45238	12.40756	8.925366
Kurtosis	8.335024	1.684732	2.810880	1.664734	2.521692	86.78983	185.6505	207.8501	103.2288
Jarque-Bera	4017.484	212.7390	566.7659	211.8926	490.5312	713496.8	3442234.	4325354.	1052856.
Probability	0.000000	0.000000	0.000000	0.000000	0.000000	0.000000	0.000000	0.000000	0.000000
Sum	1898.043	171621.4	9404.800	356509.8	22624.20	21500031	6.62E+08	1.15E+09	2.83E+08
Sum Sq. Dev.	918.7451	28247.82	73403.27	246442.1	238.0471	3.76E+12	2.69E+15	1.10E+16	3.50E+14
Observations	2438	2438	2438	2438	2438	2438	2438	2438	2438

Source: Computed Data Using EViews 9.

Empirical Analysis

According to Table 5.4, all the indicators used in this chapter are stationary at the first level.

Table 5.4: Unit Root Test.

Method	Statistic	Prob.**	Cross-sections	Obs
Null: Unit root (assumes common unit root process)				
Breitung t-stat	−2.13655	0.0163	12	25236
Levin, Lin & Chu t*	−4.39744	0.0000	12	25248
Null: Unit root (assumes individual unit root process)				
ADF – Fisher Chi-square	884.118	0.0000	12	25248
PP – Fisher Chi-square	2008.92	0.0000	12	25382
Im, Pesaran and Shin W-stat	−36.9680	0.0000	12	25248

**Asymptotic Chi-square distribution is used to compute Fisher test probabilities. For all other tests, asymptotic normality is assumed.
Source: Computed Data Using EViews 9.

For examining heteroskedasticity, Breusch-Pagan-Godfrey has been applied to detect heteroscedasticity as per Table 5.5, as the observed R square's probability Chi-Square is 0.5574, the null hypothesis is accepted, indicating that there is homoscedasticity between the variables. There is no heteroscedasticity in this data.

Table 5.5: Breusch-Pagan-Godfrey Heteroskedasticity Test.

F-stat	2.443852	Prob. F (16,2409)	0.5436
Obs*R squared	38.74862	Prob. Chi-Square (16)	0.5574
Scaled explained SS	157.2326	Prob. Chi-Square (16)	0.6350

Source: Computed Data Using EViews 9
Serial Correlation: The Breusch-Godfrey Serial Correlation LM Test has been used to analyse serial correlation.
Ho = No serial correlation exists
Ha = The model contains serial correlation.

Table 5.6: Serial Correlation LM Test: Breusch-Godfrey.

F-stat	2.161930	Prob. F(4,2405)	0.0709
Obs*R squared	8.691974	Prob. Chi-Square(4)	0.0693

Source: Computed Data Using EViews 9.
*Significant at 5 per cent level.

According to Table 5.6, the observed R-square has a probability chi-square value of 0.0693, implying that the null hypothesis is accepted; the model has no serial correlation.

Table 5.7: Bound Test.

Test Stat	**Value**	**k**
F-stat	78.28948	8
Critical Value Bounds		
Significance	**I0 Bound**	**I1 Bound**
10%	1.95	3.06
5%	2.22	3.39
2.5%	2.48	3.7
1%	2.79	4.1

Source: Computed Data Using EViews 9.

Table 5.8: F-Statistic for Assessing Long-Run Relationship Existence Error Correction Representation of ARDL (3, 0, 0, 0, 0, 1, 0, 0, 4) Dependent Variable Return on Assets.

Variable	**Coefficient**	**Std. Error**	**t-Statistic**	**Prob.***
RETURN_ON_ASSETS(-1)	0.049507	0.019254	2.571188	0.0102
RETURN_ON_ASSETS(-2)	0.018343	0.020183	0.908831	0.3635
RETURN_ON_ASSETS(-3)	0.049455	0.018860	2.622263	0.0088
EXCHANGE_RATE	−0.031988	0.051688	−0.618876	0.5361
GDP	−0.001548	0.004222	−0.366633	0.7139
INFLATION_RATEBASE_YEAR_	0.015231	0.025986	0.586132	0.5578
LENDING_INTEREST_RATE	0.339077	0.359959	0.941987	0.3463
PROFIT_AFTER_TAX	9.73E-08	3.91E-07	0.249208	0.8032
PROFIT_AFTER_TAX(-1)	−7.99E-07	2.29E-07	−3.484881	0.0005
SIZE	3.95E-07	2.15E-07	−1.839992	0.0459
TOTAL_ASSETS	8.60E-08	8.66E-08	0.993671	0.3205
TOTAL_EXPENSES	5.93E-07	1.34E-07	4.412341	0.0000
TOTAL_EXPENSES(-1)	−2.67E-08	2.98E-08	−0.896476	0.3701
TOTAL_EXPENSES(-2)	−3.88E-08	2.32E-08	−1.673593	0.0943
TOTAL_EXPENSES(-3)	−6.99E-08	1.62E-08	−4.311686	0.0000
TOTAL_EXPENSES(-4)	9.40E-08	2.83E-08	3.317910	0.0009
C	−2.420805	3.724076	−0.650042	0.0031
R-squared	0.101195	Mean dependent var		0.777406
Adjusted R-squared	0.095226	S.D. dependent var		0.614978
S.E. of regression	0.584964	Akaike info criterion		1.772451
Sum squared resid	824.3193	Schwarz criterion		1.813052
Log-likelihood	−2132.983	Hannan-Quinn criteria.		1.787213
F-statistic	16.95167	Durbin-Watson stat		1.997855
Prob(F-statistic)	0.000000			

Source: Computed Data Using EViews 9.

According to Table 5.7, Since the F- statistics value exceeds the upper bound value, cointegration is present. The variables have a long-term relationship. It can be said that both the long- and short-term ARDL models are applicable.

The findings of the ARDL model's error correction representation are shown in Table 5.8. The variables' coefficients revealed the short-run elasticity. According to the results, Profit after Tax (−1) is the most important component (with the negative coefficient) to evaluate Return on Assets in the near term. It suggested that the link between Profit after Tax at Lag 1 and Return on Assets at a 5% level of significance is negative (−7.99) and significant (0.0005). The dependent variable, return on assets, and Total expenses at lag 3 have a similar negative and substantial connection. A negative coefficient indicates the convergence of the independent variables to equilibrium. Nonetheless, there is a positive and significant association between Return on Assets at Lag 1 and Lag 3 as well as between Size at Lag 0 and Total Expenses at Lag 0 and Lag 4. Inferred from this statement is that the independent variables are veering towards equilibrium. Even in the short term, the Return on Total Assets is not greatly impacted by the Inflation Rate, Lending Interest Rate, or Gross Domestic Product.

At a five per cent level, the coefficient of error correction term (−2.420) is substantial. The error correction term's highly significant negative symbol supports the longevity of the long-term link between the variables.

Table 5.9: Correlation Between Independent Variables And Dependent Variables During Pre-Covid, Covid & Post Covid Period.

Period	**2018, 2019**	**2020**	**2021**
Particulars	**Return_On_Assets**	**Return_On_Assets**	**Return_On_Assets**
GDP	−0.016	−0.018	−0.015
Exchange_Rate	0.016	0.014	0.015
Inflation_Ratebase_Year	0.016	0.020	0.022
Profit_After_Tax	0.033	0.037	0.010
Size	−0.157	−0.153	−0.150
Total_Assets	−0.188	−0.191	−0.181
Total_Expenses	0.090	0.091	0.075

Source: Computed Data Using EViews 9.

Table 5.9 depicts the comparative study between the performance of selected manufacturing firms in India before the outbreak of COVID (2018 & 2019), During COVID (2020) and post-COVID period (2021). A correlation between Return on assets (dependent variable) and Macroeconomic Factors & Corporate attributes (independent variables) was conducted. It indicates that GDP influences negatively on ROA, meaning that higher GDP will lead to decreased ROA. In the current study, it has been seen that the ROA of the firms decreased in all situations, i.e., pre covid, during covid in the year 2020, and again, it decreased in the year 2021 as compared to the year 2020. The exchange rate and the Firms ROA is very weekly correlated, and it has been clearly seen in Table 5.9, which shows the value of r = 0.016 in the year 2018 and 2019 and r = 0.014 and again r = 0.015 in year2021 which implies that there is very less difference between all the values yearly depicts that there is less impact of covid on the performance of manufacturing firms. The inflation rate and the Firms ROA is very weekly correlated, and it has been clearly seen in Table 5.9, which shows the value of r = 0.016 in the year 2018, 2019 and r = 0.020 and again r = 0.022 in the year 2022, implying that after covid the firms have performed better as compared to pre covid and during covid period. Profit after tax of firms have decreased during covid and after covid tear, i.e., for the whole year of 2020, firms have not performed well. The size of the firms has gradually increased and has less correlation between the size and ROA of firms during covid and after covid. The correlation between total assets with ROA and total Expenses with ROA is also very showing a weak correlation that implies that it has not been affected so much during and post covid.

Findings and Discussion

H_1: Loan interest rates have an impact on the return on assets (ROA) of particular enterprises. According to the "List of Companies Under Study," this impact was positive but not statistically significant (t: 0.941987; pW0.05). As there is "no substantial influence of lending interest rate on ROA of selected enterprises," the study rejects the alternative hypothesis and supports the null.

H_2: There is evidence that the rate of inflation has a positive but insignificant impact on the return on assets (ROA) of a sample of businesses (t: 0586132; pW0.05). As there is "no substantial effect of interest rate on ROA of selected firms," the study accepts the null and rejects the alternative hypothesis.

H_3: Exchange rates have an impact on the return on assets (ROA) of particular companies. The "List of Companies Under Study" revealed that exchange rates had a detrimental but not statistically significant impact on ROA (t: 0.618876; pW0.05). As there is "no substantial effect of interest rate on ROA of selected firms," the study accepts the null and rejects the alternative hypothesis.

H_4: There is an influence of GDP growth rate on the ROA of selected enterprises. The "List of Companies under Study" revealed that the GDP growth rate had a negative but non-significant impact on ROA (t: 0.366633; pW0.05). As there is "no substantial effect of interest rate on ROA of selected firms," the study accepts the null and rejects the alternative hypothesis.

H_5: There is a relationship between business size and ROA for the sampled firms; the "List of companies under research" revealed that this relationship was negative but significant (t: 1.8399; pW0.05). As a result, the study accepts the alternative, "significant effect of interest rate on ROA of chosen firms," and rejects the null hypothesis.

H_6: There is a relationship between PAT and ROA for a subset of businesses; the "List of Companies under Study" revealed that PAT had a favourable but insignificant relationship with ROA (t: 0.249208; pW0.05). As there is "no substantial effect of interest rate on ROA of selected firms," the study accepts the null and rejects the alternative hypothesis.

Nonetheless, PAT at lag 1 had a negative yet statistically significant impact on ROA (t: −3.4848; pW0.05). It was stated that the dependent variable, or ROA, in the year 2021 was significantly and negatively impacted by the profits after tax realised in the year 2020. As a result, the analysis rejects the null hypothesis and goes with "significant influence of PAT at lag one on ROA of stated firms" as the alternative.

H_7: Total assets have an impact on the return on assets (ROA) of chosen businesses, and the "List of Companies under Study" revealed that this impact was positive but not statistically significant (t: 0.99367; pW0.05). The alternative hypothesis is therefore rejected by the study, which accepts the null of "no substantial influence of interest rate on ROA of stated enterprises."

H_8: Selected enterprises' ROA is impacted by total costs.
According to the "List of Companies under Study," total expenses significantly and favourably impacted ROA (t: 4.4123; pW0.05). The alternative, "significant effect of total expenses on ROA of stated businesses," is adopted because the investigation rejects the null hypothesis.

Conclusion

The purpose of the study was to look at the relationships between business traits, macroeconomic factors, and the financial performance of specific Indian firms. Studies show that a firm's financial success is influenced by the interaction of micro and macro elements. Although it has some control over micro variables, management has no comparable power over macro factors because they happen outside of the company. The interest rate, inflation, and exchange rate are only a few macroeconomic factors that have drastically changed in India. Over the period, these had not hampered a firm's performance, but a firm's performance also depended on how these elements combined with a firm's unique qualities. Because choices about funding and liquidity are solely the manager's domain. In light of this, there is a need for information to support the linkages between macroeconomic factors, corporate characteristics, and financial performance in developing countries.

Recommendations

The study makes the following recommendations:

1. Management must take lending rates into account when making borrowing choices since they can alter the cost of debt.
2. Given that it negatively affects the utilization of industrial capacity, the government should be concerned about the current inflation rate.
3. The government should endeavour to maintain a stable exchange rate so that businesses can access resources from other countries.
4. The government and regulatory bodies should continue to work to guarantee a sustainable GDP growth rate by implementing laws that support the growth of regional manufacturing businesses.
5. Proprietors should explore attempts at development and broaden due to the favourable effects of business size on a firm's growth potential.
6. A business's leverage situation should be closely managed by management since a heavily geared firm may have poor performance over time; and
7. Managers should evaluate a business's liquidity posture; a focus on business and across–firm assessment may be employed in observing a firm's condition in reference to rivals.

References

Abeyrathna, S. P. G. M., & Priyadarshana, A. J. M. (2019). "Impact of Firm Size on Profitability", *International Journal of Scientific and Research Publications*, *9*(6), 561–564.

Adeoye, A. O., & Elegunde, A. F. (2012). "Impacts of external business environment on organisational performance in the food and beverage industry in Nigeria", *British Journal of Arts and Social Sciences*, *6*(2), 194–201.

Akadiri, S. S., & Adebayo, T. S. (2022). "Asymmetric nexus among financial globalization, non–renewable energy, renewable energy use, economic growth, and carbon emissions: impact on environmental sustainability targets in India", *Environmental Science and Pollution Research*, *29*(11), 16311–16323.

Akben–Selcuk, E. (2019). "Corporate social responsibility and financial performance: The moderating role of ownership concentration in Turkey", *Sustainability*, *11*(13), 3643.

Awadzie, D. M., & Garr, D. K. (2020). "The Effect Of Macroeconomic Variables On Capital Market Performance: A Case Of Ghana Stock Exchange", *International Journal of Business Management and Economic Review*, *3*(5), 44–54.

Bahmani-Oskooee, M., Harvey, H., & Hegerty, S. W. (2012). "Exchange-rate volatility and industry trade between the US and Korea", *Journal of Economic Development-Seoul*, *37*(1), 1.

Baker, P., Santos, T., Neves, P. A., Machado, P., Smith, J., Piwoz, E., . . . & McCoy, D. (2021). "First-food systems transformations and the ultra-processing of infant and young child diets: The determinants, dynamics and consequences of the global rise in commercial milk formula consumption", *Maternal & child nutrition*, *17*(2), e13097.

Bala–Keffi, L. R., Mbaka, D. G., & Usman, N. (2020). "Alternative Core Inflation Measures in Nigeria: An Examination", *Applied Economics and Finance*, *7*(4), 112–120.

Barakat, M. R., Elgazzar, S. H., & Hanafy, K. M. (2016). "Impact of macroeconomic variables on stock markets: Evidence from emerging markets", *International Journal of Economics and Finance, 8*(1), 195–207.

Broadstock, D. C., Shu, Y., & Xu, B. (2011). "Do macroeconomic conditions affect firm-level earnings forecasts?", *International Journal of Trade, Economics and Finance, 2*(5), 450.

Coad, A., Segarra, A., & Teruel, M. (2013). "Like milk or wine: Does firm performance improve with age?", *Structural Change and Economic Dynamics, 24*, 173–189.

Damani, A., & Vora, V. (2018). "An Empirical and Analytical Study of the Factors Affecting the Exchange Rate Fluctuation in India", *International Journal of Innovative Studies in Sociology and Humanities, 3*(3), 1–14.

Dang, C., Li, Z. F., & Yang, C. (2018). "Measuring firm size in empirical corporate finance", *Journal of Banking & Finance, 86*, 159–176.

Das, S., & Barai, P. (2016). "Size, value and momentum in stock returns: evidence from India", *Macroeconomics and Finance in Emerging Market Economies, 9*(3), 284–302.

Devi, S., Warasniasih, N. M. S., Masdiantini, P. R., & Musmini, L. S. (2020). "The impact of the COVID-19 pandemic on the financial performance of firms on the Indonesia stock exchange", *Journal of Economics, Business, & Accountancy Ventura, 23*(2), 226–242.

Drempetic, S., Klein, C., & Zwergel, B. (2020). "The influence of firm size on the ESG score: Corporate sustainability ratings under review", *Journal of Business Ethics, 167*, 333–360.

D'Souza, J., Megginson, W., & Nash, R. (2005). "Effect of institutional and firm-specific characteristics on post-privatization performance: Evidence from developed countries", *Journal of Corporate Finance, 11*(5), 747–766.

Dunn, A., Grosse, S. D., & Zuvekas, S. H. (2018). "Adjusting health expenditures for inflation: a review of measures for health services research in the United States", *Health services research, 53*(1), 175–196.

Fifield, S. G. M., Power, D. M., & Sinclair, C. D. (2002). "Macroeconomic factors and share returns: an analysis using emerging market data", *International Journal of Finance & Economics, 7*(1), 51–62.

Gay, R. D. (2016). "Effect of macroeconomic variables on stock market returns for four emerging economies: Brazil, Russia, India, and China", *International Business & Economics Research Journal (Iber), 15*(3), 119–126.

Ghareli, S., & Mohammadi, A. (2016). "A study on the effect of macroeconomic variables and firm characteristics on the quality of financial reporting of listed firms in the Tehran Stock Exchange", *Journal of Fundamental and Applied Sciences, 8*(2), 1777–1797.

Giri, A. K., & Joshi, P. (2017). "The impact of macroeconomic indicators on Indian stock prices: An empirical analysis", *Studies in Business and Economics, 12*(1), 61–78.

Greenstone, M., Mas, A., & Nguyen, H. L. (2020). "Do credit market shocks affect the real economy? Quasi-experimental evidence from the great recession and" normal" economic times", *American Economic Journal: Economic Policy, 12*(1), 200–225.

Henry, I. P. (2022). "Processes of political, cultural, and social fragmentation: changes in the macro-environment of sport policy and management: c. 1980–c. 2022", *European Sport Management Quarterly, 22*(5), 705–725.

Hitt, M. A., & Collins, J. D. (2007). "Business ethics, strategic decision making, and firm performance", *Business Horizons, 50*(5), 353–357.

Hu, G., Wang, X., & Wang, Y. (2021). "Can the green credit policy stimulate green innovation in heavily polluting enterprises? Evidence from a quasi-natural experiment in China", *Energy Economics, 98*, 105134.

Ibrahim, M. H., & Aziz, H. (2003). "Macroeconomic variables and the Malaysian equity market: A view through rolling subsamples", *Journal of economic studies. 30*(1), 6–27.

Issah, M., & Antwi, S. (2017). "Role of macroeconomic variables on firms' performance: Evidence from the UK", *Cogent Economics & Finance, 5*(1), 1405581.

Itani, N., & Mason, K. (2014). "A macro–environment approach to civil aviation strategic planning", *Transport Policy,33*, 125–135.

Kandir, S. Y. (2008). "Macroeconomic variables, firm characteristics and stock returns: Evidence from Turkey", *International research journal of finance and economics, 16*(1), 35–45.

Khan, F., Khan, H., Khan, S. U. R., Jumaa, M., & Jan, S. U. (2019). "Macroeconomic Sensitivity, Risk-Return Trade-Off and Volatility Dynamics Evidence From Developed and Developing Markets", *International Journal of Corporate Finance and Accounting (IJCFA), 6*(1), 1–16.

Khan, H., Bajuri, N. H., Yoke, L. B., & Khan, F. (2014). "The Impacts of Corruption, Macroeconomic Instability and Market Competitiveness on Bank's Profitability", *International Journal of Information Processing and Management, 5*(3), 17.

Khanna, Vikas and Sharma, Renuka (2017). "Customer Switching Behavior in Retail Banking in India", *International Journal of Applied Business and Economic Research*, 15(9) 427–441.

Khatib, S. F., & Nour, A. (2021). "The impact of corporate governance on firm performance during the COVID-19 pandemic: Evidence from Malaysia", *Journal of Asian Finance, Economics and Business, 8*(2), 0943–0952.

Liu, J. (2021). "Big Data–Driven Macroeconomic Forecasting Model and Psychological Decision Behavior Analysis for Industry 4.0", *Complexity, 2021*, 1–11.

Mbonu, C. M., & Amahalu, N. N. (2021). "Effect of firm characteristics on the capital structure of insurance companies listed on the Nigeria stock exchange", *International Journal of Management Studies and Social Science Research, 3*(5), 217–228.

McNamara, R., & Duncan, K. (1995). "Firm performance and macro-economic variables", *Bond University, School of Business*, pp. 66, 1–22.

Mehta, K., Sharma, R., & Vyas, V. (2019). "Efficiency and ranking of sustainability index of India using DEA-TOPSIS", *Journal of Indian Business Research, 11*(2), 179–199. https://doi.org/10.1108/JIBR-02-2018-0057.

Mehta, K., Sharma, R., Vyas, V. & Kuckreja, J.S. (2022). "Exit strategy decision by venture capital firms in India using fuzzy AHP", *Journal of Entrepreneurship in Emerging Economies, 14*(4), 643–669. https://doi.org/10.1108/JEEE-05-2020-0146

Menegaki, A. N. (2014). "On energy consumption and GDP studies; A meta–analysis of the last two decades", *Renewable and sustainable energy reviews, 29*, 31–36.

Mnang'at, S. A., Namusonge, G. S., & Oteki, E. B. (2016). "The effects of interest rate on the financial performance of micro-enterprises: a case study of Makutano Township in West Pokot County", *International Journal of Novel Research in Marketing Management and Economics, 3*(3), 22–29.

Mwangi, C. I., & Jerotich, O. J. (2013). "The relationship between corporate social responsibility practices and financial performance of firms in the manufacturing, construction and allied sector of the Nairobi Securities Exchange", *International Journal of Business, Humanities and Technology, 3*(2), 81–90.

Ngene, A. N., Nwele, J., & Uduimoh, A. (2016). "Evaluation of Manufactured Goods Import and the Manufacturing Sector Productivity in Nigeria", *Saudi Journal of Business and Management Studies, 1*(4), 186–95.

Nisha, N. (2015). "Impact of macroeconomic variables on stock returns: evidence from Bombay Stock Exchange (BSE)", *Journal of Investment and Management, 4*(5), 162–170.

Okorie, I. E., & Ohakwe, J. (2018). "Forecasting Nigeria's inflation and the world prices of her major agricultural export commodities with probability distributions via VaR and ES and estimating their dependence via copula", *Communications in Statistics: Case Studies, Data Analysis and Applications, 4*(1), 28–45.

Pal, K., & Mittal, R. (2011). "Impact of macroeconomic indicators on Indian capital markets", *The Journal of risk finance, 12*(2), 84–97.

Sahu, P. (2021). "A study on the dynamic behaviour of headline versus core inflation: Evidence from India", *Global Business Review, 22*(6), 1574–1593.

Sari, I. A., & Rahmantika, D. N. (2021). "The Effect of Firm Characteristics and Entrepreneur Characteristics on the Success of MSME Business in Central Java Province", *Jurnal Manajemen Dayasaing*, *23*(1), 26–35.

Sharma, A. & Sharma, R. (2022). "Exploring Tax Decision Factors: A Perspective from North Indian Tax Practitioners", *Journal of Tax Reform*, *8*(3): 285–297. https://doi.org/10.15826/jtr.2022.8.3.122

Sharma, R., Mehta, K. & Goel, A. (2022). "Non-linear relationship between board size and performance of Indian companies", *Journal of Management and Governance* (2022). https://doi.org/10.1007/s10997-022-09651-8

Shergill, G. S., & Sarkaria, M. S. (1999). "Impact of Industry Type and Firm Characteristics on Firm–level Financial Performance – Evidence from Indian Industry", *The Journal of Entrepreneurship*, *8*(1), 25–44.

Štangová, N., & Víghová, A. (2021). "Company liquidity as a reflection of receivables and payables management", *Entrepreneurship and sustainability issues*, *9*(2), 238.

Stock, J. H., & Watson, M. (2009). "Forecasting in dynamic factor models is subject to structural instability", *The Methodology and Practice of Econometrics. A Festschrift in Honour of David F. Hendry*, *173*, 205.

Tymon Jr, W. G., Stout, D. E., & Shaw, K. N. (1998). "Critical analysis and recommendations regarding the role of perceived environmental uncertainty in behavioural accounting research", *Behavioral Research in Accounting*, *10*, 23.

Velte, P. (2020). "Does CEO power moderate the link between ESG performance and financial performance? A focus on the German two-tier system", *Management Research Review*, *43*(5), 497–520.

Vyas, V., Mehta, K., Sharma, R. (2023). "The nexus between toxic–air pollution, health expenditure, and economic growth: An empirical study using ARDL", *International Review of Economics and Finance*, *84*, 154–166 https://doi.org/10.1016/j.iref.2022.11.017

Yadav, I. S., Pahi, D., & Gangakhedkar, R. (2022). "The nexus between firm size, growth and profitability: new panel data evidence from Asia–Pacific markets", *European Journal of Management and Business Economics*, *31*(1), 115–140.

Yang, C. S. (2017). "Local labour markets and criminal recidivism", *Journal of Public Economics*, *147*, 16–29.

Priya Rana and Mahesh Sarva

6 Exploring Individual Investor Intentions Towards Socially Responsible Investment

Abstract: The aim of the study is to investigate the indirect impact of perceived risk, perceived return, trust, and morality through the mediating variable attitude towards intentions of Indian stock market investors. A sample from 213 Indian investors from the different districts of Haryana was collected to depict their responses utilizing a questionnaire with a five-point Likert scale. To do the analysis, the data were evaluated using Smart PLS v3.2. The Indian government's Ministry of Corporate Affairs (MCA) published the National Guidelines on Responsible Business Conduct (NGRBC). In NGRBC, Sustainable Development Goals (SDGs) were projected. Investors need to understand the good and negative results from their investments and related activities; endeavour to influence such outcomes in relation to the SDGs. The outcomes of the study indicate that the model depicts mediation of attitude between trust, perceived risk, perceived return, and morality towards intentions of individual investors who are currently holding accounts in the stock market.

Keywords: Socially Responsible Investment (SRI), Perceived risk, Perceived return, Trust, Morality, Attitude, Intentions

Introduction

In the 18th century, people used this concept of socially responsible investment to become a part of religious and ethical groups; later, people applied this philosophy of avoiding investment in sin stocks like gambling, prostitution, and cigarettes. In 1920 Methodist used this concept for negative screening (Broadhurst, 2003) Thereafter during the apartheid movement and the Vietnam War, chemical deployment activists tried to focus on socially responsible investment (Shapiro, 1992).

Investors who are socially responsible apply a combination of both affirmative and negative screening in their investing; the positive screening means investing in companies which support environmental protection, human and labour rights, animal rights, use renewable energy and avoiding companies which deal with or support such activities like racism, nuclear weapon, pesticide use, arms exporter, pornography, gambling, production of alcohol and weaponry products, tobacco, firearms and Irresponsible Foreign Operations (Hamilton, 1993; McLachlan, 2004; Geczy & Stambaugh, 2005).

Priya Rana, Mahesh Sarva, Lovely Professional University, Jalandhar

https://doi.org/10.1515/9783111170022-006

Only about 0.05% of the world's assets in sustainable funds come from funds in India. Six of India's eight ESG-themed funds were introduced in the year 2020, demonstrating the country's growing interest in and desire for sustainable investing. Various regulators and international organizations have been attempting to standardize the sustainability-related disclosures made by listed firms in relation to ESG-related reporting by companies. The SEBI–produced Business Responsibility and Sustainability Report, a fresh version of the sustainability and social reporting criteria, has replaced the Business Responsibility Report. The most prominent 1000 listed companies by market capitalization will have to submit BRSRs beginning with the fiscal year 2022–2023. There is an option for other companies to voluntarily declare BRSR (SEBI Consultation Paper, 2022). In India, these are the top ESG funds available (see Table 6.1).

Table 6.1: ESG Funds with Their Inception Date.

Top ESG Funds		Inception Date
1.	SBI Magnum Equity ESG Fund	August 2018
2.	Quantum India ESG Equity Fund	July 2019
3.	Axis ESG equity regular growth	Feb 2020
4.	ICICI Prudential ESG Fund	Oct 2020
5.	Mirae Asset ESG sector Leaders ETF	Nov 2020
6.	Aditya Birla ESG Fund	Dec 2020
7.	Kotak ESG Opportunities Fund	Dec 2020

MSCI, which is an American investment agency supporter globally, has used ESG ratings to measure the company's operation financially according to its ESG opportunities and risk (see Table 6.2).

Table 6.2: ESG Ratings and Categories.

Leaders	AA & AAA
Average	A BB & BBB
Laggards	B & C

Global citizens embrace outcome-based investment and demand full transparency. During Covid 19 pandemic, many investors demand greater visibility to measure Social Responsibility. Environmental concerns have been incorporated into the 125-year-old BSE (Bombay Stock Exchange) India's basic values. As a result of a long-term environmental responsibility-focused goal, the S&P BSE CARBONEX and GREENEX indices were developed. Among the top firms in this index, Tata Consultancy Services, Reliance Industries, Hindustan Unilever Limited, Housing Development Finance Corporation and Infosys demonstrate exceptionally high standards for ESG concerns. The Indian Institute of Corporate Affairs is creating a unique index specifically for Indian businesses related to sustainability, which will concentrate on problems concerned with business environmental consciousness in India (Vyas et al., 2020; Sharma et al., 2020). NSE has also made many ESG indexes like the NSE ESG index, NSE enhanced ESG index etc. Examples of impact investments include microfinance, social welfare funding, sustainable agriculture, sustainable sources, conservation, microfinance, and affordable and efficient necessities including housing, healthcare, education, and clean technology. Like this (Hellsten & Mallin, 2006) have substituted "socially responsible investments" for "ethical investments."

For mutual fund marketers, trust is a major concern with socially responsible investment profiles. The public does not trust what is underpinning social movement, and there are fewer chances to invest in socially responsible investments. On the other hand, return-driven investors could join in socially responsible investments just based on expected financial Success (Mehta & Sharma, 2017; Nilson, 2007; Sharma et al., 2021). As a result, it is critical for a country like India to comprehend the goals and make decisions about investment concerned with attitude and intentions, particularly about investor trust, their perceived risk, return, and morality concerns to develop an attitude toward intents to make an investment in socially responsible products. Further the role of depositories, environmental factors and switching behaviour has also impacted the decision making by retailers (Mahajan & Sharma, 2017; Khanna & Sharma, 2017; Vyas et al., 2023).

However, the literature lacks sufficient data to determine whether it will be possible for attitude to mediate interactions between trust, morality, perceived risk, perceived return, and the intention to make investments in socially conscious companies. This study tries to investigate the mediating role in the connection between trust, morality, perceived risk, perceived return and the intention to purchase an investment in the Indian Stock Market. The study's findings will advance the field of behavioural finance literature and show how investors make decisions in the Stock Market of India.

Literature Review

Perceived Risk

According to the consumer's goals, the likelihood of loss, and the overall evaluation of unfavourable outcomes measure the potential or predicted discontent with the purchase (Kim & Lennon, 2013; Pires et al., 2004). It has also been referred to as a function of ambiguity over loss or gain in a certain transaction (Cunningham, 1967). Focus is only placed on potential negative effects when examining perceived risk in consumer behaviour, and it differs between individuals and products (Stone & Gronhang, 1993). Through investing performance, it is demonstrated the indirect impact of perceptions of risk and intended investments. The level of risk that Indonesian stock investors perceive has a substantial impact on their motivation to invest. According to the study's findings, intention to invest and perceptions of risk are strongly correlated (Phung & Trang, 2017; Sharma et al., 2022; Nirmayantina, 2021; Shehata et al., 2021). According to the findings, having a high level of risk tolerance is important when attempting for a decision to purchase stocks. The goal of the current study is to determine how investors' attitudes and intentions come in favour of investing in socially responsible investments related to perceived risk.

Perceived Returns

According to traditional economic theory, perceived risk and return are linked to the likelihood of investing, and risk and return together drive investment behaviour. Volatility, performance predictability, and time horizon are all combined to determine the perceived return. The perceived returns have a significant impact on attitude when predicting future intentions (MacGregor et al., 1999). Return perception can influence investor conduct in a good or bad way. It depends on whether investors view the investment return and how financially savvy they are (Saleem, 2021). The anticipation that someone will participate in the stock market by purchasing stocks is the outcome of high returns relative to other types of investing. The higher the person's purpose of investing is, the greater the return received, such as unusual returns and dividends. The expectation that someone will invest in the stock market because of its high returns in comparison to other types of investment (Kurniawana, 2021). The stronger the person's purpose of investing, the greater the return received, such as unusual returns and dividends. Investors link fantastic stocks with both prospective returns and safety, believing that they are exclusively issued by trustworthy organizations, which helps to create views about risk and return (Hoffman, 2017).

Trust

To measure trust, one must be prepared to be vulnerable to the trustee. Perceived danger, in part, moderates the connection between trust and the willingness to take risks. The degree of trust is a sign of how much risk a person is prepared to accept. Trust is known as the "willingness to take risks." According to research by Mayer and Davis (2007), trust has an impact on long-term partnerships. For high- and low-relational clients, trust plays varied roles in the prediction of future intentions. Trust failed to predict investors' attitudes towards a brand while investing (Doney & Cannon, 1997; Garbarino, 1999; Ali, 2011). There are two factors that affect whether someone decides to be trustworthy. 1) Success of stock indexes is highly connected with indicators of economic trust, such as the consumer confidence index. 2) Investors that see social responsibility as a financial advantage may choose to act considering psychological research on the importance of dependability or because they really think that acting morally will make their money. When measured against other predictors of trustworthiness, trustworthiness's practical value will increase.

Morality

The moral sense of guilt has a favourable impact on how people act towards immoral activity). According to studies, moral responsibility perception has a substantial impact on one's purpose and behaviour. People opted for the moral result in order to uphold their moral principles and avoid immoral assets (Rubaltelli et al., 2015: Chen et al., 2017; Perspectives et al., 2020). The growing market demand for socially conscious investments suggests that other advantages, like attitude and moral concerns, affect investment decisions in addition to financial ones. Guilt from using immoral ways of earning devalues morality and makes individuals more eager to risk it for greater rewards. In the study, moral meaning is included as a new way to categorize mental accounts. It demonstrates how investing is impacted by the morality of the financial source, which is characterized by arbitrary values and guilt-based mental representations (Hofmann et al., 2007). Investment choices are favourably correlated with ethical perceptions. In addition to the fact that the desire for high returns is not the sole factor influencing investment decisions, non-financial factors also have a role in how financial Success is assessed (Keith et al., 2015).

Attitude Towards Socially Responsible Investment

According to Ajen (1991), an attitude influences one's intentions, which in turn influences one's behaviour. An individual is more likely to have a favourable motive to engage in a behaviour if they have a favourable attitude towards it. In addition to the actual environmental advantages, the psychological effects may enhance attitudes towards renewable energy brands and increase intentions to buy. Most pension beneficiaries express support for social screening, along with environmental screening in pension investments. Even investors who do not participate in Socially responsible investment exhibit a more meaningful value on the scale which measures attitude, indicating that attitudes are increasing because of their actions (Borgers & Pownall, 2014; Hartmann & Apaolaza-Ibáñez, 2012). It has been observed that Positive attitudes about social responsibility have an influence on respondents' pension investing. It is challenging to persuade this category of investors to adopt SRI equities funds because of their behavioural traits, which include having more favourable views about risk and savings while exhibiting less interest in sustainability concerns. There are results which support the idea that environmental attitudes and intentions to make green purchases have a favourable relationship (Nilsson, 2007; Chekima, 2015; Lagerkvist, 2020)

Intention of Investors Towards Socially Responsible Investment

Ajzen (1991) asserts that attitude towards activity determines conduct intention. According to the framework, a person's attitude towards the activity affects whether they think to invest in the stock market. Ajen (1991) claims that a person is more likely to engage in a particular behaviour if all the conditions – subjective standards, perceived behavioural control and attitude – are favourable. Researchers suggest that a person's attitude towards behaviour has an impact on whether they intend to invest in the stock market. The level of stock repurchases that investors intend and desire. The link is essential since the indirect effect has a deliberate influence (Akhtar & Das, 2019; Trang & Tho, 2017; Talha et al., 2013). The process of making ethical decisions have had an impact, and moral intensity helps to shape perceptions and intents. Positive relationships exist between attitudes towards environmentally friendly products and plans to make green purchases. It means overcoming the rise in consumer purchase intent for goods will require a positive outlook (Indriani et al., 2019; Goles et al., 2016) The connections between behavioural intention and its determinants, as well as between psychological elements and investment attitude, have been studied in Vietnamese individual investors (Phan & Zhou, 2014).

Methodology

Formulation of the Hypothesis and Framework for the Study

Hypotheses of the Study

Figure 6.1 shows the conceptual model of the study. In the following section the hypotheses of the study has been developed.

Hypothesis 1 (H1). Perceived risk has a considerable positive impact on investors' attitudes toward making socially responsible investments.

Hypothesis 2 (H2). The perceived return has a considerable positive impact on investors' attitudes toward making socially responsible investments.

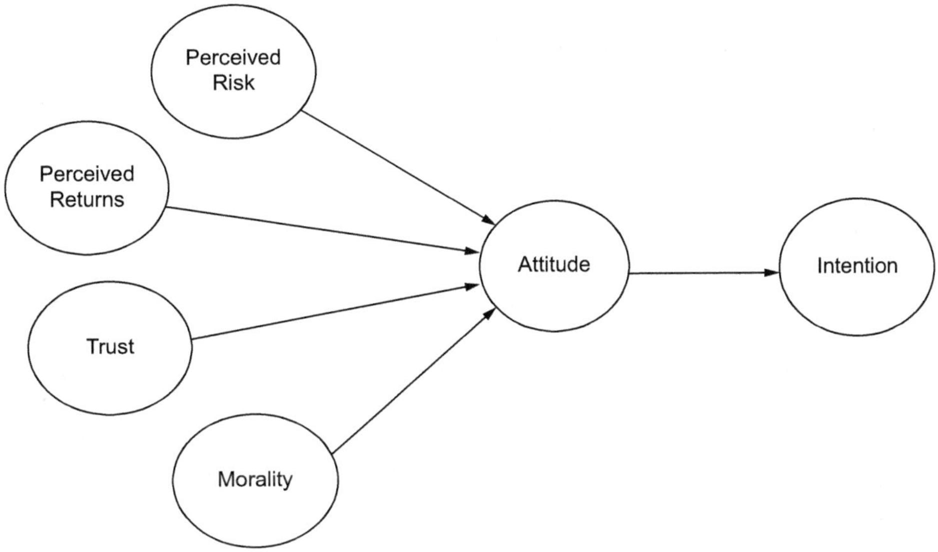

Figure 6.1: Conceptual Framework of the Study.

Hypothesis 3 (H3). Trust has a considerable positive impact on investors' attitudes toward making socially responsible investments.

Hypothesis 4 (H4). Morality has a considerable positive impact on investors' attitudes to make socially responsible investments.

Hypothesis 5 (H5). The Perceived risk has a considerable positive impact on investors' intentions to make socially responsible investments.

Hypothesis 6 (H6). The Perceived return has a considerable positive impact on investors' intentions to make socially responsible investments.

Hypothesis 7 (H7). Trust has a considerable positive impact on investors' intentions to make socially responsible investments.

Hypothesis 8 (H8). Morality has a considerable positive impact on investors' intentions to make socially responsible investments.

Hypothesis 9 (H9). The intention to make socially responsible investments is significantly influenced favourably by attitude.

Hypothesis 10 (H10). Investors' attitudes towards making socially responsible investments act as a positive mediator between perceived risk and intentions.

Hypothesis 11 (H11). Investors' attitudes towards making socially responsible investments act as a positive mediator between perceived return and intentions.

Hypothesis 12 (H12). Investors' attitudes towards making socially responsible investments act as a positive mediator between trust and intentions.

Hypothesis 13 (H13). Investors' attitudes towards making socially responsible investments act as a positive mediator between morality and intentions.

Measurement

To gather the essential data for the study, the researcher created a questionnaire. The questionnaire has six sections (i.e., perceived risk, perceived return, trust, morality, attitude, and intentions) to explore the investor's intentions towards socially responsible investment (for details see Table 6.3). To accomplish this, the researcher relied on a 5-point Likert scale with the following grades: strongly agree, agree, neutral, disagree, and strongly disagree (Shehata et al., 2021; Trang & Tho, 2017; Garbarino & Johnson, 1999; Raut & Kumar, 2018).

Table 6.3: Research Instrument of the Study.

Latent variable	code	Items	Adapted from
Perceived risk	PRi1	Socially responsible stocks have uncertain futures.	Shehata et al., 2021; Azwadi, 2011; Trang & Tho, 2017
	PRi2	Making an investment in socially conscious stocks is risky.	
	PRi3	The phrase "possible loss" instantly enters my mind when I hear the terms "socially responsible stocks" or "ESG (environment, social, and governance) stocks."	
	PRi4	I better invest my funds somewhere else than investing in Socially conscious stocks.	
	PRi5	Investing in socially conscious stocks allows me to accept some risks.	
Perceived return	PRe1	Socially Responsible stocks are financially sound.	Trang & Tho, 2017; Azwadi, 2011
	PRe2	I consider stock investing in socially responsible companies to be quite profitable.	
	PRe3	I believe that the average market return rate is greater or on par with the rate of return from equities that uphold social responsibility.	

Table 6.3 (continued)

Latent variable	code	Items	Adapted from
	PRe4	Investment in Socially Responsible stocks seems to be able to generate low returns. ***	
	PRe5	Socially Responsible stocks in which I invest have sufficiently long-term futures.	
Trust	TR1	I rely on the promises made by Socially Responsible Companies	Azwadi, 2011
	TR2	All Socially Responsible stocks are consistently of high quality.	
	TR3	Socially Responsible investments are unreliable and a waste of time. ***	
	TR4	Socially Responsible stocks usually meet expectations.	
	TR5	I think ethical businesses won't hide crucial information from their shareholders.	
Morality	MO1	Investing in socially conscious equities enables investors to have a beneficial impact on the environment.	Hoffman et al., 2007; Chen et al., 2017
	MO2	By purchasing socially conscious equities, investors can have an impact on societal issues.	
	MO3	It makes no difference if I put my money into socially conscious stocks because one investor cannot significantly impact society on their own. ***	
	MO4	It is useful for investors to think about issues like workplace rights, child labour, gambling, Tabaco and alcohol, sexual harassment etc.	
Attitude	AT1	It is beneficial to invest in socially responsible stocks	Raut & Kumar, 2018; Kirmani & Khan, 2016; Ali, 2011
	AT2	It is valuable to invest in Social Responsible stocks.	
	AT3	Investing in Socially Responsible stocks gives you inner satisfaction.	
	AT4	socially responsible stocks are nothing other than a big gambling casino	

Table 6.3 (continued)

Latent variable	code	Items	Adapted from
Intentions	INT1	Socially responsible stocks will definitely be one of choice to invest	Shehata et al., 2021; Trang & Tho, 2017; Hoffmann & Thomas, 2007; Raut et al., 2020
	INT2	I intend to suggest socially responsible stocks to others for investment.	
	INT3	Will you intend to put a larger sum of money in socially responsible funds/stocks while making a portfolio?	
	INT4	I intend to use my investment in sustainability to bring a change in society.	
	INT5	I intend to avoid those stocks which are harming society, ethics and the environment.	

*** Reverse items

Data Collection

By distributing the questionnaire both online and offline from May to August 2022, the researcher gathered the data for this study. Two hundred thirteen stock market investors in India provided the researcher with a good response.

Sampling

The research is qualitative in nature. Because the total population is unknown, we used a nonprobability sampling strategy and convenience sampling. As the population of Haryana is 27,388,008 (in 2022), Using the method developed by Krejcie and Morgan (1970), the research sample size was determined to be 385. However, due to the issue of the offline mode of sampling, many investors needed personal attention in filling out the questionnaire. Thus, above 300 survey questionnaires have been distributed among districts of Haryana (Ambala, Kurukshetra, Karnal, Yamuna Nagar, Panchkula, Panipat, and Gurugram). The researcher received correct responses from 213 Indian participants investing in the stock market. Both online and offline distribution methods of these questionnaires were used, and the participants were made aware of the study's objectives.

Analysis and Results

As suggested by prior research, the measurement model was evaluated using individual item reliability, Cronbach alpha, and convergent reliability (Hair et al., 2016).

Individual Item Reliability (Loadings): Outer loadings of each item for every framework are advised in order to evaluate the dependability of each component individually. According to earlier research, each item's dependability has to be at least 0.70 or equivalent to zero (Hair et al. 2011). In the present study, item loadings of perceived risk (PRi2) are less than the acceptable limit, but the composite reliability, Cronbach alpha and AVE are in favour of the construct, so the researcher decided to keep the item (Hair et al. 2016). Attitude (ATT4) also shows less relevance in its loading, but the overall impact of the hypothesis is significant (see Table 6.4).

Composite reliability (CR): The current study has shown a 0.6 or higher internal consistency reliability level (Bagozzi & Yi, 1998). For the current study, it was determined that each item's composite reliability ranged between 0.60 and above, indicating that all constructs had enough internal consistency.

Convergent validity (AVE): The average Variance has been proposed as a tool to evaluate the convergent validity (Fornel & Larcker, 1981). The Average Variance Extracted should be at least 0.50 or greater, to evaluate the convergent validity of each notion (Chin, 1998). Investor intentions are predicted to be around 0.50, with the exception of attitude, which has attained the bare minimum level of 0.50 (Dijkstra & Henseler, 2015) (see Table 6.4).

Cronbach alpha (CA): According to the current study, values of Cronbach alpha are within the acceptable range of 0.70 to 0.90 (Dijkstra & Henselet, 2015). Since Cronbach's alpha tends to favour brief scales of two or three items, as in the current situation, this slight discrepancy (i.e. PRi & ATT) that fell well short of the threshold for an adequate confirmatory scale would typically be overlooked (Garson, 2016) (see Table 6.4).

Discriminant Validity DV: The heterotrait-monotrait ratio of correlations was used to evaluate the discriminant validity (Henseler et al., 2015). The cut-off values for calculating the HTMT criterion should be less than 0.9, according to the HTMT (Jörg et al., 2015) presented for an estimate for evaluating discriminant validity. The fact that all values in Table 4 are below the specified value ranges below 0.9 indicates a strong discriminant validity (see Tables 6.4, 6.5 and 6.6).

Analysis of Mediation

We employed the VAF to assess and classify the mediating impact. The suggested values for variance accounting are VAF > 80% for whole mediation, VAF 20% for the absence

Table 6.4: Outcomes of Reflective Model.

Item code	Loading	Outer weight	Cronbach Alpha	Composite reliability	Average Variance extracted
PRi1	0.485	0.25	0.638	0.801	0.545
PRi2	0.306	0.032			
PRi3	0.542	0.165			
PRi4	0.736	0.421			
PRi5	0.722	0.65			
PRe1	0.88	0.297	0.899	0.925	0.711
PRe2	0.839	0.289			
PRe3	0.832	0.256			
PRe4	0.595	0.166			
PRe5	0.796	0.231			
TRU1	0.703	0.292	0.67	0.806	0.531
TRU2	0.646	0.244			
TRU3	0.582	0.243			
TRU4	0.838	0.317			
TRU5	0.719	0.32			
MOR1	0.889	0.395	0.851	0.894	0.632
MOR2	0.892	0.425			
MOR3	0.384	0.178			
MOR4	0.626	0.322			
ATT1	0.877	0.42	0.685	0.702	0.337
ATT2	0.886	0.403			
ATT3	0.771	0.32			
ATT4	0.176	0.158			
INT1	0.923	0.236	0.739	0.828	0.494
INT2	0.817	0.25			
INT3	0.829	0.291			
INT4	0.816	0.215			
INT5	0.827	0.195			

Source: Authors' estimation.

Table 6.5: HTMT (Heterotrait–Monotrait ratio).

	Attitude_	Intentions___	Morality	Perceived Return_	Perceived Risk	Trust
Attitude_						
Intentions___	0.864					
Morality	1.093	0.866				
Perceived Return_	0.997	0.746	1.003			
Perceived Risk	0.776	0.464	0.643	0.647		
Trust	1.136	0.766	1.139	0.932	0.674	

Source: Authors' estimation.

Table 6.6: Hypothesis Testing & Path Coefficients.

RELATIONSHIP OF ITEMS	Original Sample (O)	Sample Mean (M)	Standard Deviation (STDEV)	T Statistics (|O/ STDEV|)	P Values	Hypothesis support
Attitude_ -> Intentions___	0.727	0.727	0.043	17.001	0	**(H9) SUPPORTED**
Morality -> Attitude_	0.156	0.163	0.07	2.224	0.027	**(H4) SUPPORTED**
Morality -> Intentions___	0.113	0.119	0.053	2.136	0.033	**(H8) SUPPORTED**
Perceived Return_ -> Attitude_	0.262	0.23	0.093	2.805	0.005	**(H2) SUPPORTED**
Perceived Return_ -> Intentions___	0.19	0.168	0.069	2.759	0.006	**(H6) SUPPORTED**
Perceived Risk -> Attitude_	0.155	0.183	0.079	1.977	0.049	**(H1) SUPPORTED**
Perceived Risk -> Intentions___	0.113	0.132	0.055	2.057	0.04	**(H5) SUPPORTED**
Trust -> Attitude_	0.389	0.387	0.065	5.936	0	**(H3) SUPPORTED**
Trust -> Intentions___	0.282	0.282	0.052	5.46	0	**(H7) SUPPORTED**

Note: (95% confidence interval) Note: t-values > 1.96 and p-value < 0.05.

Table 6.7: Analysis of Mediation.

Items	Indirect effect	Total effect	VAF	Hypothesis supported
PERCEIVED RISK -> ATTITUDE-> INTENTION	**33.61**	**34.024**	**98.8%**	**Full mediation, H(10)supported**
PERCEIVED RETURN -> ATTITUDE-> INTENTION	**47.69**	**47.804**	**99.7%**	**Full mediation, H(11)supported**
TRUST -> ATTITUDE->INTENTION	**100.92**	**101.167**	**99.8%**	**Full mediation, H(12)supported**
MORALITY>ATTITUDE>INTENTION	**19.23**	**19.66**	**97.8%**	**Full mediation, H(13)supported**

of mediation, and 20% to 80% for partial mediation (Joseph et al., 2013). Given that the VAF in Table 6.7 is more than 80%, the results demonstrate complete mediation.

Table 6.8: Goodness of Model.

Construct	R2	Adj R2	F2	Q2	VIF	SRMR
Intentions	0.528	0.526	1.121	0.359	1.00	0.175

Table 6.9: Significance of Total Indirect Effect.

Relationship	Original Sample (O)	Sample Mean (M)	Standard Deviation (STDEV)	T Statistics (|O/ STDEV|)	P Values	Significance
ATTITUDE -> INTENTIONS	0.727	0.724	0.044	16.382	0	Significant
MORALITY -> ATTITUDE	0.156	0.166	0.076	2.056	0.04	Significant
PERCEIVED RETURN -> ATTITUDE	0.262	0.237	0.092	2.832	0.005	Significant
PERCEIVED RISK -> ATTITUDE	0.155	0.178	0.076	2.037	0.042	Significant
TRUST -> ATTITUDE	0.389	0.382	0.07	5.566	0	Significant

Note: (95% confidence interval) t-values > 1.96 & p-value < 0.05.

Table 6.10: Significance of Total Direct Effect.

Relationship	Original Sample (O)	Sample Mean (M)	Standard Deviation (STDEV)	T Statistics (|O/ STDEV|)	P Values	Significance
Perceived risk -> Intentions	0.414	0.394	0.078	5.286	0	Significant
Perceived return -> Intentions	−0.114	−0.1	0.088	1.295	0.196	Not Significant
Trust -> Intentions	0.247	0.261	0.075	3.309	0.001	Significant

Note: (95% confidence interval) t-values > 1.96 & p-value < 0.05.

Relevance of the Model

For the analysis of the study, the researcher used R2, SRMR, Q2, F2, and VIF, which are all indicators used in smart PLS to define model fit.

Several framework misspecifications are found using SRMR (Dijkstra & Henseler, 2015a; Henseler et al., 2015). The root means the square difference between the observed correlations and the model-implied correlations is a critical parameter for the SRMR. Zero represents a perfect fit because the SRMR is an absolute measure of fit. A

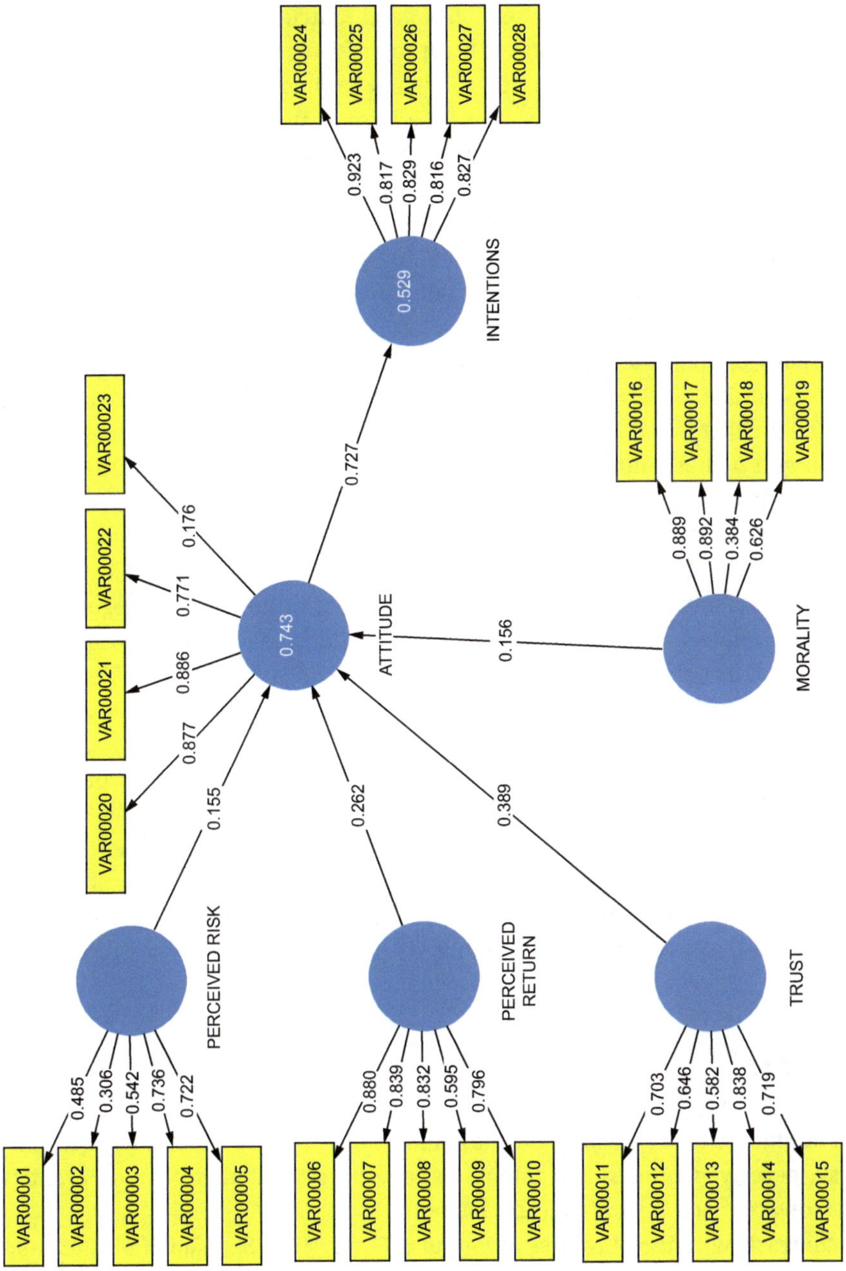

Figure 6.2: Framework of the Model.
Source: Outputs of Smart PLS software.

value of less than 0.08 is frequently seen as a good match (Hu & Bentler, 1998). The SRMR of the model, which is 0.175, makes it appropriate for study.

Q2 ought to be greater than zero (Hair, Ringle & Sarstedt, 2011). Values above zero indicate that the observed values are successfully recreated and that the model has predictive relevance (Q2), while values below zero evaluate a lack of predictive relevance (Henseler, Ringle, & Sarstedt, 2015). The coefficient of determination is used to evaluate the structural model. The Q2 score of 0.359 for the model suggests that it is appropriate for study (see Tables 6.8, 6.9 and 6.10).

This coefficient, which measures the model's capacity for prediction, is created using the R2 score, which is between the values of a certain endogenous construct that are actually observed and those that are anticipated. The authors are (Heenseler, Ringle, & Sarstedt 2015). R2, which measures how much of the dependent variable can be accounted for by the independent variable, can be examined. The R2 number goes from 0 to 1, and higher values indicate greater degrees of forecasting accuracy. It is challenging to provide general guidelines for optimal R2 values because they vary subject to the complexity of the model and the area of study. The model is suitable for research because R2 in Table 6 is 0.528.

Values of 0.02(small), 0.15(medium), and 0.35(large) influence the exogenous latent variable, as determined by the F2 calculation criteria. According to (Hair et al., 2016), effect sizes less than 0.02 indicate the lack of an effect. The model's F2 attitude impact on investor intentions to invest in socially responsible investments is a good and appropriate 1.121.

To evaluate the level of collinearity in PLS-SEM, the Variance Inflation Factor (VIF) is assessed. There are two often-used rules: According to (Hair, Ringle, & Sarstedt, 2016), there can be a collinearity issue if the VIF value is five or higher. According to (Johnston et al., 2018), VIF > 2.5 denotes significant collinearity, VIF > 5 denotes cause for concern, and VIF > 10 denotes a serious collinearity problem (see Tables 6.8, 6.9 and 6.10). The output of our model exhibits substantial collinearity (see Figure 6.2).

Discussion

The current study has well explained the relation of investors' trust, morality, perceived risk, perceived returns and intentions to ascertain whether attitude predicts intentions towards socially conscious investment.

This contrasts with the outcomes of Phung & Trang, 2017, Shehata et al., 2021 and Nirmayantina, 2021, which explained a positive correlation between perceived risk towards attitude and intentions to invest in socially responsible investment.

First, the findings support the research by Phung & Trang (2017) and Shehata et al. (2021) that attitude and intention are positively correlated with perceived risk (Nirmayantina, 2021). According to MacGregor et al.(1999), the perceived return has a second favourable indirect influence on investment intentions (Kurniawana, 2021). But it doesn't provide a direct correlation to intentions (Saleem 2021). Thirdly, research demonstrated that trust has a positive effect on attitudes and intentions in both direct and indirect relationships (Garbarino, 1999). Studies support the fact that morality has a direct and indirect link with intentions (Chen C, Chen J, He G, 2017) (Hoffman, 2007) MOR3 has contributed less to attitude than expected; additional research is necessary (Chen et al., 2017; Hoffman, 2007). Fifthly, attitude toward intentions always has a good influence (Ajen, 1999; Akhtar & Das 2019; Goles, 2016).

Implications

The most significant result is that both the social and financial components of investing appear to affect investors' behaviour. The study may be able to advise stock market corporations that there is a need to concentrate on investors' attitudes and intents in relation to the social and environmental components of the theory of investing. It could be crucial to express certain issues in quantitative terms so that they have a specific impact on investor intentions. Examples of such issues include environmental protection, good governance, social issues, gambling, alcohol-producing companies, treatment of animals, sustainability issues, etc.

However, there is a particular need for stock market businesses to highlight their beneficial effects on the environment, society, and governance. This might encourage individual investors to be more thoughtful about their investment choices and help solve the sustainability challenge. The findings demonstrate that merely factors influencing investors' attitudes are insufficient; these factors must also result in their deliberate behaviour to invest. The Stock Exchange Board of India, also known as SEBI, is required to offer reliable and pertinent information on the potential for investing in socially responsible projects.

Investors must be aware of the quantitative and qualitative indicators of socially responsible investments before they can make comparisons. The most effective way to spread awareness about this type of investment is through investor awareness on television and online. Investing through socially responsible channels may become a trend for people and financial advisers in the future since such conduct could protect investors from the likelihood of a global financial catastrophe. Even after the epidemic, many investors continued to use the same traditional approach to investing since there was no standard on investor understanding of ethical investing. Before making a social investment, investors should consider factors like perceived risk and trust, perceived return and morality. These considerations can only be made with broad domain awareness. Although investors appear to be moral, their motives sometimes seem to be corrupted by their desire for high profits. Sometimes perceived returns in the stock market can be overshadowed by the risk of losing money.

Additionally, it is important to convey the message that on the basis of financial performance, socially responsible investments provide investors with the same opportunities as conventional investments. It is highly recommended that investors and investment agencies must provide information on sustainability as an essential aspect along with profitability. There is a strong need to acknowledge the ESG (environmental, social and governance) rating of firms before making an investment; in this way, companies will put more focus on their sustainability factors which will, in return, make the globe less prone to environmental threats. The study generally takes the stance that when investors decide to make socially responsible investments, both their attitude and deliberate considerations matter.

Conclusion

The goal of the study was to establish whether attitude predetermines intentions by investigating the relationship between morality, perceived risk, expected returns, and trust. It also aimed at confirming the mediating role of attitude between independent and dependent variables. The investigation was conducted in a natural environment.

The study demonstrates how attitude affects intentional investor behaviour with regard to socially responsible investment goals. That is an investor's deliberate conduct when investing is shaped by their thinking, which is not always purely motivated by the goal of profit maximization.

Instead of making investment decisions, investors, to a certain extent, take into account their attitudes toward things like perceived risk, perceived return, trust, and morality in building the intent to invest.

It Demonstrated the significance of a favourable relationship between trust, morality, perceived risk, perceived return and intentions to invest in socially responsible investment. The findings also indicate that all construct shows a direct effect. Only perceived return is not significant to impact the intentions of investors to invest towards socially responsible investment.

The results imply that in order to reduce losses that may be likely to occur in the future due to the sustainability of the global environment, investors should enhance their study on the risks associated with the companies trading on the Indian stock market. It may also be noted that investors have a bad tendency to view and evaluate investments. People who are recognized for being socially conscious investors want to influence the world with their attitudes and want to invest in companies that share their values.

Investors should carefully weigh the pros and drawbacks of investment ideas before investing in order to affect Sustainable Development Goals. In the Indian capital market, there is more need to follow ESG norms and spread awareness to investors about the company's policies for sustainability. After the COVID pandemic, there has been an increase in socially responsible investment options in India.

This study had some limitations. First of all, it was exceedingly challenging to get responses from respondents since investors have less understanding about investing in socially responsible investments in India. There is a need for promotion and awareness of these investment policies with the help of applications and software; much like accounting ratios, ESG points are also displayed on the top side of the screen; there is a need for implementing regulations to enlarge the perspective of socially responsible investing. Secondly, demography could also become part of the study.

References

Ajzen, I. (1991). "The Theory of Planned Behavior", *Organizational Behavior and Human Decision Processes, 50*, 179–211.

Akhtar, F. & Das, N. (2018). "Predictors of investment intention in Indian stock markets: Extending the theory of planned behaviour", *International Journal of Bank Marketing*. 37. 10.1108/IJBM-08-2017-0167.

Ali, A. (2011). "Predicting Individual Investors' Intention to Invest: An Experimental Analysis of Attitude as a Mediator", *World Academy of Science, Engineering and Technology. 50*, 994–1001.

Aren, S. & Akgüneş, A. (2018). "The Effect of Risk and Trust in Investment Decision Making", *Conference: 11th International Conference on Future Challenges in Management and Business, İstanbul*

Bagozzi R. P., and Yi Y. (1988). "On the evaluation of structural equation models", *Journal of the Academy of marketing science*, 16(1), 74–94. 96.

Boffo, R., and R. Patalano (2020). "ESG Investing: Practices, Progress and Challenges", *OECD Paris*,

Borgers, A. C.T. & Pownall, R. A.J. (2014). "Attitudes towards socially and environmentally responsible investment", *Journal of Behavioral and Experimental Finance*, *1*, 27–44. doi:10.1016/j.jbef.2014.01.005

Broadhurst, D., Watson, J., Marshall, J., & Molthan, P. (2003). "Ethical and Socially Responsible Investment", K.G. Saur.

Chekima B, Syed Khalid Wafa SAW, Igau O. A., Chekima S., & Sondoh Jr SL (2015). "Examining Green Consumerism Motivational Drivers: Does Premium Price and Demographics Matter to Green Purchasing?", *Journal of Cleaner Production* doi: 10.1016/j.jclepro.2015.09.102.

Chen C, Chen J, & He G (2017). "Correction: Immorally obtained principal increases investors' risk preference", PLOS ONE 12(5): e0178892. https://doi.org/10.1371/journal.pone.0178892

Chin W. W. (1998). "The partial least squares approach to structural equation modelling", *Modern Methods for business research*, 295(2), 295–336.

Cohen, J. (1988). "Statistical Power Analysis for the Behavioral Sciences" (2nd ed.). Hillsdale, NJ: Lawrence Erlbaum Associates, Publishers.

Cunningham, S. (1967). "The major dimensions of perceived risk", in Cox, D. F. (ed.), *Risk Taking and Information Handling in Consumer Behaviour*, Harvard University Press, Boston, MA, 82–108

Diacon, S. & Ennew, C. (2001). "Consumer Perceptions of Financial Risk", *The Geneva Papers on Risk and Insurance – Issues and Practice. 26.* 389–409. 10.1111/1468-0440.00125.

Dijkstra T. K., and Henseler J. (2015). "Consistent partial least squares path modelling", *MIS Quarterly*, 39(2).

Doney, P. M., & Cannon, J. P. (1997). "An Examination of the Nature of Trust in Buyer-Seller Relationships", *Journal of Marketing*, 61(2), 35. doi:10.2307/1251829

Duarte P. A. O., and Raposo M. L. B. (2010). "A PLS model to study brand preference: An application to the mobile phone market", *In Handbook of partial least squares* (pp. 449–485): Springer. 94.

Fornell C., and Larcker D. F. (1981). "Evaluating structural equation models with unobservable variables and measurement error", *Journal of marketing research*, 18(1), 39–50. 97.

Garbarino, E. & Johnson, M. S. (1999). "The Different Roles of Satisfaction, Trust, and Commitment in Customer Relationships", *Journal of Marketing*, 63(2), 70–87. American Marketing Association URL: http://www.jstor.org/stable/1251946

Garson, G.D. (2016). "Partial Least Squares: Regression and Structural Equation Models", *Statistical Associates Publishers*, Asheboro.

Geczy, C. C., Stambaugh, R. F., & Levin, D. (2005). "Investing in Socially Responsible Mutual Funds", SSRN's eLibrary, http://dx.doi.org/10.2139/ssrn.416380

Goles, T. & White, G. & Beebe, N. & Dorantes, A. & Hewitt, B. (2006). "Moral Intensity and Ethical Decision-Making: A Contextual Extension", *ACM SIGMIS Database*, *37*, 86–95. 10.1145/1161345.1161357.

Hair J. F. Jr, Hult G. T. M., Ringle C., and Sarstedt M. (2016). "A primer on partial least squares structural equation modelling (PLS-SEM): Sage publications.

Hair, F., Sarstedt, Jr, J., Hopkins, M. L. & Kuppelwieser, V. (2014). "Partial least squares structural equation modelling (PLS-SEM): An emerging tool in business research", *European Business Review*, *26*(2), 106–121. https://doi.org/10.1108/EBR-10-2013-0128

Hair, J. F., Ringle, C. M., & Sarstedt, M. (2011). "PLS-SEM: Indeed, a silver bullet", *Journal of Marketing Theory and Practice*, *19*(2), 139–152. doi https://doi.org/10.2753/MTP1069-6679190202.

Hair, J. F., Ringle, C. M., & Sarstedt, M. (2013). "Partial least squares structural equation modelling: rigorous applications, better results and higher acceptance", *Long Range Planning*, *46(*1–2), 1–12. doi https://doi.org/10.1016/j.lrp.2013.01.001.

Hamilton, S. & Jo, H. & Statman, M. (1993). "Doing Well While Doing Good? The Investment Performance of Socially Responsible Mutual Funds", *Financial Analysts Journal* – FINANCIAL J. 49. 62–66. 10.2469/far.v49.n6.62

Hartmann, P., & Apaolaza-Ibáñez, V. (2012). "Consumer attitude and purchase intention toward green energy brands: The roles of psychological benefits and environmental concern", *Journal of Business Research*, *65*(9), 1254–1263. https://doi.org/10.1016/j.jbusres.2011.11.001

Hellsten, S. & Mallin, C. (2006). "Are 'Ethical' or 'Socially Responsible' Investments Socially Responsible?", *Journal of Business Ethics*, *66*, 393–406. 10.1007/s10551-006-0001-x.

Henseler, J., Hubona, G., & Ray, P. A. (2016). "Using PLS path modelling in new technology research: updated guidelines", *Industrial Management & Data Systems*, *116*(1), 2–20. doi: https://doi.org/10.1108/IMDS-09-2015-0382.

Henseler, J., Ringle, C. M., & Sarstedt, M. (2015). "A new criterion for assessing discriminant validity in variance-based structural equation modelling", *Journal of the Academy of Marketing Science*, *43(*1), 115–135. doi: https://doi.org/10.1007/s11747-014-0403-8

Hoffmann, A. & Post, T. (2017). "How return and risk experiences shape investor beliefs and preferences", *Accounting & Finance*, *57*, 10.1111/acfi.12169.

Hofmann, E., Hoelzl, E., & Kirchler, E. (2007). *"A Comparison of Models Describing the Impact of Moral Decision Making on Investment Decisions", Journal of Business Ethics, 82(1), 171–187.* doi:10.1007/s10551-007-9570-6

Hofmann, E., Meier-Pesti, K., & Kirchler, E. (2007). "The decision process for ethical investment", *Journal of Financial Services Marketing*, *12(*1), 4–16. doi:10.1057/palgrave.fsm.4760057

Hu, L., & Bentler, P. M. (1998). "Fit Indices in Covariance Structure Modeling: Sensitivity to Under parameterized Model Misspecification", *Psychological Methods*, *3*, 424–453.

Hulland J. (1999). "Use of partial least squares (PLS) in strategic management research: A review of four recent studies", *Strategic Management Journal*, *20*(2), 195–204.

Indriani, I., Rahayu, M., & Hadiwidjojo, D. (2019). "The Influence of Environmental Knowledge on Green Purchase Intention the Role of Attitude as Mediating Variable", *International Journal of Multicultural and Multireligious Understanding*, *6*, 627. 10.18415/ijmmu.v6i2.706.

Johnston R, Jones K, & Manley D. (2018). "Confounding and collinearity in regression analysis: a cautionary tale and an alternative procedure, illustrated by studies of British voting behaviour", *Qual Quant*, *52*(4):1957-1976. doi:10.1007/s11135-017-0584-6

Keller, C., & Siegrist, M. (2006). "Investing in stocks: The influence of financial risk attitude and values–related money and stock market attitudes", *Journal of Economic Psychology, 27(2), 285–303.* doi:10.1016/j.joep.2005.07.002

Khanna, V. & Sharma, R. (2017). "Customer Switching Behavior in Retail Banking in India", *International Journal of Applied Business and Economic Research, 15(*9), 427–441.

Kim, J., & Lennon, S. J. (2013). "Effects of Reputation and website quality on online consumers' emotions, perceived risk and purchase intention", *Journal of Research in Interactive Marketing, 7(*1), 33–56. doi:10.1108/17505931311316734

Kirmani, M. & Mohammed K. N. (2016). "Environmental concern to attitude towards green products: Evidence from India", *Serbian Journal of Management, 11*, 10.5937/sjm11-9241.

Lagerkvist, C., Edenbrandt, A., Tibbelin, I & Wahlstedt, Y. (2020). "Preferences for sustainable and responsible equity funds -A choice experiment with Swedish private investors", *Journal of Behavioral and Experimental Finance*, *28*, 100406. 10.1016/j.jbef.2020.100406.

Lewis, A., & Webley, P.A. (2002). "Socially and ethical investing: Beliefs, preferences and the willingness to sacrifice financial return".

MacGregor, D.G., Slovic, P., Berry, M.A., & Evensky, H.R. (1999). "Perception of Financial Risk: A Survey Study of Advisors and Planners", *Household Finance eJournal*.

Mahajan, V and Sharma, R (2017). "Future of Depository with Introduction of Payment Bank– A Game Changer to Capital Market", *International Journal of Applied Business and Economic Research, 15(*9), 343–356.

McLachlan, J. & Gardner, J. (2004). "A Comparison of Socially Responsible and Conventional Investors", *Journal of Business Ethics*, *52*, 11–25. 10.1023/B:BUSI.0000033104.28219.92.

Mehta K. & Sharma R. (2017), "Contrarian and Momentum investment strategies: Evidence from Indian Stock Market", *International Journal of Applied Business and Economic Research*, *15*(9), 107–118.

Mehta, K., Sharma, R., Vyas, V.(2019). "Efficiency and ranking of sustainability index of India using DEA-TOPSIS", *Journal of Indian Business Research*, *11*(2), pp. 179–199. https://doi.org/10.1108/JIBR-02-2018-0057.

Michael S. & Cvetkovich, G. (2000). "Perception of Hazards: The Role of Socially Trust and Knowledge", *Risk Analysis 20(5), 713–720.* doi:10.1111/0272-4332.205064

Nilsson, J. (2007). "Investment with a Conscience: Examining the Impact of Pro-Socially Attitudes and Perceived Financial Performance on Socially Responsible Investment Behavior", *Journal of Business Ethics, 83(2), 307–325.* doi:10.1007/s10551-007-9621-z

Nirmayantina, Y. & Arifin, A.Z. & Bangun, N. (2021). "The Influence of Product Knowledge and Perceived Risk on Investment Intention of Stock Investors in the Covid-19 Pandemic Era", 10.2991/assehr.k.210805.074.

P. Iwan Kurniawana (2021). "Effect of Expected Return, Self-Efficacy, and Perceived Risk on Investment Intention: An Empirical Study on Accounting", Masters Degree in Udayana University, Bali.

Palacios-González, M. M. & Chamorro-Mera, A. (2019). "Analysis of the intention to invest in a socially responsible manner: segmentation of the Spanish investor", Spanish *Journal of Finance and Accounting* / Revista Española de Financiación y Contabilidad, DOI: 10.1080/02102412.2019.1598700

Pasewark, W. R., & Riley, M. E. (2010). "It's a matter of principle: The role of personal values in investment decisions", *Journal of Business Ethics*, *93*, 237–253.

Pattit, K. (2009). “Understanding Socially Responsible Investing: The Effect of Decision Frames and Trade-off Options”, *Journal of Business Ethics, 87*, 41–55. 10.1007/s10551-008-9800-6.

Perspectives, Gen–Y., Ismah, O., Subramaniam, G., Mohamad, S., Hanif, A., Hassan, F., & Yaakob, S. (2020). “The Adoption of Socially Responsible Investments”, *Malaysian Journal of Consumer and Family Economics, 22*, 194–222.

Phan, C.K. & Zhou, J. (2014). “Vietnamese individual investors’ behaviour in the stock market: an exploratory study”, *Research Journal of Socially Science & Management, 3*(12), 46–54.

Pires, G., Stanton, J., & Eckford, A. (2004). “Influences on the perceived risk of purchasing online”, *Journal of Consumer Behaviour, 4*(2), 118–131. doi:10.1002/cb.163

Ramayah, T., Cheah, J., Chuah, F., Ting, H., & Memon, M. A. (2018). “Partial least squares structural equation modelling (PLS-SEM) using smartPLS 3.0. In *An Updated Guide and Practical Guide to Statistical Analysis”*, Pearson.

Raut, R. K., Kumar, R., & Das, N. (2020). “Individual investors’ intention towards SRI in India: an implementation of the theory of reasoned action”, *Socially Responsibility Journal*, ahead-of-print (ahead-of-print). doi:10.1108/srj-02-2018–0052

Ringle, C. M., Wende, S., & Becker, J. M. (2015). “SmartPLS 3. SmartPLS gmbH, Boenningstedt”, *Journal of Service Science and Management, 10*(3)

Rubaltelli, E., Lotto, L., Ritov, I. & Rumiati, R. (2015). “Moral investing: Psychological motivations and implications”, *Judgment and decision making, 10*, 64–75.

Sahi, S. K. (2017). “Psychological biases of individual investors and financial satisfaction”, *Journal of Consumer Behaviour*. https://doi.org/10.1002/cb.1644

Saleem, S., Mahmood, F., Usman, M., Bashir, M., & Shabbir, R. (2021). “Determinants of Investment Behavior in Mutual Funds: Evidence From Pakistaz”, *Frontiers in Psychology*, p. *12*, 666007. https://doi.org/10.3389/fpsyg.2021.666007

Sallehhuddin, M. A., Masoud, M.S. and Said, A.M.A. (2013) ‘An analysis of moral intensity, intention and socially responsible investment behaviour among fund managers of Malaysian unit trust companies’, *International Journal Managerial and Financial Accounting*, 5(2), 162–177.

Schoorman, F. & Mayer, R. & Davis, J. (2007). “An Integrative Model of Organizational Trust: Past, Present, and Future”, *Academy of Management Review, 32*, 10.5465/AMR.2007.24348410.

SEBI consultation paper on “Environmental, social and governance (ESG) rating providers for securities markets”, 2022.

Shapiro, J. (1992). “What is Socially Investing? Who are Socially Investors?” In Kinder, P., Lydenberg, S. and Domini, A. (eds) The Socially Investment Almanac: A Comprehensive Guide to Socially Responsible Investing, New York, NY, Henry Holt and Company, pp. 8–23

Sharma, A. & Sharma, R. (2022). “Exploring Tax Decision Factors: A Perspective from North Indian Tax Practitioners”, *Journal of Tax Reform, 8*(3): 285–297. https://doi.org/10.15826/jtr.2022.8.3.122.

Sharma, R., Mehta, K. & Goel, A. (2022). “Non-linear relationship between board size and performance of Indian companies”, *Journal of Management and Governance* (2022). https://doi.org/10.1007/s10997-022-09651-8.

Sharma, R., Mehta, K. and Sharma, O. (2021). “*Exploring Deep Learning to Determine the Optimal Environment for Stock Prediction Analysis*”, 2021 International Conference on Computational Performance Evaluation, ComPE 2021, 148–152

Sharma, R., Mehta, K., & Vyas, V. (2020). “Responsible Investing: A Study on Non–Economic Goals and Investors’ Characteristics”, *Applied Finance Letters, 9(*SI), 63–78. https://doi.org/10.24135/afl.v9i2.245

Shehata, S. M., Alaa M. Abdeljawad, L. A. Mazouz, Lamia Yousif Khalaf Aldossary, Maryam Y. Alsaeed, & Mohamed Noureldin Sayed. (2021). “The Moderating Role of Perceived Risks in the Relationship between Financial Knowledge and the Intention to Invest in the Saudi Arabian Stock Market”, *International Journal of Financial Studies, 9*, p. 9. https://doi.org/10.3390/ijfs9010009

Singhapakdi, A., Vitell, S., & Franklin, G.R. (1999). "Antecedents, Consequences, and Mediating Effects of Perceived Moral Intensity and Personal Moral Philosophies," *Journal of the Academy of Marketing Science*, *27*,(1), 19–36.

Singhapakdi, A., Vitell, S., and Kraft, K. (1996). "Moral Intensity and Ethical Decision-Making of Marketing Professionals," *Journal of Business Research*, 36(3), 245–255.

Stanga, K.G. & Kelton. A. S. (2015). "Ethicality And Moral Intensity Of Earnings Management" *In Research on Professional Responsibility and Ethics in Accounting*. 19–40.http://dx.doi.org/10.1016/S1574-0765(08)13002–3

Stanga, K. G. & Kelton, A. S. (2015). "Ethicality and Moral Intensity of Earnings Management." In Research on Professional Responsibility and Ethics in Accounting. Published online: 08 Mar 2015; 19–40.

Stone, R. N. & Grønhaug, K. (1993). "Perceived Risk: Further Considerations for the Marketing Discipline", *European Journal of Marketing*, 27(3), 39–50. doi:10.1108/03090569310026637

Talha, M., Salahuddin, A., Masoud, M.S. and Said, A.M.A. (2013). "An analysis of moral intensity, intention and socially responsible investment behaviour among fund managers of Malaysian unit trust companies", *International Journal Managerial and Financial Accounting*, *5*(2), 162–177.

Thai, P., Trang, M., & Tho, N. H. (2017). "Perceived Risk, Investment Performance and Intentions in Emerging Stock Markets", *International Journal of Economics and Financial Issues*, *7*(1), 269–278.

Thaler, Richard H. 2015. "Misbehaving: The Making of Behavioral Economics", New York: W. W. Norton.

Valls Martínez, M., Cruz Rambaud, S., & Parra Oller, I. M. (2020). *"Sustainable and conventional banking in Europe", PloS one*, *15*(2), e0229420. https://doi.org/10.1371/journal.pone.0229420

Von Wallis, M., & Klein, C. (2015). "Ethical requirement and financial interest: a literature review on socially responsible investing", *Journal of Business Research*, 8,61–98. https://doi.org/10.1007/s40685-014-0015-7

Vyas, V., Mehta K., & Sharma, R. (2020). "Investigating socially responsible investing behaviour of Indian investors using structural equation modelling", *Journal of Sustainable Finance & Investment*, DOI: 10.1080/20430795.2020.1790958

Vyas, V., Mehta, K., Sharma, R. (2023). "The nexus between toxic-air pollution, health expenditure, and economic growth: An empirical study using ARDL", *International Review of Economics and Finance*, 84,154–166 https://doi.org/10.1016/j.iref.2022.11.017

Weber, E. & Milliman, R. (1997). "Perceived Risk Attitudes: Relating Risk Perception to Risky Choice". *Management Science*, *43*, 123–144. 10.1287/mnsc.43.2.123.

William, S., Céline, L., & Roland, P. (2011). "Critical Studies on Corporate Responsibility, Governance and Sustainability] Finance and Sustainability: Towards a New Paradigm? A Post-Crisis Agenda", *The Experimental Approach to Trust in Socially Responsible Investment Funds*, *2*, *169–183*. 10.1108/S2043-9059(2011)2().

Williams, G. (2005). "Some Determinants of the Socially Responsible Investment Decision: A Cross Country Study", *Journal of Behavioral Finance*, *8*, 10.2139/ssrn.905189.

Wood, R. & Zaichkowsky, J. L. (2004). "Attitudes and Trading Behavior of Stock Market Investors: A Segmentation Approach", *Journal of Behavioral Finance*, *5*(3), 170–179. doi:10.1207/s15427579jpfm0503_5

Yu-Cheng Lin, Chiung-Yao Huang, & Yu-Shan Wei (2018). "Perfectionist decision-making style and ethical investment willingness: A two-factor causal mediation model", *Management Decision*, https://doi.org/10.1108/MD-05-2017-0492

Kiran Mehta, Renuka Sharma, and Archana Goel

7 Ownership Structures and Performance of SMEs: An Empirical Analysis

Abstract: Ownership structure and its impact on corporate performance have been a prominent and debatable subject within the framework of Corporate Governance. Empirically, the studies have checked the non-linear impact of various ownership structure variables individually on firm performance but not together. The current study uses multiple theoretical perspectives to examine whether the non-linear relationship of multiple ownership variables on the performance of Indian-listed small-cap corporates moves in the same direction or they move in the opposite direction. Promotor(s), Institutional Investor(s), and Non-Institutional Investor(s) are some of the ownership structure variables. Market-based measure, i.e., Tobin's Q, is utilized to capture firm performance. Panel regression indicates that an initial increase in the promoter holdings of small-cap corporates makes them more entrenched in extracting private benefits, which increases the agency cost and reduction in the performance of corporates. However, when the promoter holdings surpass a limit, they have much more incentive and control to oversee the company's performance. On the contrary to it, when the institutional holdings are below a level, any marginal increase in it would significantly increase their monitoring role due to the efficient monitoring hypothesis. After this, numerous institutional investors could trigger "conflicting" interests, thereby hurting the companies' performance. Also, the non-institutional holdings adversely impacted Indian corporate performance. The findings result in specific implications to be addressed by the corporates, government and policymakers.

Keywords: Ownership structure, Firm performance, Promoter ownership, Institutional ownership, Non-institutional ownership, Non-linear, Corporate governance

Researchers have previously shown a strong interest in the influence of corporate governance in increasing business performance (Mishra et al., 2021; Mendoza-Velazquez et al., 2022, Sharma et al. 2022; Goel & Sharma, 2017). Corporate governance (CG) is described as certain rules which define a company's management's responsibility and ensures shareholders' best interests (Madaan et al., 2021; Nashier & Gupta, 2020). Among the various internal and external CG mechanisms to solve CG issues, ownership structure has been considered a crucial factor in shielding the interests of the shareholders from the exploitation of the managers (Neralla, 2022; Sharma et al., 2022; Nashier & Gupta, 2020; Vyas et al., 2023). The literature on ownership structure has highlighted the

Kiran Mehta, Renuka Sharma, Archana Goel, Chitkara Business School, Chitkara University, Punjab, India

https://doi.org/10.1515/9783111170022-007

issue of whether the owner should be concentrated or diffused (Dwivedi & Jain, 2005). While concentrated ownership can lead to better monitoring of the managers, it can also lead to the expropriation of minority shareholders by the majority ones (Nashier & Gupta, 2020; Selarka, 2005; Shleifer Vishny, 1997; Hart, 1995; Sharma & Sharma, 2022). In case the ownership is scattered among the small shareholders, it would lead to the appointment of managers who could serve their interests instead of shareholders. Thus, the question of whether or not ownership and management should be kept entirely distinct from one another is consistently ranked among the most controversial and essential topics.

Corporate governance has traditionally been associated with large, publicly traded companies, but its importance for small and medium-sized enterprises (SMEs) is increasingly being recognized. SMEs face unique challenges when it comes to corporate governance, including limited resources, a lack of specialized knowledge and expertise, and a higher level of dependence on key individuals. Several studies have shown that good corporate governance practices can help SMEs to improve their performance and increase their access to financing. For example, a study by Uddin et al. (2021) found that SMEs in Bangladesh that had better corporate governance practices had higher levels of profitability and were more likely to receive loans from banks. Another study by Hernández-Cánovas et al. (2016) explored the impact of corporate governance on the financial performance of SMEs in Spain. The study found that SMEs that had implemented good corporate governance practices had higher levels of profitability and were more likely to survive in the long term. However, implementing effective corporate governance practices can be challenging for SMEs. A study by Christen et al. (2013) found that SMEs in Swiss faced several obstacles when it came to implementing good corporate governance practices, including a lack of understanding of the importance of corporate governance, limited resources, and a lack of legal and regulatory frameworks to support corporate governance. Despite these challenges, there are several strategies that SMEs can use to improve their corporate governance practices. For example, SMEs can establish a board of directors or advisory board to provide oversight and guidance, implement internal controls and risk management systems, and establish transparent reporting and disclosure practices. Overall, the literature suggests that good corporate governance practices are important for SMEs and can help them to improve their performance, attract financing, and establish a strong foundation for long-term growth and success. However, implementing effective corporate governance practices can be challenging and requires a commitment to continuous improvement and learning.

Notwithstanding the plethora of studies devoted to the relationship between ownership structure and corporate performance, empirical evidence is mixed. For instance, while some revealed that institutional shareholders positively impact the performance of investee companies (e.g., Mishra & Kapil, 2017; Yeh, 2019; Rashid, 2020), others observed their adverse impact (e.g., Pathak & Pradhan (2012). Ullah, 2017; Tsouknidis, 2019). Similar to this, some studies on the impact of insider ownership on corporate performance came up with favourable findings (e.g., Nguyen et al., 2015; Darko et al., 2016); while others found adverse (e.g., Yasser & Mamun, 2015) or non-linear results (e.g., Selarka, 2005; Balsmeier & Czarnitzki (2017)). However, only a few studies have checked the non-linear impact of either insider or institutional ownership, which may complicate the role of corporate governance (Agrawal & Knoeber, 1996). Therefore, studying the non-linear impact of these ownership variables together might help reconcile contradictory results on the links between various kinds of ownership and the performance of corporates and provide a better comprehension of corporate governance. This study integrates multiple theoretical perspectives to analyze non-linear links of various ownership structure variables together with Indian small-cap corporates' performance. Prior literature has mainly focussed on large-cap companies. More specifically, this study examines whether the non-linear relationship of multiple ownership variables moves in the same direction, i.e., U-shaped or inverted U-shaped, or they move in the opposite direction.

Earlier research on ownership structure and firm performance has mainly focused its attention on developed economies like Europe, the US, New Zealand, Taiwan, and Japan (Chen et al., 2008; Tsionas et al., 2012; Hsu & Wang, 2014; Ullah, 2017; Tsouknidis, 2019). Institutional holdings and corporate performance linkages have been explained using the efficient monitoring, strategic alignment and conflict of interest hypotheses (Pound (1988), whereas in promoter ownership and performance linkage, agency theory along with incentive alignment and managerial entrenchment hypotheses have been commonly employed (Shleifer & Vishny, 1989; Shleifer & Vishny, 1997). Recently the research has focused on developing and emerging economies like Muscat, Jordan, Morocco, China, Pakistan, and India (Ali et al., 2018; Pandey & Sahu, 2019; Banik & Chatterjee (2021) Din et al., 2021; Alodat et al., 2021; Queiri et al., 2021). Thus, it highlights the significance of studying ownership structure and the performance of corporates around the world.

There are many reasons why India was chosen as the setting for this investigation. First, in Indian companies' promoters, who are either members of the family or organizations, hold the majority of the shares (Mishra & Kapil, 2017). A circular issued by the Securities and Exchange Board of India (SEBI) in June 2013 limited the minimal promoter holdings to 25% and the maximal promoter holdings to 75%. Second, according to OECD (2020), Institutional investors in India have invested around USD 400 billion in the equity market, which is 30 per cent of India's overall market capitalization. Such funds have increasingly become a significant driver of India's capital market and generated a 34 per cent market capitalization for the largest 500 listed companies in 2018. Third, in his budget proposal for 2019–20, the honourable finance minister suggested raising the requirement of minimal shareholding of the public in registered firms from 25% to 35%, which does not appear to be well received by the business.

The current study examines the non-linear link between ownership structure and performance of 213 Indian small-cap companies registered on BSE from 2001 to 2019. Tobin's Q represents corporate performance. Institutional holdings, non-institutional holdings and promoter holdings make up the ownership structure. According to the outcome from the fixed effect panel regression models, institutional ownership-performance linkage is inverted U-shaped, and promoter holdings-performance linkage is U-shaped. It demonstrates that institutional and promoter ownership is moving oppositely.

The research provides several contributions to the existing literature: First, it brings promoter ownership, institutional holdings, and non-institutional holdings together to investigate their non-linear link with the performance of Indian registered corporates. Second, the time period of the study includes substantial years before and after major revisions in the companies act 2013. Thus, it would help to see the overall impact of these changes on the ownership structure and corporate performance link. Third, the study has focussed on small-cap companies instead of large-cap companies, which are mostly focused on by the prior studies. Moreover, there is a lack of high-quality corporate governance in these companies as the management's entire focus is on profitability targets instead of governance structures. This provides motivation to study the corporate governance of these companies.

The rest of the chapter is structured as follows: The literature review that led to the hypotheses is covered in Section 2. The methodologies employed for the investigation are thoroughly explained in Section 3. The panel data regression model and findings are outlined in Section 4. The findings and their consequences are discussed in Section 5. The conclusion and ideas for additional research are outlined in Section 6.

Review of the Literature and Formulation of Hypotheses

Institutional Ownership and Firm Performance

Several hypotheses provided by Pound (1988) showed various techniques institutional investors could employ. The first efficient monitoring hypothesis argues that effective monitoring by institutional investors prevents the managers from serving their interests and aligning themselves with the interest of shareholders. Hence a high degree of institutional ownership boosts the company's performance (McConnell & Servaes, 1990; Pound, 1988). These investors also help their companies in getting the funds in case of requirement. Additionally, they aid in lowering insiders' dominance, which improves the efficiency of their businesses (Lin & Fu, 2017). Empirically studies have identified positive contributions from institutional shareholders to the companies in which they invest. For example, Deb and Chaturvedula (2003) confirmed that the institutional holdings-performance link of 443 Indian companies for the year ended in 2003 is affirmative. Tsai and Gu (2007) showed a favourable link between institutional ownership and the Q-measured performance of casinos. Because of the efficient monitoring hypothesis, Chen et al. (2008) discovered a favourable impact of institutional holdings on the enterprise's performance in New Zealand, evaluated by Q and ROE. Thanatawee (2014) found that domestic institutional holdings had a favourable influence on 323 Thai firms from 2007 to 2011, as assessed by Q, whereas foreign institutional holdings adversely impacted the performance of companies. According to Hsu and Wang (2014), stable institutional holdings had a favourable impact on the adj. Q and adj. ROA performance of 647 Taiwanese companies from 2005 to 2009. According to Arouri et al. (2014), institutional holdings favourably impacted the 2010 performance of 58 GCC-registered banks as measured by MBVR and Q. According to the research by Nashier and Gupta (2016), institutional holdings held by foreign institutional investors had an affirmative impact on 1392 Indian enterprises' performance between 2007 and 2014, as assessed by Q. Domestic institutional ownership, in contrast, had little impact on corporate performance. The performance of 2465 registered Chinese enterprises, as assessed by Q and ROA, showed institutional ownership -performance correlation to be affirmative, which Lin and Fu (2017) attribute mostly to pressure-resistant, large and international shareholders. Tobin's Q of 391 Indian companies is positively impacted by institutional and foreign institutional ownership, according to Mishra and Kapil (2017). Yeh (2019) observed that institutional holdings affirmatively impacted the ROA and Q of 15 Taiwanese tourism enterprises from 2011 to 2015. Rashid (2020) found that institutional ownership affirmatively impacted the performance of 527 Bangladeshi businesses from 2015 to 2017; this effect was somewhat mediated by board size as well as independent directors of the board. Focussing on 81 non–financial firms in Jordan for 2014–18, Alodat et al. (2021) also observed that institutional ownership affirmatively impacts ROE. When the performance was measured using Q and ROA, Queiri et al. (2021) obtained comparable results for 14 Oman firms over seven years. By adopting ROE, Tobin's Q, and EVA as performance metrics, Banik and Chatterjee (2021) discovered a favourable influence of domestic institutional holdings on the performance of 364 Indian corporates between 2009 and 2017. Din et al. (2021), focusing on 146 Pakistani companies, posited a favourable institutional ownership-performance link for the years 2003–12. For 126 registered shipping businesses from 33 different nations, Drobetz et al. (2021) discovered affirmative institutional holdings and performance links. For businesses with a limited investment horizon and high stock liquidity, this effect was more pronounced.

Conversely, the second conflict of interests hypothesis assumes that a notable institutional holding may engender conflict among them, thereby diminishing the effectiveness of their monitoring. Hoskisson et al. (2002) reinforced this notion by arguing that various categories of owners have distinct and contradictory preferences for taking decisions. Consequently, disputes arise among them, which could impair corporate performance. Similarly, the third strategic alignment hypothesis also suggests that aligning the interest between institutional investors and managers expropriates the firm's resources, thereby exploiting the interest of shareholders (Pound, 1988). It lessens the supervision by institutional investors, which inversely impacts the performance of corporates. While several studies have concluded that institutional shareholders have a favourable effect on the investee companies, some have also identified negative outcomes. For instance, Liang et al. (2011) investigated the linkage between institutional holdings and business performance in Taiwan, which was categorized according to different life cycle stages and quantified by ROA. The 2SLS regression showed an unfavourable link between institutional holdings and corporate performance, particularly in the mature stage of the enterprises. Pathak et al. (2012) revealed that institutional holdings adversely impact the ROA-measured performance of all manufacturing Indian corporations. According to Ullah (2017), institutional holdings had a detrimental 19-year influence on the performance of 1392 Japanese enterprises from 1991 to 2009. Ali et al. (2018) disclosed that institutional ownership adversely affects the performance of 2637 Chinese corporations. According to Tsouknidis (2019), institutional holdings adversely affected the ROA-gauged performance of US shipping companies from 2002 to 16. For the Moroccan enterprises, Satt et al. (2021) found institutional ownership- firm performance linkage to be inverse, with ROA as a performance metric. In the sample of S&P 1500 enterprises between 1996 and 2006, Huang and Lu (2022) discovered an opposing influence of institutional blockholders on the variability in the performance of corporates.

The countervailing arguments presented above highlight the non-linear influence of institutional holdings on corporate performance, which is corroborated by prior empirical studies. For instance, a U-shaped connection between institutional ownership, state ownership, and Chinese SOEs performance from 1991 to 2001 was established by Wei et al. (2005). Farooque et al. (2007) discovered a U-shaped interface between institutional holdings and the performance of Bangladeshi enterprises. For the period 2000–2006, Bertin et al. (2012) found that the interface between the two, as assessed by the market-to-book ratio, was inverted U-shaped in the countries with common law and U-shaped in the countries with civil law.

This study applies a similar logic to Indian small-cap companies and predicts that there could be a non-linear link between institutional holdings and corporate performance. Therefore, the hypothesis is developed as follows:

H_1: Institutional ownership has a non-linear impact on the performance of companies.

Promoter Ownership and Firm Performance

Similar to other countries, promoters own a disproportionate amount of ownership in India (Kumar & Singh, 2013). Agency theory suggests that providing significant shares to the promoters would effectively alleviate agency problems by harmonizing their interest with the managers. It has been elucidated by the incentive alignment hypothesis provided by Shleifer and Vishny (1997). An opposing argument, however, emphasizes the effects of management entrenchment brought about by considerable insider ownership (e.g., Shleifer & Vishny, 1989). With an excessive increase in insider ownership, their chances of extracting private benefits also increase (Holderness, 2003; Bozec & Dia, 2015). In such cases, insider ownership is presumed to correlate negatively with firm performance. The trade-off between incentive alignment and entrenchment that these substantial block holders in a company face determine the overall influence of insider holdings on the performance (Selarka, 2005).

These conflicting arguments are mirrored in the available prior empirical literature. Many studies have found a positive linkage between promoter holdings as well as corporate performance. For instance, Tsionas et al. (2012) observed that concentrated ownership positively impacts the performance of 107 registered shipping corporations in Europe, Asia and America, calculated via ROA and ROE. Abdullah et al. (2012) obtained similar results, and for 183 registered Pakistani companies, gauged via Q and ROA. Alipour (2013) also discovered a favourable interface between ownership concentration and ROE and inverse linkage with ROA and Q. In Singapore and Vietnam, Nguyen et al. (2015) found that concentrated ownership positively impacted the performance via Q over 2008–11. Ownership concentration does not significantly increase the value of the enterprise in Singapore when the national government is of high calibre. It increases the value of the company in Vietnam, where the national government is not of high calibre. The performance of 20 enterprises in Ghana over five years, from 2008 to 2012, was positively impacted by ownership concentration, according to Darko et al. (2016). Mangena et al. (2012) posited that concentrated ownership had a favourable association with the ROA of Zimbabwean corporates from 2000 to 2005. Pandey and Sahu (2019) displayed that promoter ownership had affirmatively influenced the performance of 91 Indian companies from 2009–16, gauged via Tobin's Q. When using ROA, EVA, ROE, and Tobin's Q to quantify performance for 364 Indian enterprises between 2009 and 2017, Banik and Chatterjee (2021) found comparable results. Similar results were obtained by Mehrotra et al. (2021) for 68 Indian SMEs, measured via ROA for the period 2013–18. Din et al. (2021) also posited positive promoter ownership-firm performance linkage for 146 Pakistani firms for the period 2003–12. Ghalke et al. (2022) found that promoter holdings positively affected 446 family enterprises in SME markets.

Despite the positive linkage between promoter ownership and the performance of corporates, many studies have also exhibited opposing results. According to Lepore et al. (2017), concentrated ownership adversely impacted the company's performance in Italy and France, countries with slow-moving courts where disposal times were longer. The performance of businesses is, however, least affected by the rise in ownership concentration in nations with high levels of judicial efficiency, like Germany and Spain. Additionally, ownership concentration and performance are positively correlated for enterprises in Italy with a high disposition time. On the other hand, ownership concentration and performance are only marginally related in Germany, where disposal time is short. Yasser and Mamun (2015) found that ownership concentration showed a negative correlation with EVA for 95 Pakistani enterprises over five years, from 2007 to 2011, but a negligible correlation with ROA, ROE, and Q. In their 2015 study, Hamadi and Heinen examined the relationship between 194 Belgian companies' 1991–2006 performance and ownership concentration. The results showed that until ownership was 75–80% concentrated, it had a beneficial effect on performance.

The result is a conclave in a small way. Family businesses have a high incidence of this non-linear effect, which increases up to 30% before stabilizing between 30% and 40% and then begins to decline. Balsmeier and Czarnitzki (2017) found an inverted U-shaped link between concentrated ownership and private company performance in 28 Central and Eastern European Transition Economies with weak institutional settings. Lozano et al. (2016) showed a U-shaped connection between concentrated ownership and the valuation of 1064 enterprises from 16 different European nations between 2000 and 2009. Despite special regulatory requirements by SEBI, Ganguli and Deb (2016, 2021) found that promoter ownership had a non-linear influence on the performance of 265 Indian corporates between 2009 and 2013.

Mishra and Kapil (2017) found that low promoter holdings adversely impacted the performance of 391 Indian enterprises, but rising holdings improved performance. Institutional ownership and foreign institutional ownership favourably impacted Tobin Q. Kumar and Singh (2013) observed that promoter ownership is adversely linked to the corporate performance below a threshold of 40% but favourably linked as soon as that level was crossed. For the period 2001–2006, Park and Jang (2010) found an inverted U-shaped association between insider ownership and restaurant performance. Pant and Pattanayak (2007) showed that promoter ownership and corporate performance are non-monotonic, i.e., it raises performance, then declines, and then rises. Deb and Chaturvedula (2003) observed a non-linear link between insider holdings and corporate performance. They noticed that an association between the two is positive, up to 30%, and over 60%, due to the alignment effect. Due to the entrenchment effect, it is inverted between 30 and 60 per cent. Selarka (2005) discovered a curved U-shaped relationship between insider shareholding and company value. Due to insider expropriation, it initially declined by up to 45–63% before beginning to rise. According to Pathak and Pradhan (2012), promoter shareholdings did not affect the ROA-measured performance of all Indian manufacturing enterprises. According to Hoang et al. (2017), block ownership did not affect the Q-measured performance of 76 Vietnamese enterprises from 2007 to 2015.

Given the arguments above, this study expects that there would be a non-linear association between promoter ownership and Indian small-cap corporate performance. Hence, the hypothesis is developed as follows:

H_2: Promoter ownership has a non-linear impact on the performance of companies.

Individual Ownership and Firm Performance

Non-institutional investors are the general public or organizations who invest in securities for themselves via an agent or a bank. They are dispersed shareholders making modest purchases, and after covid 19, individual ownership has increased a lot (Sharma et al., 2020; Arora et al., 2022). As a result of this scattered ownership, block holders may expropriate assets. Dispersed ownership may initially be advantageous to the business since it frees it from the large outside investor's oversight (Pagano & Roell, 1998). However, it might harm corporate performance. Blockholder ownership, according to Shleifer and Vishny (1986), provides them with the incentive to effectively track managers' performance. It was recently revealed that these block holders might begin to assume a dominant position and attempt to abuse their authority by taking advantage of the interests of minority shareholders (La Porta et al., 1999). The disparity in interests between the majority and minority owners could result in an agency issue (Shleifer & Vishny, 1997). According to empirical data from Alipour (2013), individual ownership was negatively correlated with the ROA and Q-measured performance of 60 Iranian enterprises from 2005 to 2009. Individual shareholdings do not affect the performance of all manufacturing enterprises as measured by ROA, according to research by Pathak and Pradhan (2012) conducted in India.

H_3: Individual ownership has a negative impact on the performance of companies.

Research Methods

Sample and Data Sources

The sample initially constitutes BSE 250 small-cap index over the period from 2001 through 2019. Though these companies are small in size, they have huge growth potential. The following companies are not part of the final sample: First, banks (7) and financial companies (21) have varied regulations related to corporate governance (Kumar & Singh, 2013; Mishra & Kapil, 2017; Ganguli & Deb, 2021). In addition, companies (9) were either not registered during the entire sample period (Kumar, 2003) or had missing figures because their annual reports were unavailable (Arora & Sharma, 2016; Kumar & Singh, 2013). After omitting these companies, the sample consists of 213 companies with 3834 observations. The data is mainly provided by the *Prowess database* and annual reports of companies. E views ten is used to calculate the results.

Variables

In line with the previous studies (Ganguli & Deb, 2021; Nashier & Gupta, 2016; Mishra & Kapil, 2017), this study utilizes a log of Tobin's Q as a *dependent* variable to correct for the skewed distribution of corporate performance. Tobin's Q is determined by dividing the market value of equity plus total liabilities by the book value of assets. It reflects the present value of the estimated future profits that will result from shareholders' investment in the corporate assets (Short & Keasey, 1999). The value of Q above one indicates that shareholders anticipate these companies to generate more revenue using their current resources in the future. Contrarily, corporates with Q values below one show that they aren't using their resources efficiently, which implies they will generate less revenue in the future from those resources.

The *independent* variable of the study is shares held by promoters, non-promoter institutional and non-institutions holdings. Promoter holdings depict the %age of shares held by promoters. Institutional holdings represent how much of the company shares are owned by institutions. Non-promoter non-institutional ownership is the percentage of shares held by people who are neither the company's founders nor the members of an institution.

The study also utilizes three *control variables*. The first control variable- firm size, is calculated by taking the log of total assets (Kumar & Singh, 2013; Nashier & Gupta, 2016). Large businesses make huge profits which makes it harder for new enterprises to start up (Short & Keasey, 1999); they employ highly experienced workers, which eventually boosts business performance. Additionally, they can get the funds at a cheap rate and may diversify too. The second variable- firm age, is obtained by taking the log of the current year minus the year it was incorporated (Serlaka, 2005). Older businesses with greater experience and knowledge benefit from economies of scale. Compared to newly founded businesses, they make more money. While older organizations have reached the last stage of their product life cycle, newer enterprises still need to create their brand in the market. Leverage (LEV) is calculated as the total outside liabilities divided by total assets (Mishra & Kapil, 2017; Nashier & Gupta, 2016; Kumar & Singh, 2013). If LEV is higher, a more significant burden of principal and interest would be imposed on the company. Consequently, the company would be unable to produce sufficient cash flow to repay its debt commitments, and thus LEV is hoped to dwindle its financial performance.

Table 7.1: Descriptive Statistics.

	Mean	Median	Minimum	Maximum	Std. Dev
Q	2.41	1.48	0.09	47.42	2.79
TPH	51.99	52.06	0	99.59	17.14
NPI	20.61	18.92	0	76.45	13.94
NPNI	26.89	24.68	0	90.7	14.34
FS	4.45	4.3	1.4	13.09	1.17
FA	1.58	1.58	0.3	2.66	0.27
LEV	3.92	2.5	0	132	5.26
Obs.	3834	3834	3834	3834	3834

Source: *Author's self-compilation.*

Table 7.1 contains descriptive data for each study variable. The Q values ranged from 0.09 to 47.42, with an average value of 2.41. The estimates appear reasonable as the level of Q for most firms is just above one. The TPH ranged from 0% to 99.59%, with an average of 51.99% and a large standard deviation of 17.14, indicating that promoter ownership concentration is considerable and fluctuates across small-cap firms. NPI ranges from 0% to 76.45%, averaging 20.61 with a standard deviation of 13.94. TPH appears to be much higher. The mean of NPNI is 26.89%, with the minimal and maximal values as 0% and 90.7%, respectively. Non-promoter non-institutions control those companies where promoters don't. FS ranges from 1.4 to 13.09, with a mean of 4.45. The FA's minimum and maximum values are 0.30 and 2.66, with an average of 1.58. The average leverage is 3.92, with a minimal and maximal values of 0 and 132.

Table 7.2: Pearson Correlation Matrix.

	TPH	NPI	NPNI	FS	FA	LEV	Q
TPH	1						
NPI	−.551**	1					
NPNI	−.547**	−.247**	1				
FS	−.130**	.317**	−.159**	1			
FA	−.093**	.207**	−.104**	.148**	1		
LEV	.019	.016	−.024	−.007	−.099**	1	
Q	.151**	.038**	−.210**	−.033**	.122**	.014	1

** Correlation is significant at the 0.01 level (2-tailed). * at the 0.05 level (2 tailed)
Source: *Author's self-compilation.*

In Table 7.2, the correlation coefficients vary from −0.551 (between institutional holdings and promoters) to 0.317 (between the size of the firm and institutional holdings). If the correlation is below 0.60, there is no multicollinearity concern (Manna et al. 2016).

Results and Analysis

This study employs panel data regression because the data contains observations about various cross-sectional across time. Panel regression can model both individual and common behaviours of the group of data. It provides more useful, diverse data with reduced collinearity (Baltagi, 2008). This technique comprises pooled OLS, fixed effects and a random effects model.

Linear Relationship

The study aims at determining the following linear linkages between ownership structure and the performance of Indian small-cap corporates.

$$Q_{it} = \alpha_0 + \beta_1\ TPH + \beta_2\ NPI + \beta_3\ NPNI + \beta_4 FS + \beta_5 FA + \beta_6 LEV + \omega_{it} \tag{1}$$

where,
Q_{it}= Tobin's Q; α_0 = Constant term; TPH= Percentage of promoter ownership; NPI= non-promoter institutional ownership; NPNI= non-promoter non-institutional ownership; FS=Log of total assets; FA= log of firm age; LEV= Leverage; ω_{it} = Composite error term.

The pooled OLS approach presupposes a continuous link between the sample variables over both time and cross-section. If there is time or cross-sectional heterogeneity, the results will be biased. In such cases, the fixed-effect model accounts for unobserved variability in a time-invariant, cross-sectional intercept. It considers that time-invariant qualities are distinctive to each individual and shouldn't be connected. The slope coefficient is constant across cross-sections and across time. In the fixed-effect model, the intercepts of all the organizations are assumed to be distinct due to the unique characteristics of each company, such as the managerial style. So, we need to control it, which is possible by introducing each company's differential intercept dummy variable.

Table 7.3: Fixed Effect Regression Results with Log Q.

	Log Q			
	Model 1		Model 2	
Variables	**Coefficient**	**T statistic**	**Coefficient**	**T statistic**
(Constant)	−1.26	−14.16*	−1.19	−13.32*
TPH	0.003	5.21*	−0.003	−2.08**
TPH²			7.02e-05	4.14*
NPI	0.003	4.23*	0.009757	7.29*
NPI²			−0.000136	−5.66*
NPNI	−0.003	−5.66*	−0.003	−5.29*
TPH*NPI				
TA	−0.06	−4.19*	−0.07	−4.78*
FA	1.04	16.16*	1.06	16.51*
LEV	−0.005	−4.82*	−0.005	−4.92*
R^2	0.59		0.59	
Adjusted R^2	0.56		0.57	
F statistic	23.81*		24.02*	
D-W statistic	0.84		0.86	
Number of observations	3834		3834	

Note: Significance at 1% level (*), at 5% level (**): D–W: DurbinWatson.
Source: Author's Compilation.

In the random-effects method, the constants are random parameters for each section. The Hausman (1978) test shows that the fixed-effect approach is the appropriate estimation method (χ^2 = 123.94; d_f = 6; p= 0.00). The outcome of the fixed effect regression model 1 in Table 7.3 summarizes the effects of TPH, NPI, and NPNI on the performance of Indian small-cap enterprises. The coefficients of TPH (β= 0.003) and NPI (β= 0.003) on Q appear to be favourable at the 1% significance level, whereas the coefficients of NPNI (β= −0.003) on Q appear to be unfavourable at the 1% significance level. The results are consistent with Darko et al. (2016), Yeh (2019), and Rashid (2020). It implies that ownership structure directly affects the performance of small-cap corporates.

Non-Linear Relationship

Following Balsmeier and Czarnitzki (2017) and Mishra and Kapil (2017), this chapter incorporated TPH and NPI along with its square in the model to check the possible U-shaped or an inverted U-shaped ass. The following regression tests were performed:

$$Q_{it} = \alpha_0 + \beta_1 TPH + \beta_2 TPH^2 + \beta_3 NPI + \beta_4 NPI^2 + \beta_5 NPNI + \beta_6 FS + \beta_7 FA + \beta_8 LEV + \omega_{it} \quad (2)$$

Using the context of Model 2 of Table 7.3, the curvilinear linkages between ownership structure and the performance of Indian small-cap corporates exist if β_1 and β_2 vary significantly from zero. Specifically, in an inverted U-shaped interface between the two variables, $\beta_1 > 0$ and $\beta_2 < 0$. Similarly, in a U-shaped linkage between the two variables, $\beta_1 < 0$ and $\beta_2 > 0$. In Model 2, a point of inflexion for TPH is calculated using the formula $\beta_{1/}2\beta_2$. Similarly, the point of inflexion for NPI is calculated as $\beta_{3/}2\beta_4$. The Hausman (1978) test shows that the fixed-effect approach is the appropriate estimation method (χ2 =135.74; df=8; p= 0.00). Model 2 in Table 7.3 summarizes the outcome of panel regression of the effect of TPH, TPH^2, NPI, NPI^2 and NPNI on the performance of Indian small-cap corporates. The coefficients of both TPH (β= −0.003) and TPH^2 (β= 7.02e) on Q vary considerably from zero and $\beta_1 < 0$ and $\beta_2 > 0$. In other words, the interface between total promoter holdings, i.e., TPH and the performance of Indian small-cap companies in terms of Q is U-shaped. The infection point is 21.37%. The results are consistent with Selarka (2005); Lozano et al. (2016); Mishra and Kapil (2017), and inconsistent with Balsmeier and Czarnitzki (2017); Park and Jang (2010). Similarly, the coefficients of both NPI (β= 0.010) and NPI^2 (β= −0.001) on Q vary considerably from zero and $\beta_1 > 0$ and $\beta_2 < 0$. In other words, the interface between NPI and Q is also curvilinear and, more specifically, inverted U-shaped. The infection point is 35.87%. The results are consistent with Bertin et al. (2012), who also observed an inverted U-shaped association. In contrast to it, the coefficients of NPNI on Q (β= −0.003) are significantly negative at the 1% level. The results are similar to the findings of Alipour (2013) and inconsistent with the outcome of Pathak et al. (2012).

Robustness Check

To ensure that the results are accurate, a robustness analysis has been done. First, the fixed–effect regression has been repeated by using an alternative performance variable, i.e., Return on Assets (ROA). The result reported in Table 7.4 support the findings exhibited in Table 7.3. Second, time series dummies have been incorporated into the model. Since the period is of 18 years, i.e., 2001–2019, so 17-time dummies have been introduced in the model. The result reported in Table 7.5, supports the finding exhibited in Table 7.3.

Third, endogeneity is a problem that frequently arises in the corporate governance literature, making it challenging to interpret the findings. According to Demsetz (1983) and Cho (1998), ownership structure and corporate performance are determined endogenously. Since Im and Chung (2017) analyzed all the factors linked to ownership structure and control variables at 1-year lagged values, the current study also performed a regression analysis on firm performance in a similar way. The outcomes presented in Table 7.6 align with those in Table 7.3.

Table 7.4: Fixed Effect Regression Results with ROA.

Variables	ROA				
	Model 1			Model 2	
	Coefficient	Coefficient	T statistic	Coefficient	T statistic
(Constant)	−1.26	3.75	1.57	4.37	1.81***
TPH	0.003	0.04	2.52**	−0.02	−0.54
TPH^2				0.001	1.48
NPI	0.003	0.07	3.90*	0.18	5.02*
NPI^2				−0.002	−3.57*
NPNI	−0.003	−0.05	−3.34*	−0.05	−3.27*
TPH*NPI					
TA	−0.06	−1.45	−3.87*	−1.58	−4.19*
FA	1.04	5.32	3.08*	5.49	3.18*
LEV	−0.005	0.19	7.24*	0.18	7.15*
R^2	0.45			0.45	
Adjusted R^2	0.42			0.42	
F statistic	13.77*			13.74*	
D-W statistic	1.01			1.02	
Number of observations	3834			3834	

Note: Significance at 1% level (*), at 5% level (**), at 10% level (***): D–W: DurbinWatson.
Source*:* Author's Compilation.

Table 7.5: Fixed Effect Regression Results with Log Tobin's q and Year Dummies.

Variables	Model 1		Model 2	
	Coefficient	T statistic	Coefficient	T statistic
(Constant)	0.26	2.18**	0.31	2.63*
TPH	0.003	6.57*	−0.001	−1.01
TPH^2			5.22e-05	3.52*
NPI	0.003	5.04*	0.001	8.34*
NPI^2			−0.001	−6.55*
NPNI	−0.002	−3.78*	−0.002	−3.55*
TPH*NPI				
TA	−0.17	−11.43*	−0.18	−12.07
FA	0.19	2.74*	0.20	2.91*
LEV	−0.004	−4.38*	−0.004	−4.55*
Year Dummies	Yes		Yes	
R^2	0.689		0.69	
Adjusted R^2	0.668		0.67	
F statistic	33.93*		34.25*	
D-W statistic	0.80		0.82	
Number of observations	3834		3834	

Note: Significance at 1% level (*), at 5% level (**): D–W: DurbinWatson.
Source: Author's Compilation.

Table 7.6: Fixed Effect Regression Results of Lagged Independent and Control Variables with Q.

Variables	Model 1		Model 2	
	Coefficient	T statistic	Coefficient	T statistic
(Constant)	−1.24	−13.02*	−1.18	−12.32*
TPH_{t-1}	0.002	3.74*	−0.004	−2.57*
TPH^2			7.18e-05	4.10*
NPI_{t-1}	7.69e-05	0.12	0.005	3.62*
NPI^2			−9.09e-05	−3.61*
$NPNI_{t-1}$	−0.002	−3.69*	−0.002	−3.21*
TPI*NPI				
TA_{t-1}	−0.07	−4.43*	−0.07	−4.85*
FA_{t-1}	1.10	15.34*	1.13	15.70*
LEV_{t-1}	−0.003	−3.28*	−0.003	−3.26*
R^2	0.59		0.59	
Adjusted R^2	0.56		0.565	
F statistic	22.31*		22.35*	
D-W statistic	0.87		0.88	
Number of observations	3834		3834	

Note: Significance at 1% level (*), at 5% level (**): D–W: DurbinWatson.
Source: Author's Compilation.

Discussion and Implications

The findings offer a breakthrough within the growing literature on ownership structure and performance of small-cap companies. The study finds that promoter ownership favourably impacts the performance of Indian small-cap corporates. It implies that because promoters are insiders, they have greater knowledge of the business. The incentive and control to oversee the managers are better with more promoter holdings, which improves business performance. Thus, it backs up agency theory, which states that greater ownership results in incentive alignment and eventually lowers agency costs. The findings also observed the presence of a U-shaped interface between promoter holdings and corporate performance in India. It implies that there is an optimal promoter holding in the Indian listed companies, with a trade-off between benefits (i.e., incentive alignment) and drawbacks (i.e., entrenchment). The optimal promoter holdings beyond which the performance of Indian companies maximizes is 21.37%. The findings indicate that future growth prospects (Q) could be maximum if the promoter holdings reach 21.37%. More precisely, an initial increase in the promoter holdings makes them more entrenched in extracting private benefits, which increases the agency cost and reduction in corporate performance. However, they gain additional incentive and power to oversee the company's performance after their holdings exceed 21.37%. They gain a great deal of authority and the ability to scrutinize the management's behaviours and actions while also applying pressure on them. It lessens the issue of free riders that comes with distributed holdings (Hart, 1995).

Concerning institutional holdings, the study finds a significantly positive impact on the Indian small-cap companies' performance, supporting the efficient monitoring hypothesis provided by Pound (1988). One rationale is that as institutional ownership increases, their interests overlap with other investors, giving them the ability to directly or indirectly affect management decisions. Additionally, their well-equipped tools and in-depth expertise enable them to monitor the management's behaviour and discourage them from advancing their interests, which improves business performance. The results also noted an inverted U-shaped linkage between institutional ownership and Indian small-cap companies' performance, implying that both the efficient monitoring hypothesis and conflict of interest hypothesis exist simultaneously in Indian companies, i.e., there is an optimal institutional holding of 35.87%. The results indicate that Q can be maximum when the institutional holdings are 35.87 per cent. More precisely, when the institutional holdings are less than 35.87 per cent, any marginal increase in it would significantly increase their monitoring role due to the efficient monitoring hypothesis. When the institutional ownership rises above 35.87 per cent, the numerous institutional investors could trigger "conflicting" interests among them, leading to a detrimental impact on the company's performance (e.g., Hoskisson et al., 2002; Mehta et al. 2022). Concerning the non-promoter non-institutional holdings, the study finds their inverse effect on performance, thereby supporting agency theory.

The study has ramifications for regulators, investors, corporations, and academicians. Given the average and optimal promoter holdings of 52% and 21.37%, respectively, most of the Indian listed companies already enjoy the benefits of the incentive alignment hypothesis and have promoter holdings of more than 21%. Any subsequent growth in the promoter holdings would boost the performance of small-cap corporates. Concerning Institutional holdings, the mean is 22%, and optimal institutional holdings are 35.87%; the Indian listed small cap should increase their institutional holdings up to 35.87% to reap the optimal performance. Since promoter and institutional holdings affect corporate performance nonlinearly, large stock ownership should be developed to improve it. It is notable that as ownership rises to a level, institutions would be dedicated, and promoters could lead to entrenchment. However, once these levels are surpassed, the promoters would be more committed, and institutions could be poisoned. These findings may suggest how to design and practice the promoter's incentive alignment and institutions' efficient monitoring to promote the firm's performance. The shareholders can benefit from these results to decide the optimal promoter and institutional holdings for the Indian-listed small-cap companies. Moreover, the findings also contradict the government's plan to boost public shareholding from 25% to 35%. Therefore, the government and regulatory bodies can derive motivation for reforms relating to the ownership structure of Indian small-cap companies.

Conclusion and Future Research Directions

The present research jointly investigated the linear and non-linear interface between ownership structure variables, i.e., promoter holdings, non-promoter institutional and non-institutional holdings and the performance of listed small-cap corporates in India. The findings reveal a U-shaped association between promoter ownership and small-cap company performance in India by employing Tobin's Q as a performance metric and fixed effect regression technique. It implies that an initial increase in the promoter holdings makes them more entrenched in extracting private benefits, which increases the agency cost and reduction in the performance of corporates. However, when the promoter holdings surpass 21.37%, they have much more incentive and control of overseeing the small company's performance. The findings thus confirmed that both the entrenchment and incentive alignment hypotheses apply to the Indian-listed small-cap companies. Similarly, Institutional holdings and Indian small-cap companies' performance have a U-shaped association. It implies that when the institutional holdings are less than 35.87%, any marginal increase in it would significantly increase their monitoring role due to the efficient monitoring hypothesis. When institutional ownership reaches 35.87%, numerous institutional investors could trigger "conflicting" interests, thereby hurting the small companies' performance. Therefore, the study validates that efficient monitoring and conflict of interest hypothesis both apply to the Indian listed small cap companies. Also, the non-promoter non-institutional holdings harm the performance of Indian small-cap corporates.

The study suggests that Indian companies could increase their promoter holdings beyond 52%. Since the Indian small-cap companies have witnessed a significant increase in institutional holdings, the findings suggest that it should not go beyond 35%. Moreover, the results don't support the government's plan to boost public shareholding from 25% to 35%. Therefore, the government and regulatory bodies can derive motivation for reforms relating to the ownership structure of Indian small-cap companies. The study findings are useful for investors too who are looking for style investment strategies for obtaining extra ordinary returns (Mehta & Sharma, 2017). The study is subjected to certain limitations also. It solely includes well-governed listed companies. Future studies may include mid-cap and private companies. Moreover, future studies can check the interaction effect between various ownership types and firm performance.

References

Abdullah, F., Shah, A. & Khan, S. U. (2012). "Firm performance and the nature of agency problems in insiders-controlled firms: Evidence from Pakistan", *The Pakistan Development Review, 51*(4): 161–182.

Agrawal, A. & Knoeber, C. R. (1996). "Firm performance and mechanisms to control agency problems between managers and shareholders", *Journal of Financial and Quantitative Analysis, 31*(3): 377–397.

Al Farooque, O., Van Zijl, T., Dunstan, K. & Karim, A. W. (2007). "Corporate Governance in Bangladesh: Link between ownership and financial performance", *Corporate Governance: An International Review, 15*(6), 1453–1468.

Ali, A., Qiang, F. & Ashraf, S. (2018). "Regional dynamics of ownership structure and their impact on firm performance and firm valuation", *Review of International Business and Strategy, 28*(1): 129–147.

Alipour, M. (2013). "An investigation of the association between ownership structure and corporate performance", *Management Research Review, 36*(11): 1137–1166.

Alodat, A. Y., Salleh, Z., Hashim, H. A. & Sulong, F. (2021). "Corporate governance and firm performance: empirical evidence from Jordan", *Journal of Financial Reporting and Accounting*, doi https://doi.org/10.1108/JFRA-12-2020-0361.

Arora, A. & Sharma, C. (2016). "Corporate Governance and firm performance in developing countries: evidence from India", *Corporate Governance, 16*(2), 420–436.

Arora, M., Sharma, R., & Mehta, K. (2022). "Personality Effects on Financial Responses Caused by the Perceived Financial Threat during the COVID-19 Pandemic", *Journal of Wealth Management, 25*(3), 72–89.

Arouri, H., Hossain, M. & Muttakin, M. B. (2014). "Effects of board and ownership structure on corporate performance", *Journal of Accounting in Emerging Economies, 4*(1), 117–130.

Balsmeier, B. & Czarnitzki, D. (2017). "Ownership concentration, institutional development and firm performance in Central and Eastern Europe", *Managerial and Decision Economics, 38*(2); 178–192. https://www.jstor.org/stable/26608104

Baltagi, B. (2008). "Econometric analysis of panel data". John Wiley & Sons.

Banik, A. & Chatterjee, C. (2021). "Ownership pattern and governance–performance relation: Evidence from an emerging economy", *Global Business Review, 22*(2): 422–441.

Bozec, R. & Dia, M. (2015). "Governance practices and firm performance: Does shareholders' proximity to management matter?", *International Journal of Disclosure and Governance, 12*(3): 185–209.

Chen, J., Blenman, L. & Chen, D. H. (2008). "Does institutional ownership create values? The New Zealand case", *Quarterly Journal of Finance and Accounting, 47*(4): 109–124.

Cho, M. H. (1998). "Ownership structure, investment, and the corporate value: an empirical analysis", *Journal of Financial Economics, 47*(1):103–121.

Christen, A., Halter, F., Kammerlander, N., Künzi, D., Merki, M., & Zellweger, T. (2013). "Success Factors for Swiss SMEs – Company Succession in Practice", 10.13140/2.1.4635.4889.

Darko, J., Aribi, Z. A. & Uzonwanne, G. C. (2016). "Corporate Governance: The impact of director and board structure, ownership structure and corporate control on the performance of listed companies on the Ghana stock exchange", *Corporate Governance, 16*(2), 259–277.

Deb, S. S. & Chaturvedula, C. V. (2003). "Ownership structure and firm value: an empirical study on corporate governance system of Indian firms", doi: https://papers.ssrn.com/sol3/papers.cfm?abstract_id=594221

Demsetz, H. (1983). "The structure of ownership and the theory of the firm", The Journal of Law and Economics 26(2): 375–390.

Din, S. U., Khan, M. A., Khan, M. J. & Khan, M. Y. (2021). "Ownership structure and corporate financial performance in an emerging market: a dynamic panel data analysis", *International Journal of Emerging Markets*, doi https://doi.org/10.1108/IJOEM-03-2019-0220.

Drobetz, W., Ehlert, S. & Schröder, H. (2021). "Institutional ownership and firm performance in the global shipping industry", *Transportation Research Part E: Logistics and Transportation Review 146*, 102152.

Dwivedi, N. & Jain, A. K. (2005). "Corporate Governance and performance of Indian firms: The effect of board size and ownership", *Employee Responsibilities and Rights Journal, 17*(3): 161–172.

Ganguli, S. K. & Guha Deb, S. (2021). "Board composition, ownership structure and firm performance: New Indian evidence", *International Journal of Disclosure and Governance, 18*(3): 256–268.

Ganguli, S. K., & Guha Deb, S. (2016). "Board composition, ownership structure and firm performance: new Indian evidence in a unique regulatory environment", doi: https://papers.ssrn.com/sol3/papers.cfm?abstract_id=2746773

Ghalke, A., Haldar, A. & Kumar, S. (2022). "Family firm ownership and its impact on performance: evidence from an emerging market", *Review of Managerial Science*, 1–20.

Goel, A. & Sharma, R. (2017). "Disclosures, Board Size & Composition, Ownership Structure and Firm's Performance: Finding Future Research Perspectives" International Journal of Applied Business and Economic Research (SCOPUS), Volume 15:9 (May 2017) Pages: 199–220.

Hamadi, M. & Heinen, A. (2015). "Firm performance when ownership is very concentrated: Evidence from a semiparametric panel", *Journal of Empirical Finance 34*, 172–194.

Hart, O. (1995). "Corporate governance: some theory and implications". *The Economic Journal*, 105(430), 678–689.

Hausman, J. A. (1978) "Specification tests in econometrics", *Econometrica: Journal of the Econometric Society*, 1251–1271.

Hernández-Cánovas, G., Mínguez-Vera, A., & Sánchez–Vidal, J. (2016). "Ownership structure and debt as corporate governance mechanisms: an empirical analysis for Spanish SMEs", *Journal of Business Economics and Management, 17*(6), 960–976.

Hoang, L. T., Nguyen, C. C., & Hu, B. (2017). "Ownership structure and firm performance improvement: does it matter in the Vietnamese stock market?" *Economic Papers: A Journal of Applied Economics and Policy*, 36(4), 416–428.

Holderness, C. G. (2003). "Joint ownership and alienability", *International Review of Law and Economics, 23*(1), 75–100.

Hoskisson, R. E., Hitt, M. A., Johnson, R. A. & Grossman, W. (2002). "Conflicting voices: The effects of institutional ownership heterogeneity and internal Governance on corporate innovation strategies", *Academy of Management Journal*, *45*(4): 697–716.
Hsu, M. F. & Wang, K. (2014). "The level and stability of institutional ownership and firm performance: Evidence from Taiwan", *Emerging Markets Finance and Trade 50*(sup2), 159–173.
Huang, P. & Lu, Y. (2022). "Institutional block holders and the variability of firm performance", *International Journal of Managerial Finance*, *18*(1), 118–137.
Im, J. & Chung, Y. (2017). "The effects of insider ownership and board composition on firm performance in the restaurant industry", *The Journal of Hospitality Financial Management 25*(1) 4–16.
Jara-Bertin, M., López-Iturriaga, F. J. & López-de-Foronda, Ó. (2012). "Does the influence of institutional investors depend on the institutional framework? An international analysis", *Applied Economics*, *44*(3), 265–278.
Kumar, J. (2003). "Ownership structure and firm corporate performance". Indira Gandhi Institute of Development Research. Processed.
Kumar, N. & Singh, J. P. (2013). "Effect of board size and promoter ownership on firm value: some empirical findings from India", *Corporate Governance: The International Journal of Business in Society 13*(1), 88–98.
La Porta, R., Lopez-de-Silanes, F. & Shleifer, A. (1999). "Corporate ownership around the world", *The Journal of Finance*, *54*(2), 471–517.
Lepore, L., Paolone, F., Pisano, S. & Alvino, F. (2017). "A cross-country comparison of the relationship between ownership concentration and firm performance: Does judicial system efficiency matter?", *Corporate Governance: The International Journal of Business in Society*, *17*(2), 321–340.
Liang, C. J., Lin, Y. L. & Huang, T. T. (2011). "Does endogenously determined ownership matter on performance? Dynamic evidence from the emerging Taiwan market", *Emerging Markets Finance and Trade*, *47*(6), 120–133.
Lin, Y. R. & Fu, X. M. (2017). "Does institutional ownership influence firm performance? Evidence from China", *International Review of Economics & Finance*, *49*, 17–57.
Lozano, M. B., Martínez, B. & Pindado, J. (2016). "Corporate Governance, ownership and firm value: Drivers of Ownership as a good corporate governance mechanism", *International Business Review*, *25*(6), 1333–1343.
Madaan, D.A., Mehta, K. & Sharma, R. (2021). "A Revisit to Research on Corporate Governance Using Systematic Literature Review", *ECS Transactions*, 107(1), DOI 10.1149/10701.4035ecst
Mangena, M., Tauringana, V. & Chamisa, E. (2012). "Corporate boards, ownership structure and firm performance in an environment of severe political and economic crisis", *British Journal of Management*, *23*, S23–S41.
Manna, A., Sahu, T. N. & Gupta, A. (2016)." Impact of ownership structure and board composition on corporate performance in Indian Companies", *Indian Journal of Corporate Governance*, *9*(1), 44–66.
McConnell, J. J. & Servaes, H. (1990). "Additional evidence on equity ownership and corporate value", *Journal of Financial Economics*, *27*(2), 595–612.
Mehrotra, S., Mohanty, B. & Sharma, T. (2021). "Do board quality and promoters' holdings affect firm performance? Evidence from small and medium-sized enterprises", *FIIB Business Review*, 1–9.
Mehta, K. & Sharma, R. (2017). "Contrarian and Momentum investment strategies: Evidence from Indian Stock Market", *International Journal of Applied Business and Economic Research*, *15*(9), 107–118.
Mendoza-Velázquez, A., Ortuño-Barba, L. C. & Conde-Cortés, L. D. (2022). "Corporate governance and firm performance in hybrid model countries", *Review of Accounting and Finance*.
Mishra, A. K., Jain, S. & Manogna, R. L. (2021). "Do corporate governance characteristics influence firm performance in India? Empirical evidence using dynamic panel data analysis", *International Journal of Disclosure and Governance*, *18*(1), 71–82.

Mishra, R. & Kapil, S. (2017). "Effect of ownership structure and board structure on firm value: evidence from India", *Corporate Governance: The International Journal of Business in Society, 17*(4), 700–726.

Nashier, T. & Gupta, A. (2016). "The effect of institutional ownership on firm performance", *IUP Journal of Corporate Governance, 15*(3), 36–56.

Nashier, T. & Gupta, A. (2020). "Ownership concentration and firm performance in India", *Global Business Review*, 1–18.

Neralla, N. G. (2022). "Can corporate governance structure effect on corporate performance: an empirical investigation from Indian companies", *International Journal of Disclosure and Governance*, 1–19.

Nguyen, T. H., Nguyen, X. M., Nguyen, T. T. H. & Tran, Q. T. (2017). "Ownership structure and performance of professional service firms in a declining industry: Evidence from Vietnamese securities firms", *Business & Economic Horizons, 13*(2), 142–151.

Nguyen, T., Locke, S. & Reddy, K. (2015). "Ownership concentration and corporate performance from a dynamic perspective: Does national governance quality matter?", *International Review of Financial Analysis, 41*, 148–161.

Pagano, M. & Röell, A. (1998). "The choice of stock ownership structure: Agency costs, monitoring, and the decision to go public", *The Quarterly Journal of Economics, 113*(1), 187–225.

Pandey, K. D. & Sahu, T. N. (2019). "Concentrated promoters' ownership and firm value: Re–examining the monitoring and expropriation hypothesis", *Paradigm, 23*(1), 70–82.

Pant, M. & Pattanayak, M. (2007). "Insider ownership and firm value: Evidence from Indian corporate sector", *Economic and Political Weekly, 42*(16), 1459–1467.

Park, K. & Jang, S. S. (2010). "Insider ownership and firm performance: An examination of restaurant firms", *International Journal of Hospitality Management, 29*(3), 448–458.

Pathak, R. & Pradhan, S. (2012). "The role of ownership structure in firm performance: A study of Indian manufacturing firms", *IUP Journal of Corporate Governance, 11*(3), 36–47.

Pound, J. (1988). "Proxy contests and the efficiency of shareholder oversight", *Journal of Financial Economics 20*, 237–265.

Queiri, A., Madbouly, A., Reyad, S. & Dwaikat, N. (2021). "Corporate governance, ownership structure and firms' financial performance: Insights from Muscat securities market (MSM30).", *Journal of Financial Reporting and Accounting, 19*(4), 640–665.

Rashid, M. M. (2020). "Ownership structure and firm performance: the mediating role of board characteristics", *Corporate Governance: The International Journal of Business in Society, 20*(4), 719–737.

Satt, H., Nechbaoui, S., Hassan, M. K. & Halim, Z. A. (2021). "Institutional ownership and firm performance: the case of Morocco", *Macroeconomics and Finance in Emerging Market Economies*, 1–17.

Selarka, E. (2005). "Ownership concentration and firm value: A study from the Indian corporate sector", *Emerging Markets Finance and Trade, 41*(6), 83–108.

Sharma, R., Mehta, K. & Goel, A. (2022). "Non-linear relationship between board size and performance of Indian companies", *Journal of Management and Governance* (2022). https://doi.org/10.1007/s10997-022-09651-8

Sharma, R., Mehta, K., & Vyas, V. (2020). "Responsible Investing: A Study on Non–Economic Goals and Investors' Characteristics", *Applied Finance Letters, 9*(SI), 63–78. https://doi.org/10.24135/afl.v9i2.245.

Sharma, A. & Sharma, R. (2022). "Exploring Tax Decision Factors: A Perspective from North Indian Tax Practitioners", *Journal of Tax Reform, 8*(3): 285–297. https://doi.org/10.15826/jtr.2022.8.3.122

Mehta, K., Sharma, R., Vyas, V. & Kuckreja, J.S. (2022). "Exit strategy decision by venture capital firms in India using fuzzy AHP", *Journal of Entrepreneurship in Emerging Economies*, 14(4), 643–669. https://doi.org/10.1108/JEEE-05-2020–0146.

Shleifer, A. and Vishny, R. W. (1986). "Large shareholders and corporate control", *Journal of Political Economy, 94*(3, Part 1): 461–488.

Shleifer, A. & Vishny, R. W. (1989). "Management entrenchment: The case of manager–specific investments", *Journal of Financial Economics, 25*(1), 123–139.

Shleifer, A. & Vishny, R. W. (1997). "A survey of corporate Governance", *The Journal of Finance*, *52*(2), 737–783.

Short, H. & Keasey, K. (1999) "Managerial Ownership and the Performance of Firms: Evidence from the UK", *Journal of corporate finance*, *5*(1), 79–101.

Thanatawee, Y. (2014). "Institutional ownership and firm value in Thailand", *Asian Journal of Business and Accounting*, *7*(2), 1–22. https://papers.ssrn.com/sol3/papers.cfm?abstract_id=2543058.

Tsai, H. & Gu, Z. (2007). "The relationship between institutional ownership and casino firm performance", *International Journal of Hospitality Management*, *26*(3), 517–530.

Tsionas, M. G., Merikas, A. G. & Merika, A. A. (2012). "Concentrated ownership and corporate performance revisited: The case of shipping", *Transportation Research Part E: Logistics and Transportation Review*, *48*(4): 843–852.

Tsouknidis, D. A. (2019). "The effect of institutional ownership on firm performance: the case of US-listed shipping companies", *Maritime Policy & Management*, *46*(5), 509–528.

Uddin, M. N., Hosen, M., Chowdhury, M. M., Tabassum, T., & Mazumder, M. A. (2021). "Does corporate governance influence firm value in Bangladesh? A panel data analysis", *Economics and Management*, *24*(2), 84–100.

Ullah, W. (2017). "Evolving corporate Governance and firm's performance: evidence from Japanese firms", *Economics of Governance 18*(1), 1–33.

Vyas, V., Mehta, K., & Sharma, R. (2023). "The nexus between toxic-air pollution, health expenditure, and economic growth: An empirical study using ARDL", *International Review of Economics and Finance*, *84*, 154–166 https://doi.org/10.1016/j.iref.2022.11.017.

Wei, Z., Xie, F. & Zhang, S. (2005). "Ownership structure and firm value in China's privatized firms: 1991–2001", *Journal of Financial and quantitative analysis*, *40*(1), 87–108.

Yasser, Q. R. & Abdullah, Al M. (2015). "Effects of ownership concentration on firm performance: Pakistani evidence", *Journal of Asia Business Studies*, *9*(2), 162–176.

Yeh, C. M. (2019). "Ownership structure and firm performance of listed tourism firms. International", *Journal of Tourism Research*, *21*(2), 165–179.

Kapil Shrimal, Nidhi Solanki, CS. Priyanka Mathur

8 Short-Run Pricing Performance of Selected Indian IPOs During COVID-19 for Alternative Investment Avenue

Abstract: Small and Medium Enterprises (SMEs) act as a backbone for income generation in the economic growth of India. The new edge of funds generation in small and medium companies through public offering has been reasonably emerging, and the growth of SME IPOs in the secondary market has been extremely good. It can be noticed that numerous IPOs experience a quick surge in their trading prices on the day they are listed. Newly issued stocks often conclude their first trading day at a significantly higher price than their initial offering price. The present study examines the pricing and performance of SME IPOs issued on Indian Stock Exchanges for Alternative Investment Market (AIM) during the COVID-19 duration of two years, from 1st January 2020 to 31st December 2021. The aim of the research is to analyze the returns generated by BSE SME IPOs on the day of listing, in addition to the returns offered by the BSE SME IPO Index. A total of 87 SMEs have issued IPO during this period, and for the present study, 84 companies' data are taken as a sample based on the availability of data. The study of SME IPOs holds practical significance for investors in making informed decisions, for issuers in monitoring IPOs as a fresh source of investment, and for regulators in ensuring compliance with due diligence. The results showed that there is no significant effect of independent variables, i.e. Issue Size and Issue Price, on the dependent variable MAER (Market Adjusted Excess Return) during the Covid-19 pandemic.

Keywords: SME, IPO, Short run performance, MAER

Introduction

The Micro, Small, and Medium Enterprises (MSME) sector in India plays a crucial role in the country's economic development, contributing significantly to employment and income generation (Mehta et al., 2017). In recent years, the fund generation trend for Small and medium-sized enterprises (SMEs) through Initial Public Offerings (IPOs) has gained momentum, and the secondary market prices of SME IPOs have been impressive. However, the COVID-19 pandemic has had an adverse impact on the Indian

Kapil Shrimal, National Institute of Securities Markets (NISM), Mumbai
Nidhi Solanki, Prestige Institute of Management and Research, Indore
CS. Priyanka Mathur, Prestige Institute of Management and Research, Indore

https://doi.org/10.1515/9783111170022-008

economy, causing market uncertainty and volatility. The impact of the pandemic on the short-run pricing performance of selected Indian SME IPOs during Covid-19 in the Alternative Investment Markets (AIM) has been a subject of interest for investors, regulators, and policymakers. MSMEs have a big impact on the overall business ecosystem (Mehta et al., 2019; 2022b). The small venture of today will become big corporates of tomorrow and therefore, board composition of such firms plays a significant role in the overall performance in future (Sharma et al., 2022).

SMEs which are important for economic growth and job creation, have struggled to raise money during this time. Start-ups and new enterprises, often small or micro businesses, are common in many countries (Mehta et al., 2022b). One way for SMEs to get money is through initial public offerings (IPOs) in the alternative investment market. However, the success of SME IPOs during the pandemic may depend on various factors, such as market conditions, investor perception, and regulatory changes. It is, subsequently, imperative to dissect the estimated execution of certain Indian SME IPOs amid the widespread COVID-19 to get what impacts their victory within the brief term. It is, therefore, important to analyze the pricing performance of certain Indian SME IPOs during the COVID-19 pandemic to understand what influences their success in the short term.

The study employs the BSE SME IPO Index as the benchmark for comparison and uses the Market Adjusted Excess Returns (MAER) as the dependent variable and; Issue Size and Issue Price as independent variables. Similarly, there are various other firm specific factors are used by researchers to examine their contribution in the overall attainment of wealth maximization role (Sharma et al, 2021).

The findings of this research will provide insights into the short-run pricing performance of selected Indian SME IPOs during Covid-19 in the AIM. The study's results can guide investors, issuers, and regulators in making informed investment decisions and monitoring the performance of SME IPOs. Additionally, the study's practical implications will be helpful for making investment decisions for investors and monitoring IPO listing gain/loss for company regulators and policymakers.

The objective of this study is to analyze the pricing and performance of the Indian Stock Exchange's Alternative Investments (MAI) Small and Medium Enterprises (SME) Initial Public Offerings (IPOs) during the COVID-19 period from 1st January 2020 to 31st December 2021. Specifically, the study focuses on the listing day returns offered by BSE SME IPOs compared to the BSE SME IPO Index. Out of the 87 SMEs that issued IPOs during this period, data from 84 companies were selected as a sample based on data availability for the study.

Initial Public Offering

An IPO is a kind of exit strategy for a private company or early investors to earn full profit out of the complete private investment. An initial Public Offering is when the company decides to offer stock of the company on a public platform. It happens when the private limited plans to launch its company shares on a public platform in new stock issuance. An IPO allows the company to raise funds through public investors. These Companies need to meet requirements by exchanges and the Securities and Exchange Commission (SEC) to launch this IPO. It provides companies with an opportunity to obtain capital by offering shares through the primary market. The companies hire investment banks to market, gauge demand, and set the IPO price and date. This IPO can be seen as a strategy for the company's founders and early investors, realizing the full profit from their private investment. IPO is an economical option than a loan for raising funds. They also become beneficial in terms of better capital generation options that are risk-free. Before qualifying for an IPO, the company needs to register itself with the SEBI (Securities Exchange Board of India) and appoint underwriters to assist in the process of selling shares. After that, only SEBI gives permission to individual investors for IPO. Furthermore, this IPO issue shares are listed on National Stock Exchange and Bombay Stock Exchange, with the company becoming a publicly listed company.

With different categories of investors who invest in IPO, it could be further classified as short term and long-term investors who are classified based on returns, they expect. It has been noticed that long-term returns from IPO are risky in comparison to short-term investments in IPO. It has also been observed that about 60% IPOs give listing day returns in double digits, and only a fifth of them end up with the listing day in the red zone. As a result of this, it has encouraged a trend of utilizing them as a temporary investment option. In the last few years, within these IPO processes, a separate way of raising funds has emerged for small and medium companies called SME IPO. Although the recent research studies have focused on the agenda of sustainability too (Sharma et al., 2020; Vyas et al., 2023; Mehta et al., 2019) but that the current research has not included the same in its scope.

Small and Medium Enterprise IPO

An SME IPO is a method for a small or medium-sized business to sell its stocks to the public for the first time and be listed on the BSE SME or NSE Emerge platform. Retail investors in India can apply for SME IPOs by filling out an online application form through their stockbroker or bank. To qualify for an SME IPO, the company must adhere to higher standards of corporate governance and financial transparency. The COVID-19 pandemic has emphasized the significance of having sufficient liquidity and cash reserves to endure unforeseen circumstances, during which business activities may be halted while continuing expenses such as salaries and rent still have to be met. By being listed, a company can easily generate cash from the liquidity of the market and unlock the wealth of its business assets.

Listing Criteria of SME IPO

SME platforms were made after considering worldwide encounters, household capital showcase substances, and challenges confronted by SMEs, as well as the encounter of the OTCEI (Over-The-Counter Trade of India) (see Table 8.1). Agreeing to SEBI rules, SME trades ought to be built up as corporatized substances with a 1000 million net worth at least. SEBI has, moreover, loose posting standards for SME trades, as backers are not required to have a track record of distributable benefits for three a long time, as is the case for posting on most boards.

Table 8.1: Listing Norms Parameters on SME Exchange.

Parameters	SME Exchange
Paid-up Capital (Post-issue)	Not exceeding ₹ 250 million
Minimum number of allottees	50
IPO Application Size	At Least ₹ 1 lakh
Surveillance on draft red herring prospectus (DRHP)	By Exchange
Track record	Relaxed norms for track record
IPO Underwriting	Compulsory (100% underwritten, out of which 15% forcibly by merchant banker)
Market Making	Compulsory (All market makers in scrip will provide two-way quotes for 75% time during a trading day)
listing time frame	2–3 months
Reporting requirements	Half-yearly

Note: Adapted from SEBI and BSE.

The new initiative of capital financing of SMEs through IPOs has been quite encouraging, and the secondary market performance of SME IPOs has also been very good. However, it seems that is risky for investors, as there is not enough liquidity and the turnover. Considering these problems, market regulator SEBI has issued guidelines to keep away small investors from investing in SME IPOs. To make the market liquid,

SEBI guidelines stipulate that merchant bankers should act as market makers in such stocks for three years. However, after the stipulated period of three years, the stocks may face the problem of liquidity again. To avoid such a scenario, the present chapter suggests the need for more transparency and increased institutional participation in companies listed on SME platforms.

Also, stock exchanges where this com The new initiative of capital financing of SMEs through IPOs has been quite encouraging, and the secondary market performance of SME IPOs has also been very good. However, it seems that this is risky for investors, as there is not enough liquidity, and the turnover is also low. Considering these problems, market regulator SEBI has issued guidelines to keep away small investors from investing in SME IPOs. To make the market liquid, SEBI guidelines stipulate that merchant bankers should act as market makers in such stocks for three years. However, after the stipulated period of three years, the stocks may face the problem of liquidity again. To avoid such a scenario, the present chapter suggests the need for more transparency and increased institutional participation in companies listed on SME platforms.

The new initiative of capital financing of SMEs through IPOs has been quite encouraging, and the secondary market performance of SME IPOs has also been very good. However, it seems that this is risky for investors, as there is not enough liquidity, and the turnover is also low. Considering these problems, market regulator SEBI has issued guidelines to keep away small investors from investing in SME IPOs. To make the market liquid, SEBI guidelines stipulate that merchant bankers should act as market makers in such stocks for three years. However, after the stipulated period of three years, the stocks may face the problem of liquidity again. To avoid such a scenario, the present chapter suggests the need for more transparency and increased institutional participation in companies listed on SME platforms. Also, stock exchanges where these companies are listed should provide sustained handholding to the management of these companies.

Literature Review

Several studies have been conducted in recent years around the world to evaluate the pricing and success of SME IPOs, utilizing varied techniques and giving varying results. Several studies have produced contradictory results. A few financial specialists purchase within the IPO showcase for short-term picks up or posting picks up, whereas others may need to hold it for a long time. When advertising approaches verifiable levels, numerous financial specialists accept that IPO advertising is relentless. To justify the outcomes of our research, we reviewed many papers that shed light on various factors.

Adanan et al. (2021) did a consideration on the execution of Malaysian IPOs amid the travel control arrangement and found that underestimates were tall at this time.

Their thinking looked at the relationship between how IPO continues was utilized (such as for speculation and development, working capital, and obligation reimbursement) and their starting victory. The data was collected from a variety of sources, including the prospectus, the company's website, and the DataStream database, covering 65 IPOs from 2016 to the present. Analysis including pairwise correlation and OLS regression shows that although fewer IPOs were issued during a Movement Control Order (MCO), a significant proportion of them received initial returns. Positive (undervalued). It has also been found that there is a significant negative initial return on IPOs to investment and growth, as well as debt repayment. These discoveries include, in the proceeding, talk about approximately corporate back procedures and venture techniques for potential speculators. Commerce extension, as well as obligation lessening. These discoveries include in the proceeding discussion almost company fund methodologies and venture techniques for potential financial specialists.

Arora and Singh (2021) investigated the long-term performance of small business IPOs and found they outperformed other markets. The research findings indicate that small and medium-sized enterprise (SME) IPOs in India show superior performance over the long term, which is contrary to international evidence that suggests underperformance. This outperformance is especially evident when using buy-and-hold abnormal returns (BHAR) as the performance measure. Hypothetical results related to disagreements, fads, and windows of opportunity suggest that issue size and oversubscription adversely affect BHAR. Conversely, the reputation of auditors, underwriters, hot markets, undervaluation, reverse issue price, and pre-listing earnings all have a positive impact on long-run pricing performance. However, there was no significant relationship found between company age, size, leverage, volatility, and long-term performance as measured by BHAR. Due to limited pricing, this study used a one-year event-time methodology to measure aftermarket performance. For more meaningful results, this study can be extended to analyze aftermarket returns over 3–5 years, and the calendar time method can be used to calculate anomalous returns.

Kuswanto (2021) examined the under-pricing marvel of IPO firms recorded within the Indonesia Stock Trade amid the widespread COVID-19. A test of 34 IPO firms after the widespread declaration was chosen utilizing a purposive testing strategy. The study used a paired sample t-test to examine the closing prices and returns of IPO equities on days 1, 5, 10, 15, and 20. According to the findings, while underpricing persisted throughout the pandemic, it was only statistically significant on the first day of trading. The stock's returns were continually low after the first trading day and were considered statistically insignificant at T5, T10, T15, and T20. This study adds to our understanding of the phenomena of under-pricing and its behaviour over the pandemic period.

Yadav et al. (2021) looked at the relationship between free factors and the subordinate variable under/overpricing. As it were, the proposed cost value had a positive connection with the IPO cost esteem, while the price adjustment final and rate alter in the cost band had a somewhat negative relationship. The captured and coefficients of eight autonomous factors speaking to the degree of alteration within the Clever Near were decided to utilize multivariate direct relapse investigation. The consideration affirmed two investigative speculations, proposing that under-pricing/overpricing impacted IPO membership but did not have an adequate interaction to make significant changes in cruel stocks.

Sharma and Wazal (2020) analyzed the effectiveness of SMEs and fundamental main-board IPOs in terms of cost disclosure from 2000 to 2019. The study revealed that while SME IPOs had a better under-pricing rate than fundamental board IPOs, there was a lower request for SME IPOs compared to fundamental board IPOs. Rajvanshi and Kalyani (2020) considered the impact of profit on possession weakening, under-pricing, and long-run victory of SME IPOs from the year 2016 to 2018. The examination found that changes in proprietorship were to fault for the under-pricing seen in IPOs. Samantha et al. (2018) conducted research 2018 analysing 117 IPOs issued for subscription in India between 2009 and 2013. They studied the short-term performance of these IPOs using MAER and aimed to determine the factors that affect their performance. Past investigations have demonstrated that IPOs tend to perform ineffectively in the long run but bid great short-run returns. The present study used regression analysis to identify correlation coefficients among the factors assumed to affect short-term IPO performance. The chapter recommends that financial specialists ought to be mindful of these components sometime recently contributing, and it serves as a directing rule for surveying abundance showcase returns.

Dhamija and Arora (2017) studied the success of IPOs listed on the newly formed SME indices of BSE and NSE for small and medium-sized firms were investigated. The analysis discovered indications of under-pricing consistent with foreign studies, albeit at a lower level when compared to IPOs listed on India's main board stock markets. The low amount of SME IPO oversubscription shows a lack of investor interest. The study identifies numerous characteristics that influence under-pricing, including issue type and size, promoter holding, and lead management status. SME IPOs beat the benchmark index after listing, which contradicts earlier research on main-board exchanges. The ramifications of these discoveries are significant for regulators, issuers, and investors.

Tripathi et al. (2017) studied the performance of IPOs listed on the BSE SME, and NSE EMERGE platforms are examined in this study. According to the data, the number of difficulties listed on these platforms is growing with time, and the average issue size is encouraging. On average, SME IPOs are under-priced by 10.60%, which is consistent with the initial under-pricing phenomenon. Although the degree of under-pricing is diminishing, the contrast isn't measurably critical. The study also uncovers a connection between under-pricing and membership rates. The discoveries have repercussions for financial specialists, little businesses, speculation financiers, and administrative offices. The study provides insights into the performance of IPOs listed on these platforms and highlights the need to consider subscription rates as a crucial factor when analysing under-pricing. This information can help investors and regulatory bodies make more informed decisions and assist small businesses in raising capital through IPOs.

Gupta and Saini (2016) examined the market-adjusted pricing performance of initial public offerings on the BSE SME index from the commencement to the end of 2015. According to the study, while most IPOs did well at first and generated significant profits, they were unable to maintain the same level of momentum in the long run. Jain et al. (2015) addressed the importance of increasing openness and institutional involvement in companies listed on the SME Platform. A new platform has been developed by stock exchanges to assist small and medium-sized firms (SMEs) in meeting their equity funding requirements. While preliminary statistics reveal encouraging equity resource mobilization, these companies' issue floatation costs are greater. Given the poor liquidity and trading volume, the sudden rise in the BSE SME IPO Index is cause for concern. Right now, as it was educated that financial specialists with risk-taking cravings are taking an interest in the SME stages, the administration of recorded companies ought to increment money-related straightforwardness to guarantee reasonable estimating. In arrange to address the issue of a need for liquidity, SEBI (Securities and Trade Board of India) has commanded that guarantors must serve as showcase producers for a period of three a long time. Be that as it may, after the three-year period, the execution of the file may posture an issue due to the illiquidity of these scrips. Excessive reliance on underwriters to create the market discourages reputable investment banks from entering the market and increases costs for issuers. Another weak link in this segment is the weak participation of institutional investors. Bansal and Khanna (2012) analyzed the differences in the undervaluation of the IPOs issued through fixed-price offers and book-building procedures were examined, and disparities in undervaluation were identified.

From the above studies, we have found that most of the researchers attempted the short and long-run performance analysis of main board companies listed on exchanges in India and abroad. But none of the studies has been done on short-run performance analysis of SME IPO listed in India, especially during covid 19 period.

Rationale of the Study

The initiative to introduce financing of SMEs through IPOs has been successful in past years, and their performance in the secondary market has been quite good. SME IPOs are gaining popularity as they attract a growing number of investors. The proliferation of stocks and higher returns are among the factors contributing to the rise in investor interest in SMEs. The Indian market is favourable for SME IPOs, with support from the exchange board and investors. However, low liquidity and turnover can make it challenging for investors to sell their shares in the secondary market. Also, the market for SME shares is comparatively small and more sensitive to price swings; hence it is difficult to predict the value of the investment. SEBI guidelines issued in this respect can enhance liquidity by mandating merchant bankers to act as market makers. This study suggests that institutional participation and increased transparency in SMEs could help to avoid this scenario. Additionally, stock exchanges should provide support to the management of these companies. This study may benefit small and medium-sized investors, portfolio managers and institutional investors. The pandemic has also highlighted the importance of liquidity and cash reserves for SMEs. The conceptual model of the study is presented in Figure 8.1.

Objectives of the Study

The main objectives performed in the present study are:
- To evaluate the short-run performance of SME IPO listed on an exchange, i.e. from the date of the offer to the public to the date of listing (listing day gain/loss).
- To find out the relationship between Market Adjusted Excess Return (MAER) with Issue size and Issue Price.
- To study the trends in SME IPOs during the study period.

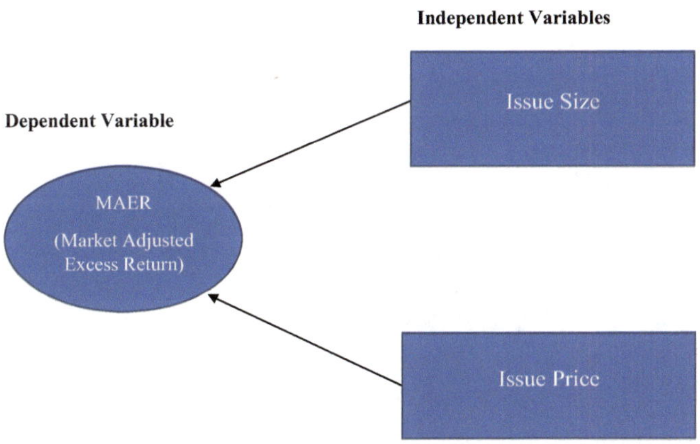

Figure 8.1: Conceptual Framework of the Study.
Source: Authors' compilation.

Research Methodology

Study Type: The research conducted is descriptive in nature and is based on secondary data sources.

Method of Data Collection: To conduct this study, secondary data was collected from the reports and articles on the web portals of SEBI, NSE and BSE.

Population & Sample Size: For the present study, 84 companies were selected as a suitable sample size based on the data available.

Duration of the study: The period of this study is two years beginning from 1st January 2020 to 31st December 2021.

Research Tools: The collected data have been analyzed with the help of relevant statistical tools like descriptive analysis, correlation, and multiple regression analysis (see Figure 8.2).

Hypothesis: To study the relationship between MAER with issue size and issue price, the following hypotheses have been developed and tested:

Relationship between MAER and Issue size:

H_1: There is no significant effect of issue size on the MAER of selected SME IPOs in India during the Covid-19 period.

Relationship between MAER and Issue price

H_2: There is no significant effect of issue price on MAER of selected SME IPOs in India during the Covid-19 period.

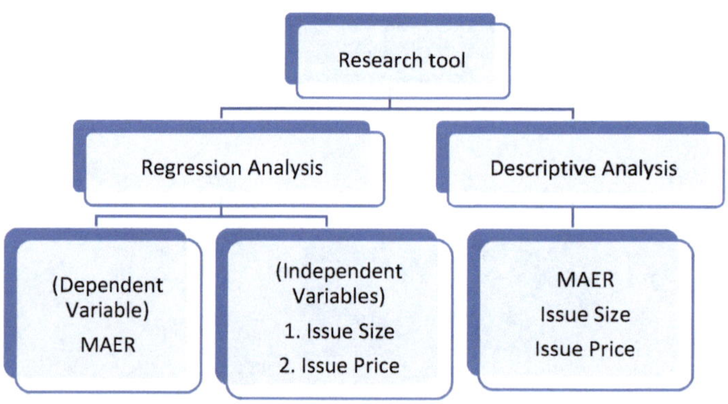

Figure 8.2: Research Tools Employed.
Source: Authors' compilation.

Results and Discussion

After analysing the collected data in line with the study's objective, the following key findings were obtained:

The Table 8.2 shown below shows the total number of IPOs launched in the year 2020 and their respective issue sizes. The highest number of IPOs were launched

Table 8.2: Number of SME IPO, Along with Their Monthly Issue Size Monthly For The Year 2020.

Month	Jan-20	Feb-20	Mar-20	Apr-20	May-20	Jun-20	Jul-20	Aug-20	Sep-20	Oct-20	Nov-20	Dec-20
No. of SME IPO	6	0	6	0	0	3	0	2	8	2	1	0
Issue Size (₹ in Cr.)	63.54	0	2.78	0	0	17	0	11.44	65.45	5.31	2.7	0

Source: Author computed.

in September 2020, with an issue size of ₹ 65.45 crores. The total number of SME IPO in the year 2020 was 28.

Table 8.2 shows the number of SME IPOs and the corresponding issue size in crores of rupees for each month from January 2020 to December 2020. The highest number of IPOs were issued in September 2020, along with the highest issue size of ₹ 65.45 crores. It is important to notice that the number of SME IPOs and their issue sizes can vary greatly from month to month, depending on various factors such as market conditions and investor sentiment (see Figure 8.3).

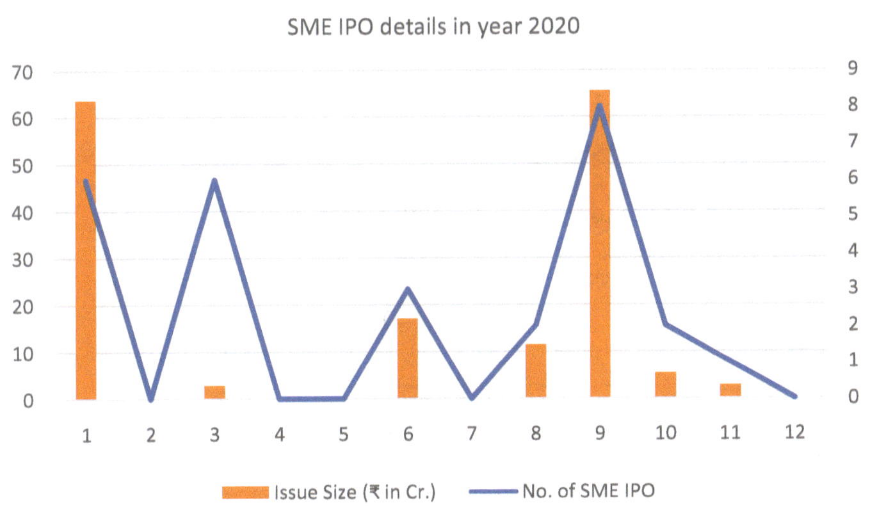

Figure 8.3: Details of SME IPOs in the Year 2020.
Note: This graph clearly shows the movement of Issue Size and No of IPOs monthly starting from January 2020 to December 2020. It is showing rapid changes throughout the entire year.
Source: Author generated.

Table 8.3 shows the total number of IPOs launched in the year 2021 and their respective issue sizes. The highest number of IPOs were launched in September 2021, with an issue

Table 8.3: Number of SME IPO, Along with Their Issue Size on a Monthly Basis for the Year 2021.

Month	Jan-21	Feb-21	Mar-21	Apr-21	May-21	Jun-21	Jul-21	Aug-21	Sep-21	Oct-21	Nov-21	Dec-21
No. of SME IPO	0	3	10	1	0	6	4	2	17	3	3	11
Issue Size	0	40.69	145.01	1.12	0	31.18	31.55	106.13	194.91	69.25	50.49	146.81

Source*:* Author computed.

Figure 8.4: Details of SME IPOs in the Year 2021.
Note: This graph is prepared for the year 2021 and shows the movement of Issue Size and No of IPOs monthly starting from January 2021 to December 2021. It can be observed that fluctuations in Issue size and No. of SME IPOs monthly is not very wide as compared to the year 2020.
Source: Author generated.

Table 8.4: Comparative Analysis of No. of IPOs and Issue Size in the Years 2020 & 2021.

Year	No. of IPO	Issue Size (₹ in Cr.)
2020	**28**	**168.22**
2021	**60**	**817.14**

Notes: This table gives a comparative analysis of the total no. of SME IPOs issued and their respective issue sizes for the financial year 2021–22 and the year 2022–23.
Source: Author computed.

size of ₹ 194.91 crores (Figure 8.4). The total number of SME IPO in the year 2021 was 60. A comparison of IPO during 2020 and 2021 is shown in Figures 8.5, 8.6 and Table 8.4.

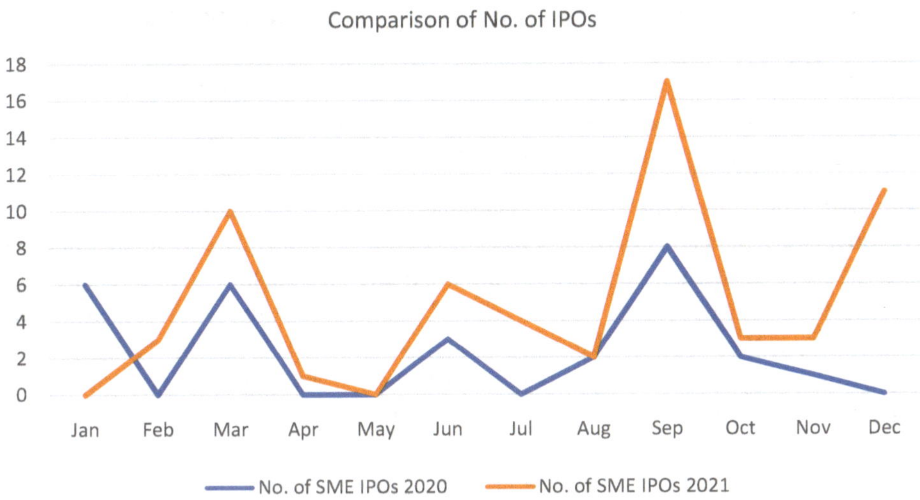

Figure 8.5: Comparison of No. of IPOs for the Years 2020 and 2021.
Note: The above graph shows the flow of no. of SME IPOs issued in the years 2020 and 2021.
Source: Author generated.

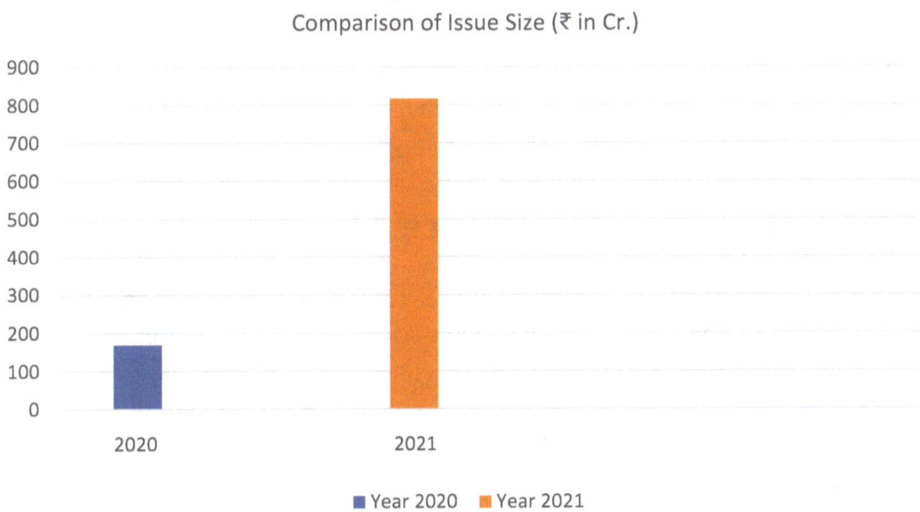

Figure 8.6: Comparison of Issue Size (₹ in Cr.) of IPOs for the Years 2020 and 2021.
From Table 8.4 and Figure 8.6, it can be clearly observed that there is a drastic change in IPOs from 2020 to 2021. In comparison to 2020, the number of SME IPOs has gone more than doubled in 2021, and the issue size is over four times larger.

Factors Considered for the Short-Term Performance of SME IPOs

Issue Size: It has anticipated by the investors that the larger is the size of the issue, the better is the short-run price performance. The regression analysis performed in the study will either endorse or nullify this assumption.

Issue Price: For the present study, an assumption is considered that the listing day price performance of the shares depends contrariwise on the offer price. Slighter the offer price, the more the demand will be, and the better the performance will be, as the price performance on the listing day has been selected as an indicator of short-run price performance, whereas the raw return represents the initial return on IPOs. Firstly, the relationship between the dependent and independent factors needs to be studied to analyse to what extent the co-relation exists between them. Next, regression analysis will be applied to study the impact of each independent factor on the dependent factor, and a regression equation shall be framed. Short-run MAER is the dependent factor, and independent factors include issue price and issue size. The multiple regression analysis using the OLS technique is used to test the influence of the explanatory variables mentioned above. To predict the correlation, Pearson's two-tailed test is conducted so as to test the starting assumption of the hypothesis that there is no correlation between the dependent and independent factors. The regression equation provided the value constant alpha and the beta values. The Beta shows the degree of impact that each independent factor has on the dependent factor. The study went ahead with both methods of 'correlation and regression' separately to analyze the influence using two different approaches of analysis.

Short-Term Price Performance Analysis

'Returns are calculated as the difference between the closing price of the stock on the first day of trading and the offer price of that stock divided by the offer price'.

$$Ri = ((P1 - P0)/P0) * 100$$

Where Ri is the Raw return of the stock i
P1 = Closing price of the stock on listing day
P0 = Offer price

The market return is equal to the difference between the closing value of the market return on an index on the listing day and the closing value of that index on the offer closing date divided by the closing value of the index on the offer closing day. The market return is equal to the following:

$$Mi = ((M1 - M0)/M0) * 100$$

Where M1 = Closing value of Nifty on the first day of trading of stock i

M0 = Closing value of Nifty on the offer closing date of stock i

$$\text{MAER} = ((\text{P1} - \text{P0})/\text{P0}) - ((\text{M1} - \text{M0})/\text{M0}) * 100$$

Data Interpretation

Table 8.5: Descriptive Analysis of MAER, Issue Size and Issue Price.

Descriptive Statistics			
	MAER	**Issue Size (₹ in Crores)**	**Issue Price**
Mean	5.930381109	11.7852381	66.88095238
Standard Error	3.516542766	1.623752334	5.518845946
Median	2.799808286	6.36	51
Standard Deviation	32.22964682	14.88193596	50.58105859
Sample Variance	1038.750134	221.472018	2558.443488
Kurtosis	27.81855658	15.76689597	1.372883318
Skewness	4.658188773	3.362222257	1.379539378
Range	254.6313643	100.52	215
Minimum	−28.6114723	1.12	10
Maximum	226.019892	101.64	225
Sum	498.1520132	989.96	5618
Count	84	84	84

Source: Author computed.

The data in Table 8.5 describes three variables related to initial public offerings (IPOs) that are MAER (Mean Absolute Error Rate), Issue Size (in crores of Indian Rupees), and Issue Price. The mean MAER is 5.9304, indicating that, on average, the predicted values of the IPOs deviated from the actual values by 5.9304 (see Table 8.6). The mean Issue Size is 11.7852 crores of Indian Rupees, with a range from 1.12 to 101.64 crores. The mean Issue Price is 66.8810, with a range from 10 to 225. The median MAER is 2.7998, which is lower than the mean, suggesting that the distribution of MAER values may be skewed. The median Issue Size is 6.36 crores, which is also lower than the mean, indicating that there may be some larger IPOs that are increasing the mean. The median Issue Price is 51, which is significantly lower than the mean, indicating that there may be some high-priced IPOs that are increasing the mean.

The standard deviation of MAER, Issue Size, and Issue Price are 32.2296, 14.8819, and 50.5811, respectively, indicating that there is significant variability in these variables across the sample of 84 IPOs. The skewness values for all three variables are positive, indicating that the distribution is skewed to the right, with more extreme values in the positive direction. The kurtosis values for MAER and Issue Size are very high, indicating that the distribution of these variables is heavily tailed and that there are a few extreme values in the sample.

Overall, this data suggests that there is significant variability in the MAER, Issue Size, and Issue Price of IPOs, with some extreme values influencing the mean values.

Table 8.6: Correlation Analysis Between MAER, Issue Size, and Issue Price.

	Correlation Analysis		
	MAER	**Issue Size**	**Issue Price**
MAER	1		
Issue Size	-0.082857444	1	
Issue Price	-0.01643803	0.337436281	1

Source: Author computed.

The correlation coefficient measures the strength and direction of the linear relationship between two variables, with a value ranging from –1 to +1. A value of 1 indicates a perfect positive correlation. A value of 0 indicates no correlation between the variables. Based on the given correlation coefficient:

- The correlation between MAER and itself is always 1, as it is the correlation of the variable with itself.
- 'There is a weak negative correlation between MAER and Issue Size (₹ in crores) with a correlation coefficient of −0.082. This indicates that as the issue size increases, the MAER tends to decrease slightly, although the relationship is not strong.
- 'There is a weak positive correlation between the issue price and issue size (₹ Crores) with a correlation coefficient of 0.337. This indicates that as the issue size increases, the issue price tends to increase slightly, although the relationship is not strong.
- There is a very weak negative correlation between MAER and Issue price with a correlation coefficient of –0.0164. This indicates that there is almost no linear relationship between these two variables.

Overall, these correlation coefficients suggest that there is no strong linear relationship between these variables, and any relationship that does exist is weak.

Table 8.7: Multiple Regression Analysis – Model Summary.

Regression Statistics	
Multiple R	0.083756474
R Square	0.007015147
Adjusted R Square	−0.017502998
Standard Error	32.51048101
Observations	84

Source: Author computed.

The statistics given above are related to multiple regression analysis between the dependent variable and one or more independent variables (see Table 8.7).

- The multiple R-values of 0.0838 indicates a weak positive correlation between the dependent variable and the independent variable(s).
- The R-squared value of 0.00701 indicates that only a very small proportion (0.7%) of the variability in the dependent variable can be explained by the independent variable(s).
- The adjusted R-squared value of -0.0175 is negative, which suggests that the independent variable(s) used in the regression model are not useful in explaining the variation in the dependent variable. This may be due to the inclusion of irrelevant or weakly correlated independent variables in the model.
- The standard error value of 32.5105 indicates the average distance that the observed values fall from the predicted values in the regression model. This value is used to determine the accuracy of the regression model. The observations value of 84 indicates the number of data points used in the regression analysis.

Overall, the regression statistics suggest that the independent variable(s) included in the model are not strongly related to the dependent variable.

Table 8.8: Results of ANOVA.

	ANOVA				
	Df	**SS**	**MS**	**F**	**Significance F**
Regression	2	604.8197457	302.4098728	0.286120632	0.751928013
Residual	81	85611.4414	1056.931375		
Total	83	86216.26114			

Source: Author computed.

The given data represents the results of an ANOVA (analysis of variance). See Table 8.8 for regression analysis. The table is divided into three parts: Regression, Residual and Total.

- Regression: This section displays the result of the regression analysis, which shows how much of the variation in the dependent variable is explained by independent variables. The regression section includes the degree of freedom (df), sum of squares (ss), mean sum of squares (MS), F-Statistic (F), and significance F.

In Table 8 (ANOVA) given above, the Regression section shows that there are 2 degrees of freedom, indicating that there are two independent variables in the model. The sum of squares for regression is 604.8197457, which represents the amount of variability in the dependent variable that is explained by the independent variables. The mean sum of squares for regression is 302.4098728, which is the sum of squares divided by the degrees of freedom. The F-statistic is 0.286120632, which is a ratio of the variability between groups to the variability within groups. The significance F value is 0.751928013, which represents the probability of obtaining an F-value as large as the one observed, if the null hypothesis (no relationship between the dependent and independent variables) is true.

- *Residual*: This section displays the results of the analysis of the unexplained variability in the dependent variable. The Residual section includes the degrees of freedom (df), sum of squares (SS), and mean sum of squares (MS).

In the given ANOVA table, the Residual section shows that there are 81 degrees of freedom, which is the number of observations minus the number of independent variables. The sum of squares for residual is 85611.4414, which represents the unexplained variability in the dependent variable. The mean sum of squares for residual is 1056.931375, which is the sum of squares divided by the degrees of freedom.

- *Total*: This section displays the results of the overall variability in the dependent variable. The Total section includes the degrees of freedom (df) and the sum of squares (SS).

In the given ANOVA table, the Total section shows that there are 83 degrees of freedom, which is the total number of observations minus 1. The sum of squares for the total is 86216.26114, which represents the total variability in the dependent variable.

Overall, the ANOVA table indicates that the F-value for the regression model is not significant, as the significance F-value is higher than the commonly used alpha level of 0.05. This suggests that the independent variables in the model do not significantly explain the variability in the dependent variable. The residual sum of squares and the total sum of squares are relatively high, indicating that there is still a lot of unexplained variability in the dependent variable that is not accounted for by the independent variables in the model.

Table 8.9: Coefficients.

	Coefficients	Standard Error	t Stat	P-value
Intercept	7.603072247	6.046818367	1.257367393	0.212233897
Issue Size (Rs Cr)	−0.188944705	0.254726743	−0.74175449	0.460381453
Issue Price	0.00828438	0.074945586	0.110538593	0.912255673

Source: Author computed.

Table 8.9 represents the results of a multiple regression analysis, which includes the coefficients, standard error, t-statistic, and p-value for each independent variable.

- Intercept: The intercept value of 7.603072247 represents the predicted value of the dependent variable when the independent variables (Issue Size and Issue Price) are equal to zero. The standard error value of 6.046818367 indicates the average distance that the observed values fall from the predicted values for the intercept term. The t-statistic value of 1.257367393 indicates the degree to which the intercept differs from zero. The p-value of 0.212233897 represents the probability of obtaining a t-statistic as large as the observed one, if the null hypothesis (no relationship between the dependent and independent variables) is true. Since the p-value is greater than the commonly used alpha level of 0.05, the intercept term is not statistically significant.

- Issue Size (₹ Cr): The coefficient value of -0.188944705 represents the change in the dependent variable for a one-unit change in the Issue Size independent variable, holding all other variables constant. The standard error value of 0.254726743 indicates the average distance that the observed values fall from the predicted values for the Issue Size variable. The t-statistic value of -0.74175449 indicates the degree to which the Issue Size coefficient differs from zero. The p-value of 0.460381453 represents the probability of obtaining a t-statistic as large as the observed one, assuming that the null hypothesis (no relationship between the dependent and independent variables) is true. Since the p-value is greater than the commonly used alpha level of 0.05, the Issue Size variable is not statistically significant.
- Issue Price: The coefficient value of 0.00828438 represents the change in the dependent variable for a one-unit change in the Issue Price independent variable, holding all other variables constant. The standard error value of 0.074945586 indicates the average distance that the observed values fall from the predicted values for the Issue Price variable. The t-statistic value of 0.110538593 indicates the degree to which the Issue Price coefficient differs from zero. The p-value of 0.912255673 represents the probability of obtaining a t-statistic as large as the observed one, assuming that the null hypothesis (no relationship between the dependent and independent variables) is true. Since the p-value is greater than the commonly used alpha level of 0.05, the Issue Price variable is not statistically significant.

In other words, in the regression analysis, the constant value of the sample is 7.60, whereas the coefficient of correlation between the dependent and independent variables is 0.083, which is less than 0.30; however, the coefficient value of the issue size is −0.188, and the issue price is 0.0082848. In relation to this P value of the issue, the price is 0.9122, which is more than 0.05, and the test value of issue size is also 0.460, which is again more than 0.05 at a 5% level of significance, which leads us to fail and reject the null hypothesis. In other words, we can say that there is no significant relationship between MAER with both Issue size and issue price during the time of covid-19.

The findings of this study have important implications for SMEs, investors, and policymakers. SMEs planning to go public during the pandemic need to consider the challenging market conditions and investor sentiment while setting IPO offer prices. Investors should carefully evaluate the pricing performance of SME IPOs during the pandemic and consider factors such as market conditions and regulatory changes while making investment decisions. Policymakers need to monitor the regulatory environment and consider appropriate measures to support SMEs in accessing capital through IPOs during challenging times.

Limitations of the Study

We have conducted the research for only two years with a limited number of variables. The study only includes two independent variables, Issue Size (₹ Cr) and Issue Price, which may not capture the full range of factors that could influence the dependent variable. Including additional variables could help to improve the predictive power of the model and identify other factors that may be important in explaining the variation in the dependent variable. Other factors that are important predictors of the dependent variable but were not included in the study could exist. Incorrect conclusions regarding the link between the independent and dependent variables can result from omitting crucial factors. The sample size of 84 is modest, which may restrict the generalizability of the findings to larger populations. A greater sample size may yield more robust results while lowering the likelihood of sampling error. The adjusted R-squared value of -0.017502998 indicates that the model does not fit the data well, implying that the independent variables do not explain a significant percentage of the variation in the dependent variable. This could be due to missing variables that could improve the model's fit. Furthermore, studies can be conducted by taking increasing periods of study with a greater number of variables, and research can also analyze long-term performance, which can help investors and companies make long-term investment strategies for planning investment in the SME Equity market.

Future Scope

This study offers up various opportunities for future research, such as analyzing the long-term performance of SME IPOs during the COVID-19 pandemic to understand post-IPO performance and the sustainability of IPO pricing performance. The impact of investor attitude on the pricing performance of SME IPOs during the pandemic can be investigated further by considering characteristics such as investor risk appetite, market sentiment, and investor behaviour. The role of regulatory changes during the pandemic on IPO pricing performance can be further investigated by analysing the specific regulatory measures taken by policymakers and their impact on SME IPO pricing. It may be valuable to conduct similar analyses within specific industries to identify industry-specific patterns and trends. This could provide more targeted insights into the factors that affect IPO returns in different industries. Conducting a longitudinal analysis could help to identify how the relationship between independent and dependent variables changes over time. This could provide insights into how the IPO market is evolving and how different factors may become important over time. Lastly, comparing the results of this study with similar studies conducted in different countries or regions could provide insights into how factors that affect IPO returns vary across different markets and regulatory environments.

Conclusion

This chapter provides insights into the short-run pricing performance of selected Indian SME IPOs during the COVID-19 pandemic in the alternative investment market. The findings suggest that SME IPOs launched during the pandemic exhibit different pricing performance compared to those launched in the pre-pandemic period. Market conditions, investor sentiment, and regulatory changes are identified as significant factors influencing the pricing performance of SME IPOs during the pandemic.

The major finding is to decide and recognize the extreme alter in the performance of SME IPOs within the brief run beginning day returns post covid-19. To meet the first objective of this study, i.e. measuring the initial listing performance of IPOs, the MAER analysis has been conducted for short-run listing gain/loss. Next, to meet the second objective, regression analysis was done, and the results showed that there was no significant effect between the variables. Lastly, to meet the third objective in the study, a graphical analysis was done, and it was found that the trend has increased in the year 2021 as compared to the previous year, 2020; the number of SME IPO in 2021 is more than double of SME IPO in 2020 and fundraising in 2021 is more than three times (issue size) as compared to that raised in the year 2020. It can be concluded that SME IPO could be a prospective unused speculation road for financial specialists in essential advertising. Overall, this research contributes to the understanding of SME IPO pricing performance during the COVID-19 pandemic in the alternative investment market and provides directions for future research in this area.

References

Adanan, S.A., Bustamam, K.S., Abd Samad, K., Abdullah Sani, A., Saidin, A., & Mamat, S.N. (2021), "Does Intended Use Influence the Initial Returns of Initial Public Offering (IPO) Amidst Economic Crisis of Covid-19", *International Journal of Academic Research in Accounting, Finance and Management Sciences, 9* (3), 629–643.

Arora, N., & Singh, B. (2020). "The long-run performance of SME IPOs in India: empirical evidence from Indian stock market", *Journal of Asia Business Studies, 15*(1), 88–109.

Baig, A. S., & Chen, M. (2022). "Did the COVID-19 pandemic (really) positively impact the IPO Market? An Analysis of information uncertainty", *Finance Research Letters, 46*, 102372.

Baluja, G. (2018). "Does Size Matter for IPO Survival? Empirical Evidence from India", *Vision*, *22*(1), 88–104. https://doi.org/10.1177/0972262917750249

Bansal, R., & Khanna, A. (2012). "Pricing mechanism and explaining under pricing of IPOs, evidence from Bombay stock exchange India", *International journal of research in finance and marketing*, *2*(2), 205–216.

Chaudhary, R., Bakhshi, P., & Gupta, H. (2020). "The performance of the Indian stock market during COVID-19", *Investment Management and Financial Innovations*, *17*(3), 133–147.

Chiraphadhanakul, S., & Gunawardana, P. (2012). "An empirical study of factors affecting IPO performance of Thai firms", *Journal of Applied Business Research (JABR)*, *28*(5), 921–934.

Dhamija, S., & Arora, R. K. (2017). "Initial and aftermarket performance of SME IPOs in India", *Global Business Review*, *18*(6), 1536–1551.

Ellikkal, A., Rajamohan, S., & Prakash, M. O. (2022). "IPOs in Indian Stock Market: Analyzing Pricing and Performance of IPO Listed in 2021", *Journal of Management*, *10*(2), 1–8.

Gupta Varsha & Saini Jasmer Singh. (2016). "IPO Financing: An alternative source of financing for SMEs in current era", *IOSR Journal of Business and Management*, *18*(7), 119 – 125

Gupta, V., Singh, S., & Yadav, S. S. (2021). "Disaggregated IPO returns, economic uncertainty and the long-run performance of SME IPOs", *International Journal of Emerging Markets* (ahead-of-print).

Handa, R., & Singh, B. (2017). "Performance of Indian IPOs: an empirical analysis", *Global Business Review*, *18*(3), 734–749.

Hawaldar, I. T., K.R., Kumar N. & Mallikarjunappa, T. (2018) "Pricing and Performance of IPOs: Evidence from Indian Stock Market", *Cogent Economics & Finance*, *6*(1), 1–20. DOI: 10.1080/23322039.2017.1420350., Available at SSRN: https://ssrn.com/abstract=3504459 or http://dx.doi.org/10.2139/ssrn.3504459

Jain, R. K., Shukla, A. K., & Singh, K. (2013). "SME financing through iPOs–An Overview", *Reserve Bank of India Occasional Papers*, *34*(1), 138–151.

Kuswanto, R. (2021). "IPO Stock Performance amidst the COVID–19 Pandemic: Has It Been Undervalued?", *Journal Dinamika Akuntansi dan Bisnis*, *12*(1), 105–116.

Mazumder, S., & Saha, P. (2021). "COVID-19: Fear of pandemic and short–term IPO performance", *Finance research letters*, *43*, 1–10.

Mehta, K., Sharma, R. & Chugh, A. (2017). "Management of Forex Risk Exposure: A Study of SMEs and Unlisted Non–Financial Firms in India", *International Journal of Applied Business and Economic Research (SCOPUS)*, *15*(9) (May 2017), 43–54.

Mehta, K., Sharma, R., & Vyas, V. (2019). "Efficiency and ranking of sustainability index of India using DEA-TOPSIS", *Journal of Indian Business Research*, *11*(2), 179–199. https://doi.org/10.1108/JIBR-02-2018–0057.

Mehta, K., Sharma, R., & Vyas, V. (2022). "A quantile regression approach to study the impact of aluminium prices on the manufacturing sector of India during the COVID era", *Materials Today: Proceedings*, *65*(8), 3506-3511, ISSN 2214–7853, https://doi.org/10.1016/j.matpr.2022.06.087.

Mehta, K., Sharma, R., Vyas, V. & Kuckreja, J.S. (2022). "Exit strategy decision by venture capital firms in India using fuzzy AHP", *Journal of Entrepreneurship in Emerging Economies*, *14*(4), 643–669. https://doi.org/10.1108/JEEE-05-2020-0146

Nagesh, G. P., & Murugaiah, V. (2019). "Book building-A Strategic Mechanism for Issue Price Determination in IPOs-A Study on Indian Companies". https://www.ijrar.org/papers/IJRAR1AHP003.pdf

Rajvanshi, V. & Kalyani, S. T. (2020). "Earnings Management and Ownership Dilution in Small and Medium Enterprises: Evidence from Indian IPOs", *Indian Institute of Management Calcutta, Working Paper Series.*

Roopa. P & Nishitha. P (2021). "COVID Impact on IPOs in SME Platforms in India: Before and After the Lockdown", *Pacific Business Review International*, *14*(6), 1–9.

Samanta, P. K., Dam, S., Saluja, R. S., Bansal, S., & Chhabra, N. (2018). “Short-Run Performance Analysis of IPOs in the Indian Market”, *IUP Journal of Management Research*, *17*(1).

Sharma, R., Mehta, K. & Goel, A. (2022). “Non-linear relationship between board size and performance of Indian companies”, *Journal of Management and Governance* (2022). https://doi.org/10.1007/s10997-022-09651-8

Sharma, R., Mehta, K. & Sharma, O. (2021). “Exploring Deep Learning to Determine the Optimal Environment for Stock Prediction Analysis”, *International Conference on Computational Performance Evaluation, ComPE 2021*, 148–152.

Sharma, R., Mehta, K., & Vyas, V. (2020). “Responsible Investing: A Study on Non–Economic Goals and Investors’ Characteristics”, *Applied Finance Letters, 9(SI)*, 63–78.

Sharma, S. K., & Wazal, M. S. (2020). “Comparative analysis of underpricing and subscription of SME IPOs and main board IPOs in India”, *Comparative Analysis of Underpricing and Subscription of SME IPOs and Main Board IPOs in India (6th February 2020). Published in Our Heritage*, *68*(27).

Singh, A. K., & Anand, A. (2020). “A study on listing day price performance of BSE SME IPOs and its determinants”, *Indian Journal of Finance*, *14*(5–7), 44–61.

Tripathi, A. R., Pradhan, G. P., & Pandey, S. N. (2017). “SME IPOs in Indian Capital Market”, *SCMS Journal of Indian Management*, *14*(3).

Vyas, V., Mehta, K., & Sharma, R. (2020). “Investigating socially responsible investing behaviour of Indian investors using structural equation modelling”, *Journal of Sustainable Finance & Investment*, 1–23 DOI: 10.1080/20430795.2020.1790958

Vyas, V., Mehta, K., & Sharma, R. (2023). “The nexus between toxic-air pollution, health expenditure, and economic growth: An empirical study using ARDL”, *International Review of Economics and Finance, 84*, 154–166 https://doi.org/10.1016/j.iref.2022.11.017

Yadav, A., & Prosad, J. (2021). “Pricing and Performance of IPOs: Empirical Evidence from Indian Stock Market”, *Turkish Online Journal of Qualitative Inquiry*, *123*(3).

Navpreet Kaur, Renuka Sharma, and Kiran Mehta

9 Emerging Green: Exploring Strategic Factors for SMEs' Adoption of Green Technology and Innovation in India

Abstract: The association between general innovation and green growth is well acknowledged. Green innovation is advantageous to keep the environment clean, aids in trash recycling, and might even conserve non-biodegradable energy. Additionally, green technology could lead to sustainable development. Due to awareness and environmental concerns, small and medium-sized businesses must embrace environmentally friendly practices in emerging nations. In order to succeed, core sector enterprises must maximize production efficiency, reduce waste, and improve return on investment. In our opinion, effective automation and power management provide the best path to achieving this. Progressively gaining traction are ideas like integrated power management and infrastructure monitoring. There is a paradigm change among SME shareholders, who want to replace traditional processes with green ones and are working to remove obstacles to green innovation in an emerging economy. Studies concentrating on SMEs in developing nations are still few, even though their existence in developing areas and countries is still crucial and has been favored in economic organizations. The current research has explored various determinants supporting SMEs' adoption of green technology and innovation. The study's findings have provided a future pathway for the researcher to explore several new dimensions in helping SMEs adopt green innovation and technology.

Keywords: SMEs, Innovation, Technology, Green practices, Literature survey

Introduction

The discovery of artificial resources has significantly increased, thanks to advancements in technology and research, making life better for everyone. However, the opulent use of artificial resources has come at the expense of ecology and sustainability. The association between general innovation and green growth is well acknowledged. Green innovation is advantageous to keep the environment clean, aids in trash recycling, and might even conserve non-biodegradable energy. Additionally, green technology could lead to sustainable development. Small and medium-sized businesses must embrace environmentally friendly practices in emerging nations due to aware-

Navpreet Kaur, Renuka Sharma, Kiran Mehta, Chitkara Business School, Chitkara University, Punjab, India

https://doi.org/10.1515/9783111170022-009

ness and environmental concerns. Our existence depends on the environment, which in turn depends on the labor that we do to make a livelihood. Environmental sustainability and industrialization are interdependent. We must adopt green technology that will set us on a road of sustainable development if we are to excel in both the environment and industrialization. The key to maintaining the environment's sustainability is to make environmentally responsible decisions and take appropriate steps to protect the environment, with an emphasis on maintaining the capacity of the environment to continue supporting our existence.

For organizational and environmental performance, green innovation is a crucial and prime subject. Thus, the purpose of this study is to investigate how green innovation affects environmental performance, which in turn affects organizational performance in a developing economy. Green innovation is now widely recognized as a viable concept in the modern period as environmental challenges and global warming gain importance on a worldwide scale. Because sustainability is regarded to be the primary obligation for firms participating in the universal competitive climate organizations must embrace green growth strategies.

Companies are becoming more aware of the urgency of the issue and the necessity to address it because of the corporate sector's increased demands in the area of environmental responsibility. Information and communication technologies (ICTs) businesses contributed about 2% of global CO2 emissions in 2015 (GeSI, 2015), escalating environmental issues. Green information technology (GIT) efforts can assist firms in reducing their environmental impacts. Green information technology (GIT) enhances the company's value development and financial success. Businesses that use GIT solutions see their operating margins permanently decline and their cost-to-sales ratios increase.

Indian enterprises are aware of the advantages they would enjoy by implementing these solutions, and responses from industries including oil and gas, electricity, and pharmaceutical have been promising. Companies struggle with high adoption and implementation costs compared to their size. Technology adoption is hindered by issues such as a lack of trained workers who can overcome technological obsolescence via ongoing advancements. Ten years ago, there was little awareness, and market education took some time. However, it is reasonable to infer that the market is undoubtedly more advanced and aware presently.

To succeed, core sector enterprises must maximize production efficiency, reduce waste, and improve return on investment. Effective automation and power management, in our opinion, provide the best path to achieving this. Progressively gaining traction are ideas like integrated power management and infrastructure monitoring. The biggest challenge of our time is inventing sustainable technologies, particularly in poor nations. Although technology has contributed significantly to the challenges we confront, it may also contribute significantly to their solution.

Many small and medium-sized enterprises are beginning to understand the importance of sustainability and are making investments in green technologies. These businesses are becoming more conscious of the advantages of utilizing green technologies. SMEs are a key source of income, dynamism, increased livelihood, and competitiveness. They may also help the economy evolve enough. In compared to multinational firms, SMEs have a greater direct impact on social issues like poverty reduction. When SMEs are successfully incorporated into the overall economy, there is an increased use of material and people resources in that nation (Leo, 2011; Fahad & Wang, 2018, Mehta et al., 2017).

In response to growing awareness of the environmental risks associated with economic activities, stakeholders are increasingly interested in the environmental and social costs of goods and services. Businesses are therefore under pressure to conduct their operations within a framework for sustainable development. To win the trust of stakeholders, companies are highlighting their concrete efforts to promote sustainable development. The emergence of the three pillars of sustainability has led to a global push for businesses to adopt novel practices that protect the environment through rules and procedures. In this new era of environmentalism, green innovation practices have become necessary actions that positively contribute to reducing carbon emissions, conserving resources, and managing the detrimental effects of global warming. Due to the impact of sustainability on corporate performance and competitiveness, green innovation adoption has emerged as a crucial issue in modern business and innovation literature. Hansen and Klewitz (2012) highlight the unique characteristics of SMEs, such as flexibility, market responsiveness, and agility, that make them both favorable and unfavorable for green innovation and note that SMEs operate differently from large firms in terms of their approach to green innovation.

The increasing importance of green practices has become a global trend. As consumers become more aware of environmentally friendly products, the performance of SMEs is now a major concern. Failure to adopt green practices may lead to a significant decline in performance for businesses. When a company's leadership is committed to using green practices, they inspire their staff to do the same and offer opportunities for experimentation with green product innovation. Entrepreneurial leadership is a vital component in fostering innovative behavior among businesses, resulting in product innovation and exceptional performance for SMEs. In the current environmentally conscious era, adopting a green entrepreneurial orientation is a key performance indicator. The Resource-based view considers it a crucial resource for the enterprise as entrepreneurial orientation itself is a resource that can provide a competitive advantage.

Climate change has become one of the most pressing global issues as businesses are ranked among the top polluters in the world. To address this issue, it is imperative to implement green innovation strategies and practices. As customers and stakeholders are increasingly concerned about environmental protection, innovation becomes critical. Thus, it requires traditional business models to adapt and shift towards a corporate culture that promotes green innovation. Unlike traditional innovation, which aims to create competitive advantages by adding value to the company, green innovation focuses more on reducing the negative impact of processes or products on the environment.

The three categories of green innovation practices include managerial, systemic, and process, as defined by Chen (2008). Green innovation refers to the implementation of improved methods or services that reduce environmental impact. In order to uphold their social responsibility values, companies should utilize innovative, environmentally friendly technology in their manufacturing practices, recognizing the link between innovation and sustainability practices. Corporate social responsibility aims to integrate wealth, social justice, and environmental protection. To create and execute new business models, traditional SMEs often invest in hiring workers with digital skills and expertise in innovative domains. SMEs are increasingly involved in social, environmental, and green initiatives as they can benefit from reduced costs and expenses through grants and subsidies. Incentives and subsidies support green initiatives, thereby advancing green practices and innovation within SMEs.

Research Methodology

The current research has systematically reviewed the literature in a rigorous and comprehensive manner. It has synthesized the existing research on the theme of the study. The methodology involves carefully defining the research scope, extensively searching multiple databases, and selecting studies based on predefined inclusion and exclusion criteria. The included studies are then critically appraised, data is extracted, and findings are synthesized to explore the strategic factors affecting the SMEs decision to adopt green technology and innovation. The review of studies conducted in this research encompasses eight distinct sub-themes, each contributing to a comprehensive understanding of the topic under investigation. These sub-themes serve as crucial building blocks that not only facilitate the organization and categorization of the existing literature but also provide a broader list of constructs or factors that future researchers can explore. The research studies shortlisted for this study involved an exhaustive search across multiple databases, viz., Sciencedirect, Springer, Emerald, Wiley and Taylor & Francis etc., ensuring the inclusion of relevant studies from diverse sources. The sub-themes explored within the review encompassed a range of interconnected dimensions, shedding light on various aspects of the phenomenon being studied. By analyzing and synthesizing the findings within each sub-theme, the review offers a nuanced and multifaceted perspective on the research topic, enhancing our understanding of its complexity and contributing to the existing body of knowledge. This comprehensive approach not only helps identify commonalities and consistencies among studies but also highlights gaps and discrepancies, paving the way for future research endeavors to delve deeper into specific sub-themes or explore new avenues within the overarching topic. Thus, the review of literature based on these eight sub-themes provides a valuable resource for researchers to explore and expand upon, fostering further advancements and insights in the field.

Review of Literature

Innovation Strategy

Small and Medium Enterprises (SMEs) play a critical role in the economic growth and development of any nation. SMEs are known for their flexibility, agility, and ability to respond to changing market conditions. Innovation is a key driver for the success of SMEs, as it enables them to stay ahead of the competition and adapt to changing market conditions. The literature on innovation strategies of SMEs highlights various factors that influence innovation in SMEs, including organizational culture, leadership, resources, and external environment.

Morrow and Rondinelli (2002) emphasize the importance of having a formal strategy or plan for adopting green innovation in SMEs. This includes defining goals, identifying key stakeholders, allocating resources, and monitoring progress. By having a formal strategy, SMEs can ensure that they are aligned with their organizational goals and can track their progress towards becoming more environmentally sustainable. According to Huang and Wang (2021), SMEs that prioritize innovation as a core strategy tend to have better performance outcomes than those that do not. These outcomes include increased sales, profitability, and competitiveness. Innovation can take many forms, such as product innovation, process innovation, and business model innovation. SMEs that are successful in innovation tend to have a culture that fosters creativity and encourages experimentation. Leadership is another important factor that influences innovation in SMEs. According to Baum and Locke (2004), transformational leadership styles, which emphasize vision, inspiration, and intellectual stimulation, are associated with higher levels of innovation in SMEs. This is because transformational leaders are able to create a vision for innovation and inspire their employees to work towards that vision.

In terms of external environment, SMEs that have access to external resources, such as knowledge networks, funding, and partnerships, are more likely to innovate. This is because external resources can provide SMEs with new ideas, expertise, and resources that they may not have internally. According to Kitzinger and Lettl (2018), open innovation strategies, which involve collaboration with external partners, can help SMEs overcome resource constraints and accelerate innovation. Boiral (2009) focuses on the importance of setting specific goals or targets for reducing environmental impact in SMEs. This involves identifying specific areas where the SME can reduce its environmental impact, such as reducing waste or energy consumption, and setting measurable targets for improvement. By setting specific goals, SMEs can track their progress and identify areas for further improvement.

Albino, Balice, and Dangelico (2012) argue that regular review and update of green innovation strategies is critical for SMEs to remain competitive and adapt to changing market conditions. This includes assessing the effectiveness of current strategies, identifying new opportunities for innovation, and ensuring that the SME remains aligned with its organizational goals. By regularly reviewing and updating their green innovation strategies, SMEs can stay ahead of the competition and continue to improve their environmental sustainability.

In conclusion, the literature on innovation strategies of SMEs highlights various factors that influence innovation, including organizational culture, leadership, resources, and external environment. SMEs that prioritize innovation and foster a culture of creativity and experimentation tend to have better performance outcomes than those that do not. Additionally, access to external resources and collaboration with external partners can help SMEs overcome resource constraints and accelerate innovation.

Resource Allocation

Resource allocation is a crucial aspect of innovation practices, particularly for small and medium-sized enterprises (SMEs) that may face resource constraints. In recent literature, scholars have explored the factors that influence SMEs' resource allocation decisions towards green innovation and technology practices. According to the study by Huang and Wang (2021), SMEs with a clear innovation strategy are more likely to allocate resources towards green innovation practices. In addition, the study found that SMEs with higher levels of dynamic capabilities, such as sensing, seizing, and transforming capabilities, were more likely to allocate resources towards green innovation practices. This suggests that a clear innovation strategy and dynamic capabilities can help SMEs overcome resource constraints and prioritize green innovation.

Chen and Chang (2012) noted that SMEs that allocate a dedicated budget for green innovation are more likely to adopt and implement green technology and innovation practices. This allocation of funds helps SMEs in financing their green innovation efforts and demonstrates their commitment towards sustainable development and environmental conservation. Similarly, the study by Brouthers et al. (2020) found that SMEs with a greater commitment to sustainability were more likely to allocate resources towards green innovation. The study found that SMEs that had adopted green practices, such as reducing waste or energy consumption, were more likely to invest in green innovation. This suggests that SMEs that have already made progress in reducing their environmental impact are more likely to allocate resources towards green innovation.

However, the study by Purwandani and Michaud (2021) found that while SMEs recognized the importance of green innovation, they often faced challenges in allocating resources towards these practices. The study found that SMEs faced a range of barriers, including a lack of financial resources, lack of knowledge and skills, and lack of stakeholder pressure. This suggests that while SMEs may recognize the importance of green innovation, they may struggle to allocate resources towards these practices due to a range of internal and external factors.

Providing training and development opportunities for employees to improve their skills in green innovation can be a crucial factor in enhancing the effectiveness of green innovation practices in SMEs, as noted by Weng et al. (2015). These opportunities can include workshops, training sessions, and seminars that equip employees with the knowledge and skills required to develop and implement green innovation practices effectively. Such initiatives also serve to engage employees and foster a culture of sustainability within the organization, contributing to the overall success of green innovation practices in SMEs. According to Majali et al. (2022), the designation of staff or a team responsible for green innovation is an effective way for SMEs to ensure that green innovation practices are integrated into their daily operations. The designated team can oversee the implementation of green technology and innovation practices, monitor the progress, and ensure that the initiatives align with the company's overall sustainability objectives.

Overall, these studies suggest that SMEs' resource allocation decisions towards green innovation and technology practices are influenced by a range of factors, including a clear innovation strategy, dynamic capabilities, commitment to sustainability, and internal and external barriers. Future research can further explore these factors and provide insights into how SMEs can overcome resource constraints and prioritize green innovation practices.

Collaboration

Large enterprises have a comparative advantage over SMEs when it comes to implementing green innovation practices due to their greater resources and infrastructure. SMEs, on the other hand, often struggle to implement green innovation practices due to resource constraints and a lack of expertise. Building innovation linkages with partners in the supply chain such as consumers, suppliers, competitors, universities, R&D laboratories, and consultants is essential for SMEs to overcome these barriers and effectively collaborate for green innovation (Love et al., 2014). Green market orientation (GMO) is a promising approach for SMEs to address environmental challenges and promote sustainability by aligning their operations with green market demands (Wang, 2020). This approach allows SMEs to take advantage of new opportunities in the growing green market while also improving their environmental performance.

Collaborating with suppliers is an effective strategy for SMEs to reduce the environmental impact of their supply chain. Wang et al. (2018) suggested that by working together, SMEs and suppliers can identify ways to minimize waste, reduce energy consumption, and use eco-friendly materials. Such collaborations can lead to a more sustainable supply chain, which benefits both the SME and the environment. Collaborating with customers is another way SMEs can promote green innovation. Hart (2005) argued that involving customers in the development of green products or services not only provides valuable insights into what consumers want but also creates a sense of ownership and loyalty. SMEs can gain a competitive advantage by meeting customer demand for environmentally friendly products while also reducing their carbon footprint. Participating in industry-wide initiatives is also an effective way for SMEs to promote green innovation. Sarkis and Cordeiro (2012) noted that industry-wide initiatives offer SMEs opportunities to network with other businesses, learn from each other's experiences, and gain access to knowledge and resources that may not be available otherwise. Such collaborations can lead to the development of new ideas and strategies for promoting green innovation in industry. SMEs that participate in industry-wide initiatives can also enhance their reputation and credibility as environmentally responsible businesses.

The literature on green practices in SMEs highlights the importance of collaboration with external stakeholders, including suppliers, customers, and industry-wide initiatives, to promote green innovation Wang et al. (2018) found that collaboration with suppliers is crucial for SMEs to reduce the environmental impact of their supply chain. Hart (2005) emphasized that collaborating with customers can lead to the development of new green products or services, resulting in a competitive advantage. Sarkis and Cordeiro (2012) argued that participating in industry-wide initiatives can help SMEs access knowledge, resources, and networks to promote green innovation. However, these collaborations require trust, shared vision, and communication among stakeholders. Therefore, several studies have emphasized the role of relational capabilities, such as trust, communication, and commitment, in facilitating collaborative green innovation (e.g., Zsidisin & Wagner, 2010; Zahra et al., 2020, David et al., 2022; Mehta et al., 2022a). The literature also highlights the need for SMEs to develop absorptive capacity, which refers to the ability to identify, assimilate, and apply external knowledge, to effectively collaborate for green innovation (e.g., JpJ et al., 2009; Annamalah et al., 2022). Overall, the literature suggests that collaboration with external stakeholders can be an effective strategy for SMEs to promote green innovation and enhance their performance.

Employee Involvement

Chen and Chang (2012) found that SMEs that provide training to their employees on green innovation are more likely to achieve success in adopting green practices. Providing employees with the necessary skills and knowledge to implement green innovation initiatives can help SMEs overcome the lack of expertise and resources that often hinder green innovation in smaller firms.

According to Weng et al. (2015), encouraging employee suggestions for improving environmental performance is crucial for SMEs to successfully adopt green practices. By involving employees in the process, SMEs can benefit from their knowledge and creativity, which can lead to the development of more innovative and effective green practices. Boiral (2009) argued that recognizing and rewarding employees who contribute to green innovation initiatives can be an effective way to motivate and engage employees in the adoption of green practices. Recognition and rewards can range from financial incentives to public recognition and can help SMEs create a culture of sustainability where employees are committed to environmental performance.

Over the last five years, literature has focused on the importance of providing training to employees on green innovation practices. Researchers have argued that providing training to employees is a critical step for SMEs to successfully implement green innovation strategies (Rodrigues & Franco, 2023). Additionally, it has been found that training can lead to increased employee engagement and participation in green innovation initiatives (Zhang et al., 2021). Moreover, some studies have suggested that SMEs that invest in employee training on green innovation can achieve better financial performance and gain a competitive advantage (Haiyan Li, 2022; Fang et al., 2022; Mehta et al., 2022b). Another area of focus in the literature has been employee involvement in green innovation initiatives. Researchers have highlighted the need for SMEs to encourage employee suggestions for improving environmental performance. It has been suggested that this can lead to increased employee commitment, job satisfaction, and organizational performance (Zaid & Jaaron, 2022). Furthermore, studies have shown that employee involvement in green innovation initiatives can lead to a more innovative and sustainable organizational culture (Yang et al., 2017).

The literature has also emphasized the importance of recognizing and rewarding employees who contribute to green innovation initiatives. Studies have suggested that rewarding employees for their contributions can increase employee motivation and engagement in green innovation activities (Bekhit et al., 2023). Furthermore, recognition and rewards can also help SMEs to retain talented employees and attract new talent.

Overall, the literature suggests that SMEs that invest in training, encourage employee involvement, and recognize and reward employee contributions to green innovation initiatives can achieve better environmental and financial performance, and gain a competitive advantage in the marketplace.

Environmental Performance

In 2015, international organizations such as the World Meteorological Organization (WMO) designated it as the year in human history when atmospheric carbon dioxide levels reached 400 parts per million. Policymakers and managers have come to realize the importance of green innovation in achieving sustainable company performance, given that environmental challenges are increasingly affecting corporate performance. To ensure the sustainability of green innovation, these authors argue that it must simultaneously address social, economic, and environmental considerations and be implemented alongside the Triple Bottom Line Model.

Green process innovation refers to measures aimed at reducing material and energy consumption, and thereby minimizing waste, by using renewable energy sources to increase the efficiency of industrial processes and reduce environmental impacts. This type of environmentally friendly innovation focuses on concerns such as pollution control, waste recycling, energy conservation, and eco-friendly design. Green entrepreneurial orientation has a positive impact on green innovation and can enhance return on investments, establish industry leadership in the adoption of green practices, and address the issue of resource costs through process innovation. A company's social, economic, and environmental performance benefits from the positive effects of green entrepreneurial orientation on green innovation. Therefore, green innovation is a crucial and popular topic for achieving both environmental and organizational success. The use of energy-efficient technology is one of the most adopted green innovation practices among SMEs. Many studies have shown that the adoption of energy-efficient technology can significantly reduce energy consumption and costs, leading to improved financial performance (Yang et al., 2011; Ali et al., 2021; Sharma et al., 2021a). Additionally, it can also lead to reduced carbon emissions, which is a critical step towards achieving sustainability goals.

SMEs are increasingly adopting renewable energy sources to reduce their carbon footprint. Renewable energy sources, such as solar and wind power, are becoming more accessible and affordable, making it easier for SMEs to adopt them. Studies have shown that the adoption of renewable energy sources can not only reduce carbon emissions but also improve a firm's reputation and brand image, leading to increased customer loyalty and sales (Nulkar, 2014).

Waste management is another crucial area where SMEs can adopt green innovation practices. By implementing a waste management system that reduces waste output, SMEs can not only reduce their environmental impact but also save costs associated with waste disposal. Studies have suggested that adopting a waste management system can lead to improved operational efficiency and reduced costs, leading to improved financial performance (De et al., 2020; Sharma et al., 2022). Moreover, it can also help SMEs comply with environmental regulations and enhance their reputation as socially responsible firms. Waste management is another area of focus in the literature on sustainable practices in SMEs. Several studies have highlighted the importance of implementing waste management systems that reduce waste output.

Over the last five years, literature has emphasized the importance of implementing sustainable practices within SMEs. Several studies have highlighted the benefits of adopting energy-efficient technology for reducing energy consumption in SMEs. For instance, Parrilli et al. (2023) found that the use of energy-efficient technology can help SMEs reduce their energy consumption and lower their operational costs. Similarly, some studies have investigated the impact of renewable energy sources on SMEs' carbon footprint. Caragliu (2021) found that the adoption of renewable energy sources can significantly reduce the carbon footprint of SMEs and improve their environmental performance. Furthermore, some studies have investigated the role of government policies and incentives in promoting sustainable practices in SMEs. For instance, several studies have highlighted the importance of government subsidies and incentives for encouraging SMEs to adopt sustainable practices. Additionally, researchers have suggested that government policies that promote sustainable practices can create a level playing field for SMEs and larger enterprises, thereby enabling SMEs to compete on an equal footing (Hrovatin et al., 2021; Graafland, & Smid, Hugo, 2016).

Customer Demand

As creatures of habit, humans engage in a multitude of daily routines that impact the environment, from transportation choices and purchasing decisions to waste disposal practices. To encourage sustainable consumer behaviors, it is essential to break harmful habits and foster positive ones. Green innovation is positively influenced by customer participation, particularly among Millennials who prioritize sustainability and purpose in their consumption choices. As a result, there has been a significant shift in the market demand for sustainable innovative products, prompting SMEs to reengineer their production processes and allocate renewable resources. This not only helps reduce manufacturing costs but also decreases the carbon footprint. To identify customer demand for eco-friendly goods and services, SMEs conduct market research, as noted by Hart (2005). Consequently, customers are increasingly aware of the need to choose long-lasting, eco-friendly products, driving SMEs to produce sustainable goods. According to Hart (2005), the SME has conducted market research to identify customer demand for green products or services. This research may have included surveys or focus groups to determine the environmental values and preferences of the target market. By understanding customer demand, the SME can tailor its green innovation initiatives to meet the needs and expectations of its customers, thereby increasing its competitive advantage and improving its environmental performance.

Sarkis and Cordeiro (2012) suggest that the SME has developed new green products or services in response to customer demand. This may involve redesigning existing products or creating new ones that align with the company's environmental values and meet customer needs. Developing green products or services can also help the SME differentiate itself from competitors and appeal to environmentally conscious consumers. Additionally, regular feedback can help the SME identify areas for improvement and potential opportunities for further green innovation (Xin et al., 2023).

One study by Finisterra et al. (2009) emphasized the importance of market research in identifying customer demand for green products and services. The researchers found that SMEs that conducted market research were more likely to succeed in their green innovation initiatives and were better able to meet the needs and preferences of their target market. Boiral (2009) asserts that the SME regularly solicits feedback from customers on its environmental performance and uses this feedback to improve its green innovation initiatives. By engaging with customers and incorporating their feedback into its green innovation initiatives, the SME can continuously improve its environmental performance and increase customer satisfaction.

Over the past five years, there has been significant research conducted on the topic of green innovation and its importance for small and medium-sized enterprises (SMEs). A study by Alyahya et al. (2023) focused on the importance of customer feedback in improving environmental performance. The researchers found that SMEs that regularly solicited feedback from customers were better able to identify areas for improvement and implement effective green innovation initiatives. Customer feedback was also found to be crucial in enhancing customer satisfaction and loyalty. Another study by Mauricio (2020) explored the role of product development in green innovation. Many studies have focused on various aspects of green innovation, including market research, product development, and customer feedback. The researchers found that SMEs that developed new green products or services were able to increase their competitive advantage and appeal to environmentally conscious consumers. Additionally, product development was found to be a key driver of green innovation for SMEs.

Similarly, a study by Ali et al. (2021) emphasized the importance of customer engagement in driving green innovation. The researchers found that SMEs that actively engaged with customers on environmental issues were more likely to succeed in their green innovation initiatives and were better able to identify new opportunities for innovation. Finally, a study by Jun et al. (2019) explored the factors that influence the adoption of green innovation by SMEs. The researchers found that factors such as financial constraints, lack of awareness, and inadequate government support can hinder the adoption of green innovation by SMEs. However, factors such as environmental values, customer demand, and competitive advantage were found to be strong drivers of green innovation for SMEs.

Overall, these studies highlight the importance of market research, product development, customer feedback, and customer engagement in driving green innovation for SMEs (Li et al., 2023). Additionally, the studies emphasize the need for government support and financial incentives to encourage the adoption of green innovation by SMEs.

Regulatory Compliance

Environmental conservation is of utmost importance, and regulatory compliance is a critical factor in implementing sustainable practices for manufacturing Small and Medium-sized Electric Vehicles (SMEVs). SMEVs that adhere to environmental regulations are better equipped to take actions that benefit the environment in the present, without jeopardizing the ability of future generations to meet their needs. Regulatory compliance, as supported by stakeholder theory, ensures that companies follow the standards set by the government to promote environmental preservation. The primary motivation for environmentally compliant SMEVs is environmental conservation, which translates to following the law. These companies strive to meet legal requirements and believe that complying with regulations is the right thing to do. Their management places a higher priority on protecting the environment. Pas studies have suggested that compliance with environmental regulations is crucial for promoting green development and sustainability practices. Similarly, it is documented that environmental compliance certification is a critical enabler of environmental sustainability. Furthermore, several studies have explored the link between environmental compliance and innovation in SMEs. It is found that environmental regulations can drive SMEs to innovate by promoting resource efficiency, eco-design, and green production practices. It is evidenced that SMEs can use environmental regulations as a source of competitive advantage by developing innovative eco-friendly products and services (Zhang & Ding, 2023; Ullah et el., 2021; Zhao et al., 2021; U et al., 2022; Yi et al., 2019).

Over the last five years, several research papers have highlighted the importance of environmental compliance and performance for SMEs. It is found that compliance with environmental regulations positively affects SMEs' financial performance. Furthermore, SMEs that go beyond compliance and adopt proactive environmental management practices can achieve greater environmental and economic benefits. Sendawula et al. (2021) emphasized the importance of complying with environmental regulations and standards at the local and national level for small and medium-sized enterprises (SMEs). Compliance not only helps SMEs avoid legal and financial penalties but also contributes to sustainable development and protects the environment. Wang et al. (2018) suggested that SMEs can develop policies and procedures to ensure compliance with environmental regulations. These policies can help SMEs identify environmental risks and implement measures to mitigate them. Moreover, such policies can enhance the credibility of SMEs and improve their reputation among stakeholders. According to Sarkis and Cordeiro (2012), environmental regulations can serve as a driver for innovation and improvement in SMEs' environmental performance. By complying with regulations, SMEs can identify areas for improvement and innovation, leading to increased efficiency and reduced environmental impact. Such practices can also result in cost savings and improved competitiveness in the market.

Overall, the literature suggests that environmental compliance and performance can benefit SMEs in various ways, including financial gains, enhanced reputation, and increased competitiveness. Policymakers and business leaders need to recognize the importance of environmental sustainability and implement measures to promote sustainable practices in SMEs.

Innovation Culture

Green product innovation involves making changes to product design, quality, and safety, as well as reducing the environmental impact of the entire product lifecycle, such as by minimizing production toxins, improving energy efficiency, and utilizing biodegradable packaging. In today's digitally competitive world, Small and Medium-sized Enterprises (SMEs) must develop internal digital skills to quickly adapt to market changes, support innovative performance, and drive development. Along with investing in human capital to increase employee digital literacy, the sociotechnical changes associated with Industry 4.0 production systems necessitate digital transformation through the use of digital technologies. Organizational learning, encompassing knowledge acquisition, behavioral and cognitive factors, and organizational aspects such as adaptability, engagement, mission, and consistency, all play a role in cultivating an innovation culture. SMEs are crucial to the economy, but they have only a marginal impact on innovation. While product innovation aims to enhance profitability, process innovation often leads to cost reduction (and consequently, greater productivity) and/or improvements in quality (Muisyo & Qin, 2020).

Encouraging experimentation and risk-taking can be an effective strategy for promoting green innovation within SMEs. The researchers suggested that by providing a supportive environment for trying out new ideas and taking calculated risks, SMEs can foster a culture of innovation that promotes sustainable practices. This approach may lead to the development of new green products, processes, and services that contribute to the company's long-term success. Providing resources and support to employees is critical to the success of green innovation initiatives within SMEs (Sharma et al., 2021a). Majali et al. (2022) suggest that creating an organizational culture that prioritizes environmental sustainability requires investing in human resources. By providing training, mentorship, and other resources, SMEs can empower employees to develop and implement green innovation initiatives. This approach may lead to the creation of new green products and services that enhance the company's competitiveness and reputation.

Creating a culture of continuous improvement through collaboration and innovation can help SMEs achieve their environmental sustainability goals. Boiral (2009) suggests that by engaging employees in ongoing discussions about environmental performance and encouraging collaboration across departments and functions, SMEs can develop new ideas for reducing their environmental impact. This approach may lead to the implementation of innovative practices and technologies that improve the company's environmental performance over time. Additionally, it can help SMEs build strong relationships with customers and other stakeholders who value sustainable practices.

Over the last five years, research on environmental sustainability has highlighted the importance of small and medium-sized enterprises (SMEs) in driving progress towards sustainability. One key area of focus has been on the role of SMEs in promoting green innovation, particularly through experimentation and risk-taking. To succeed in green innovation, SMEs must also provide resources and support for employees to develop and implement green initiatives (Majali et al., 2022; Wang et al., 2022).

Collaboration and knowledge sharing have also been identified as key drivers of sustainability in SMEs. By working together and sharing information, SMEs can promote innovation and progress in sustainability (Boiral, 2009; Wang et al., 2018; Yang et al., 2017). Furthermore, SMEs can also benefit from digital transformation and industry 4.0 production systems to enhance their innovative performance and development.

Overall, the literature suggests that SMEs play a crucial role in driving progress towards sustainability through green innovation, regulatory compliance, collaboration, and digital transformation. By promoting sustainability, SMEs can enhance their overall performance and build stronger relationships with stakeholders while also contributing to a more sustainable future.

Conclusion

The concept of green innovation and its significance in the current business and innovation landscape is highlighted in this summary. As stakeholders increasingly prioritize environmental and social considerations, companies are compelled to adopt sustainable development frameworks and showcase their efforts in promoting sustainability. Green innovation practices, such as recycling, eco-design, and energy conservation, have emerged as essential strategies for reducing carbon emissions, conserving resources, and mitigating the effects of global warming. The adoption of green practices is particularly relevant for small and medium-sized enterprises (SMEs), which possess characteristics that both favor and hinder green innovation. The commitment of leadership and the integration of green practices throughout the organization contribute to improved performance and competitiveness in the market.

Resource allocation plays a crucial role in the implementation of green practices. SMEs that fail to adopt green practices may experience a decline in performance due to increasing consumer awareness of environmentally friendly products. Entrepreneurial leadership and a green entrepreneurial orientation fosters innovative behavior and product innovation, resulting in exceptional performance for SMEs. Collaboration is another essential aspect of green innovation, as businesses need to adapt traditional models and cultivate a corporate culture that promotes green practices. While large enterprises may find it easier to execute green innovation due to their resources, SMEs need more resources and expertise. Establishing innovation linkages with various partners, including consumers, suppliers, competitors, and research institutions, can support green innovation in SMEs.

Employee involvement is crucial in driving green innovation practices within organizations. Green innovation encompasses managerial, systemic, and process-oriented practices that aim to minimize environmental impacts. For example, companies that prioritize social responsibility and employ innovative and environmentally friendly technologies contribute to integrating sustainability principles in their manufacturing processes. Additionally, SMEs are more inclined to engage in social, environmental, and green initiatives as they can lower costs and expenses through grants and subsidies.

The performance of SMEs is significantly influenced by green innovation. Environmental challenges and increasing awareness have led to a elaborated clarity of the significance of sustainable practices for corporate performance. Green process innovation, focused on minimizing material and energy consumption and employing renewable energy sources, contributes to environmental sustainability. In addition, green entrepreneurial orientation positively affects green innovation and overall organizational performance.

Customer demand plays a pivotal role in driving green innovation. Customers, particularly Millennials, express a preference for businesses that prioritize sustainability. As a result, SMEs have shifted from traditional products to sustainable, innovative products to meet market demands. Market research helps SMEs identify customer demand for green products and services, leading to re-engineering production processes and reducing the carbon footprint.

Regulatory compliance is essential for implementing environmental sustainability practices in manufacturing SMEs. Adhering to environmental standards enhances the chances of engaging in actions that benefit the environment. Stakeholder theory emphasizes the importance of regulatory compliance to ensure adherence to governmental regulations and promote environmental preservation.

Fostering an innovation culture is crucial for green product innovation. Product design, quality, and safety changes that reduce environmental impacts are essential components of green innovation. In addition, SMEs must invest in human capital and digital literacy to adapt to market changes and support innovation. Organizational learning, knowledge acquisition, and behavioral and cognitive factors contribute to an innovation culture within SMEs.

In summary, green innovation has become a critical topic in modern business and innovation literature due to the increasing awareness of environmental concerns. With their unique characteristics, SMEs face challenges and opportunities in implementing green practices. Innovation strategy, Resource allocation, collaboration, employee involvement, environmental performance, customer demand, regulatory compliance, and fostering an innovation culture are essential aspects of green innovation that contribute to sustainable business performance.

References

Ahmed, Z., & Ayham, J. (2022). "The Impact of Green Human Resource Management Practices with Sustainable and Operational Performance: A Conceptual Model", *Innovation of Businesses, and Digitalization during Covid-19 Pandemic*, 10.1007/978–3-031-08090–6_37 (583–610).

Albino, V., Balice, A., & Dangelico, R. M. (2012). "Environmental strategies and green product innovation in small and medium-sized enterprises (SMEs)", *Sustainability*, 4(8), 1518–1538.

Ali, Y., Younus, A., Khan, A.U. and Pervez, H. (2021), "Impact of Lean, Six Sigma and environmental sustainability on the performance of SMEs", *International Journal of Productivity and Performance Management*, 70(8), 2294–2318. https://doi.org/10.1108/IJPPM-11-2019-0528

Alyahya, M., Agag, G., Aliedan, M., & Abdelmoety, Z. H. (2023). "A cross-cultural investigation of the relationship between eco-innovation and customers boycott behaviour." *Journal of Retailing and Consumer Services*, 72, 103271.

Annamalah, S., Aravindan, K. L., Raman, M., & Paraman, P. (2022). "SME Engagement with Open Innovation: Commitments and Challenges towards Collaborative Innovation", *Journal of Open Innovation: Technology, Market, and Complexity*, *8*(3), page 146. https://doi.org/10.3390/joitmc8030146

Baum, J. R., & Locke, E. A. (2004). "The Relationship of Entrepreneurial Traits, Skill, and Motivation to Subsequent Venture Growth", *Journal of Applied Psychology*, *89*(4), 587–598. https://doi.org/10.1037/0021-9010.89.4.587

Bekhit, K., Leithy, E. W & Mahmoud, A. (2023). "The Impact of Green Human Resource Management Practices on Employee Retention and Environmental Sustainability: A Conceptual Model", 22. 1005–1034. 10.37896/YMER22.01/78.

Boiral, O. (2009). "Greening the corporation through organizational citizenship behaviors", *Journal of Business Ethics*, *87*(2), 221–236.

Brouthers, K. D., Gao, Y., & McNicol, J. P. (2020). *"The relationship between environmental sustainability and innovation in SMEs: The moderating role of stakeholder pressure" Journal of Business Research*, *113*, 173–183. doi: 10.1016/j.jbusres.2019.09.008

Caragliu, A. (2021). "Energy efficiency–enhancing policies and firm performance: Evidence from the paper and glass industries in Italy", *Energy Policy*, *156*, 112415 https://doi.org/10.1016/j.enpol.2021.112415.

Chen, Y. S., & Chang, C. H. (2012). "Enhancing firm sustainability through green supply chain management: A theoretical framework and empirical evidence", *Transportation Research Part E: Logistics and Transportation Review*, *48*(1), 25–38.

Chen, Y. S. (2008). "The Driver of Green Innovation and Green Image – Green Core Competence", *Journal of Business Ethics*, *81*, 531–543. https://doi.org/10.1007/s10551-007-9522-1

David S-V., Marcela Y. M., Néstor M. B., Jose A. G., & Katherine P. G. (2022). "Worldwide Research on Open Innovation in SMEs", *Journal of Open Innovation: Technology, Market, and Complexity*, *8*(1), 20.

De, D., Dey, P., Ghosh, S. & Pappu, R. (2020). "Impact of Waste Management Practices of Indian Small and Medium-Sized Manufacturing Enterprises on Their Financial Performance", 10.1007/978–981-13-7071-7_5.

Fahad, S., & Wang, J. (2018). "Farmers' risk perception, vulnerability, and adaptation to climate change in rural Pakistan", *Land Use Policy*, *79*, 301–309. doi:10.1016/j.landusepol.2018.08.

Fang, L., Shi, S., Gao, J., Li, X. (2022). "The mediating role of green innovation and green culture in the relationship between green human resource management and environmental performance", PLoS ONE 17(9): e0274820. https://doi.org/10.1371/journal.pone.0274820

Finisterra do Paço, A., Barata Raposo, M. & Filho, W. (2009). "Identifying the green consumer: A segmentation study", *Journal of Targeting, Measurement and Analysis for Marketing*, 17, 17–25 (2009). https://doi.org/10.1057/jt.2008.28

Gelenbe, E. & Caseau, Y. (2015). The impact of information technology on energy consumption and carbon emissions. *Ubiquity*, 2015(June), 1–15.

Gomaa Agag, G., Durrani, B.A., Shehawy, Y. M., Alharthi, M., Alamoudi, H., El-Halaby, S., Hassanein, A., & Abdelmoety, Z. H. (2023). "Understanding the link between customer feedback metrics and firm performance", *Journal of Retailing and Consumer Services*, *73*, 103301,

Graafland, J. & Smid, H. (2016). "Reconsidering the relevance of social license pressure and government regulation for environmental performance of European SMEs", *Journal of Cleaner Production*, *141*, 10.1016/j.jclepro.2016.09.171.

Haiyan, L. (2022). "Green Innovation, Green Dynamic Capability, and Enterprise Performance: Evidence from Heavy Polluting Manufacturing Enterprises in China", *Complexity*, Article ID 7755964, 13 pages, 2022. https://doi.org/10.1155/2022/7755964

Hansen, E. G. & Klewitz, J. (2012). "The Role of an SME's Green Strategy in Public-Private Eco-Innovation Initiatives: The Case of Eco profit", *Journal of Small Business and Entrepreneurship*, *25*(4), 451–477.

Hart, S. L. (2005). "Capitalism at the crossroads: Aligning business, earth, and humanity", Wharton School Publishing.

Hrovatin, N., Cagno, E., Dolšak, J., Zorić, J. (2021). "How important are perceived barriers and drivers versus other contextual factors for the adoption of energy efficiency measures: An empirical investigation in manufacturing SMEs", *Journal of Cleaner Production*, *323*, 129123.

Huang, C. Y., & Wang, S. S. (2021). "Innovation strategy and performance of SMEs: A moderated mediation model of dynamic capabilities and competitive intensity", *Journal of Business Research*, *133*, 684–693.

Jam, M. & Warda, J. (2020). "Impact of Green Human Resources Management Practices on Organizational Sustainability and Employee Retention: An Empirical Study Related to Educational Institutions", *iRASD Journal of Management. 2*, 38–48. 10.52131/joe.2020.0201.0014.

Jpj, J. D., Vanhaverbeke, W. W., Vja, V. V., & Mh, R. D. (2009). "Open innovation in SMEs: trends, motives and management challenges", Steel and Composite Structures.

Jun, W., Ali, W., Bhutto, M., Hadi, H., & Khan, N. (2019). "Examining the determinants of green innovation adoption in SMEs: a PLS-SEM approach", *European Journal of Innovation Management*. ahead-of-print. 10.1108/EJIM-05-2019-0113.

Khan, M. A. S., Du, J., Malik, H. A., Anuar, M. M., Pradana, M., Yaacob, M. R. B. (2022). "Green innovation practices and consumer resistance to green innovation products: Moderating role of environmental knowledge and pro–environmental behavior", *Journal of Innovation & Knowledge*, 7, 4, 100280.

Kitzinger, E., & Lettl, C. (2018). "Open innovation in SMEs: A systematic review of literature", *Journal of Small Business Management*, *56*(2), 191–212.

Leo, B. (2011). "New SME Financial Access Initiatives: Private Foundations' Path to Donor Partnerships", *Center for Global Development Working Paper*.

Li, B., Mousa, S., Reinoso, J. R. R., Alzoubi, H. M., Ali, A., Hoang, A. D. (2023). "The role of technology innovation, customer retention and business continuity on firm performance after post-pandemic era in China's SMEs", *Economic Analysis and Policy*, *78*, 1209–1220.

Love, J. H., Roper, S., & Vahter, P. (2014). "Learning from openness: The dynamics of breadth in external innovation linkages", *Strategic Management Journal*, *35*(11), 1703-1716.

Majali, T., Alkaraki, M., Asad, M., Aladwan, N., Aledeinat, M. (2022). "Green Transformational Leadership, Green Entrepreneurial Orientation and Performance of SMEs: The Mediating Role of Green Product Innovation", *Journal of Open Innovation: Technology, Market, and Complexity*, *8*(4), 191.

Mauricio, C.-V. (2020). "Product Innovation and Performance in SMEs: The Role of the Creative Process and Risk Taking", *Innovation: Organization & Management. 23*. 10.1080/14479338.2020.1811097.

Mehta, K., Sharma, R. & Chugh, A. (2017). "Management of Forex Risk Exposure: A Study of SMEs and Unlisted Non–Financial Firms in India", *International Journal of Applied Business and Economic Research, 15(*9), 43–54.

Mehta, K., Sharma, R., & Vyas, V. (2019). "Efficiency and ranking of sustainability index of India using DEA-TOPSIS", *Journal of Indian Business Research*, 11(2), 179–199. https://doi.org/10.1108/JIBR-02-2018–0057.

Mehta, K., Sharma, R., & Vyas, V. (2022). "A quantile regression approach to study the impact of aluminium prices on the manufacturing sector of India during the COVID era", *Materials Today: Proceedings*, *65*(8), 3506-3511, ISSN 2214-7853, https://doi.org/10.1016/j.matpr.2022.06.087.

Mehta, K., Sharma, R., Vyas, V. & Kuckreja, J.S. (2022). "Exit strategy decision by venture capital firms in India using fuzzy AHP", *Journal of Entrepreneurship in Emerging Economies*, *14*(4), 643–669. https://doi.org/10.1108/JEEE-05-2020–0146

Morrow D. & Rondinelli, D. (2002). "Adopting corporate environmental management systems: motivations and results of ISO 14,001 and EMAS certification", *European Management Journal*, *20*(2), 159–171.

Muisyo, Paul Kivinda & Qin, Su. (2020). "Enhancing the FIRM'S green performance through green HRM: The moderating role of green innovation culture", *Journal of Cleaner Production*, *289*, 125720.

Nulkar (2014). "SMEs and Environmental Performance – A Framework for Green Business Strategies", *Procedia – Social and Behavioral Sciences*, *133*, 130–140.

Parrilli, M. D., Balavac-Orlić, M., Radicic, D. (2023). "Environmental innovation across SMEs in Europe", *Technovation*, 119, 102541.

Purwandani, J. A., Michaud, G. (2021). "What are the drivers and barriers for green business practice adoption for SMEs?", *Environment Systems and Decisions*, *41*, 577–593. https://doi.org/10.1007/s10669-021-09821-3

Quang-Huy Ngo (2022). "The Adoption of Green Market Orientation in Logistic Industries – Empirical Evidence from Vietnamese SMEs", *Journal of Open Innovation: Technology, Market, and Complexity*, *8*(4), 199.

Rodrigues, M., & Franco, M. (2023). "Green Innovation in Small and Medium-Sized Enterprises (SMEs): A Qualitative Approach", *Sustainability*, *15*(5), 4510. MDPI AG. Retrieved from http://dx.doi.org/10.3390/su15054510

Sarkis, J. & Cordeiro, J. (2012). "Ecological Modernization in the Electrical Utility Industry: An Application of a Bads-Goods DEA Model of Ecological and Technical Efficiency", *European Journal of Operational Research*, *219*, 386–395. 10.1016/j.ejor.2011.09.033.

Sendawula, K., Turyakira, P., Ikiror, C. M. and Bagire, V. (2021), "Regulatory compliance and environmental sustainability practices of manufacturing entrepreneurial ventures in Uganda", Asia Pacific Journal of Innovation and Entrepreneurship, *15*(1), 62–74. https://doi.org/10.1108/APJIE-08-2020-0122

Sendawula, K., Bagire, V., Mbidde, C.I., & Turyakira, P. (2021). "*Environmental commitment and environmental sustainability practices of manufacturing small and medium enterprises in Uganda*." *Journal of Enterprising Communities: People and Places in the Global Economy*, 15(4), 588–607. https://doi.org/10.1108/JEC-07-2020-0132

Sharma, S., Prakash, G., Kumar, A., Mussada, E. K., Antony, J., Luthra, S. (2021). "Analysing the relationship of adaption of green culture, innovation, green performance for achieving sustainability: Mediating role of employee commitment", *Journal of Cleaner Production*, *303*, 127039.

Sharma, R., Mehta, K. & Goel, A. (2022). "Non-linear relationship between board size and performance of Indian companies", *Journal of Management and Governance* (2022). https://doi.org/10.1007/s10997-022-09651-8

Sharma, R., Mehta, K. and Sharma, O. (2021). "Exploring Deep Learning to Determine the Optimal Environment for Stock Prediction Analysis", *2021 International Conference on Computational Performance Evaluation, ComPE 2021*, 148–152.

Shouwen Wang, S., Abbas, J., Sial, M.S., Álvarez-Otero, S., Cioca, L. I. (2022). Achieving green innovation and sustainable development goals through green knowledge management: Moderating role of organizational green culture, *Journal of Innovation & Knowledge*, *7*(4), 100272.

u, G., Xu, Q., Niu, X. and Tao, L. (2022). "How Does Government Policy Improve Green Technology Innovation: An Empirical Study in China", *Frontiers in Environmental Science*, *9*:799794. doi: 10.3389/fenvs.2021.799794

Ullah, R., Ahmad, H., Rehman, F. U. & Fawad, A. (2021). "Green innovation and Sustainable Development Goals in SMEs: the moderating role of government incentives", *Journal of Economic and Administrative Sciences*. ahead-of-print. 10.1108/JEAS-07-2021-0122.

Wang, C. H. 2020. "An environmental perspective extends market orientation: Green innovation sustainability," *Business Strategy and the Environment*, Wiley Blackwell, vol. 29(8), pages 3123-3134.

Wang, J. & Ran, B. (2018). "Sustainable Collaborative Governance in Supply Chain", *Sustainability*. 10. 171. 10.3390/su10010171.

Wang, J., Zhang, Y., & Goh, M. (2018). "Moderating the role of firm size in sustainable performance improvement through sustainable supply chain management." *Sustainability*, *10*(5), 1654.

Weng, H.-H., Chen, J.-S., & Chen, P.–C. (2015). "Effects of Green Innovation on Environmental and Corporate Performance: A Stakeholder Perspective", *Sustainability*, *7*(5), 4997–5026. MDPI AG. Retrieved from http://dx.doi.org/10.3390/su7054997

Wu, G. Z., & You, D. M. (2019). "The influence mechanism of environmental regulation on technology innovation and green total factor productivity: Based on the moderating effect of fiscal decentralization", *Journal of Industrial Engineering and Management*, *33*, 37–50. (In Chinese). doi:10.13587/j.cnki.jieem.2019.01.005

Xin, Y., Khan, R. U., Dagar V., & Qian, F. (2023). "Do international resources configure SMEs' sustainable performance in the digital era? Evidence from Pakistan." *Resource Policy*, *80*, 103169.

Yang, M., Hong, P. & Modi, S. (2011), "Impact of lean manufacturing and environmental management on business performance: an empirical study of manufacturing firms", *International Journal of Production Economics*, *129*(2), 251–261.

Yang, Z., Sun, J., Zhang, Y., & Wang, Y. (2017). "Green, green, it's green: A triad model of technology, culture, and innovation for corporate sustainability." *Sustainability*, *9*(8), 1369.

Yi, M., Fang, X., Wen, L., Guang, F., and Zhang, Y. (2019). "The heterogeneous effects of different environmental policy instruments on green technology innovation", *Ijerph 16*, 4660. doi:10.3390/ijerph16234660

Zahra, S., Hossein, T., Royston, M. & Gary, G. (2020). "Supply chain digitalization: past, present and future", *Production Planning & Control*, 31:2–3, 96–114, DOI: 10.1080/09537287.2019.1631461

Zaid, A. A., Jaaron, A. A., & Bon, A. T. (2018). "The impact of green human resource management and green supply chain management practices on sustainable performance: An empirical study." *Journal of cleaner production*, 204, 965–979.

Zhang, B., Yang, L., Cheng, X., & Chen, F. (2021). "How Does Employee Green Behavior Impact Employee Well-Being? An Empirical Analysis", *International journal of environmental research and public health*, *18*(4), 1669. https://doi.org/10.3390/ijerph18041669

Zhang, Z., Dai, X., & Ding, Y. (2023). "Government environmental governance and firms' green innovation: Evidence from listed firms in heavy pollution industries of China", *Finance Research Letters*, 103848.

Zheng, M., Feng, G. F., Jiang, R. A., & Chang, C. P. (2023). "Does environmental, social, and governance performance move together with corporate green innovation in China?" *Business Strategy and the Environment*, *32*(4), 1670–1679.

Zhao, Y., Peng, B., Elahi, E., & Wan, A. (2021). "Does the extended producer responsibility system promote the green technological innovation of enterprises? An empirical study based on the difference-in-differences model", *Journal of Cleaner Production*, *319*, 128631. doi:10.1016/j.jclepro.2021.128631
Zhaojun, Y., Jun, S., Yali, Z., Ying, W., & Lisha, C. (2017). "Employees' collaborative use of green information systems for corporate sustainability: motivation, effort and performance", *Information Technology for Development*, 10.1080/02681102.2017.1335281, 23, 3 (486–506).
Zsidisin, G. A. and Wagner, S. M. (2010). "Do Perceptions Become Reality? The Moderating Role of Supply Chain Resiliency on Disruption Occurrence", *Journal of Business Logistics*, *31*, 1-20. https://doi.org/10.1002/j.2158-1592.2010.tb00140.x

Anupam Sharma* and Shivani Bajaj*

10 Impact of Sustainability and Green Finance on SMEs to Promote Green Growth

Abstract: In the current scenario, the entire functionality of the Indian economy can be transformed by Green Economy as it helps the nation's healthy growth and promotes a green economy. Green growth with minimal carbon emissions depends on green finance. As it connects the environmental improvement, financial industries and economic growth of the country for a country like India to sustain and survive in the long run in this competitive world, Green finance is required in the country. Generally, the term green finance is also referred to as an innovative tool in the area of Finance as it depicts various forms of financing for various projects, environment-based technologies, businesses or industries. The main aim of this chapter is to make their operation Green. This means minimizing or reducing those activities or operations which contain a harmful impact on the economy.

Apart from green ginance, for green economy and economic growth, sustainability finance is also required in the country as it supports better development and funding for the nation's and the world's economic growth. Corporations, International Financial institutions, and banks are the key Sustainable finance providers to companies and MSMEs through various Financial instruments like Green Bonds, Climate Funds, impact Finance, Social Bonds, SIDBI Sustainable green finance scheme for funding, NABARD, Microfinance, Make in India.

The study demonstrates that government actions have given the MSME sector a tremendous chance to supply the right product, quality, and solution at a competitive price and better contribute to the nation's green economic growth. Additionally, banks and other financial institutions have been able to advance this growth thanks to the guidelines set by the RBI. The government's and the RBI's policy directives will assist businesses in implementing environmentally friendly practices that promote economic growth.

The main aim of this chapter is to explore the term green finance. And how it is helpful in India for Micro, Small, and Medium Enterprises if it uses its various products and services. The focus of this chapter is to explore the impact of Sustainability, Green Finance on Micro, Small, and Medium enterprises to promote Green Growth.

Note: We have no conflicts of interest to disclose. All co-authors have seen and agree with the contents of the manuscript and there is no financial and non-financial interest to report. We certify that submission is original work.

***Corresponding author: Anupam Sharma**, MM Institute of Management, MMDU, Mullana,
e-mail: anupam.sharma@mmumullana.org
***Corresponding author: Shivani Bajaj**, MM Institute of Management, MMDU, Mullana
e-mail: shivani.bajaj@mmumullana.org

https://doi.org/10.1515/9783111170022-010

This chapter also increases academic understanding by emphasizing opportunities available to various sectors.

Keywords: Green economy, Green finance, Green finance initiatives, Sustainability finance, Sustainable Development Goals, MSMEs

Introduction

In today's scenario, the overall functionality of the economy can be shaped by the Green Economy; Green Finance is necessary for the country's sustainable growth and a greener economy. It is an integral part of low-carbon green growth as it connects the environmental improvement of financial industries and the country's economic growth. For a country like India to sustain itself and survive in the long run in this competitive world, Green Finance is required in the country; this has become crucial for businesses as well as for the environment also. Generally, the term Green Finance is also referred to as an innovative tool in the area of Finance as it depicts a wide range of funding for various projects, environment-based technologies, businesses, or industries. It refers to the principle of 'Green Credit'. It means various financial institutions and commercial banks conduct research to generate facilities for pollution treatment for ecological protection. Green Finance refer as corporate social responsibility so that every firm should do something for society similarly (Carroll, 1979). Expert also said firms like mutual fund companies, banks, and stock companies conduct some CSR activity in terms of Green financing, which may not be profitable but focused on some environmental improvement, economic growth and ultimately finance industry development (Koo, 2010).

As such, there is no prescribed definition of Green Finance; in simple terms, Green Finance refers to money-related assistance for the development terms of 'Green', which helps decrease the air poison discharges and ozone depletion substances. 'IFC' defines this as the organization's financing that provides a win-win situation for both environmental quality improvement and economic development. Zadek and Flynn define this as Green Investment. It has a variety of definitions and connotations in both academia and industry. According to UNFCCC, "Green finance" refers to "local, national or transnational financing drawn from the private, public and various alternative sources of financing that help to adapt actions that lead to climate change". Green development focuses on vitality imperatives, changes in the environment, and finance-related emergencies in the whole world. Green growth or development means balanced green economic growth (see Figure 10.1). This represents growth with a new driving force, i.e. "Green", to acquire various eco-friendly opportunities and improve companies' manufacturing process by adopting green knowledge and technology and using the resources and energy (Noh, 2010). As in the rest of the globe, the ecological imbalance is brought on by excessive emissions of gases into the atmosphere, such as carbon dioxide, which causes global warming. Because of this concept of Green investment, Green Technology, Green funding, and many more Green initiatives come into the picture that comes under one head, 'Green Finance' (Chopra et al., 2005). Government should boost green consumption by promoting green products. Green finance is an integral part of the green economy and growth as it provides funding business opportunities, and if this is not strong, then there will be no sale of green products (Rutherford, 1994).

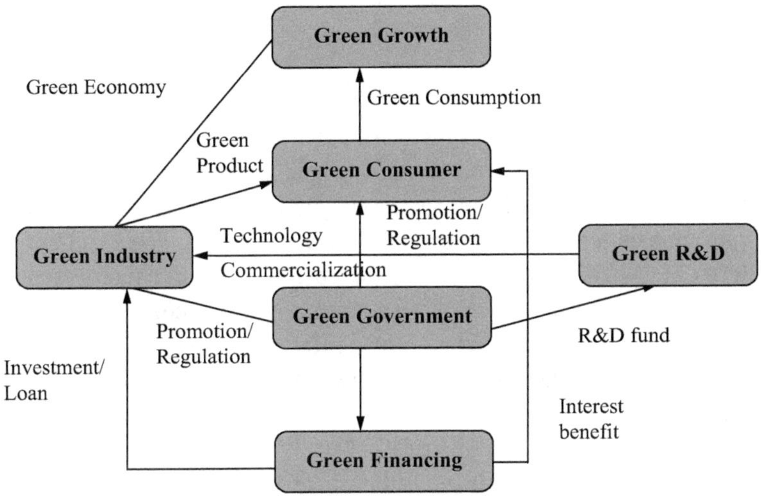

Figure 10.1: Relationship Between Green Finance and Green Growth.
Source: Koo (2010).

Green economy refers to the economy in which growth of income and employment is derived from the investment of private and public that minimized pollution and carbon emissions and prevented the loss of the ecosystem. Green growth can be defined as an approach of ecological principles for shaping the economic processes for generating income and employment opportunities and reducing environmental impact. Green finance is an approach to transforming low-carbon and resource-efficient economies to adapt to climate change (Figure 10.2). This refers to a strategy for government and financial institutions to address an issue like biodiversity loss and climate change (Dziwok & Jager, 2021).

Working green finance is based on various Green technologies and Green industries, but all these are at different maturity levels and require different funding from different sources. These are classified into three sources- Domestic public finance (direct funding from the government), international public finance (funding from multinational corporations and multilateral banks), and private sector finance are the three main categories (funding from both domestic as well as international). Green Finance provides the following benefits to the economy.

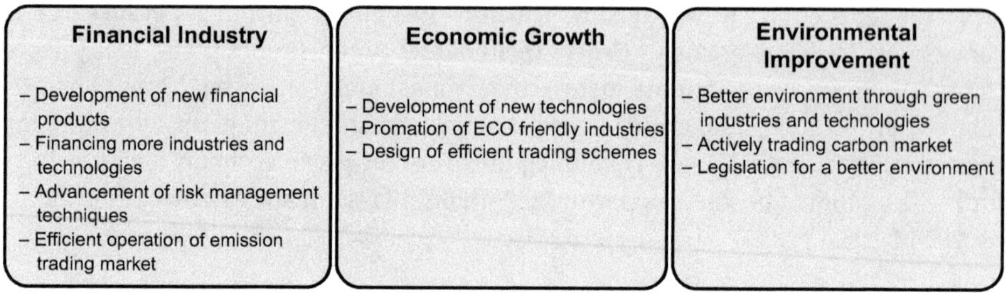

Figure 10.2: Green Finance.
Source*:* Noh (2010).

For Green Growth, the following green products are required to study such (i) Retail Financial services that include items like green mortgages, green home loans, green commercial building loans, green car loans, green credit cards, and green home equity loans. (ii) Asset management consists of Natural Disaster Bonds, Eco Funds, Carbon Funds, Eco RTFs, and Treasury Funds. (iii) Corporate Finance covers carbon financing, green project financing, green private equity, green securitization, and green technology leasing. (iv) Insurance covers autos, catastrophes, carbon emissions, and the environment. Through Green financing, the government is trying to fulfill the following objectives:

- Financial support for green growth industries.
- Creating innovative financial solutions that promote green, low-carbon growth.
- To build green infrastructure and attract private investments.

Apart from green finance, for green economy and economic growth, sustainability finance is also required in the country as It supports greater development and finance for the nation's and the world's economic progress. Sustainability finance is the process of considering Environment, Social, and Governance into account while making or taking financial-related decisions in the financial sector leading to increased economic projects and activities. Sometimes green finance is also known as Environmental Finance, Sustainability Finance, Green Investment, and Climate Finance; the ultimate goal of all these is to benefit the economy as a whole.

Micro, small, and medium-sized enterprises somehow helped the economy achieve this goal as approximately 6.5 crore MSMEs in India are working and contributing almost 30% to the GDP, employing almost 11 crores individuals and contributing 40% in exports. Because of this large size and impact, active participation of micro, small, and medium-sized enterprises is important for achieving a low-carbon transition. Moreover, in MSMEs, there is a clear 'Green transition' globally because of private and public finance or investment flows, and this provides an opportunity to strengthen their performances, improve operational efficiency and reduce risk.

Literature Review

Nowadays, green finance is referred to as an emerging indicator of economic growth as it considers both economic and environmental development. This is referred to as a futuristic tool that focuses on economic growth, environmental protection, and the development of the industry. Even before the global financial crisis, green growth attracted interest as a new economic growth driver that was capable of both environmental and economic development. In this way, green financing plays a crucial part in promoting green growth. Small and medium-sized businesses should concentrate on establishing their companies on the sustainable development, waste management, and resource conservation concepts that are essential for the green economy. For SMEs, implementing green technologies and environmentally friendly practices might be difficult due to a lack of funding, awareness, and education. In addition to infrastructure issues, SMEs often have issues with access to funding, which worsens their condition and casts doubt on their ability to survive and expand. For SMEs to grow their businesses and create new products, financing is crucial.

Generally speaking, green finance is future-focused and works to advance the financial sector, the economy, and environmental conservation. Green finance targets economic activities that are green, like venture financing, SME business financing, and export financing. It can be divided into two categories: funding for green growth and funding for reducing environmental costs. Micro, small, and medium-sized enterprises are the supporter of economic growth and the national economy.

An extensive literature review on sustainable finance has been done, and the impact of sustainability and green finance on MSMEs was observed from various studies to find out inclusive growth, MSMEs have a great potential for job creation. There are various indicators of sustainability regarding sustainability development (Freimann, ham & Mijoc, 2014). Experts explored that various nations have created Green Growth in terms of infrastructure and protection of the environment, and for all these, there is a need for Green Technology innovation like the use of renewable and non-renewable resources (Acemoglu & et al., 2016). Government can support robust micro, small, and medium-sized enterprises only when government accomplishes SDGs. A positive correlation between financial performance, innovation, and economic growth, and he also explored that MSMEs in India are more focused on the environment via sustainable innovation (Oncioiu et al., 2017).

Developing strong SMEs would be necessary for countries to achieve the SDGs. The researcher emphasized the need for policies to establish a positive business climate in order to increase the productivity of SMEs while discussing the significance of SMEs in innovation, employment generation, gender equality, inclusive development, etc. (Kamal-Chaoui, 2017). He expressed concern about the funding of SMEs, their involvement in global value chains, banking sector reforms, and innovative methods of financing.

It was discovered in the study that going green has the potential to improve the performance of Micro, Small, and Medium-Sized Enterprises in India due to increased sales and decreased cost expenses, which ultimately results in the creation of jobs and financial gain (Koirala, 2018).

The goals of sustainability and the capacity of micro, small & medium-sized enterprises to achieve sustainability just because of the support from government initiatives and the use of Ministry policies approaches of promoting industry waste management, credit finance approach, lean manufacturing, and MSMEs entrepreneur's awareness programs.

The term Sustainability finance is nothing but the process of considering Environment, Social, and Governance into the account while making or taking financial-related decisions in the financial sector leading to increased economic projects and activities. Globally, it has become a powerful movement led by institutional investors, asset managers and regulators. Sustainability, however, is a very evolving and complex area. Sustainability development restores and protects the country's ecological system. The World Bank, SIDBI, and NITI Aayog pave the way for sustainable finance to inspire and motivate companies to develop from small and medium-sized businesses into very large organisations and industries that have a profound global effect.

Micro, small, and medium-sized companies (MSME) produce 33.4% of India's manufacturing output, which contributes to the nation's economic growth, as well as 6.11% and 24.63% of the GDP of the nation, respectively. SIDBI employs these strategies to fund MSMEs, bringing sustainable financing to MSMEs to support long-term environmental initiatives. Promoting low carbon, effective renewable resource use, and increased MSMEs' profitability are the main objectives of funding the green revolution.

The study sheds light on green growth via sustainable technology and innovation. His study concluded that a sustainable society and increased economic growth are benefits of enterprise, government, and consumers. Early 1970s government policy, collaboration in technical development, and the concept of "green growth" were all highlighted in the report. These factors have a favorable effect on reducing climate change (Fernandes et al., 2021).

More foreign direct investment should be promoted in the development of cutting-edge technologies in MSMEs. Collaboration with international partners is essential to addressing climate change, and major corporations are switching to green energy to reduce their negative environmental effects and align regulations with the green economy (Mahesh et al., 2022).

The findings indicate that MSMEs' use of digital platforms for marketing, promotion, and communication, as well as their creative financial practices during a crisis, had a favourable and significant impact on their long-term financial performance. Additionally, the financial assistance provided by the government through banking waivers and Covid-19 positively impacted MSMEs' ability to survive and recover financially. This research makes a contribution by highlighting the crucial aspect of successful policymaking that has been shown to mediate the link between financial support from the government and the long-term success of MSMEs (Kurniawan et al., 2023).

In this chapter, the focus is more on Sustainable and Green Financing for Micro, Small, and Medium-Sized Enterprises to promote Green Growth in India.

Objectives

- To study and explain the term Sustainable Finance and Green Finance.
- To understand the role of MSMEs in achieving Green Growth.
- To assess the development of Sustainable Finance in India.

Research Methodology

In order to support green growth, this study examined the effects of sustainability and green finance on SMEs using available sources and secondary data. A descriptive approach is used for this study. Data was collected from various well-known articles, magazines, journals, Internet websites, and various other sources. Most of the data was collected from the United Indian Nations website and the Indian Government Ministry of Micro, Small, and Medium-sized Enterprises.

Data Analysis & Interpretation

Explanation of Green Finance and Sustainable Finance

In simple terms, green finance refers to money-related assistance for the development in terms of 'Green', which helps in decreasing air poison discharges and ozone depletion substances. Green finance' refers to "local, national or transnational financing drawn from the private, public and various alternative sources of financing that help to adapt actions that leads to climate change". It is a strategy for changing economies to be low-carbon and resource-efficient in order to adapt to climate change. This refers to a strategy for government and financial institutions to address an issue like biodiversity loss and climate change (Dziwok & Jager, 2021). It is a type of Financing that contribute to the environment and promotes sustainability in the nation. The term Sustainability finance is nothing but the process of considering Environment, Social, and Governance into the account while making or taking financial-related decisions in the financial sector leading to increased economic projects and activities.

Role of MSMEs in Achieving Green Growth

In earlier times, Sustainable and Green finance was the primary concern for the Indian government. Various initiatives were taken by the Indian government to balance the economic as well as sustainability development like 'Make in India' and 'Zero Defect and Zero Effect'. Despite various challenges, MSMEs play a significant role in the growth of the economy by generating a variety of job possibilities and fostering ecosystems, which helps to promote social and economic development. As per the FICCI report on MSMEs, it was observed that MSMEs sectors are contributing almost 45% in output of manufacturing, 40% in exports, 95% in Industries, and almost 30% in GDP and creating job opportunities for almost 60 million individuals in rural areas. They have ownership of natural resources. Because of this, they are more conscious of the environment. Because of this, MSMEs have a positive impact on understanding and tackling climate change and implementing sustainability in production as well as consumption strategies.

United Nations, in 2015, adopted several sustainability development goals worldwide to end poverty and to protect the environment so that individuals can enjoy peace & prosperity by 2030.

Role of MSMEs in Achieving Sustainability Development

- Provide jobs to almost 60 million individuals in 11 lakh organisations and businesses all over India.
- The goal of sustainable development is to reduce or end up hunger by 2030. Understand the sustainable food production system and make up the farmers and food producers by providing access to land, equipment, market, and technology.
- Under this, they are arranging various awareness camps across India, especially in rural areas providing facilities regarding free health checks, medical checks, free ambulance services, etc., to enhance good health and well-being.
- In this goal, SDG's target is to provide quality education across India, and MSMEs support them by opening various schools in backward and rural areas. Basically, they are developing the talents of youngsters in rural areas. To know more about SDGs see Figure 10.3.
- Ending all discrimination among females, they are empowering women and advancing gender equality. Almost in India, there are around 123 lakh women entrepreneurs.
- The scarcity of water affects almost 40% of individuals and raises temperature also. To come out of these, they invest in infrastructure, reduce containment levels, provide sanitation facilities, eliminate dumping activities, encourage hygiene, and restrict the release of hazardous material, which increase water quality and sanitation.

- Developing infrastructure and advancing technology to generate more renewable energy and energy-efficient products.
- Promote sustainable economic growth. Creating jobs and encouraging startups is key to this as they increased the contributions of industries in exports, Job creation, and GDP.
- Contributing almost 40% in output of manufacturing units and 45% in total export.
- Various initiatives were taken, like the urban renewal project, that led to sustainable cities or more inclusive ones.
- Implemented responsible production and consumption practices that are more inclined towards renewable resources and decreasing the release and use of harmful waste.
- Focused more on the environment by adopting green manufacturing strategies and by using green resources.
- Observe the life underwater and focus on waste management, water purity and cleaning up of the environment.
- Restriction on the overuse of resources from the forest.
- Restriction on the exploitation of females and use of child labour.
- To attain self-sufficiency, there is a requirement to attain collaboration between commercial and public sectors.

Figure 10.3: Sustainable Development Goals.
Source*:* undp.org.

Assessment of Development of Sustainable Finance in India

- Climate change was estimated by the World Bank, which has an impact on the standard of living of individuals and can reduce the GDP of India by 3%.
- Neev funds, SBI Cap, and SBI gives 100 million dollars to various firms in India for the development of waste management, electronic vehicles, and optimum utilization of resources.
- Various CSR activities, international solar alliances of organizations like the UN, G20, OECD, EIB, etc., various banks, national-international financial institutions, institutional investors, and governments are the key players for Green or sustainable finance in India.
- It was estimated that 50 million new job opportunities will be created by the green economy of India by 2030 and 15 trillion by 2070.
- As part of the overall sustainable development and green growth of the economy, many organizations like the RBI, NABARD, SIDBI, and NITI Ayog have taken the following steps:
- In the years 2012 and 2015, By examining the environmental risk to the development of agricultural goods, RBI devised a number of projects for sustainable development in the areas of social infrastructure, housing, and renewable energy. SIDBI had launched sustainable finance schemes for MSME development. They also finance MSMEs with the intention that MSME uses renewable resources and low carbon. NABARD made accessibility of climate finance to MSMEs for sustainable development and also provided green technology for the development of various projects. NITI Ayog also launched a program by the name 'Shoonya'- the adoption of electric vehicles in urban areas, which directly and indirectly reduces the demand for petrol and diesel, CO2, and GHG emissions.

Conclusion

The implementation of climate change requires international cooperation, and MSMEs are converting to green energy to lessen the environmental effect of their operations and draw regulatory attention to the green economy. All ESG funds are Sustainable finance that helps not only the environment and the economy but also investors and businesses. To draw in more foreign direct investment, MSMEs are urged to develop cutting-edge technologies in waste management, renewable energy, ecotourism, organic agriculture, and ecotourism. The government must initiate the policy changes necessary to embrace green or sustainable finance in the ESG global wave.

Using the research as a foundation, we have some suggestions. It would be possible for MSMEs to acquire more sophisticated manufacturing methods and increase their efficiency in terms of value and quantity if MSMEs and TNC (Transnational Corporations) affiliates had better connections. High-growth suppliers can promote more investment and even boost the development benefits of foreign direct investment. The Indian government must create distinct financial institutions for advising and refinancing financial intermediaries regarding appropriate policy, regulation, climate transition risks, and legal and market changes to support the Sustainable Development Goals (SDGs) for MSMEs and a low-carbon, climate–resilient world.

These organizations must also incorporate governance, social, and environmental. To decrease pollution and increase the use of electric vehicle charging stations, an economically and environmentally sound answer is required. The institutional credit support mechanism needs to be improved. A support network must be created in addition to lending options so that MSMEs can discuss their problems and seek advice from authorities. The credit plus plan of Mudra Bank is one such support program.

References

Acemoglu, D., Autor, D., Dorn, D., Hanson, G. H., & Price, B. (2016). Import competition and the great US employment sag of the 2000s. *Journal of Labor Economics, 34*(S1), S141–S198.

Bharati, D., & Patra, G. (2022). "The Challenges For SMEs In Green Finance Initiatives Adoption", *Journal of Positive School Psychology, 6(2s), 313–325.*

Carroll, A. B. (1979). A three-dimensional conceptual model of corporate performance. *Academy of management review, 4*(4), 497–505.

Carroll, A. B. (2016). "Carroll's pyramid of CSR: taking another look", *International Journal of Corporate Social Responsibility, 1(1), 1–8.*

Chopra K., Kumar P. (2005): Ecosystems and Human WellBeing: Our Human Planet: Summary for Decision Makers. Millennium Ecosystem Assessment, Island Press, Washington D.C.

Dziwok, E., & Jäger, J. (2021). "A classification of different approaches to green finance and green monetary policy", *Sustainability, 13(21), 11902.*

Fernandes, C. I., Veiga, P. M., Ferreira, J. J., & Hughes, M. (2021). Green growth versus economic growth: do sustainable technology transfer and innovations lead to an imperfect choice? *Business Strategy and the Environment*, 30(4), 2021–2037.

Freimann, A., Ham, M., & Mijoc, J. (2014, April). "Measuring Objective Well-Being and Sustainable Development." *Journal of Knowledge Management, Economics and Information Technology, IV*(2).

Ghosh, K. (2022). "Green Finance Initiatives in India", *IUP Journal of Accounting Research & Audit Practices, 21(2).*

Kamal-Chaoui, L., & Watts, M. (2017). "Climate, inequality and cities: How the world's mayors can make a difference". https://doi.org/10.1787/98d29a13-en

Kamal-Chaoui, L. (2017, April 3). Unlocking the potential of SMEs for the SDGs. Retrieved from OECD DEVELOPMENT MATTERS: https://oecd-developmentmatters.org/2017/04/03/unlocking-the-potentia lof-smes-for-the-sdgs/#fn2

Keerthi, B. S. (2013). "A Study on Emerging Green Finance in India: Its Challenges and Opportunities", *International Journal of Management and Social Sciences Research, 2(2), 49–53.*

K.M, Aithal, S., & K R S, Sharma. (2022). "Impact of Sustainable Finance on MSMEs and other Companies to Promote Green Growth and Sustainable Development", *International Journal of Applied Engineering and Management Letters, 6(1),* 60–76. 10.47992/IJAEML.2581.7000.0120.

Knaack, P., & Volz, U. (2022). "Inclusive green finance. Scaling Up Sustainable Finance and Investment in the Global South".

Koirala, S. (2019). "SMEs: Key drivers of green and inclusive growth".

Koirala, B. P., van Oost, E., & van der Windt, H. (2018). "Community energy storage: A responsible innovation towards a sustainable energy system?" Applied Energy, 231, 570–585.

Koo J.H. (2010): The Current Status and Future of Green Finance. Finance VIP series 2010–01, Korea Institute of Finance.

Koo, J., Son, D., & Jeon, Y. (2010). "Sustainable (Green) Finance: Efficient and Effective Investment Strategies for Green Technologies", *Environmental and Resource Economics Review, 19(3), 659–688.*

Kurniawan,, Maulana, A., & Iskandar, Y. (2023). "The Effect of Technology Adaptation and Government Financial Support on Sustainable Performance of MSMEs during the COVID-19 Pandemic", *Cogent Business & Management, 10(1), 2177400.*

Make the SDGs a Reality, Department of Economic and Social Affairs, Sustainable Development *Retrieved from* http://sustainabledevelopment.un.org

Mahesh, K. M., Aithal, P. S., & Sharma, K. R. S. (2022). Seven Pillars of Inclusive Ecosystem-Transforming Healthcare Special reference to MSME & SME sectors. International Journal of Case Studies in Business, IT, and Education *IJCSBE*, 6(1).

Ministry of Micro, Small & Medium Enterprises, Government of India Retrieved from http://msme.gov.in

Noh H.J. (2010a). Financial Strategy to Accelerate Innovation for Green Growth. Korea Capital Market Institute.

Noh H.J. (2010b). Strategic Approaches to Develop Green Finance. Korea Capital Market Institute.

Petrescu, A. G., Oncioiu, I., & Petrescu, M. (2017). Perception of organic food consumption in Romania. *Foods*, 6(6), 42.

Roopa, T. N., & Rajan, N. (2012). "Green Finance-The Trends and Opportunities", *Asia Pacific Journal of Management & Entrepreneurship Research, 1(2), 239.*

Rutherford, M. (1994): At what point can pollution be said to cause damage to the Environment? *The Banker, January*: 10–11.

Shubha, B. N., & Sushma, R. (2018). "Sustainable green economic growth through "green finance".

Singh, S., Jindal, J., Tikkiwal, V. A., Verma, M., Gupta, A., Negi, A., & Jain, A. (2022). "Electric vehicles for low-emission urban mobility: current status and policy review for India", *International Journal of Sustainable Energy, 41(9), 1323–1359.*

Sinha, A. K., Mishra, A. K., Manogna, R. L., & Prabhudesai, R. (2023). "Determinants of sustainable financial and innovation performance: a panel data analysis of Indian manufacturing SMEs", *International Journal of Business and Globalisation, 33(1–2), 113–129.*

Smith, T. (2018). "Adaptation of MSMEs to climate change: a review of the existing literature. Private-sector action in adaptation: Perspectives on the role of micro, small and medium-sized enterprises", *p. 19.*

Soundarrajan, P., & Vivek, N. (2016). "Green finance for sustainable green economic growth in India", *Agricultural Economics, 62(1), 35–44.*

Verma, T. L. (2019). "Role of micro, small and medium enterprises (MSMEs) in achieving sustainable development goals", *Small And Medium Enterprises (MSMEs) In Achieving Sustainable Development Goals (April 1, 2019).*

Yacob, P., Wong, L. S., & Khor, S. C. (2019). "An empirical investigation of green initiatives and environmental sustainability for manufacturing SMEs", *Journal of Manufacturing Technology Management, 30(1), 2–25.*

Bhaveshkumar J. Parmar and Chirag Rasikbhai Patel

11 Progress Intention and Sales Revenue Growth in Micro, Small and Medium Enterprises (SMEs)

Abstract: Small and Medium Enterprises (SMEs) have a pivotal role in creating new jobs and national income generation. For more than the last five decades, SMEs have proved to be vivacious and vigorous contributors to the economy of India. The Micro, small and medium enterprise sector has gained a noticeable place in the nation's socio-economic growth during the last six decades. The noticeable reforms started back in 1991 in the country, full of opportunities for SMEs to grow big. The purpose of the study was to scrutinize the Sales Revenue Growth of SMEs working in the manufacturing sector and its impact on the development of SMEs.

Keywords: Financial competitiveness, SMEs, Progress intention, Manufacturing enterprises

Introduction

The manufacturing industry in India is the main driver of growth because it helps the country's employment, agricultural, and service sectors (Mehta et al., 2022b). As a result, it is the most important part of the Indian economy, according to a joint report on the Global Manufacturing Competitiveness Index (GMCI) by Deloitte and the US Council on Various Dimensions of Competitiveness. In the years to come, India will dominate the global manufacturing sector. India is a resource-rich country that is quickly emerging as a manufacturing powerhouse for international players because of its competent and reasonably priced labour force, welcoming business incentives, and constantly growing worldwide reputation. The emergence of globalization has increased the competitive pressures on regional Micro, Small, and Medium Enterprises (SMEs) in both local and international markets, along with the expansion of regional economic integration. Despite their apparent flaws, such as their small size and limited resources, India still has a thriving, commercial, and increasingly globalized SME sector, according to a 1995 Hall quote. Since SMEs have not been eliminated by globalization and local integration, their contribution and role have changed as they fight to

Bhaveshkumar J. Parmar, School of Management Studies, National Forensic Sciences University, Gandhinagar, Gujarat, India
Chirag Rasikbhai Patel, Department of Business Management, Sankalchand Patel College of Engineering, Sankalchand Patel University, Visnagar

https://doi.org/10.1515/9783111170022-011

maintain a competitive edge in both local and international markets (Harvie & Lee, 2002a, 2005; OECD, 2006; Mehta et al., 2017). Sudan (2005) identified the obstacles to the growth of SMEs as well as the issues with policy that were brought up by several SMEs-related questions in 2005. He notes in his research that the government of India has tried to create an SME sector in all its initiatives. This has aided in the creation of a vast economy, job prospects, and financial chances. According to Subrahmanya (1995), these policy changes have extended the scope of SMEs and presented several new obstacles. Technology advancement and easy adaptation must be emphasized in such policy texts. SMEs will be able to compete and take on global issues thanks to the strong infrastructural components, particularly those relating to finance. According to Gunasekaran et al. (2011), SMEs also struggle with issues such as a lack of technical knowledge, a lack of funding, a lack of time and space, and upgrading manufacturing processes. SMEs are defined differently in every nation. Different entities have defined SMEs based on benchmarks for employment, based on all assets, in terms of sales turnover, and in terms of shareholder's funds.

Gujarat, an Indian state, has long been referred to be the "land of entrepreneurs." Gujarat has become India's most popular location for commercial investment during the past 20 years. Over the past five years, Gujarat has been able to grow at a rate of over 10% annually. This state, which frequently steals the show at international conferences, contributes 16% of the nation's industrial output and 22% of all Indian exports. Gujarat offers several benefits that make investing easy, including good infrastructure, a skilled and semi-skilled population, outstanding domestic and international connectivity, and abundant natural resources. The main differentiator for Gujarat is its investor-friendly policies and propensity for industrial development.

In terms of India, the SME sector has made a significant contribution to the nation's growth during the past 70 years on both the social and financial fronts. India's economic reforms, which got underway in 1991, allowed SMEs to expand rapidly. At the nation's current monetary valuations, manufacturing/production in SMEs accounts for about 33% of the nation's total manufacturing GV (Gross Value) of output. Additionally, the small sector had 3.31 lakh estimated SMEs, while the medium sector had 0.05 lakh, accounting for 0.52% and 0.01% of all estimated SMEs, respectively. 324.88 lakh SMEs, or 51.25 per cent of the total 633.88 SMEs, are in rural areas, and 309 lakh SMEs, or 48.75 per cent, are in urban areas. The industrial sector currently includes more than 1200 big industries and more than 3,45,000 MSMEs. According to ISED Small Enterprise Observatory (Source: Gujarat MSME Report 2013), Gujarat State is ranked first in the nation for the integration of SME performance at the national level.

The empirical research has been deemed to be lacking considering the significant economic contributions made by SMEs (Barnes, 2002; McCarthy & Leavy, 2000; Mehta et al.2022b), even though research on SMEs is evident (Peel & Bridge, 1998). Experiential research on SMEs, specifically in the manufacturing sector, is very lacking. More precisely, there is no empirical or proven study on decision-making, financial literacy, strategy formulation, performance measurements, or linkages among these topics. The level of financial competitiveness in manufacturing SMEs can be ascertained by looking at the interactions between each variable.

New worldwide opportunities are also available to SMEs. The expansion of SMEs' markets and distribution networks through international business networking results in the realization of production balance and a range of products, services, and processes. The sale and licencing of technology-based assets generate revenue for SMEs as well. Small and medium-sized businesses (SMEs) could receive assistance from the government in comprehending the advantages of global restructuring, as shown by appropriately maintaining a business environment and open policies for foreign direct investment and trade, leveraging inter-firm networking, and upgrading organizational capabilities to participate in global networks and foreign markets.

This study aims to examine the factors influencing the performance of SMEs in Gujarat's manufacturing industry as well as the sales revenue growth of SMEs categorically operating in the manufacturing sector. The goal of the study is to compare every possible classification of manufacturing SMEs using specific financial performance metrics.

Two goals were the focus of the study. First, determine how financially competitive the SME is, particularly if it operates in the manufacturing sector. The second goal is to research the financial traits of SMEs and how they affect the bottom line of SMEs operating as manufacturing firms.

Literature Review

Current research suggests that several important characteristics may distinguish SMEs from larger businesses. It is described (Addy et al., 1994; Burns & Dewhurst, 1996; Ghobadian & Gallear, 1997) as "Personalized management with little devolution of authority," "Severe resource limitations in terms of management and manpower, as well as finance," "Reliance on a small number of customers, and operating in limited markets," "Flat, flexible structures," and "High innovatory potential, reactive, and informal." SMEs are complex, diverse, and influenced by factors that cannot be depicted by static models. However, these businesses are frequently regarded as a single entity. SMEs differ from multinational corporations in terms of size, management structure, knowledge specialization, and position in the procurement and financial markets. SMEs are not considered miniature versions of large firms (Coad, 2009); therefore, they need to be studied as either distinct research objects or as a small subset of firms within the business pool.

According to Gyampah and Boye (2001), tiny businesses with limited resources perceive their business environment differently than large businesses. Small businesses are unable to devote sufficient resources and time to sustainable growth due to limited resources (Singh et al., 2010). Neneh and Vanzyl (2014) identified the factors associated with growth intention among current business proprietors, and the effect growth has on actual SME expansion. The results indicate that the growth intention of the entrepreneur determines the business's actual development potential, resulting in a significant causal relationship between growth intention and sales growth and asset growth. Levratto et al. (2010) found that factors such as a company's resources, human capital (age, experience), and market and environmental conditions play significant roles in SME growth. There should be an increased sense of responsibility among the financial backers of SMEs as we are seeing the responsible investing behavior of investors for large corporates (Sharma et al., 2020, Vyas et al., 2022).

The effective formation and establishment of small and medium-sized businesses (SMEs), as well as their constant growth and development, have always intrigued and alarmed researchers, government officials, and policymakers. This is because SMBs are becoming increasingly important to the nation's economic development. Their importance to economic activity is manifest in both tangible and intangible ways. In response to this observation, local governments have formulated and implemented a variety of policies, including the provision of legal advice and financing, to aid in the formation of new businesses and aid small and medium-sized enterprises (SMEs) to ensure their survival and promote increased growth rates. Small and medium-sized businesses (SMEs) are the backbone of the economies of numerous nations. In many nations, they account for more than 90 per cent of all businesses (Poon & Swatman, 1999; Cull et al., 2006; Ozgulbas et al., 2006).

According to a study by Boardman et al. (1997) and Hutchinson et al. (2005), the collective effect of SME growth and expansion creates distinctive financial profiles for the units. It entails not disregarding the enterprise expansion and its effect on SME financial profiles. Hutchinson (1989) defines a financial profile as "that set of accounting ratios, available from the firm's profit and loss account and balance sheet, which usefully and efficiently summarises the firm's financial aspects, such as profitability, liquidity, and gearing." McMahon and Holmes (1991) conclude in their paper that comprehensive financial management is essential for the existence, sustenance, and overall well-being of small businesses.

A study by Pramono et al. (2021) demonstrates that the development of businesses is dependent on the source of capital and education, achievement requirements, and locus of control. In their study, Sariwulan et al. (2020) determined that digital literacy has the greatest direct and indirect impact on the performance of SME entrepreneurs. Additional research revealed the significance of digital literacy in establishing business and marketing networks. According to Porcar et al. (2017), sustainability is gaining importance in society, and the creation of business ventures is one area in which sustainability is essential. Neneh and Vanzyl (2014) investigated the factors that influence the growth intention of current business owners and the effect that growth intention has on the actual expansion of their SMEs. The relationship between board size and firm performance is also identified by the researchers (Sharma et al., 2022). This study demonstrates a significant relationship between growth intentions and actual firm growth in terms of sales growth and asset growth.

In addition, researchers have conducted extensive research on the causes of small business failure. According to Berryman (1983), inadequate or irresponsible financial administration is the leading cause of failure in these industries. Significant economic problems are likely to arise for this sector because of its frequently inadequate resources, leaving small businesses gravely undercapitalized. Its strategic capabilities are determined by its financial strength (Johnson & Scholes, 1993). It can be evaluated using a variety of financial and non-financial metrics. The selection of measures is dependent on the enterprise and its competitive environment. For example, service industries have fewer fixed assets than heavier industries. Therefore, it is extremely difficult to develop a universal framework for measuring the financial fortitude of a business with a standardized instrument.

Research Methodology

The various aspects of SME performance have been empirically examined in Indian studies on firm performance and competitiveness. Still, no conclusive evidence was discovered, particularly regarding financial performance measures as a tool for enhancing SME competitiveness. The purpose of this study is to examine the financial competitiveness of small and medium-sized manufacturing companies using their financial statements from the past three years.

This study utilizes secondary data from a variety of SME financial statements. These databases were constructed using the ACE Knowledge database as a starting point. The remaining databases were utilized to supplement the ACE Knowledge database with lacking information. Accord Fintech, a private database management company that maintains a database of companies and also provides various services in India, supplied the data. Having access to such an exhaustive longitudinal database presented a one-of-a-kind opportunity.

Only manufacturing SME firms were sampled, and 175 SME firms were chosen at random based on the availability of data from a government-published database. Such a random sampling can be viewed as an advantage of the analysis conducted. Several authors have outlined the disadvantages of non-random sampling procedures, which primarily consist of extremely misleading indications of a model's "external validity" and its usefulness for decision-making purposes (Keasey & Watson, 1991; Palepu, 1986). For the period 2011 to 2013, the financial statements of the SMEs included in the sample were compiled.

Model Regression Equation

$Growth_{it} = \alpha_0 + \beta_1$ *(Total Assets)* $+ \beta_2$ *(Leverage)* $+ \beta_3$ *(Current Ratio)* $+ \beta_4$ *(Capital Productivity)* $+ \beta_5$ *(Cash flow ratio)* $+ \beta_6$ *(Debt to Equity Ratio)*

Where, Growth is defined as the difference between the logarithms of a firm's sales revenues in periods t and t – 1 (Honjo & Haranda, 2006). The other measure of growth used in the regression is the percentage change in total assets. Variables Total Assets, and Cash-Flow Ratio, represent firms' size. Variables Leverage, Debt to Equity Ratio, Current Ratio, and Capital Productivity represent the capital structure, short-term liquidity, future growth opportunities, and capital productivity, respectively (I stand for a firm, and t stands for the time period).

Several research used a CI (composite index) or multiple measures for their DV (dependent variable). Those research economic achievements (financial measures) and operational measures like Orientation of innovation or factors supporting to achieve of financial growth) (Rauch et al., 2009; Unger et al., 2011; Venkatraman & Ramanujam, 1986). A selection of samples for the literature review and major review referred to factors of growth, profitability, and performance. The application of multiple measures, between and within, and analysis through categorization.

As SMEs do not follow a stringent accounting process, data inaccuracy and sufficiency are the study's primary limitations. The most notable is the lack of complete data for proxy variables, i.e., short-term and long-term debt, intangible assets, firms' age, and ownership structure. Such proxy variables can further improve the understanding of strong competence. In addition, the empirical results are derived from a sample of 175 manufacturing SMEs working in major cities of Gujarat state. The limited sample size also may impact the study results.

Data Analysis and Interpretation

Operating Revenue as SMEs' Growth Evaluation

The growth in SMEs can be explained by traditional (such as size and age of the firm) and firm-specific (Total Assets, capital structure, capital productivity) characteristics. This section evaluates SMEs' growth by traditional characteristics (Firm size) (see Table 11.1).

Correlation and multiple regression analyses were conducted to examine the relationship between SMEs' growth and various potential predictors. Table 11.2 shows the ability to predict SMEs' growth ($R^2 = .271$). In this model value of R^2 denotes that given variables can explain only 27.1 per cent of SME growth. The residual 72.9 per cent is not defined, which means that the rest, 72.99 per cent of the growth in SMEs, is affected by other variables not shown in this model.

Table 11.1: Model Summary: Operating Revenue Regression.

Model	R	R Square	Adjusted R Square	Std. An error in the Estimate	Durbin-Watson
1	0.520	0.271	0.245	0.2344	2.196

Predictors: (Constant), Debt to Equity Ratio, Current Ratio, Leverage, Cash Flow, Capital Productivity, Total Assets.
Dependent Variable: Net Sales.
Source: Authors' calculation.

Table 11.2: Regression Analysis of SMEs' Growth Factors Coefficients.

Model		Un-standardized Coefficients		Standardized Coefficients	t	p-value
		β	Std. Error	β		
1	(Constant)	0.100	0.026		3.909	0.000
	Total Assets	0.622	0.143	0.354	4.344	0.000
	Current Ratio	−0.011	0.006	−0.125	−1.792	0.075
	Leverage	−0.078	0.096	−0.056	−0.813	0.417
	Capital Productivity	0.077	0.012	1.044	6.417	0.000
	Debt to Equity Ratio	0.004	0.003	0.087	1.234	0.219
	Cash-Flow	−0.035	0.009	−0.587	−3.834	

Source: Authors' calculation.

As seen in Table 11.2, the intercept (identified as the constant) was significant at the level of 0.05 (B = .100; t = 3.909). Three of the six independent variables are statistically significant: total assets (t = 4.344; P value = .000 < 0.05) and capital productivity (t = 6.417; P value = .000 < 0.05) and cash flow (t = −3.834; P value = .000 < 0.05). One variable leverage is statistically significant at a 0.10 significance level (P value = .075 < 0.10). When evaluating the standardized beta values or "size of influence", the greatest influence upon the dependent variable is capital productivity (beta = 1.044), followed by cash flow and total assets, respectively (beta = −.587 & .354). At the same time, variables for financial structure found no significant impact on firms' growth (Leverage: t = −0.813; P = .417 <0.05, Debt to Equity ratio: t = 1.234; P = 0.219 <0.05). The positive beta of capital productivity and total assets indicated that these constructs had a positive relationship with the growth of SMEs. It meant that the increase in productivity and asset size would lead SMEs to higher growth.

Correlation and multiple regression analyses were conducted to examine the relationship between SMEs' growth and various potential predictors. The SPSS model summary for the above correlations contains the following information: R Square = 0.431

and Adjusted R Square = 0.411. In this model the value of R^2 denotes that given variables can explain only 43.1 per cent of SME growth. The residual 56.9 per cent is not defined, which means that the rest, 56.99 per cent of the growth in SMEs, is affected by other variables not shown in this model (see Table 11.3).

Table 11.3: Model Summary: Operating Revenue Regression.

Model	R	R Square	Adjusted R Square	Std. The error in the Estimate	Durbin-Watson
1	0.656	0.431	0.411	0.2425	2.180

Predictors: (Constant), Total Assets, Debt to Equity Ratio, Current Ratio, Leverage, Cash Flow, Capital Productivity.
Dependent Variable: Net Sales.
Source: Authors' calculation.

As seen in Table 11.4, three of the six independent variables are statistically significant: total assets (t = 6.174; P value = .000 < 0.05) and capital productivity (t = 6.419; P value = .000 < 0.05) and cash flow (t = −4.004; P value = .000 < 0.05). When evaluating the standardized beta values or "size of influence" (Vogt, 1993), the greatest influence upon the dependent variable is capital productivity (beta = .576), followed by total assets and cash flow, respectively (beta = .488 & −.362). The positive beta of capital productivity and total assets indicated that these constructs had a positive relationship with the growth of SMEs. It meant that the increase in productivity and asset size would lead SMEs to higher growth. The finding concerning Total Assets is contrary to prior studies (Pramono et al., 2021) which have indicated a significant relationship between Total Assets and Net Sales.

Table 11.4: Regression Analysis of SMEs' Growth Factors Coefficients.

Model		Un-standardized Coefficients		Standardized Coefficients	t	p-value
		β	Std. Error	β		
1	(Constant)	0.005	0.020		0.278	0.781
	Total Assets	1.134	0.184	0.488	6.174	0.000
	Current Ratio	−0.014	0.009	−0.089	−1.511	0.133
	Leverage	−0.118	0.112	−0.063	−1.053	0.294
	Capital Productivity	0.037	0.006	0.576	6.419	0.000
	Debt to Equity Ratio	0.000	0.003	0.001	0.017	0.986
	Cash Flow	−0.129	0.032	−0.362	−4.004	0.000

Source: Authors' calculation.

Conclusion

A net sale has a significant impact on the development of small and medium-sized enterprises when traditional characteristics are considered. The results of the research also indicate that the growth variables chosen for the study are significant and have played a role in the growth and performance of small and medium-sized businesses classified according to their investment in plant and machinery and their average annual net sales. The variables identified in the study have a significant impact on the development of small and medium-sized enterprises (SMEs). Multiple regressions indicate that the effects of explanatory variables (total assets, current ratio, capital productivity, and cash flow) on the dependent variable (operating revenue) were statistically significant. In conclusion, SMEs are the backbone of the Indian economy, as they provide the largest employment basis, and India is moving towards an enterprise-based economy. Faced with such challenges in the coming years, this overview calls for more policy assistance and financial support for the development of small and medium-sized enterprises (SMEs) with their problem-solving and adaptable business practises; in fact, SMEs in India may soon be part of the solution rather than the problem.

References

Addy, C., Pearce, J., & Bennett, J. (1994). "Performance measures in small manufacturing enterprises: Are firms measuring what matters?", In *10th National Conference on manufacturing research (proceedings) (110–14). Loughborough: Taylor & Francis Publishing.*

Amoako-Gyampah, K., & Boye, S. S. (2001). "Operations strategy in an emerging economy: the case of the Ghanaian manufacturing industry", *Journal of Operations Management, 19*(1), 59–79.

Barnes, D. (2002). "The Manufacturing Strategy Formation Process in Small and Medium-Sized Enterprises", *Journal of Small Business and Enterprise Development, 9*(2), 130–149.

Berryman, J. (1983). "Small Business Failure and Survey of The Literature", *European Small Business Journal, 1*(4), 47–59.

Boardman, A. E., Shapiro, D. M., & Vining, A. R. (1997). "The Role of Agency Costs in Explaining the Superior Performance of Foreign MNE Subsidiaries", *International Business Review, 6*(3), 295–317.

Burns, P., & Dewhurst, J. (Eds.). (1996). "Small business and entrepreneurship", *Basingstoke: Macmillan.*

Coad, A. (2009). "The Growth of Firms: A Survey of Theories and Empirical Evidence", *Edward Elgar Publishing.*

Cull, R., Davis, L. E., Lamoreaux, N. R., & Rosenthal, J. L. (2006). "Historical Financing of Small-And Medium-Size Enterprises", *Journal of Banking & Finance, 30*(11), 3017–3042.

Ghobadian, A., & Gallear, D. (1997). "TQM and Organization Size", *International Journal of Operations & Production Management, 17*(2), 121–163.

Gunasekaran, A., Rai, B. K., & Griffin, M. (2011). "Resilience and Competitiveness of Small and Medium Size Enterprises: An Empirical Research", *International Journal of Production Research, 49*(18), 5489–5509.

Hall, C. (1995). "APEC and SME Policy: Suggestions for an action agenda", *Monash Asia Institute.*

Hall, C. (2002). "Profile of SMEs and SME issues in East Asia", *The role of SMEs in National Economies in East Asia*, 2, 21. *Cheltenham, UK Northampton, MA: Edward Elgar, c2002.*

Harvie, C., & Lee, B. C. (2002). "East Asian SMEs: Contemporary Issues and Developments-An Overview", The role of SMEs in national economies in East Asia, 1–20. *Cheltenham, UK Northampton, MA: Edward Elgar, c2002.*

Harvie, C., & Lee, B. C. (Eds.) (2002), "The role of SMEs in national economies in East Asia", *Cheltenham, UK Northampton, MA: Edward Elgar, c2002.* https://www2.deloitte.com/global/en/pages/manufacturing/articles/global-manufacturingcompetitiveness-index.html

Harvie, C., & Lee, B. C. (Eds.). (2005). Sustaining growth and performance in East Asia: The role of small and medium sized enterprises (Vol. 3). Edward Elgar Publishing.

Honjo, Y., & Harada, N. (2006). "SME policy, financial structure and firm growth: Evidence from Japan." *Small Business Economics, 27*, 289–300.

Hutchinson, K., Quinn, B., & Alexander, N. (2005). The internationalisation of small to medium-sized retail companies: towards a conceptual framework. Journal of Marketing Management, 21(1-2), 149–179.

Hutchinson, K., Quinn, B., & Alexander, N. (2005). "The Internationalisation of Small to Medium-Sized Retail Companies: Towards A Conceptual Framework", *Journal of Marketing Management, 21*(1–2), 149–179.

Hutchinson, P. J. (1989). "The Financial Profile of Growth of Small Firms: An Analysis of The Accounting Ratios of Australian Companies at and After Flotation 1964/5–1983/4" *(Doctoral dissertation, University of Bath).*

Johnson, G., & Scholes, K. (1993). Exploring Corporate Strategy: text and cases (3-rd edn), London, Prentice Hall.

Johnson, G., Scholes, K., & Whittington, R. (2008). "Exploring Corporate Strategy: Text & Cases", *Pearson Education.*

Keasey, K., & Watson, R. (1991). "The state of the art of small firm failure prediction: achievements and prognosis." *International small business journal, 9*(4), 11–29.

Keasey, K., & Watson, R. (1993). "Small Firm Management: Ownership, Finance, and Performance", *Blackwell Publication.*

Levratto, N., Tessier, L., & Zouikri, M. (2010). The determinants of growth for SMEs. A longitudinal study from French manufacturing firms. *SSRN Electronic Journal*, 28.

McCarthy, B., & Leavy, B. (2000). "Phases in The Strategy Formation Process: An Exploratory Study of Irish SMEs", *Irish Journal of Management, 21*(2), 55.

McMahon, R. G., & Holmes, S. (1991). "Small Business Financial Management Practices in North America: A Literature Review", *Journal of Small Business Management, 29(*2), 19.

Mehta, K., Sharma, R. & Chugh, A. (2017). "Management of Forex Risk Exposure: A Study of SMEs and Unlisted Non–Financial Firms in India", *International Journal of Applied Business and Economic Research, 15*(9), 43–54.

Mehta, K., Sharma, R., Vyas, V. (2022). A quantile regression approach to study the impact of aluminium prices on the manufacturing sector of India during the COVID era, *Materials Today: Proceedings, 65*(8), 3506–3511. ISSN 2214–7853, https://doi.org/10.1016/j.matpr.2022.06.087.

Mehta, K., Sharma, R., Vyas, V. and Kuckreja, J.S. (2022). "Exit strategy decision by venture capital firms in India using fuzzy AHP", *Journal of Entrepreneurship in Emerging Economies, 14*(4), 643–669. https://doi.org/10.1108/JEEE-05-2020-0146

Neneh, B. N., & Vanzyl, J. (2014). "Growth intention and its impact on business growth amongst SMEs in South Africa", *Mediterranean Journal of Social Sciences, 5*(20), 172.

Ozgulbas, N., Koyuncugil, A. S., & Yilmaz, F. (2006). Identifying the effect of firm size on financial performance of SMEs. The Business Review, Cambridge, 6(1), 162–167.

(2006). "OECD Employment Outlook 2006", Retrieved from https://www.oecd-ilibrary.org/content/publication/empl_outlook-2006–en.Palepu,

Palepu, K. G. (1986). "Predicting takeover targets: A methodological and empirical analysis." *Journal of accounting and economics, 8*(1), 3–35.

Peel, M. J., & Bridge, J. (1998). "How Planning and Capital Budgeting Improve SME Performance", *Long Range Planning, 31*(6), 848–856.

Poon, S., & Swatman, P. M. (1999). "An Exploratory Study of Small Business Internet Commerce Issues", *Information & Management, 35*(1), 9–18.

Porcar, A. T., Tierno, N. R., & Mestre, A. L. (2017). "Factors affecting entrepreneurship and business sustainability", *Sustainability, 10*, 452. https://doi.org/10.3390/su10020452

Pramono, R., sondakh, L. W., bernarto, I., juliana, J., & Purwanto, A. (2021). "Determinants of the Small and Medium Enterprises Progress: A Case Study of SME Entrepreneurs in Manado, Indonesia", *The Journal of Asian Finance, Economics and Business, 8*(1), 881–889. https://doi.org/10.13106/JAFEB.2021.VOL8.NO1.881

Sariwulan, T., Suparno, S., Disman, D., Ahman, E., & Suwatno, S. (2020). "Entrepreneurial performance: The role of literacy and skills", *Journal of Asian Finance, Economics, and Business, 7*(11), 269–280. doi.org/10.13106/jafeb.2020.vol7. no11.269

Singh, R. K., Garg, S. K., & Deshmukh, S. G. (2008). "Challenges and strategies for the competitiveness of SMEs: a case study in the Indian context", *International Journal of Services and Operations Management, 4(*2), 181–200.

Singh, R. K., Garg, S. K., & Deshmukh, S. G. (2010). Strategy development by small scale industries in India. *Industrial Management & Data Systems, 110*(7), 1073–1093.

Sharma, R., Mehta, K. & Goel, A. (2022). "Non-linear relationship between board size and performance of Indian companies", *Journal of Management and Governance*. https://doi.org/10.1007/s10997-022-09651-8

Sharma, R., Mehta, K., & Vyas, V. (2020). "Responsible Investing: A Study on Non–Economic Goals and Investors' Characteristics", *Applied Finance Letters, 9(SI)*, 63–78. https://doi.org/10.24135/afl.v9i2.245

Subrahmanya, M. B. (1995). "Reservation Policy for Small-Scale Industry: Has It Delivered the Goods?" *Economic and Political Weekly*, M51–M54.

Sudan, F. K. (2005). "Challenges in Micro and Small–Scale Enterprises Development: Some Policy Issues", *Synergy: I. T. S. Journal of IT and Management, 3*(2), 67–81.

Vyas, V., Mehta, K., & Sharma, R. (2020). "Investigating socially responsible investing behaviour of Indian investors using structural equation modelling", *Journal of Sustainable Finance & Investment*, 1–23. DOI: 10.1080/20430795.2020.1790958

Vyas, V., Mehta, K., & Sharma, R. (2022). "Investigating socially responsible investing behaviour of Indian investors using structural equation modelling." *Journal of Sustainable Finance & Investment, 12*(2), 570–592.

Dr. M. Chithra

12 Green Management Practices by Small and Medium Enterprises

Abstract: As 'Greening' the process has become norm of the day, total quality management in manufacturing sector becomes a reality only with green practices. Having green practices in place, creating awareness among the employees and adhering to the mandate on green practices sustainable practices, does have a huge impact on performance of the entities. This chapter attempts to bring together, the components of green management practices, from existing literature and contemporary practices. Green management practices enable continuous improvement and sustainability. Green Manufacturing is the most emerging sustainable manufacturing practice that has the capability to solve the most of issues that the Indian industries come across now. It covers all aspect to reduce the environmental impact by optimum use of available resources and reduction of waste. Due to various reasons, small and medium sized enterprises (SMEs) may have been left out of the regulatory and social pressures. The time has come where ignoring environmental impacts of SMEs is no longer viable. Small and medium sized firms are essential to all economies but also have a significant negative impact on the environment. Their collective footprint equates to the major contribution of industrial pollution, yet SMEs are not convinced of the necessity for behaviour change. It is imperative to understand the importance of becoming green, and act swiftly.

Keywords: Green manufacturing, SMEs, Sustainability

Background

In the current uncertain economic times, where many businesses are aiming for survival, smart businesses are exploring opportunities to sustain and grow in a green way. The common belief is to invest in greener technologies and meet the compliance requirements to get the operating license. However, things have quickly changed in the recent past, which is unprecedented. Rapid globalization, with the rise of nations like China and India as economic powerhouses, has brought to the forefront the aspirations of billions of people to live a comfortable life with all modern amenities. These aspirations have put tremendous pressure on natural resources, which is expected to intensify further. The post Covid 19 scenario has affected both small and big manufacturing firms (Mehta et al., 2022) and a new world economic order is taking

Dr. M. Chithra, Gnanam School of Business

https://doi.org/10.1515/9783111170022-012

place in terms of responsible corporate citizenship. In addition, the growing consensus on the impacts of global warming calls for more concrete actions from government, businesses, and civil society to mitigate the climate change risks.

Smart businesses have identified the associated risks and spotted the opportunity to satisfy the aspirations of individuals indulged in green innovation. 'Greening' help businesses to explore new product/services proposition, gain a social license to operate, reduce costs, build brand value, and contribute to lesser environmental degradation. Today, the green way of business is poised to be the next business differentiator akin to the quality revolution in the eighties and nineties and the IT revolution in the first decade of this century.

Across sectors, companies have begun to realize the business case of greening. Extractive industries are under constant pressure from various stakeholders to demonstrate green mining practices, focusing on minimizing pollution and waste (Sharma et al., 2020; Vyas et al. 2020). Cement companies are reducing their energy requirement by co-processing high-calorific wastes from other industries. The auto sector is forced to improve the fuel efficiency of vehicles through market and regulatory forces, thereby reducing the emission of global warming gases. The realty sector is realizing the benefits of 'green buildings', which optimize the construction cost and provide customers with savings on their utility bills. The environment degradation is duly considered by companies while taking any strategic decision (Vyas et al., 2023; Mehta et al., 2019). Electronic companies promote take–buy schemes of old products to retrieve and reuse useful components. Energy companies are focusing more on green energy production. Companies are leveraging technology to better manage their energy needs and reduce travel using video/audio conferencing facilities. Better environmental practices instil greater confidence in the investor community, and companies can access capital funds, which only invest in responsible organizations. Green practices are highlighted in dialogue and communication with regulatory agencies to gain a license to operate. Environmental initiatives are also finding their way into companies' marketing strategies to project the brand as a responsible one with care for the environment and society. Being a responsible organization also helps retain talent who would want to associate themselves with companies with high ethical and environmental standards.

However, there are many challenges in changing the business into a 'green' way. Supply chains are critical to almost all sectors, contributing to as high as 70–80 per cent of the value-creation process. More and more companies today have complex supply chains originating from unorganized and small-scale sectors. Reputed companies are realizing the benefits of greening their operations, but seldom do companies assess and act on the supply chain risks. Investment decisions in green technologies are still made with traditional return-on-investment considerations without evaluating the intangible benefits over the life cycle of the technology. Few companies have identified green aspects as part of their enterprise risk management framework to integrate those at the strategic level. Water is soon becoming a key business risk, with many parts of India listed as having water scarcity; still, water management in industries is not a high-priority operational issue. The regulators have enacted laws to prevent environmental pollution by business activities. However, the rigour in enforcing the law is missing, with many pollution control boards facing the challenges of resource constraints. There is an overall lack of knowledge among the market participants (Mahajan & Sharma, 2017) for various services provided to them by depositories. The investors' interest is affected by several factors related to internal and external environment of a business (Mehta et al., 2022). There is an increase volatility in financial markets (Sharma et al., 2021) and investors appreciated a consistent investment style resulting into extra ordinary returns to them (Mehta & Sharma, 2017). Therefore, adoption of green practices by any organization is affected by several reasons and it has long term implications.

The greening of businesses can enhance the brand value of organizations while enabling those to derive cost benefits. It allows companies to innovate for the future with clean and green products and services. The governance related issues are playing vital roles in board rooms of the companies (Sharma et al., 2022). Companies who evaluate the environmental risks and opportunities in their entire value creation process will gain from a clear business differentiator- the 'green' way of doing business. The 'green' way of doing business will set progressive and innovative companies apart from the rest in meeting the growth imperatives of tomorrow.

Why SMEs?

As per prior research, 90% of all global enterprises are SMEs, many of which constitute the global supply chain. In addition to that, 0.4% of all SMEs have more than 100 employees.

And the most important reason why SMEs should implement green practices is the majority of them, being in the manufacturing sector, share 70% of global environmental pollution, as they use plastics, non-metallic minerals, and chemicals in their manufacturing process. It's a well-known fact that such materials lead to environmental degradation. Therefore, the only way they can cut upon such hazardous effects, and minimize the environmental degradations they cause, is by implementing green practices. The increasing foreign exposure of SMEs also require more research studies focusing on SMEs (Mehta et al., 2017).

The key success factor in greening the economy is reducing the environmental impact of SMEs in the manufacturing and services sectors. Apart from improving environmental performance, if an SME tries to exhibit pro-environment behaviour, it attracts and retains stakeholders, which will continue to provide significant business opportunities. But, of course, SMEs are unaware of the benefit of attracting more opportunities if green practices are in place. Hence, they are not willing to implement green practices as they have resource constraints about the entity's size, the skillset to implement and execute such practices and most importantly, the knowledge and awareness about such initiatives.

SMEs are under this misperception that such green initiatives will cost them more, which will not have a return on their investment. They are more concerned about the payback period, as they must invest in new technologies. They are unaware that better environmental performance helps them have a competitive edge over other players in the market. They are much more bothered about the burdens and costs of such green practices rather than the win-win situation it will offer.

Objectives:

1. To do an integrated review in the area of Green Manufacturing
2. To identify the green practices at SMEs
3. To learn the challenges in implementing green practices
4. To get to know the regulations regarding implementing green practices.
5. To understand the benefits of greening SMEs

Review of Literature

In the late 1980s, Green Management (GM) practices started in Germany to establish standards for goods to be exported globally. Meanwhile, the Brundtland Commission's report (1987) on environment and development emphasized how the pursuit of development was causing a faster rate of resource depletion. Thanks to the report, the industrial community was pushed to adopt GM practices due to the quick depletion of natural resources, increased energy consumption, expanding consumer awareness of environmentally friendly products, and the necessity to adhere to strict environmental standards. The consumer switching from one organization to another due to any reason required due cognizance by the business firms (Khanna & Sharma, 2017).

Paul, Bhole, and Chaudhari (2014) provide an overview of green manufacturing, including what it is, why it is necessary, and green manufacturing techniques that reduce waste and pollution. Dissanayake, Premaratne, Ranwala & Melegoda (2019) aims to explore green practices, challenges, and strategies, as well as the necessary institutional support for implementing and maintaining such practices in manufacturing SMEs in Kochi, a region similar to Sri Lanka, to gain a priori knowledge of the reality. Shah, Naghi, Ganji & Hasan (2017) examine different avenues that allow businesses to move towards entities with high levels of environmental responsibility in an adhesive manufacturing company. Wit (2012), based on a random sample of 689 SMEs, tried to forecast their involvement of them in environmental management practices. The industrial community's requirement inspired researchers to create a framework for GM practices (Daly, 1990). Most of the GM definitions provided by researchers narrowed down to reducing negative environmental effects from conception to death, i.e., from the design stage to the end-of-life stage. Dornfeld (2014) defined GM practices as manufacturing practice that complies with environmental standards and consumer needs. In other words, GM practices are a green manufacturing design that strives to reduce waste and conserve energy (Paul et al. 2014a). GM practices were outlined by Mohanty and Deshmukh (1998) as a compilation of all actions taken to reduce waste. With the addition of resource conservation, recycling, and using green energy as GM practices, Atlas and Florida (1998) supported the same. However, according to Nair and Sodhi (2012), the environmental initiative taken by SMEs is still on par with or even greater than that of large business owners.

According to a survey of 198 Indian SMEs, most determine their immediate qualitative and quantitative gains by implementing GM instead of practising environmental protection (Sangwan, 2011). Due to a lack of the necessary skills and financial resources, many SMEs in India find it challenging to apply GM practices (Gandhi et al., 2018). But according to the research done by Sezen and Cankaya (2013), adopting GM practices enhances an SME's economic performance over time by lowering the cost of raw materials and energy in addition to its social and environmental performance. Nevertheless, many Indian SMEs are hesitant to implement GM practices, despite widespread environmental awareness campaigns and strict environmental regulations. India is under intense pressure from external shareholders or investors to adopt GM practices since it is a rising economy and a significant industrial base (Mohanty & Prakash, 2014).

The industry is understood to be implementing zero waste generation and removal methods with the goal of reducing negative environmental effects (Dupont et al., 2015). According to Thanki et al. (2016) and Dieste et al. (2019), integrating green and lean manufacturing can help manufacturing industries reduce their negative environmental effect. While the GM practices mentioned above have changed recently, India's SME sector situation is entirely different. To fulfil corporate social responsibility (CSR), the sector has established a general management practice framework, according to Gale et al. (2014). Vancheswaran and Gautam (2011) conducted a case study involving 30 Indian SMEs. While many see CSR as a marketing channel, the idea is still unclear to many others. As a result, Indian SMEs do not consistently comprehend GM practises (Yadav et al., 2018).

Few academics have addressed the obstacles to the successful adoption of GM practices; instead, they have concentrated mostly on the advantages of these practices. Govindan et al. (2015) found 12 common drivers of GM practices from a survey of 120 top enterprises in south India. Their study indicated regulatory compliance as the main driver. However, it also highlighted the possibility that all of them could be ineffective for Indian SMEs because they are unfamiliar with GM practices.

In Malaysian SMEs, Ghazilla et al. (2015) investigated the motivations behind and constraints on GM practices. Their research reveals that GM practices are driven by strict environmental standards, competition, environmental awareness, and consumer demand, while impediments include financial limitations, a lack of technical support, a lack of rules, subpar R&D, and low-level commitment from top management as deterrents. In addition, changes in operational capabilities and resource usage are necessary for businesses to undertake green initiatives (Wang & Chan, 2013). This is primarily because, even though the system typically necessitates higher operating expenses and skill sets, the deployment of GM practices requires a production system that produces less environmental pollution (Geng et al., 2017). The primary barrier to the introduction of GM is thought to be a lack of innovation in the manufacturing process, as all secondary barriers stem from this failure (Rodriguez & Weingarten, 2017).

Green Manufacturing

Green manufacturing (sustainable or environmental-friendly manufacturing) refers to transforming materials into products without giving rise to the emission of greenhouse gases, use of non-renewable or toxic materials or generation of waste (Allwood, 2009). Green manufacturing is implementing environment-friendly operations in the production processes. Green SMEs are " that embrace green processes and/or produce green products/services using green production inputs" (Ramessur, 2018). Fewer usage of natural resources, reduction in pollution and waste, recycling and reuse of materials, and moderate emissions during the manufacturing process are the essentials of "greening" the manufacturing process. There are three ways by which one can transform industrial operations into green:
(1) using green energy,
(2) producing and selling green products and
(3) employing green processes in business operations.

Green manufacturing encompasses all of these and is often misinterpreted as Lean manufacturing. Green and Lean are not the same, though the former is complementary in nature to the latter. Lean Manufacturing is a production and management system comprising different measures to increase customer satisfaction in a profitable way. The objective of lean marketing is to eliminate waste, minimize resource consumption, optimize customer satisfaction etc. In a way, lean manufacturing is the predecessor of green manufacturing. Green Manufacturing comprises a set of alternatives intending to preserve environmental quality (as being recyclable, biodegradable, or non-polluting). As industrial production releases toxic chemicals and greenhouse gases, which pollute the water, air, and soil, throughout the process, green manufacturing intends to optimize the process with minimal or no effects on the environment.

The influencing factors of green manufacturing, as stated in "*Green Manufacturing: Fundamentals and Applications*" (Dornfeld, 2014), are,
- Increasing legal pressure by regulations, laws, fines, taxes, or tax-exemptions
- A pull from the market or consumers, as they get attracted to green products.
- An increase in efficiency.
- Minimization of risks due to resource shortages.

A System Model for Green Manufacturing

The system model of green manufacturing, proposed by Ahmed M. Deif (2011), provides us with a clear roadmap on how manufacturing industries can assess their current level of greenness alongside a structured framework towards becoming greener. The system model consists of two modules, namely, a) design and planning and b) Control tools and techniques (see Figure 12.1).

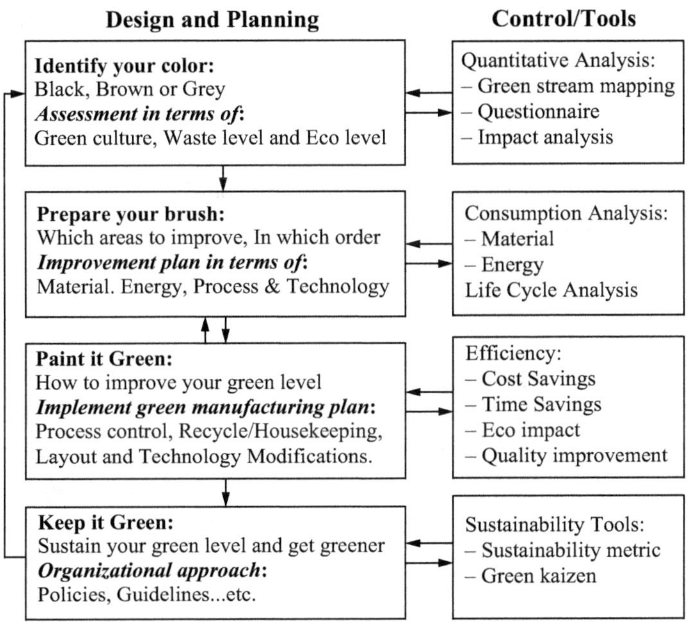

Figure 12.1: Ahmed M. Deif (2011): A System Model for Green Manufacturing.

Assessment- The green culture of the industry, Waste level and Ecological level are assessed with the help of green streaming, Questionnaire, and Impact Analysis.

Areas of Improvement- Improvement in Areas like material and energy consumption, as well as process and technology, are understood with consumption analysis and Life cycle analysis.

Implement green manufacturing- Transformations in areas like Process control, recycling, housekeeping, layout, and technology modification are brought in, and the efficiency is calculated in terms of Time savings, cost savings, ecological impact, and quality improvement.

Keep it green- Sustaining the green with the help of organizational policies, standards operating procedures, and guidelines, with the help of sustainability tools like sustainability metrics and green kaizen.

Besides this model, Dornfeld identifies general parameters for ecologically improving manufacturing processes.

- Avoid the usage of a resource in the first place.
- Reduce weight.
- Increase the yield.
- Decrease the environmental footprint of a resource.
- Increase the yield and reduce the costs of recycling.
- Leverage resource usage (meaning when the negative impact of a product is higher in the utilization phase than in the production phase (e.g., automobiles), future impact needs to be minimized by respective product development or reasonable resource usage).
- Increase the product lifespan.

Despite such research and models, Industries shy away from greening due to the resulting costs, technology barriers and a lack of suitable measurement, control, and management tools.

Green Practices at SMEs

As businesses are transforming their process into green, SMEs, too, are gearing up to green their manufacturing process, not to be left behind in the race. By bringing down the usage of energy and water, SMEs can achieve efficiency. Recycling the waste, in place of purchasing raw materials, will bring down their material cost. Compliance costs can be kept under control. And above all, it improves the company image. The following are the various ways by which green practices could be implemented in SMEs.

1. Energy efficiency

The simple yet best way to achieve energy efficiency is to cut down on the usage of energy and water. Considering future generations, and leaving behind resources for them to use, is the golden principle of sustainability. This awareness would enable the employees to contribute towards energy efficiency.

The first step towards energy efficiency is to conduct an energy audit by professionals, which investigates the source of the required energy for the production process and how it is consumed. The results are converted into energy reports, which will guide the entity in energy efficiency.

a) *Energy from renewable resources:* We are dependent on natural sources of energy to generate electricity, heat, and fuel, which might deplete them in the near future. To sustain sources of energy for future generations to come, we should use alternative renewable energy sources. Those sources include hydropower- obtaining energy from moving water, which has been happening for ages. It was one of the first sources of energy for electricity generation.

Solar – Solar technologies convert sunlight into electrical energy either through photovoltaic (PV) panels or through mirrors that concentrate solar radiation.

Ocean energy – Ocean produces two types of energy, thermal energy from the surface heat and mechanical energy from the movement of the waves.

Landfill gas – Landfill gas (LFG) is a natural by-product of the decomposition of organic material in landfills. LFG is composed of roughly 50 per cent methane (the primary component of natural gas), 50 per cent carbon dioxide (CO_2) and a small amount of non-methane organic compounds. It is a huge source of energy for electricity, and it also acts as a renewable natural gas.

Municipal solid waste – Municipal Solid Waste is trash or garbage which increases due to urbanization, population growth and technological changes. The non-recyclable waste is converted into usable heat, electricity, or fuel that could be used in the manufacturing process.

Geothermal – This renewable energy is taken from the earth's core. The heat that is generated during the original formation of the planet and the radioactive decay materials is the source of this energy. It is used in electricity generation and other heating and cooling applications.

Biomass – It is a renewable organic material that comes from plants and animals. Biomass is used for cooking and heating in developing countries. Manu developed countries use it as fuels for transportation and also for electricity generation.

Wind energy- Windmills are used to harness the power of wind and convert the kinetic energy into electricity to help power the grid.

Based on the location and the product they produce, SMEs can opt for any of the above-mentioned renewable energy to bring in energy efficiency.

2. Pollution reduction and removal

The foremost thing SMEs should be doing is to reduce pollution, which is detrimental to the environment. Choosing the right place for factories, opting for renewable energy resources, analyzing, and treating hazardous waste, running environmental impact assessments, and abiding with the regulations, are various ways by which pollution in SMEs can be brought under control.

3. Greenhouse gas reduction

On average, Industries contribute to one-fourth of Greenhouse gas emissions throughout the world. This is primarily because of burning fossil fuels for energy. And certain chemical reactions which take place while raw materials are converted into finished goods also add to greenhouse gas emissions. Using renewable energy sources would be a fitting alternative.

4. Reduce, Reuse or Recycle
Using the raw materials in an optimum way such that it meets the customer's expectation, as well as are not wasted during the production process. Alternatively, consumption of raw materials can be reduced by reusing or recycling. Refurbished old products or parts can be reused in machinery to sustain them for a few more years. Recycling is the last phase; when a product or its components cannot be reused, the materials are separated as metals or plastics.

5. Conservation of natural resources
Awareness programmes and technology upgradation would enable the Workers to conserve natural resources and indulge in organic agriculture and land management. Conserving soil, water, or wildlife would greatly contribute to energy efficiency.

Challenges in Implementing Green Practices

Green practices are not the ones which SMEs would readily embrace. Any green regulation authorities initially face resistance from the manufacturing units. Introducing and implementing green practices in their location is quite a challenging one, And the following are the various reasons why it is not readily accepted.

1. Absence of environmental laws- If the countries of the respective companies are not that particular about environmental protection, and there are no laws which would govern it, they stay away from green practices.
2. Lack of capital investment- As implementing green practices involves more capital investment, SMEs see it as an unwanted financial burden.
3. Uncertain Future- Not knowing what this extra cost would bring them, they hesitate to invest. The fear of problems keeps them away from green practices.
4. Lack of awareness- They are not aware of the benefits; such green practices would bring to their organizations.
5. Low customer demand- When there is a low or no demand from the customers for products which go through the greening process. It is a well-known fact that products which are produced through green practices will be priced slightly higher.
6. Low Top Management commitment- Even if the employees are interested in doing so, if the top management is not supportive in nature, the benefits of green practices cannot be realized.
7. Lack of resources- If the needed resources or alternative source of energy is not available, then the manufacturing facilities tend to stick to the older process.
8. Lack of skilled staff- If the employees are not competent enough or trained to accommodate the green practices, then they cannot be put into practice.

9. Lack of Research and Development (R & D)- When there are only a few or no R&D measures to understand the impact of green practices in SMEs, no one is going to feel the need.

Regulations Regarding Implementing Green Practices

SMEs are bound to the Environmental laws in India and are required to abide by the regulations. The Environmental laws comprise the water act of 1974, the air act of 1981 and the environmental protection act of 1986. Both centre and the state governments have the authority to collect information, monitor activities, implement, and inspect the facilities. If the facilities fail to comply, violations are considered criminal activities.

Water (Prevention and Control of Pollution) Act of 1974: The Water Act vests regulatory authority in State Boards, and these boards are empowered to establish and enforce effluent standards for factories that discharge pollutants into water bodies (Section 17). The Central Government has published Environment Protection Rules (EPR) as per Section 2A of the Environment Protection Act (EP Act), establishing industry-based standards for certain types of effluent discharge (Schedules I and VI, EPR). The Boards are empowered to issue directions to close facilities or withdraw their supply of power or water for violating regulations by an administrative order (Section 33A). If the facilities fail to comply, they can be prosecuted criminally, and this is punishable by fines and imprisonment (Sections 41, 42, 43, 44, 45, 45A).

Air (Prevention and Control of Pollution) Act of 1981: As per the act, the State Boards are empowered to designate air pollution control areas (Section 19), and the Boards or state governments cannot exempt a polluter if they fall within a designated area, as per the Air act. The Air Act empowers State Boards to establish emission standards for the facilities in consultation with the Central Board, mentioning the air quality standards (Section 17(g)). Emission norms for specific industries are framed under the EP Act (Schedule I, EPR), and also the general emission standards, which are concentration-based, equipment-based, and load based, are also framed (Part D, Schedule VI, EPR). Information is directly collected from facilities (Section 25); air samples are taken for analysis (Section 26); Inspections are conducted at any time (Section 24). The Boards are empowered to act during an accident or other unforeseen event that results in air pollution (Section 23). During such incidents, actions like removing the pollutants, reducing the damage, and issuing orders to the polluter prohibiting the emission of air pollutants, are also taken by the boards. If the facilities fail to comply, they can be prosecuted criminally and is punishable by fines and imprisonment (Sections 37, 38, 39).

Environment (Protection) Act of 1986: The EP Act was enacted under Article 253 of the Indian Constitution. It encompasses various activities of central and state authorities that are coordinated by the central government. The EP Act empowers the Central Government,

- To protect and improve the quality of the environment and also to prevent, control and abate environmental pollution.
- To set new standards for the quality of the environment, control emissions and effluent discharges,
- To regulate industrial locations.
- To prescribe procedures for managing hazardous substances,
- To establish safeguards for preventing accidents; and
- To collect and disseminate information regarding environmental pollution.

Similar to the Water and Air Acts, Enforcement of the EP Act is authorized to collect information, take samples for analysis and also to enter the facilities and conduct inspections at any time (Sections 10, 11, 20). If there is any accident or unforeseen event due to the discharge of environmental pollution by any facilities, emergency measures shall be taken (Section 9). The Central Government is empowered to close facilities or withdraw their supply of power or water by an administrative order (Section 5) if the facilities fail to comply. Failure to comply can be taken to the extent of criminal prosecution and is punishable by fines and imprisonment (Section 15).

Benefits of Greening SMEs

Cost Reduction

For any manufacturing facility, the costs incurred towards energy and water are of prime concern. Investing once in green practices cuts down on these expenses on a day-to-day basis. Such investments are considered annual savings, unlike quicker, short-term cost reductions.

Long-term electrical costs are reduced by switching to energy-efficient lighting. The lighting levels can be adjusted as required by the production schedule. Maintenance and regular inspection of equipment will also prove beneficial. Costs can further be reduced by the way products and supplies are packed. Using renewable energy sources like Solar and wind for power and energy requirements will greatly reduce monthly utility bills. Reducing, reusing, and recycling will enable savings in the procurement of materials.

Stakeholders' Attraction

Customers, Clients and even employees are attracted towards organizations that have got "Greenness" attached to them. It makes it more marketable and sustainable. As the corporate world is all set to green itself, it will strengthen the reputation of the company among the stakeholders. This will lead to an increase in sales. As green factors are brought under the manufacturing standards, manufacturers who look forward to government delays must implement them in their facilities. Thanks to the advent of social media and technology, the information about your green practices attracts stakeholders.

Tax Incentives

Manufacturers who had proactively implemented green practices in their premises enjoy various tax rebates from both centre and state governments. This is done in order to encourage facilities to become green.

Employee green Behaviour: Becoming green is not a one-man show. It is a collaborative effort which involves everyone in the organization, right from Top management to the first-level employees. This teamwork culture enables continuous improvement. Employee green behaviour fuels sustainable organizations and leads to a sense of pride for them. Creating awareness about sustainability among the employees, providing them with required resources and recognizing their pro-environmental behaviour positively influence the organizational culture and enable them to embrace green initiatives.

Innovation and creativity: If employees are empowered to reuse and recycle, which is one of the important aspects of green practices, that would ignite creativity and innovation. They know better how to reduce scraps or recycle waste during the manufacturing process. Green practices bring in innovation. Organizational support would lead to more idea generation. This practice would create a culture wherein green initiatives become a process that leads to organizational effectiveness and profitability.

Societal Impact

Above all, the benefits like profitability, effective organizational culture and climate, green employee behaviour, and the very act of becoming green, with all pro-environmental measures in place, make a real difference in society. Green practices help organizations to reduce their carbon footprint and reduce the detrimental impact on the environment. Such practices help us leave behind clean air, water, renewable energy sources and fewer or no landfills for future generations to be at peace.

Conclusion

As many SMEs are entrepreneur-driven, implementation of green practices needs the owner's will to adopt them. They should understand that green manufacturing and green purchasing would be beneficial for all stakeholders. As global environmental issues need immediate attention, legal pressure on SMEs to implement green practices will increase dramatically. Hence it becomes important for SMEs to gear up to brace for the future.

References

Atlas, M., & Florida, R. (1998). "Green manufacturing", *Handbook of technology management*, 1385–1393.

Allwood, J. M., & Cullen, J. M. (2009). Steel, aluminium and carbon: alternative strategies for meeting the 2050 carbon emission targets. Asamblea anual de Davos.

Borra, C. R., Pontikes, Y., Binnemans, K., & Van Gerven, T. (2015). "Leaching of rare earth from bauxite residue (red mud)", *Minerals Engineering*, *76*, 20–27.

Can Saglam, Y., Yildiz Çankaya, S., & Sezen, B. (2021). "Proactive risk mitigation strategies and supply chain risk management performance: an empirical analysis for manufacturing firms in Turkey", *Journal of Manufacturing Technology Management*, *32*(6), 1224–1244.

Daly, H. E. (1990). "Toward some operational principles of sustainable development", *Ecological economics*, *2*(1), 1–6.

Dissanayake, K., Premaratne, S. P., Ranwala, S., & Melegoda, N. (2019). "Adoption of green practices in manufacturing SMEs: some lessons from Kochi, Kerala, India", *Journal of Business*, *2*(01), 6.

Deif, A. M. (2011). "A system model for green manufacturing", *Journal of cleaner production*, *19*(14), 1553–1559.

Dieste, M., Panizzolo, R., Garza-Reyes, J. A., & Anosike, A. (2019). "The relationship between lean and environmental performance: Practices and measures", *Journal of Cleaner Production*, *224*, 120–131.

Dornfeld, D. A. (2014). "Moving towards green and sustainable manufacturing", *International Journal of Precision Engineering and Manufacturing-Green Technology*, *1*, 63–66.

Dupont, D., Raiguel, S., & Binnemans, K. (2015). "Sulfonic acid functionalized ionic liquids for dissolution of metal oxides and solvent extraction of metal ions." *Chemical Communications*, *51*(43), 9006–9009.

Gandhi, N. S., Thanki, S. J., & Thakkar, J. J. (2018). "Ranking of drivers for integrated lean-green manufacturing for Indian manufacturing SMEs", *Journal of Cleaner Production*, *171*, 675–689.

Gale, N. K., Shapiro, J., McLeod, H. S., Redwood, S., & Hewison, A. (2014). "Patients-people-place: developing a framework for researching organizational culture during health service redesign and change", *Implementation Science*, *9*(1), 1–11.

Govindan, K., Khodaverdi, R., & Vafadarnikjoo, A. (2015). "Intuitionistic fuzzy-based DEMATEL method for developing green practices and performances in a green supply chain", *Expert Systems with Applications*, *42*(20), 7207–7220.

Geng, G., Zheng, Y., Zhang, Q., Xue, T., Zhao, H., Tong, D., . . . & Davis, S. J. (2021). "Drivers of PM2. 5 air pollution deaths in China 2002–2017", *Nature Geoscience*, *14*(9), 645–650.

Ghazilla, R. A. R., Sakundarini, N., Abdul-Rashid, S. H., Ayub, N. S., Olugu, E. U., & Musa, S. N. (2015). "Drivers and barriers analysis for green manufacturing practices in Malaysian SMEs: a preliminary finding", *Procedia Cirp*, *26*, 658–663.

Khanna, V. & Sharma, R. (2017). "Customer Switching Behavior in Retail Banking in India", *International Journal of Applied Business and Economic Research*, 15(9), 427–441.

Mahajan, V. and Sharma, R. (2017). "Future of Depository with Introduction of Payment Bank- A Game Changer to Capital Market", *International Journal of Applied Business and Economic Research*, 15(9), 343–356.

Mehta, K.& Sharma, R. (2017), "Contrarian and Momentum investment strategies: Evidence from Indian Stock Market", *International Journal of Applied Business and Economic Research*, 15(9), 107–118.

Mehta, K., Sharma, R. & Chugh, A.(2017). "Management of Forex Risk Exposure: A Study of SMEs and Unlisted Non–Financial Firms in India", *International Journal of Applied Business and Economic Research*, 15(9), 43–54.

Mehta, K., Sharma, R., Vyas, V. (2019). "Efficiency and ranking of sustainability index of India using DEA-TOPSIS", *Journal of Indian Business Research*, 11(2), 179–199. https://doi.org/10.1108/JIBR-02-2018-0057.

Mehta, K., Sharma, R., Vyas, V. and Kuckreja, J.S. (2022). "Exit strategy decision by venture capital firms in India using fuzzy AHP", *Journal of Entrepreneurship in Emerging Economies*, 14(4), 643–669. https://doi.org/10.1108/JEEE-05-2020–0146

Mohanty, R. P., & Deshmukh, S. G. (1998). "Managing green productivity: some strategic directions". *Production Planning & Control*, *9*(7), 624–633.

Mohanty, R. P., & Prakash, A. (2014). "Green supply chain management practices in India: an empirical study", *Production Planning & Control*, *25*(16), 1322–1337.

Nair, N. K., & Sodhi, J. S. (2012). "CSR practices by SMEs in India: Lessons from five case studies", *Indian Journal of Industrial Relations*, 583–597.

Paul, I. D., Bhole, G. P., & Chaudhari, J. R. (2014). "A review on green manufacturing: its importance, methodology and its application", *Procedia materials science*, *6*, 1644–1649. https://doi.org/10.1016/j.mspro.2014.07.149

Ramessur, T.S. (October 2018). A Trade Action Plan for Harnessing "Green" SMEs Export Potential in Small Island Economies: A Mauritian Perspective. *Journal of Indian Ocean Rim Studies*, *1*(2), 26–55.

Rodriguez, J. A., & Wiengarten, F. (2017). "The role of process innovativeness in the development of environmental innovativeness capability", *Journal of cleaner production*, *142*, 2423–2434.

Sangwan, K. S. (2011). "*Quantitative and qualitative benefits of green manufacturing: an empirical study of Indian small and medium enterprises. In Glocalized Solutions for Sustainability in Manufacturing", Proceedings of the 18th CIRP International Conference on Life Cycle Engineering, Technische Universität Braunschweig, Braunschweig, Germany, May 2nd–4th, 2011* (371–376). *Springer Berlin Heidelberg*.

Sezen, B. & Çankaya, S. Y. (2013). "Effects of Green Manufacturing and Eco-innovation on Sustainability Performance." *Procedia – Social and Behavioral Sciences*, *99*, 154–163. ISSN 1877–0428. https://doi.org/10.1016/j.sbspro.2013.10.481.

Shah, S., Naghi Ganji, E., & Hasan, S. (2017). "An analysis of environmental management and sustainability in SMEs", *WSEAS Transactions on Environment and Development*, *12*, 353–365.

Sharma, R., Mehta, K. & Goel, A. (2022). "Non-linear relationship between board size and performance of Indian companies", *Journal of Management and Governance*. https://doi.org/10.1007/s10997-022-09651-8

Sharma, R., Mehta, K. and Sharma, O. (2021). "Exploring Deep Learning to Determine the Optimal Environment for Stock Prediction Analysis", *2021 International Conference on Computational Performance Evaluation, ComPE* 2021, 148–152.

Sharma, R., Mehta, K., & Vyas, V. (2020). "Responsible Investing: A Study on Non–Economic Goals and Investors' Characteristics", *Applied Finance Letters*, 9(SI), 63–78. https://doi.org/10.24135/afl.v9i2.245

Sun, L., Li, H., Dong, L., Fang, K., Ren, J., Geng, Y., Fujii, M., Zhang, W., Zhang, N., & Liu, Z. (2017). "Eco-benefits assessment on urban industrial symbiosis based on material flows analysis and emergy evaluation approach: A case of Liuzhou city, China." *Resources, Conservation and Recycling*, *119*, 78–88. ISSN 0921–3449. https://doi.org/10.1016/j.resconrec.2016.06.007.

Thanki, S., Govindan, K., & Thakkar, J. (2016). “An investigation on lean–green implementation practices in Indian SMEs using analytical hierarchy process (AHP) approach”, *Journal of Cleaner Production, 135,* 284–298.

Uhlaner, L.M., Berent-Braun, M.M., Jeurissen, R.J.M. et al. (2012). “Beyond Size: Predicting Engagement in Environmental Management Practices of Dutch SMEs.”, Journal of Business *Ethics* 109, 411–429 (2012). https://doi.org/10.1007/s10551-011-1137

Vancheswaran, A., & Gautam, V. (2011). “CSR in SMEs: Exploring a marketing correlation in Indian SMEs”, *Journal of Small Business & Entrepreneurship, 24*(1), 85–98.

Vyas, V., Mehta, K. & Sharma, R. (2020). “Investigating socially responsible investing behaviour of Indian investors using structural equation modelling”, *Journal of Sustainable Finance & Investment*, 1–23. DOI: 10.1080/20430795.2020.1790958

Vyas, V., Mehta, K., Sharma, R. (2023). “The nexus between toxic–air pollution, health expenditure, and economic growth: An empirical study using ARDL”, *International Review of Economics and Finance*, 84, 154–166 https://doi.org/10.1016/j.iref.2022.11.017

Wang, X., & Chan, H. K. (2013). “A hierarchical fuzzy TOPSIS approach to assess improvement areas when implementing green supply chain initiatives”, *International Journal of Production Research*, 51(10), 3117–3130.

Wit, G., Uhlaner, L., Berent-Braun, M., Jeurissen, R. (2012). “Beyond Size: Predicting Engagement in Environmental Management Practices of Dutch SMEs.” *Journal of Business Ethics, 109*. 10.1007/s10551-011-1137-x.

Yadav, G. S., Das, A., Lal, R., Babu, S., Meena, R. S., Saha, P., . . . & Datta, M. (2018). “Energy budget and carbon footprint in a no-till and mulch–based rice–mustard cropping system”, *Journal of cleaner production, 191*, 144–157.

Shefali Saluja

13 An Analysis of MSMEs' Contributions to the Promotion of SDGs in India

Abstract: Responsible and sustainable consumerism is everyone's business in today's world. No organization can ignore the environmental problems that impact us all in the face of growing worries over climate change and energy security. Micro, Small and medium-sized businesses (MSMEs) are crucial to the nation's growth. Sustainable development may be attained through socially conscious businesses and innovative MSMEs led by entrepreneurs who follow 21st-century's viewpoints and recommendations and produce new eco-friendly technology that could replenish natural resources. MSMEs can build the foundation for regional, national, and global sustainability initiatives. To successfully incorporate sustainability concepts and practices into their corporate cultures, MSMEs must understand the new opportunities and how they apply them. This chapter presents a rationale for implementing the principles of sustainable development and demonstrates how MSMEs may support it. It shows that it takes changing regulations and systemic changes in how financial markets and institutions function to fully realize the promise of MSMEs for the SDGs. This would ease the barriers that MSMEs must overcome to access financial resources and help turn informal MSMEs into formal ones. And this would have several far-reaching effects, opening more funding sources, boosting extra economic growth, and creating more job prospects.

Keywords: MSMEs, Sustainability, SDGs, India

Introduction

India has a long history of upholding the idea of independence. Jawaharlal Nehru, India's first Prime Minister, had envisioned a nation independent of imports. Small businesses were expected to supply the economic rocket fuel. Micro businesses are those with fewer than nine employees, small businesses are between 10 and 49 employees, and medium businesses are between 50 and 249 employees, according to the World Bank. However, the local definition of MSMEs, which differs from nation to country and is based on elements more than just the workforce size, such as turnaround and assets, is defined locally. MSMEs have a big impact on the overall business ecosystem (Mehta et al., 2019; 2022a). Start-ups and new enterprises, often small or micro businesses, are common in many countries (Prasetyo,2021; Mehta et al., 2022a). The impor-

Shefali Saluja, Chitkara Business School, Chitkara University, Punjab, India

https://doi.org/10.1515/9783111170022-013

tance of MSMEs in India's illustrious economic history cannot be overstated, especially if the country has the confidence to become an economic superpower. Despite having limited operating capital and funding gaps, MSMEs continue to propel countries towards economic growth. This idea was first presented by the Indian government in 2006 through the Micro, Small and Medium Enterprises Development (MSMED) Act. There are more new companies valued at over $1 billion each year, or "unicorns." Numbers paint a moving picture. According to a FICCI report, MSMEs make up around 40% of exports, 45% of manufacturing output, and 95% of industrial units, according to a recent post on Greeneconomycoalition.org. It also states that the sector is the second-largest source of income production in rural areas, behind the agriculture sector, providing employment opportunities for about 60 million people. SME financing is still a hot topic in our nation. As per the SME Rating Agency of India, to some extent, the financial opposition that MSMEs and MSMEs experience from lending institutions or investors can be overcome by a solid sustainability record. Making sustainable products can also assist MSMEs in expanding their market share, identifying new competencies, and meeting supply-chain demands. Sustainability is certain to take centre stage in discussions on the "role of SMEs in India", – which is appropriate given their status as the nation's growth engine (Arifin et al., 2021).

EU standards define SMEs as businesses with fewer than 250 employees, annual revenue of up to 50 million euros, and/or an annual balance sheet of up to 43 million euros (European Commission, 2005). The EU Central Bank estimates that SMEs account for 99.8% of all non-financial businesses in the EU, create 66.6% of jobs, and produce 56.4% of added value. But they are currently taking significant damage due to the COVID-19 pandemic that is spreading rapidly worldwide. As the epidemic has pushed approximately 70% of small and medium-sized enterprises (SMEs) to cease operations, the recovery efforts are mostly. Motivated by the Sustainable Development Goals (SDGs) by focusing on constructing more inclusive economies and societies to chart a new route for a socially just, low-carbon, and climate-resilient world where no one is left behind (PWC, 2020). Export and domestic manufacturing, operational adaptability, technology, and innovation-oriented endeavors, etc., are all areas in which India's thriving sectors play a significant role. These small and medium-sized enterprises (MSMEs) have enormously contributed to the healthy growth of India's economy. More than half of all businesses are based in rural areas, which is great news for inclusive growth and fair distribution across the country. Massive personal and financial growth is possible through MSME (Puspasari et al., 2022). By focusing on topics like gender and racial justice, low-cost non-agrarian employment prospects, impartial local development, and environmentally sustainable growth, SMEs contribute to quick economic growth and creating a diverse and reasonable populace. Approximately 1.2 million micro, small, and medium-sized firms (20%) employ approximately 40% of India's labor force, with most of these establishments in rural areas (Batalhone & Clement, 2018). Table 13.1 has explained the definition of MSME defined by Government of India.

Table 13.1: Definition of MSMEs Retrieved Official Website of MSMEs (https://msme.gov.in).

Classification	Micro	Small	Medium
Manufacturing Enterprises and Enterprises rendering services	Investment in Plant and Machinery or Equipment Not more than Rs 1 crore and Annual Turnover, not more than Rs 5 crore	Investment in Plant and Machinery or Equipment Not more than Rs 10 crore and Annual Turnover, not more than Rs 50 crore	Investment in Plant and Machinery or Equipment Not more than Rs 50 crore and Annual Turnover, not more than Rs 250 crore

What is Sustainability?

Micro, small, and medium-sized enterprises (MSMEs) that act ethically regarding their local and global social, economic, and environmental concerns adopt sustainable development. The concept emphasizes a general, long-term commitment to maintaining a balance between social, environmental, and economic concerns, as opposed to short-term gains and unplanned supplementary activity. Unfortunately, there is little research on how MSMEs function, even though the phrase has only lately started to appear in management literature, and there are usually conflicting definitions of the concept (Condon,2004).

This chapter aims to highlight the importance, function, and contributions of MSMEs to the 17 Sustainable Development Goals (SDGs). The research looks at how MSMEs fit into each of the SDGs. The chapter explores the function of MSMEs in the economy by generating. Employment and incomes, particularly for the underprivileged and marginalized groups, as providers of services (such as education, health, water, and sanitation) and as consumers of energy and environmental polluters. These perspectives allow for establishing direct and indirect connections between MSMEs and the seventeen goals.

Sustainability and its Contribution to SDGs

Unsustainable consumption and production practices worsen inequality and the depletion of natural resources as economic expansion quickens. For the Sustainable Development Goals to be met by 2030, business as usual is no longer a viable option, either in the short- or long-term. We must immediately switch to a green economy that benefits all people and places a premium on using resources effectively and protecting ecosystems for the long term. Promoting sustainable lifestyles, expanding sustainable consumption and production (SCP), and inspiring environmental entrepreneurship are all necessary steps in the transition to a green economy that benefits (Wirdani & Rachmawati, 2022). New jobs are predicted to be produced in the renewable energy and recycling industries, among others, without jeopardizing existing employment through the development of innovations, the promotion of resource efficiency, and the mainstreaming of conscientious consumer behaviour. Reduced carbon emissions, garbage, and other pollution are all possible outcomes. Unfortunately, the complexity of the sustainable landscape sometimes leaves firms confused. Micro, small, and medium-sized enterprises (MSMEs) in developing nations have difficulties due to developing rules, standards, codes of conduct, and similar activities in the global value chain. Discrimination against micro, small, and medium-sized enterprises (MSMEs) may occur if the requirements are too complex. MSMEs frequently lack the technical and financial resources to comply with the standards and provide evidence of compliance. Also, the proliferation of standards can lead to muddled thinking among MSMEs and manufacturers, higher implementation costs, and the appearance of non-tariff barriers where none existed.

SMEs are crucial for fostering globalization and prosperity that is more inclusive due to the following reasons:

- Several countries, especially those in the OECD, are struggling with the challenges of slow growth, weak trade, and investment, and rising or persistently high inequality. The public's growing displeasure with the state of affairs, which is also manifesting as a backlash against globalization and technological innovation, is another issue they must deal with. The correct conditions must be in place for open markets and technology. Innovation is more advantageous and evenly spread throughout the economy and society.
- Small and medium-sized enterprises (SMEs) play an important role in the economy and the business ecosystem. People need to be equipped with the abilities to adapt, prosper in an open environment, and actively participate in digital transformation if the economy is to expand. The globalization process is to be more equitable. Because of their ability to foster inclusive and sustainable economic growth, provide jobs and decent work for all, encourage sustainable industrialization and innovation, and decrease income inequality, small and medium-sized enterprises (SMEs) are crucial to achieving the Sustainable Development Goals (SDGs) in all countries and at all stages of development (Arner et al., 2022).
- Small and medium-sized enterprises (SMEs) make important contributions to the economy and society that could be expanded upon. When the impact of unreported businesses is factored in, small and medium-sized enterprises (SMEs) are responsible for more than half of employment and GDP in most countries (IFC, 2010). Expanding small and medium-sized enterprises (SMEs) can bolster economic stability and diversity. For resource-rich countries, this is crucial because they are more vulnerable to swings in commodity prices.

The bigger business ecosystem depends on SMEs. The main causes of net job growth in many countries are young firms, which are frequently small or micro businesses. Also, the rise in productivity is significantly influenced by business considerations

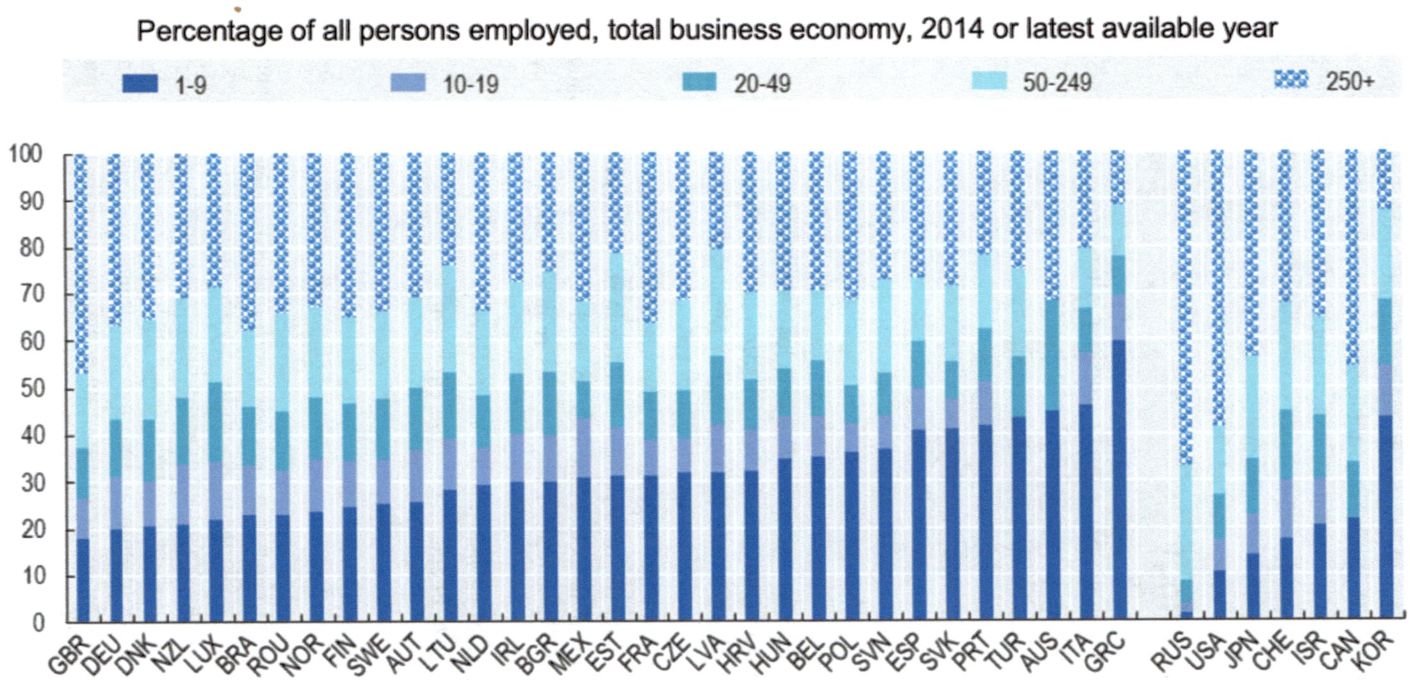

Figure 13.1: Most Business Jobs Come from Small and Medium-Sized Enterprises (SMEs).

Note: For Canada, Switzerland, Israel, Japan, Korea, the United States and the Russian Federation, Data do not Include Non-Employers. Data for Korea and Mexico are Based on Establishments. Data for the United Kingdom Exclude an Estimate of 2.6 Million Small Unregistered Business. For Austraila, Canada and Turkey the Size Class 1–9 Refers to 1–19.

Source: OCED (2017), Entrepreneurship at a Glance 2017, OECD Publishing, Paris, Forthcoming.

(OECD, 2018). Nonetheless, most new enterprises either fail within the first few years of existence or remain small (OECD, 2018). Also, rapidly growing businesses contribute significantly to job growth across various industries and age groups. Refer to Figure 13.1 to understand the jobs offered by SMEs across various countries of the world.

Research Methodology

This study examined the elements SMEs might consider when promoting the SDGs. Several databases, including:

a) Science Direct
b) Springer Link
c) Emerald
d) Web of Science
e) Scopus
f) Scimago

All the above were searched for the data. The articles were published in the past years till 2023. Moreover, the study also reviewed some latest industry reports like OECD 2018, Business Economics, MSME Government of India website, FICCI and Ministry of External Affairs

Selection of Data: The information gathered from the chosen articles concentrated on the SDGs threshold in 2030, the involvement of SMEs in sustainability, and India's entrepreneurial spirit, innovation, social responsibility, and sustainable development.

Research requisites: The articles used for this review analysis primarily addressed the following areas:

- *Empirical research articles published in academic journals.*
- *Empirical research articles in and across different countries*

MSMEs and Sustainability

Sustainability has taken center stage as a major trend in modernization. The government of India has made numerous promises on the global and national stages. The Make in India "Zero Defect and Zero Effect" launched by the Government of India was a significant move towards achieving balanced, long-term economic growth. The Indian economy needs to work together to improve conditions. The current scenario relies heavily on manufacturing sector to maintain economic growth. Governments worldwide have recently pledged to alter the global economic model to better address social and environmental concerns. These changes are in more demand from customers. All businesses, regardless of size, should be aware of the laws and regulations being updated to reflect this shift. Even though many new rules are aimed at major corporations and energy-intensive industries, even SMEs will feel the effects of this trend. Small and medium-sized enterprises (SMEs) prepare a sizable chunk of the global economy, and their cooperation with the changes is considered important if governments are to achieve their goals. Small and medium-sized enterprises (SMEs) seeking to do business with large corporations and government agencies would do well to familiarise themselves with the new responsibilities that these entities face, as these could lead to the imposition of constraints on the SMEs' suppliers (Virmani et al., 2022). However, larger organizations increasingly decide to impose their value criteria on SMEs who want to collaborate with them. Therefore, SMEs need to be aware of this trend. Because of this, supply chain SMEs should be ready to adjust their methods as required to keep their clientele happy. Governments and banks are providing new avenues of financial support to SMEs that involve making social and environmental reforms to encourage the business community to adapt to new and sustainable ways of operating. Companies, especially SMEs, willing to incorporate solutions to these problems into their operations have a better chance of accessing previously unavailable funding options. Accounting professionals have always been crucial in assisting small and medium-sized enterprises (SMEs) to become profitable, grow and adapt to new regulations. Many specific actions in the sustainability agenda can be navigated with their assistance (Mahesh et al., 2022). Professional accountants in the SME sector are in a prime position to advise their customers on how to take advantage of the opportunities presented by the sustainability agenda, in addition to helping manage compliance (Submitter et al., 2022).

MSMEs' Opportunities

Micro, small, and medium-sized businesses (MSMEs) have experienced explosive growth since the 2008 financial crisis. According to data from a recent OECD and World Bank survey, MSMEs in countries like the UK, France, and Sweden are growing, which is good news for the economy and the job market. Fifty-one per cent of the MSMEs surveyed have plans to increase staffing levels within the next three years.

To a greater extent than in other economic sectors, SMEs predominate in sectors where a large number of workers are needed but where a high level of expertise is not required, such as

Manufacturing and service industry. In contrast to large corporations, small and medium-sized businesses (SMBs) often sell their products directly to consumers through channels like the Internet and word-of-mouth advertising, or they are contracted as suppliers in the lower-value-added upstream segments of value chains dominated by multinational corporations (MNEs). Due to a lack of trust and market intelligence, MSMEs tend to work together less frequently. Since many MSMEs, and especially micro-enterprises, are run by families, hiring decisions are often made without giving much thought to whether or not the prospective employee has the necessary skills. As a result, jobs created by MSMEs may be lower-paying and less secure than those offered by large firms due to this impacting operational efficiency, quality and consistency in products and processes and competitiveness. Yet, there is relatively less data on the expansion of MSMEs in countries with developing and growing economies. According to a recent OECD-World Bank study on inclusive global value chains, the most rapid expansion of micro, small, and medium-sized enterprises (MSMEs) occur in sectors that are both labour-intensive and possess low barriers to entry, such as agricultural production and agribusiness, industrial production, and the related industries. However, many micro, small, and medium-sized enterprises (MSMEs) in developing nations are still operated in an unofficial capacity. It is also significant because small and medium-sized enterprises (SMEs) income in developing economies is increasingly capitalizing on knowledge. Knowledge-based capital, when combined with the fragmentation of value chains, could help micro, small and medium-sized enterprises (MSMEs) from developing nations carve out a place for themselves in established international marketplaces, ultimately leading to the creation of more value.

Some Common Schemes for MSMEs by Make in India

1. Micro, Small, and Medium-Sized Businesses (MSMEs) are the backbone of the Indian economy, and they have benefited greatly from the government's support through initiatives like "Made in India" and the "Atmanirbhar Bharat Abhiyaan" (Self Dependent India Campaign).
2. The Prime Minister's Employment Generation Programme (PMEGP) was established for this purpose and is managed by the "Khadi and Village Industries Commission" at the central level and by the State KVIC Directorates, "State Khadi and Village Industries Boards", "District Industries Centres" and banks at the state and local levels.
3. Khadi institutions around the country are able to get funding for their khadi programmes thanks to a new scheme called "Interest Subsidy Eligibility Certificate" (ISEC). It does So by tapping into the resources of financial institutions in an effort to close the gap between the money available from the budget and the actual amount needed.

The Role of MSMEs in Fulfilling the SDGs

Due to their wide range of activities, MSMEs can significantly contribute to several different SDG targets. Social and transformational entrepreneurs innovate with new services and methods of doing business while also providing decent work for their employees. If they are successful, it will enhance life for everyone, especially the most disadvantaged, and it will also help the economy remain stable (Taiwo et al., 2022). With the right knowledge and (digital) resources, transformational/social/humanitarian entrepreneurs and MSMEs can provide affordable, contextualized, dependable, supportable, and healthful food, teaching, health, aquatic and hygiene, energy, weather, and modern city explanations needed to speed up the implementation of the 2030 Agenda. Figure 13.2 has given a pictorial description of all 17 SDGs.

Figure 13.2: Sustainable Development Goals.
Source: https://www.un.org/en/sustainable-development-goals.

By capitalizing on the trillions of dollars in business opportunities represented by the SDGs, small and medium-sized enterprises (SMEs) can help implement these goals and create a vicious circle of transformation and environmental sustainability in their native countries. However, especially in developing and transition economies, entrepreneurs face obstacles that slow down their ability to engage in productive activities and contribute to inclusive as well as green advancement, and thus speed up the implementation of the SDGs. Competition, high electricity costs, a lack of knowledge about available business options, a widening digital divide, and a lack of capital all fall into this category. Women and minority-owned businesses are feeling the pinch of these issues more than others. With this, let us see the role of MSMEs in the contribution towards achieving SDGs:

1. MSMEs' Contribution to "No Poverty."

70% of India's entire population lives in rural areas. The majority of the rural population lives in remote and underdeveloped communities. According to the 2011 census, more than 600,000 villages are home to approximately 800 million inhabitants in rural areas (Elbers & Lanjouw, 2019). Improved living conditions and economic stability for rural residents are hallmarks of successful rural development. A key factor in the fight against poverty has been creating jobs in the private sector. MSMEs provide a substantial contribution to the private sector's process of creating jobs (Jacob et al., 2022). MSMEs created four out of every five new formal sector jobs in emerging markets or roughly 90% of all new jobs. A game-changer in the fight against poverty could be MSMEs. This is supported by the fact that more than 1109 lakh people are currently employed by more than 633 lakh MSMEs in rural areas, providing both self-employment and wage employment opportunities through entrepreneurship (Vaishnav & Surya, 2020). Data shared from the Udayam portal by Minister of State for MSMEs Bhanu Pratap Singh Verma indicates that the number of people employed by micro, small, and medium-sized enterprises (MSMEs) in fiscal year 22 was approximately 10.31 million, a 16% increase from the number of people employed by MSMEs in fiscal year 21. To increase employment, which would lead to rural development and poverty reduction, the author argues that government interventions are necessary for monetary, structural, and technical support for MSMEs. There will be a better chance for rural growth and poverty reduction if more small and medium-sized enterprises (SMBs) succeed.

2. MSMEs' Contribution to "Zero Hunger."

MSMEs support initiatives to build the capacity of small-scale farmers and MSMEs with an agricultural focus directly related to SDG Goal 2.3. 14 Small-scale farmers make up a major portion of the farming population in emerging nations. Among the nations in Africa, Asia, and Latin America for which data are available, the proportion of small-scale food producers ranges from around 40 to about 85%. The Antyodaya Anna Yojana (AAY) plan aims to end hunger in India and provide food security for all citizens over the next five years while also reforming and improving the public distribution system to help the poorest people in rural and urban areas. Operational responsibilities for lifting and distributing the food grains within the States and UTs, include identifying Below Poverty Line (BPL) families, issuing rations, as well as tracking the allocation of apportioned grain production to able to qualify cardholders through affordable grocery stores of State/UT Governments. Hence, MSMEs might been encouraged to run nutrition education and awareness programmes to enhance home eating practices. These programmes can simultaneously encourage people to eat food produced by small-scale farmers.

3. MSMEs' Contribution to "Good Health and Well-Being."

To guarantee that MSMEs continue to exhibit resilient and robust growth, providing access to affordable and accessible healthcare solutions for employees and safeguarding against personal and company risks through proper insurance coverage remains crucial. Offering health insurance to employees is essential for MSMEs as a risk reduction strategy for the company and to help shield staff members and their families from the financial burden of unforeseen health crises and scares. In addition, MSMEs are closing the healthcare gap by offering higher-quality medical treatment and a greater array of fundamental laboratory and imaging services.

4. MSMEs' Contribution to "Quality Education."

According to business economics (https://businesseconomics.in/msme-growth-path-role-education), the information below demonstrates how crucial the MSME sector is to the Indian economy and how carefully it must be nurtured. India has 6.33 billion MSMEs, of which 6.30 billion, or 99.4%, are micro-enterprises, 3.31 lakh, or 0.52%, are medium-sized businesses, and 5,000, or 0.007%, are medium-sized businesses. In India, micro, small, and medium-sized businesses employed more than 110 million people in the fiscal year 2020. The MSME industry contributes over 6000 goods to exports and 30% of GDP. Micro, small, and medium-sized enterprises (MSMEs) in education can potentially increase the public's access to these services. In order to reach SDG 4, small and medium-sized businesses (SMEs) must significantly raise possibilities for young people and women to engage in and take advantage of formal qualifications and the workplace.

5. MSMEs' Contribution to "Gender Equality."

Strengthening the capabilities of women owned and operated MSMEs is one way to help women become more financially self-sufficient. Women-owned micro, small, and medium-sized enterprises (MSMEs) are present across all economic sectors. They are more likely to be more prevalent in the retail, wholesale, healthcare, and cosmetics industries. In the industries of tourism, transportation, hotels and restaurants, services, and trade, they are on roughly equal footing. However, their presence in manufacturing, agriculture, and construction is a little bit less (Endris & Kassegn, 2022). Women-owned firms face several challenges, the most significant of which is a dearth of funding. Lack of business skills and prospects is another hindrance. Nevertheless, it is possible to encourage MSMEs, like large corporations, to implement gender-inclusive policies throughout their value chains and daily operations. This includes providing women with flexible work hours, aiding with children and childcare, promoting women to management jobs, raising gender parity in teams, and not tolerating workplace abuse.

6. MSMEs' Contribution to "Clean Water and Sanitation."

The objective is to guarantee everyone has access to water, sustainable water management, and sanitary conditions. MSMEs Working in the area could be very beneficial in addressing water and sanitation-related issues. As businesses typically have a plentiful water source for their operations, they might distribute water from their plant to the residents (Verma,2019). By decreasing contamination, eliminating dumping activities, and restricting the release of hazardous residual materials, MSMEs may contribute to improving water quality. Also, they might encourage and improve community involvement in enhancing local sanitation, water management, and water efficiency. In the same vein, they may create ponds and dams as part of their CSR responsibilities to assist in conserving and replenishing water.

7. MSMEs' Contribution to "Affordable and Clean Energy."
MSMEs can improve their ZED score by using solar energy because it lowers carbon emission and qualifies them for government incentives and subsidies. By adding solar rooftops, it lowers overall costs and the cost of electricity. Contrary to the conventional method of using coal-generated power, it provides constant access to electricity, one of its key benefits. The company's brand will grow by attracting investors and customers by demonstrating that it supports a green environment. Through funding and promoting renewable energy projects, IREDA, also known as the Indian Renewable Energy Development Agency, seeks to combat the effects of climate change and reduce pollution (Olabi et al., 2022). More loans will be funded for SMEs recently, increasing their involvement in the green energy sector. MSMEs must demonstrate significant participation in the effort to reach the 2030 goals of 500 GW of renewable energy capacity and a 50% share of energy coming from fossil fuels.

8. MSMEs' Contribution to "Decent Work and Economic Growth."
In contrast to interventions at only one level, a "productivity ecosystem" strategy entails tackling the issue of MSME productivity in an integrated manner across the levels of firm, sector, national, and subnational performance (Mehta & Sharma, 2016). In order to comprehend and solve the underlying causes of MSMEs' low production levels and growth rates, it also needs to look past the immediately apparent symptoms. Low productivity levels, for instance, may not just be the result of inadequate firm-level knowledge but may also be partially the result of more structural problems like restricted access to resources (capital, labour, and technology), unfavourable business environment conditions, and insufficient MSME policies and programmes (Ejarque & Campos, 2020). In addition, the formalization and growth of entrepreneurship as envisioned by this goal will necessitate addressing several issues that MSMEs face, such as the need for better infrastructure for MSME operations and more enabling policy and regulatory frameworks, finance, and market information access.

9. MSMEs' Contribution to "Industry Innovation and Infrastructure."
Not all micro, small, or medium-sized enterprises (MSMEs) are artistic. However, many are because they can function outside traditional frameworks, seize commercial or technological opportunities that larger enterprises may have missed, or aid in commercializing knowledge that might otherwise remain untapped (Liu, 2018) For example, MSMEs account for approximately 20% of patents in the biotechnology sector in Europe, which is an indicator of innovation. The SDGs advocate for resource efficiency and environmentally friendly manufacturing practices. The good news for the economy is that micro, small, and medium-sized businesses (MSMEs) can successfully replicate and commercialize innovations and create value in various fields, such as operating systems, nano-technology, bioengineering, and environmental protection.

10. MSMEs' Contribution to "Reduced Inequalities."

MSMEs encourage economic participation and have the potential to revitalize underserved regions of the country. Small businesses provide services to communities, demographics, and markets too small for larger companies to compete. Smaller firms can revitalize economically underdeveloped communities because research has shown that they typically spend more of the money they earn locally. Young people, women, and members of other underrepresented groups, including immigrants, members of disadvantaged ethnic groups, and people with disabilities all benefit from the opportunities for employment and entrepreneurship offered by MSMEs. Thus, micro, small, and medium-sized enterprises (MSMEs) are crucial to lifting the living standards of the world's poorest 40%.

11. MSMEs' Contribution to "Sustainable Cities and Communities."

According to Khan (2011), small and medium-sized enterprises (SMEs) in the professional services, digital, and creative industries, collectively referred to as "new work", are becoming increasingly important to cities in terms of employment and production. They can cooperate to establish and/or participate in a sustainable community that brings concerned parties to a neutral, common forum to examine, debate, and take action on urban functionality, resilience, and sustainable development issues. They can also care and consider the use of public services in transportation (Seshagiri, 2019).

12. MSMEs' Contribution to "Responsible Consumption and Production."

MSMEs are the foundation of the national economy and the international supply chains of major corporations. MSMEs individually have minimal social and environmental implications, but together, the effects are significantly more significant. MSMEs make up a sizable portion of all private sector organizations in both developed and developing nations, including Peru. Participation of MSMEs in public procurement can be hampered by green public procurement. The difficulties MSMEs encounter in green public procurement can be addressed by strengthening policies and providing capacity-building assistance for MSMEs (Milwood, 2020). MSMEs must be encouraged to embrace ethical business practices and to report on those that can be profitable for them (Romana, 2017).

13. MSMEs' Contribution to "Climate Action."

There is mounting evidence that climate change places serious risks for small, medium-sized businesses (MSMEs). MSMEs are the second-largest employers after agriculture and contribute 30% of GDP. The industry is responsible for around one-fourth of all GHG (Green House Gas) emissions in India, according to the GHG Platform India. Some of the possible hazards offered by climate change to organizations include infrastructure damage, regulatory uncertainty, financial risks, market swings, supply chain disruptions, and reputational damage (Hammond et al., 2007). The commercial argument for corporate climate action is compelling, nevertheless. Some companies, including Mahindra, Tata, and Dalmia, have sparked broader discussions about climate action, leading many others to make commitments to "net zero" and "carbon negative" goals during the coming ten years. To assist MSMEs in quickly implementing climate-smart technology and practises, provide access to low-cost climate funding. The newly signed agreement between the European Investment Bank and SBI promises to offer $100 million in equity financing for small firms focusing on combating climate change. It is anticipated to inspire MSMEs to adopt creative, environmentally friendly solutions. Provide incentives for MSMEs to engage in the SME Climate Hub, a global project developed as a one-stop-shop for SMEs to reduce carbon emissions and increase company resilience. This can be done through customizing legislation and regulations. Currently, 19 Indian MSMEs have committed to science-based goals for tackling climate change.

14. MSMEs' Contribution to "Life Below Water."

Roughly equal numbers of men and women are employed in the small-scale artisanal fishing industry across pre-harvest, harvest, and post-harvest stages. However, women are overrepresented in fish processing and small-scale fish trading. Sustainable practices like eco-labelling and traceability systems for wild catch would help MSMEs become more competitive in the face of rising consumer demand for fair exchange, natural, and bio trades product lines. The increasing demand from consumers for fair trade, organic, and bio trades products can be met by adopting sustainable practices such as eco labelling and suitability processes for a wild catch.

Recent developments have been made in marine biotechnology, ocean thermal energy conversion, wave and tidal energy generation, among other marine renewable energy sources. Commercializing sea food fit for the cosmetics industry, extracting green energy from the sea, and collecting microorganisms for use in the chemical and pharmaceutical industries are now all instances. If the marine industry is going to get the most out of the contributions of small-scale enterprises, it is crucial to recognize the value of micro, small and medium-sized enterprises (MSMEs) in these developing industries, cultivate the skills of current small business owners, and support new ventures.

15. MSMEs' Contribution to "Life on Land."

Companies, particularly those whose core offering is the ecological restoration of forests and landscapes, are coming to see the commercial potential in this field. This link may be direct, such as with tree-planting companies, or indirect, such as firms that supply tools or advice for ecological restoration. Even if a company's earnings have nothing to do with restoration, it can still be considered a restoration venture if it uses its profits to fund restoration efforts. As a Result of their contributions to the SDG, current MSMEs and start-ups will have access to new economic opportunities. However, they will need assistance in order to fully realize these opportunities.

16. MSMEs' Contribution to "Peace, Justice and Strong Institutions."

MSMEs' expansion and profitability may be aided by adopting ethical business practices and standards and encouraging their inclusion within value chains. For instance, a business that operates ethically and without the need for unlawful payments can operate more affordably. Strengthening client connections, enhancing reputation, and gaining more business can all be achieved by upholding high standards of corporate ethics and integrity. MSMEs offer employment and business opportunities that generate money for underprivileged families, women, and young people. Encouraging women- and youth-led businesses is a successful violence prevention tactic because the money earned from entrepreneurship can persuade young people not to join the armed forces or commit crimes. Helping marginalized youth- and woman-led companies can help create a more inclusive society, fostering peace (Ferrata,2019).

17. MSMEs' Contribution to "Partnerships for the Goals."
Public-private partnerships (PPPs) also involve MSMEs in providing services to meet various developmental concerns. For example, when they collaborate directly with communities, they can participate in discussions with governments and communities to identify answers to development issues. In addition, with Corporate Social Responsibility (CSR) initiatives, they can benefit society.

Conclusion

While the gap between basic connectivity and web presence is generally small, it widens when considering involvement in e-commerce and, particularly, more advanced apps. Cloud computing, which includes renting computer capacity from an external source, can allow smaller enterprises to access big data while overcoming some constraints connected with the high fixed-cost commitment. However, many countries have a significant adoption gap (Tambunan,2011). Our livelihoods are intricately linked to the health of the ecosystems in which we live. There is a direct correlation between industrialization (or just doing business) and the degradation of the natural environment (Vyas et al., 2023). We need to adopt green technology that puts us on the road to sustainable development if we want to succeed in environmental protection and industrialization. To ensure that the natural world can continue to provide for human needs in future environmental sustainability centers on making decisions and engaging in environmentally responsible activities, and protecting nature (Sharma et al., 2022). This is a pressing concern now because of the growing awareness of the damage that human activities can do to the natural world. Sustainable business is more than recycling more or turning off the lights when they're not in use; it's about creating systems that will make companies long-term fixtures in their communities and aid in the fight to save the planet by developing more effective green technologies. One of the newest trends nowadays is starting or transitioning a firm into an environmentally friendly enterprise, and many new possibilities are opening every day due to the constant stream of cutting-edge ideas, models, and techniques. More and more customers are gravitating towards green and organic products; therefore, encouraging MSMEs to become environmentally conscious and environmentally friendly is a win-win. Consumers are increasingly conscious of their purchasing decisions' impact on the earth and its inhabitants. As a result, they are increasingly choosing green and environmentally friendly options. Businesses that invest in environmentally friendly technologies see a surge in sales and a high likelihood of future expansion as consumers become more conscious of the importance of environmentally responsible products. In recent years, sustainability has emerged as a major theme in international development discussions, and the Indian government has pledged several efforts to protect the environment at home and abroad. One such initiative is the government's "Make in India" programme, which pairs the quality assurance goals of "Zero Defect & Zero Effect" with those of "Make in India," thereby expressing the will to strike a balance between economic growth, sustainability, and social inclusion while also encouraging MSMEs to maintain ever-improving product and process quality without negatively impacting the environment. Over the long term, sustainable nation-building requires contributions from agriculture, industry, and the service sector. Increased focus on the manufacturing sector as an essential part of sustainable economic development has increased the significance of resource consumption, particularly of fossil fuels and other non-renewable resources. The SDGs will be accomplished by supporting new business strategies, possibilities, and models for MSMEs. This goal is connected to the evolution of global value chains because they are components of a more cohesive global economic system (GVCs) (Sulis-wanto & Rofik, 2019). GVCs and digital transformation present MSMEs with fresh chances for global economic integration. MSMEs may have a competitive edge in international markets because of their increased flexibility, ability to modify products, and capacity to differentiate products due to their ability to react quickly to shifting market conditions and test with shorter products life cycles. MSMEs rule over several niche international markets, and inventive small enterprises are frequently significant collaborators with larger multinationals in creating new products or providing new customers. Everyone must work towards sustainable development to safeguard the environment (biome) and human health for the present and the future (Dasaraju et al., 2022). Using international standards to accomplish the SDGs enables smaller firms to take action, increase the impact of their efforts, and contribute to the solution. When corporate planning and goals are combined, new and lucrative opportunities are unlocked, higher productivity levels are encouraged, and innovation is boosted, all supporting strong economic growth. By adopting a standards-based approach to sustainability, smaller organizations will be better equipped to adapt, implement suitable internal policies, and communicate their performance to external stakeholders.

Policy Implications

Most micro, small, and medium-sized enterprises (MSMEs) are in rural areas, providing year-round non–farm employment, easing the burden on the agricultural sector while discouraging people from leaving the countryside for the city. It is important to boost the number of MSMEs operating in the formal sector of the economy, as most of these businesses now operate outside of it. Encourage business owners in this field to register their company with the Ministry of Micro, Small, and Medium Enterprises (MSME) to take advantage of the government, banking system, and other agency programmes designed to help them succeed. Tax breaks, streamlined processes, improved infrastructure, a welcoming atmosphere, and other incentives should be offered to private companies. The lack of cash flow is an issue for small businesses, which is made worse by the issue of late payments. Because most purchasers aren't vigilant about making payments on time, providing them various incentives, and having the appropriate gear on hand to quickly resolve complaints about payment delays is important.

References

Arner, D. W., Animashaun, S., Charamba, K., & Cai, Y. (2022). "MSME Access to Finance: The Role of Digital Payments", *United Nations, Economic and Social Commission for Asia and the Pacific, MSME Financing Series* (7).

Arifin, R., Ningsih, A. A., & Putri, A. K. (2021). "The Important Role Of MSMEs In Improving The Economy", *East Asia Journal of Contemporary Business, Economics and Law*, 52–59.

Ayyagari, M., Demirguc-Kunt, A., & Maksimovic, V. (2014). "Who creates jobs in developing countries?", *Small Business Economics, 43*, 75–99.

Batalhone, A. P., & Clement, D. (2018). "How sustainability standards contribute to SDG 12", International Trade Forum (3*)*, 14–15. Retrieved from https://www.proquest.com/scholarly-journals/how-sustainability-standards-contribute-sdg-12/docview/2136874420/se-2

Condon, L. (2004). "Sustainability and Small to Medium Sized Enterprises–How to Engage Them", *Australian Journal of Environmental Education*. 20. 10.1017/S0814062600002305.

Dasaraju, H., Abraham, S., Somalraju, K., & Aparna, S. (2022). "Reflections of covid-19 on MSMEs in developing economies: a case of India. *Covid-19 and its Reflection on SMEs in Developing Countries*", 41–58.

Endris, E., & Kassegn, A. (2022). "The role of micro, small and medium enterprises (MSMEs) to the sustainable development of sub-Saharan Africa and its challenges: a systematic review of evidence from Ethiopia", *Journal of Innovation and Entrepreneurship, 11*(1), 20.

Ejarque, A. T., & Campos, V. (2020). "Assessing the economy for the common good measurement theory ability to integrate the SDGs into MSMEs". *Sustainability, 12*(24), 10305

Elbers, C., & Lanjouw, P. (2019). "The distributional impact of structural transformation in rural India: Model-based simulation and case–study evidence" (No. 2019/33). WIDER Working Paper.

Ferrata, L. (2019). "Digital financial inclusion–an engine for "leaving no one behind", *Public Sector Economics, 43*(4), 445–458

Hammond, A. et al. (2007). "The Next 4 Billion Market Size and Business Strategy at the Base of the Pyramid", World Resources Institute (WRI) and the International Finance Corporation, World Bank Group

Jacob-John, J., D'Souza, C., Marjoribanks, T., & Singaraju, S. P. (2022). "Institutional pressures for SDGs in Indian food supply chains", *Social Responsibility Journal* (ahead-of-print).

Khan, A. D. (2011). "MSMEs and Their Role in Ensuring Sustainable Economic Development in India Characterized By LPG", *International Journal of Management Research and Development (IJMRD)*, *1*(1).

Liu, C. K. (2018). "Policy Brief: The Role of Micro-Small and Medium Enterprises in Achieving SDGs-1. Micro-, Small and Medium Enterprises (MSMEs) and their potential contributions to SDGs–2. MSMEs' Growth: Opportunities and Challenges".

Mahesh, K. M., Aithal, P. S., & Sharma, K. R. S. (2022). "Impact of sustainable finance on MSMEs and other companies to promote green growth and sustainable development", *International Journal of Applied Engineering and Management Letters (IJAEML)*, *6*(1), 60–76.

Mehta, K., & Sharma, R. (2016). "SMEs and corporate social responsibility: Indian perception. *SCMS Journal of Indian Management*, *13*(3), 58–67.

Mehta, K., Sharma, R., & Vyas, V. (2019) "Efficiency and ranking of sustainability index of India using DEA-TOPSIS", *Journal of Indian Business Research*, *11*(2), pp. 179–199. https://doi.org/10.1108/JIBR-02-2018–0057.

Mehta, K., Sharma, R., & Vyas, V. (2022). "A quantile regression approach to study the impact of aluminium prices on the manufacturing sector of India during the COVID era", *Materials Today: Proceedings*, *65*(8), 3506-3511, ISSN 2214-7853, https://doi.org/10.1016/j.matpr.2022.06.087.

Mehta, K., Sharma, R., Vyas, V. & Kuckreja, J.S. (2022). "Exit strategy decision by venture capital firms in India using fuzzy AHP", *Journal of Entrepreneurship in Emerging Economies*, *14(*4), 643–669. https://doi.org/10.1108/JEEE-05-2020-0146

Milwood, P. A. & Maxwell, A. (2020). "A boundary objects view of Entrepreneurial Ecosystems in tourism." *Journal of Hospitality and Tourism Management*, *44*, 243–252.

Organization for Economic Co-operation and Development (OECD) Development Centre and Emerging Markets Network (EMnet) (2018). Policy Note on Sustainability Better Business For 2030: Putting the SDGs at the Core. OECD.

Olabi, A. G., Obaideen, K., Elsaid, K., Wilberforce, T., Sayed, E. T., Maghrabie, H. M., & Abdelkareem, M. A. (2022). "Using novel indicators to assess the pre–combustion carbon capture contribution to sustainable development goals SDGs", *Renewable and Sustainable Energy Reviews*, *153*, 111710.

Puspasari, N., Sihidi, I. T., & Salahudin, S. (2022). "Analysis of challenges and potential for village economic equity through MSMEs in Tulungagung Regency", *DIA: Jurnal Administrasi Publik*, *20*(02), 196–209.

Prasetyo, P. E. (2021). "The Role of MSME on Unemployment in Indonesia", *Turkish Journal of Computer and Mathematics Education (TURCOMAT)*, *12*(13), 2519–2525.

Romana, L. L. S. (2017). "Sustainable Consumption and Production in the Philippines", In *Sustainable Asia: Supporting the Transition to Sustainable Consumption and Production in Asian Developing Countries* (pp. 239–266).

Schumacher, E. F. (1973). "Small is Beautiful: Economics as if People Mattered, *Harper & Row Publishers"*, London.

Seshagiri Rao, P. V. S. (2019). "FPO Emerging as the New MSME or Village Industry", *SEDME (Small Enterprises Development, Management & Extension Journal)*, *46*(1), 35–53.

Sharma, R., Mehta, K. & Goel, A. (2022). "Non-linear relationship between board size and performance of Indian companies", *Journal of Management and Governance*. https://doi.org/10.1007/s10997-022-09651-8

Shelly, R., Sharma, T., & Bawa, S. S. (2020). "Role of micro, small and medium enterprises in the Indian economy", *International Journal of Economics and Financial Issues*, *10*(5), 84.

Submitter, G. A. T. R., Ilmi, Z., Purwadi, P., & Sampeliling, A. (2022). "Supporting SDGs for increasing the MSMEs Industry–A correlation prediction", *Journals and Ilmi, Zainal and Purwadi, Purwadi and Y., Syaharuddin and Sampeliling, Alexander, Supporting SDGs for Increase of the MSMEs Industry–A Prediction Using Correlation (March 31, 2022). Reference to this paper should be referred to as follows: Ilmi, Z*, 47–63

Suliswanto, M. S. W., & Rofik, M. (2019). "Digitalization of micro, small & medium enterprises (MSMEs) in East Java, Indonesia", *Muhammadiyah International Journal of Economics and Business*, *2*(1), 34–43.

Taiwo, O. S., Hakan, A. C. E. T., & Savaş, Ç. (2022). "Modelling the impacts of MSMEs' contributions to GDP and their constraints on unemployment: the case of Africa's most populous country", *Studies in Business and Economics*, *17*(1), 154–170.

Tambunan, T. T. (2011). "Development of Micro, Small and Medium Enterprises and Their Constraints: A story from Indonesia", *Gadjah Mada International Journal of Business*, *13*(1), 21–43.

United Nations Global Compact. (2016). "A Guide to Traceability for SMEs The Drivers, Opportunities, Challenges and Implementation Steps for Small and Medium-Sized Enterprises (SMEs) Looking to Adopt Traceability in their Supply Chains".

Verma, T. L. (2020). "Role of MSMEs in Poverty Alleviation and Rural Development in India", *International Journal of Multidisciplinary Research and Development*, *7*(9), 61–65, Available at SSRN: https://ssrn.com/abstract=3701314

Vaishnav A, & Surya S. (2020). Definition of MSMEs. Retrieved from Definition of MSMEs, 2020. https://www.prsindia.org/theprsblog/definition-msmes

Verma, T. L. (2019). "Role of micro, small and medium enterprises (MSMEs) in achieving sustainable development goals", *Small And Medium Enterprises (MSMEs) In Achieving Sustainable Development Goals (April 1, 2019)*.

Virmani, N., Saxena, P., & Raut, R. D. (2022). "Examining the roadblocks of circular economy adoption in micro, small, and medium enterprises (MSME) through sustainable development goals", *Business Strategy and the Environment*, *31*(7), 2908–2930.

Vyas, V., Mehta, K., & Sharma, R. (2023). "The nexus between toxic-air pollution, health expenditure, and economic growth: An empirical study using ARDL", International Review of Economics and Finance, 2023, 84, pp. 154–166 https://doi.org/10.1016/j.iref.2022.11.017

Wardani, S. I., & Rachmawati, I. (2022). "The Role of Micro, Small and Medium Enterprises (MSMEs) In Promoting SDGs in Blitar", *Enrichment: Journal of Management*, *12*(5), 3678–3683.

Aveline S.

14 Impact of Innovation and Its Role in Small Medium Enterprises' Sustainability

Abstract: This conceptual chapter explores innovation's role in the sustainability of small and medium enterprises (SMEs). Innovation is acknowledged as a major factor in the expansion and success of SMEs, particularly in the current quickly evolving corporate climate. The chapter begins by defining innovation and its various types, such as product, process, and organizational innovation. Next, it examines the importance of innovation for SMEs, including its potential to enhance competitiveness, increase productivity, and improve customer satisfaction. The chapter also discusses the challenges faced by SMEs in implementing innovation, such as lack of resources, limited access to financing, and risk aversion. Finally, the chapter proposes strategies that SMEs can use to foster a culture of innovation, including investing in research and development, collaborating with partners, and leveraging technology. Overall, this chapter highlights the critical role that innovation plays in the sustainability of SMEs and provides practical recommendations for SMEs to improve their innovation capabilities.

Keywords: Small medium enterprises, Innovation, Sustainability

Introduction and Background

Small and medium-sized businesses (SMEs) are crucial to a nation's economic growth. However, SMEs face many challenges, including limited resources, competition, and environmental and social concerns (Mehta et al., 2017). Therefore, innovation has grown to be an essential tactic for SMEs to improve sustainability. Small and medium-sized businesses (SMEs) must innovate to remain competitive, satisfy the changing needs of their clients, and solve environmental issues. Innovation is essential to SMEs' sustainability. This conceptual chapter intends to investigate how innovation contributes to the sustainability of SMEs and to highlight some of the potential constraints that SMEs encounter when implementing innovative practices. For Small and Medium-sized Enterprises (SMEs) to be competitive in the quickly evolving business climate of today, technological advancement is essential. the This development enables SMEs to increase the effectiveness of their manufacturing processes, cut costs, and provide their clients with better goods and services. In this overview of the literature, we will talk about the factors that push SMEs to adopt new technology to stay competitive.

Aveline S., Business Administration Department, Madras Christian College, East Tambaram, Chennai

https://doi.org/10.1515/9783111170022-014

Globalization: Globalization has forced SMEs to compete with larger firms both domestically and internationally. This competition has created a need for SMEs to improve their technological capabilities to remain competitive. As a result, SMEs can access new markets and compete globally by adopting new technologies that help them reduce costs, improve quality, and enhance their production efficiency.

Customer Demands: Customer demands are constantly changing, and SMEs must keep up with these changes to remain competitive. Advances in technology have made it possible for SMEs to better understand customer needs and preferences. SMEs can use this knowledge to develop better products and services that meet customer expectations.

Government Regulations: Government regulations are becoming increasingly strict, and SMEs must comply with these regulations to avoid penalties and remain competitive. Advances in technology have made it easier for SMEs to comply with regulations by automating their processes and reducing their environmental impact.

Access to Funding: Access to funding is essential for SMEs to invest in new technologies and remain competitive. Advances in technology have made it easier for SMEs to access funding through crowdfunding platforms and online lending marketplaces.

Collaboration: Collaboration among SMEs can help them share resources and knowledge, enabling them to adopt new technologies and remain competitive. Advances in technology have made it easier for SMEs to collaborate by providing them with communication tools and cloud-based collaboration platforms.

Education and Training: Education and training are crucial for SMEs to adopt and implement new technologies successfully. Advances in technology have made it easier for SMEs to access education and training programs online, enabling them to acquire new skills and knowledge at a lower cost.

Contribution of Innovation to SMEs' Sustainability

Innovation can contribute to SMEs' sustainability in the following ways Cost Reduction: Innovation can help SMEs reduce their operational costs, energy usage, and waste production, translating into long-term sustainability benefits.

New Market Opportunities: Innovation can help SMEs identify new market opportunities, particularly in sustainable products and services, and expand their customer base. Improved Resource Efficiency Innovation can result in new technologies, goods, and procedures that maximise resource efficiency, reduce waste, and conserve natural resources.

Enhanced Customer Relationships: Innovation can help SMEs build stronger relationships with customers by providing them with innovative and sustainable solutions that meet their changing needs and expectations.

Increased Resilience: Innovation can help SMEs adapt to changing market conditions and environmental challenges, such as climate change, by developing new products and services that are more resilient and sustainable. Innovation is essential to the survival of SMEs because it enables them to lower costs, develop new market opportunities, increase resource efficiency, improve client connections, and become more resilient. SMEs should therefore prioritise innovation as a crucial tactic for ensuring their long-term sustainability.

Innovation and the Sustainability of SMEs

Innovation is creating and using novel concepts, procedures, goods, or services that add value to organisations and society. Innovation is the process of coming up with brand-new concepts, items, or procedures that benefit consumers, companies, and society at large. Product, process, and organisational innovation are just a few examples of the various shapes that innovation can take. Product innovation is the process of creating new or enhanced goods or services that better satisfy consumer wants or open new business prospects. Process improvement involves finding more efficient ways of producing or delivering products or services, such as through automation or improved supply chain management. Organizational innovation consists in implementing new business models or management practices that increase efficiency, productivity, and agility. In the context of SMEs, innovation plays a crucial role in enhancing their sustainability by providing them with a competitive edge, reducing their environmental impact, and meeting their customers' evolving needs and expectations. Innovation can help SMEs achieve sustainability in several ways. Dasgupta (2021) has found that the scope of the problems in the environment and society Businesses of all sizes are being urged to provide creative alternatives that are workable from an economic, environmental, and social perspective.

The results of sustainable innovation initiatives made by small and medium-sized businesses (SMEs) and small business owners (SBEs). First, innovation can result in the creation of brand-new goods and services that are more eco-friendly, socially conscious, and energy efficient. For example, SMEs can adopt renewable energy sources, use biodegradable materials, and develop eco-friendly products that meet the needs of environmentally conscious consumers. Second, innovation can help SMEs decrease waste generation and improve resource efficiency. For instance, SMEs can monitor their energy use, reduce water use, and improve production processes using cutting-edge technology like artificial intelligence and the Internet of Things.

Third, innovation can help SMEs create new market opportunities and expand their customer base. For example, SMEs can develop innovative products and services that address emerging social and environmental challenges, such as climate change, sustainable transportation, and circular economy. Hilke & Jacke (2009) has identified a focus on novel sustainable development strategies. This research blends insights from innovation theory, sustainable development practice, and small company characteristics to provide new insight into the factors that influence how sustainable innovation inside small and medium-sized firms (SMEs) is converted into practice.

Challenges and Opportunities for SMEs' Sustainability

Dorian & Mora (2019) has determined that the most pertinent factors were the financial outlay that businesses would need to make and the length of time it would take them to embrace these new technologies. The most significant concerns were the increased unemployment brought on by adopting new technologies, the data's manipulation susceptibility, and the devices' interconnection. Device connectivity may allow for more efficient production management. Ndesaulwa & Kikula (2016), "Clarification is necessary on two aspects of innovation's beneficial effects on the productivity and performance of businesses. In the traditional approach to finance and accounting, expenditures in innovation and technology should be viewed as factors that increase a company's efficiency rather than as expenses that drain the organisation. The second consideration is that such investments must be connected to production". New market entry is challenging for SMEs.

Additionally, they cannot influence market prices because bigger companies interfere to set them. This last factor is merely an exception in the case of "hidden champions." Smaller companies that are extremely powerful in specific niche areas are known as hidden champions. Despite the potential benefits of innovation, SMEs face several challenges in adopting innovative practices. For example, SMEs often lack the financial and human resources to invest in research and development and implement innovative solutions. Moreover, SMEs may lack the knowledge and skills to identify and implement innovative practices. Das, Rangaraja & Dutta (2020) have explored that in large firms, corporate sustainability is a well-practised area. Literature indicates that things are different for SMEs, nevertheless. Particularly in emerging markets, SMEs excessively disregard social and environmental practices. In the literature already in existence, it is mentioned that a cooperative operating style, government policy and facilitation, and supportive organisational culture can all have a good impact on an SME's sustainability performance and, as a result, their financial success.

However, SMEs also have many opportunities to overcome these challenges and adopt innovative practices. For example, SMEs can work with academic and research institutions to gain access to knowledge and experience in innovation. SMEs can also join innovation networks and clusters to share resources and knowledge and gain from one another's experiences.

The role of innovation in enhancing SMEs' sustainability has been widely discussed in previous studies. Small and medium-sized businesses (SMEs) must innovate to increase their competitiveness and sustainability. Importance of Innovation for SMEs: Innovation can help SMEs to develop new products, services, and processes, which can enhance their competitiveness and sustainability. According to a study by Bessant and Tsekouras (2001), innovation is a critical factor for SMEs to achieve long-term growth and success. Moreover, innovation can enable SMEs to enhance good associations with customers and vendors, which is essential for their success. SMEs can use various innovative strategies to increase their sustainability, including organisational, process, and product innovation. A study by Adam & Alarifi (2021) found that SMEs focusing on product and process innovation are more likely to achieve sustainable growth and competitiveness. Moreover, organizational innovation, such as adopting new management practices and business models, can help SMEs improve their efficiency and effectiveness.

SMEs confront several obstacles to innovation, including a lack of funding, expertise, and teamwork. A study by Lindholm-Dahlstrand and Jacobsson (2003) found that SMEs that lack resources and knowledge are less likely to adopt innovation strategies, negatively affecting their sustainability and competitiveness. Moreover, SMEs may face challenges in collaborating with other firms, research institutions, and government agencies, which can limit their access to external knowledge and resources. Increased innovation can lead to several benefits for SMEs, such as improved performance, enhanced reputation, and reduced costs. According to a study by Hu and Mathews (2008), SMEs that focus on creativity can achieve higher levels of productivity and profitability. Moreover, increased innovation enables SMEs to enhance better associations with customers, suppliers, also other stakeholders, which can improve their overall reputation and brand image. Additionally, increased innovation can help SMEs to reduce costs by improving their overall efficiency and effectiveness.

Innovation as a Key Strategy for SMEs Sustainability

Innovation has been identified as a key strategy for SMEs to enhance their sustainability. A study by Dasgupta (2023) found that innovation positively affects SMEs' sustainability by improving their competitiveness, reducing their environmental impact, and enhancing their social responsibility. Another study by Rao et al. (2022) highlighted the role of innovation in improving SMEs' resilience and adaptive capacity to environmental and social challenges. Innovation is a critical component of SMEs' sustainability as it provides opportunities to improve their competitiveness, develop new products or services, and enhance their operational efficiency. The review of literature on innovation as a key strategy for SMEs sustainability is presented below with references.

Kafouros et al. (2008) have emphasized the significance of innovation for the long-term survival of SMEs. They explained that innovation helps SMEs to adjust to market changes and create novel offerings that cater to the evolving needs of customers. The authors noted that innovation allows SMEs to adapt to changing market conditions and develop new products or services that meet customer needs. Sánchez et al. (2011) have examined how innovation impacts the sustainable performance of SMEs. They discovered that innovation has a favourable influence on the sustainable performance of SMEs, encompassing economic, environmental, and social aspects. De Sá et al. (2016) examined the role of innovation in enhancing SMEs' competitiveness. The study found that innovation is a critical factor in improving SMEs' competitiveness, especially in dynamic and fast-changing markets. Chesbrough (2006) discussed the concept of open innovation and its application in SMEs. The author argued that open innovation could help SMEs to access external knowledge and resources, which can contribute to their innovation capabilities and competitiveness. González-López et al. (2019) identified key factors that impact innovation management within SMEs. The research indicated that factors such as leadership, organizational culture, and human resource management practices play a crucial role in facilitating innovation in SMEs. A study has found that innovation can enhance SMEs' export performance, providing them with opportunities for growth and increased revenue. The authors' research revealed a positive correlation between innovation and the export performance of SMEs. According to a study investigated that there is a strong link between innovation and the long-term viability of SMEs. The findings showed that SMEs that are innovative are more likely to thrive and expand over time, in contrast to SMEs that do not prioritize innovation. Even at the time of exit decisions, the financial backers of the new ventures consider innovation practices as an important factor in decision making (Mehta et al., 2022).

Challenges and Opportunities for Innovation in SMEs

SMEs face several challenges in adopting innovative practices, including limited resources, lack of knowledge and expertise, and risk aversion. However, SMEs also have many opportunities to overcome these challenges and leverage the potential benefits of innovation. For example, SMEs can collaborate with universities and research institutions to access knowledge and expertise in innovation, as highlighted by Pereira & Franco (2021). SMEs can participate in innovation networks and clusters, which enables them to exchange information and resources and gain insights from other SMEs' experiences. Innovation is essential for the success of small and medium-sized enterprises (SMEs). However, SMEs face several challenges and opportunities when it comes to innovation. The board size of the firms also affects its decisions and hence affect the performance (Sharma et al., 2022).

Piatkowski and Gupta (2015) have discussed the role of innovation in SMEs and outlined the opportunities and challenges that SMEs encounter in the innovation process. The authors highlighted that SMEs confront various obstacles to innovation, such as insufficient financial resources, restricted access to external knowledge and expertise, and a reluctance to take risks. Chen et al. (2019 revealed a connection between innovation capabilities and the performance of SMEs. The findings suggested that SMEs with robust innovation capabilities tend to exhibit better levels of innovation performance, which can enhance their competitiveness and provide them with growth opportunities. Howells et al. (2017) investigated the significance of open innovation in SMEs and asserted that it could enable SMEs to acquire external knowledge and resources. This, in turn, can assist SMEs in overcoming obstacles that impede their innovation process. Paredes-Frigolett et al. (2020) explored the link between intellectual property and innovation in SMEs. The research indicated that SMEs that allocate resources to intellectual property tend to exhibit better levels of innovation performance, which can improve their competitiveness and market success.

Digital Innovation and SMEs the study by Abou-Shouk et al. (2021) discussed the importance of digital innovation in SMEs and contended that it could offer new prospects for SMEs to enhance their operations, products, and services and to expand into new markets. Saunila and Ukko (2015) investigated the role of collaboration in promoting innovation in SMEs. The study found that SMEs that engage in collaborative activities with other firms, universities, or research organizations have higher levels of innovation performance, which can lead to increased competitiveness and growth opportunities.

Small and medium-sized enterprises have the option to utilize various forms of innovation, such as product innovation, process innovation, and organizational innovation, in order to improve their sustainability. A study by Klewitz & Hansen (2014) found that SMEs often choose product innovation as the primary form of innovation to improve their sustainability. However, process innovation and organizational innovation are also essential for improving SMEs' resource efficiency and reducing their environmental impact, as highlighted by Dasgupta (2023) and Rao et al. (2022). Zighan, et al. (2023). SMEs have varying perspectives on sustainable innovation, which leads to diverse methods for incorporating it into their operations. The definition of sustainable innovation is not clear-cut, and there are many different interpretations, which can make it difficult for SMEs to adopt a fixed approach to sustainable innovation. Both internal and external factors can drive sustainable innovation in SMEs. The success of sustainable innovation in terms of cooperation, work team integration, agreement, activity formulation, consistency, and dedication to the firm's goals largely depends on the organizational culture, as well as the skills and abilities of SMEs and their members. These elements interact, strengthen one another, and have a favourable effect on the sustained innovation of SMEs.

Innovation and Sustainable Development Goals (SDGs)

Innovation can contribute to achieving the Sustainable Development Goals (SDGs) by addressing environmental and social challenges and promoting sustainable development. Earlier studies and reports highlighted that innovation plays a vital role in meeting Sustainable Development Goals by creating sustainable products and services, embracing circular economy principles, and promoting social innovation.

For small and medium-sized enterprises (SMEs), reducing costs is an essential element in guaranteeing their sustainability.

Cost Reduction is a Key Strategy for SMEs' Sustainability: Cost reduction has been identified as a key strategy for SMEs to enhance their sustainability. Cost reduction is essential for SMEs to remain competitive and survive in a challenging economic environment. The study found that SMEs that implement effective cost-reduction strategies can achieve significant cost savings, which can enhance their profitability and sustainability. SMEs face several challenges in reducing their costs, including limited resources, lack of economies of scale, and limited access to finance. However, SMEs also have many opportunities to overcome these challenges and reduce their costs. For example, SMEs can leverage digital technologies to streamline their operations and reduce their overhead costs, as highlighted by a study by Schlegelmilch and Bohm (2018). Moreover, SMEs can collaborate with suppliers to achieve cost savings through joint purchasing and logistics optimization, as highlighted by a study by Demeter and Matyusz (2019).

Cost Reduction Strategies for SMEs' Sustainability

SMEs can adopt different cost-reduction strategies to enhance their sustainability, including process optimization, supply chain management, and energy efficiency. A study by Acosta et al. (2018) found that process optimization is the most common cost-reduction strategy adopted by SMEs. However, supply chain management and energy efficiency are also essential for reducing SMEs' costs and enhancing their sustainability, as highlighted by Demeter and Matyusz (2019). Cost reduction and innovation are closely related, and SMEs can leverage innovation to achieve cost savings and enhance their sustainability. According to a study by Parry et al. (2017), SMEs that adopt a culture of innovation can achieve significant cost savings by improving their efficiency, reducing their waste, and optimizing their resources. Moreover, SMEs can utilize innovation to create new products and services that align with their customers' needs and expectations, ultimately improving their competitiveness and long-term viability.

New Market Opportunities

Identifying and exploring new market opportunities is crucial for the growth and sustainability of businesses. The review of literature on new market opportunities is presented below with references. Identifying New Market Opportunities play a vital role in SMEs' sustainability; Gliem and Hsuan (2017) identified the key factors that contribute to the identification of new market opportunities. The study found that environmental scanning, customer insights, and entrepreneurial orientation are essential for identifying new market opportunities. Sanzo et al. (2017) investigated the association between market orientation and recognizing novel market opportunities. The authors have argued that companies that possess a robust market orientation tend to be more adept at recognizing and capitalizing on emerging market opportunities. Vanhaverbeke et al. (2018) examined the role of technology in creating new market opportunities. The authors argued that technology can create new markets by enabling new products and services or by disrupting existing markets. Elbanna and Child (2017) investigated the role of internationalization can be an effective means of generating fresh market opportunities, as it allows firms to access untapped markets and reach out to new customers.

Social Media and New Market Opportunities have been the recent developments in the economy. The study by Zott and Amit (2018) examined the role of social media in creating new market opportunities. The authors argued that social media can provide firms with new ways to engage with customers and identify new market opportunities. Zawislak et al. (2019) investigated the relationship between business model innovation and new market opportunities. The study found that companies which undertake business model innovation are more inclined to discover and leverage new market opportunities.

Small and medium-sized enterprises (SMEs) play a crucial role in stimulating economic growth and generating employment opportunities in numerous nations. However, they face several challenges in sustaining their operations and achieving growth. One key strategy for SMEs to enhance their sustainability and growth prospects is to identify and exploit new market opportunities.

Importance of New Market Opportunities for SMEs

New market opportunities are critical for SMEs to enhance their sustainability and growth prospects. According to a study by Blackburn and Schaper (2012), new market opportunities can help SMEs to diversify their customer base, reduce their reliance on existing customers, and increase their revenues and profits. Moreover, new market opportunities can enable SMEs to expand their product and service offerings, increase their market share, and enhance their competitiveness.

SMEs can identify new market opportunities through various sources, including market research, customer feedback, and networking. A study by Birley and Westhead (1994) found that market research is the most common source of new market opportunities for SMEs. However, customer feedback and networking can also provide valuable insights into emerging customer needs and market developments, as highlighted by a study by Sharma et al. (2020). SMEs face several challenges and risks in identifying and exploiting new market opportunities, including limited resources, lack of market knowledge, and market uncertainty. According to a study by Lindelof and Lofsten (2005), SMEs that enter new markets without adequate preparation and knowledge are more likely to experience failure and financial losses. Therefore, SMEs need to carefully evaluate new market opportunities and develop appropriate market entry strategies to mitigate the risks and challenges.

SMEs can adopt various strategies to exploit new market opportunities and enhance their sustainability and growth prospects. These strategies include product innovation, market segmentation, and internationalization. A study by Andersson et al. (2014) found that SMEs that involve themselves in product innovation tend to have an enhanced capacity to recognize and capitalize on new market opportunities. Additionally, market segmentation can aid SMEs in focusing on specific customer segments and customizing their products and services to cater to their demands and preferences, as highlighted by a study by Blackburn (2012). Finally, internationalization offers SMEs the potential to access new markets and customers, as well as the chance to acquire knowledge and innovate from diverse market environments., as highlighted by a study by Zahra and George (2002).

Improved Resource Efficiency

Importance of Improved Resource Efficiency for SMEs: Improved resource efficiency is crucial for SMEs to enhance their sustainability and competitiveness. According to a study by Majid et al. (2023), improved resource efficiency can lead to cost savings, enhanced productivity, and reduced environmental impact. Moreover, improved resource efficiency can help SMEs to comply with environmental regulations, attract customers and investors who value sustainability, and improve their reputation and brand image. Several drivers and barriers influence SMEs' adoption of improved resource efficiency practices. The main drivers include economic benefits, environmental regulations, customer demands, and internal motivations. A study by Ayadi and Amara (2016) found that SMEs that adopt resource efficiency practices are more likely to experience cost savings, enhance their competitiveness, and comply with environmental regulations. However, SMEs encounter various obstacles in implementing resource efficiency practices, including insufficient financial resources, inadequate technical expertise, and insufficient managerial support. SMEs can adopt various strategies to improve their resource efficiency and enhance their sustainability and competitiveness. These strategies include energy and water conservation, waste reduction, and green supply chain management. Hervani. et al. (2005) found SMEs that adopt green supply chain management practices are more likely to enhance their resource efficiency and reduce their environmental impact. Moreover, by adopting energy and water conservation measures as well as waste reduction practices, SMEs can experience financial savings and environmental advantages., as highlighted by a study by Aslam et al. (2021).

Technology and innovation play a critical role in improving resource efficiency for SMEs. Small and Medium Enterprises can adopt various technologies and innovations to enhance their resource efficiency, such as renewable energy, smart grids, and eco-design. A study by Phan et al. (2019) found that SMEs that adopt renewable energy technologies are more likely to enhance their resource efficiency and reduce their environmental impact. Moreover, SMEs can improve the sustainability of their products and services while boosting their competitiveness and customer satisfaction by incorporating eco-design principles.

Enhanced Customer Relationships

For small and medium-sized enterprises (SMEs), building and improving customer relationships is vital to bolstering their sustainability along with competitiveness. Building strong relationships with customers is critical for the success and sustainability of SMEs. The review of literature on enhanced customer relationships in SMEs is presented below with references.

Ndubisi and Wah (2015) investigated the role of CRM in enhancing customer relationships in SMEs. The study found that effective use of CRM can help SMEs build and maintain strong relationships with their customers. Homburg et al. (2017) examined personalization can play a significant role in strengthening customer relationships for SMEs by allowing them to customize their products and services to match the unique requirements of their customers. García-Villaverde et al. (2017) investigated discovered that for SMEs, prioritizing the establishment of trust with their customers can result in long-term and mutually beneficial relationships. Hsu and Tsou (2018) examined the role of social media in enhancing customer relationships in SMEs. The authors argued that social media could offer SMEs fresh means of interacting with their customers and developing stronger relationships. Adomako and Opoku (2018) revealed that SMEs that actively solicit and act upon customer feedback are more likely to establish loyal and robust customer relationships. Jiang et al. (2020) examined the role of service quality in enhancing customer relationships in SMEs. The authors argued that SMEs that prioritize service quality and provide excellent customer service are more likely to build strong and long-lasting relationships with their customers.

Building and maintaining strong customer relationships is essential for SMEs to enhance their sustainability and competitiveness. According to a study by Alniacik and Alniacik (2012), SMEs that develop strong customer relationships are more likely to enhance customer loyalty, increase sales, and improve their reputation and brand image. Moreover, strong customer relationships can help SMEs to identify and respond to customer needs and preferences, which is critical for their long-term success. SMEs can adopt various strategies to enhance their customer relationships and improve their sustainability and competitiveness. These strategies include customer engagement, customer service, and social media marketing. A study by O'Cass and Ngo (2011) found that SMEs that engage their customers through personal interactions and customized offerings are more likely to enhance their customer relationships and improve their competitive position. Moreover, effective customer service and social media marketing can help SMEs to build and maintain strong customer relationships while reaching a wider audience.

Enhanced customer relationships can lead to several benefits for SMEs, such as increased sales, enhanced customer loyalty, and improved brand image. According to a study, SMEs that build strong customer relationships are more likely to achieve higher levels of sales growth and profitability. Moreover, strong customer relationships can help SMEs to differentiate themselves from competitors, enhance customer satisfaction, and improve their overall reputation. Small and medium-sized enterprises (SMEs) encounter various obstacles in creating and sustaining robust customer relationships, including limited resources, inadequate customer knowledge, and insufficient technology infrastructure. A study by Pan and Chen (2019) found that SMEs that lack resources and technology infrastructure are less likely to adopt customer relationship management practices, which can negatively affect their sustainability and competitiveness.

Increased Resilience

Small and medium-sized enterprises (SMEs) must prioritize building resilience to improve their sustainability and endure economic, environmental, and social disruptions. Here are some key features of increased resilience.

SMEs can adopt various strategies to build resilience and enhance their sustainability, such as risk management, innovation, and collaboration. A study by Seville et al. (2015) found that SMEs that have a proactive risk management approach are more likely to build resilience and improve their ability to respond to disruptions. Moreover, innovation can help SMEs to develop new products and services, which can enhance their competitiveness and sustainability. Collaboration with other SMEs, government agencies, and other stakeholders can also help SMEs to build resilience and share resources and knowledge. Resilience is the ability of SMEs to anticipate, prepare for, and adapt to various challenges and disruptions. SMEs that are resilient can withstand economic downturns, natural disasters, and other unexpected events. According to a study by Naldi et al. (2015), resilience is a critical factor for SMEs to achieve long-term sustainability and competitiveness. Moreover, resilience can help SMEs to build strong relationships with customers, suppliers, and other stakeholders, which is essential for their success.

Increased resilience can lead to several benefits for SMEs, such as improved performance, enhanced reputation, and reduced costs. According to a study by OECD (2022), SMEs that build resilience can achieve higher levels of productivity and profitability. In addition, enhanced resilience can aid SMEs in establishing better relationships with stakeholders like customers and suppliers, boosting their reputation and brand image in the process. Additionally, increased resilience can help SMEs to reduce costs by minimizing the impact of disruptions and avoiding potential risks. SMEs face several challenges in building resilience, such as a lack of resources, lack of knowledge, and lack of awareness. A study by Kotsios (2023) found that SMEs that lack resources and knowledge are less likely to adopt resilience strategies, which can negatively affect their sustainability and competitiveness. Moreover, SMEs may face challenges in accessing external resources and support, such as funding, training, and technical assistance.

Methodology

This research has adopted a qualitative methodology. The study has adopted techniques such as case studies, interviews, and surveys to collect data from SMEs and analyze the impact of innovation on their sustainability. The data has been analyzed thematically. A systematic literature review was adopted to identify previous research on the topic and to develop a comprehensive understanding of the existing literature in this area. Overall, the methodology used in the study has involved a combination of qualitative and quantitative methods, theoretical frameworks, and systematic literature reviews to develop a comprehensive understanding of the impact of innovation on SME sustainability.

Discussion and Conclusion

There is an increased number of research work produced by researchers related to innovation and sustainability (Mehta et al., 2019; Mehta et al., 2022). Be it a field of consumer behavior or investor behavior, the retention of consumers and investors in the capital market depends upon the sustainable practices in the related field by the corporates (Khanna & Sharma, 2017; Mahajan & Sharma, 2017; Mehta &Sharma, 2017; Vyas et al., 2020). Innovation is a critical factor for SMEs to enhance their sustainability and competitiveness. SMEs can adopt various types of innovation to achieve sustainable growth and success, such as creativity in product, process, and organization.

However, to overcome the barriers to innovation, SMEs must assess their innovation strategies critically and adopt appropriate measures to improve their sustainability and competitiveness. The challenges SMEs face in innovation include insufficient resources, inadequate knowledge, and limited collaboration. Innovation plays a crucial role in enhancing SMEs' sustainability by improving their competitiveness, reducing their environmental impact, and meeting their customers' evolving needs and expectations. SMEs face several challenges in adopting innovative practices, but they also have many opportunities to overcome these challenges and leverage the potential benefits of innovation. Cost reduction is essential for SMEs to enhance their sustainability by improving their profitability, competitiveness, and resource efficiency. SMEs face several challenges in reducing their costs, but they also have many opportunities to overcome these challenges and achieve significant cost savings. The literature reviewed above emphasizes cost reduction as a crucial strategy for the long-term sustainability of small and medium-sized enterprises (SMEs).

Identifying and exploiting new market opportunities is essential for SMEs to enhance their sustainability and growth prospects. SMEs can adopt various strategies to identify and exploit new market opportunities, including market research, customer feedback, and networking. However, SMEs also face several challenges and risks in exploiting new market opportunities, including limited resources, lack of market knowledge, and market uncertainty. Therefore, SMEs need to carefully evaluate new market opportunities and develop appropriate market entry strategies to mitigate the risks and challenges.

Improved resource efficiency is critical for SMEs to enhance their sustainability and competitiveness while reducing their environmental impact. Small and medium-sized enterprises (SMEs) can utilize multiple tactics to enhance their resource efficiency, such as conserving energy and water, minimizing waste, and implementing green supply chain management. However, Small and medium-sized enterprises (SMEs) may encounter obstacles to implementing resource efficiency practices, including insufficient financial resources, inadequate technical knowledge, and limited management support. Therefore, SMEs need to carefully evaluate their resource use and adopt appropriate practices and technologies to enhance their sustainability and competitiveness. Building and maintaining strong customer relationships is essential for SMEs to enhance their sustainability and competitiveness.

SMEs can adopt various strategies to enhance their customer relationships, such as customer engagement, customer service, and social media marketing. Enhanced customer relationships can lead to several benefits for SMEs, such as increased sales, enhanced customer loyalty, and improved brand image. However, SMEs often face resource constraints, which can make it difficult for them to invest in customer relationship management systems or technologies. They may also lack the necessary customer knowledge or data to understand their customers' needs and preferences. Additionally, they may not have the technological infrastructure to support effective communication and engagement with their customers. These challenges can make it difficult for SMEs to build and maintain strong customer relationships. Therefore, small and medium-sized enterprises need to carefully evaluate their customer relationships and adopt appropriate strategies to enhance their sustainability and competitiveness.

Building resilience is critical for SMEs to enhance their sustainability and withstand various challenges and disruptions. SMEs can adopt various strategies to build resilience, such as risk management, innovation, and collaboration. Increased resilience can lead to several benefits for SMEs, such as improved performance, enhanced reputation, and reduced costs. However, SMEs may face challenges in building resilience due to various factors, such as limited financial resources, lack of knowledge about risk management, and limited awareness about the potential disruptions that could affect their business. These challenges may make it difficult for SMEs to identify and prioritize resilience-building strategies and implement them effectively. Additionally, SMEs may lack the necessary networks and partnerships to effectively manage risks and respond to disruptions. Therefore, small and medium-sized enterprises need to carefully evaluate their resilience and adopt appropriate strategies to enhance their sustainability and competitiveness.

Recommendations for SMEs that are looking to adopt innovative practices to enhance their sustainability:

Conduct a sustainability assessment: SMEs should conduct a sustainability assessment to identify their strengths, weaknesses, opportunities, and threats in terms of sustainability. This will help them to develop a sustainability strategy that is aligned with their business objectives and priorities.

Develop a culture of innovation: SMEs should develop a culture of innovation that encourages creativity, experimentation, and learning. This can be achieved by providing employees with training and development opportunities, fostering collaboration and communication, and recognizing and rewarding innovative ideas and practices.

Collaborate with stakeholders: SMEs should collaborate with their stakeholders, such as customers, suppliers, and community organizations, to identify opportunities for innovation and to develop solutions that meet their needs and expectations.

Adopt sustainable business practices: SMEs should adopt sustainable business practices, such as energy and water conservation, waste reduction, and green supply chain management, to enhance their environmental performance and reduce their operating costs.

Leverage technology: SMEs should leverage technology to enhance their sustainability, such as by adopting digital platforms and tools to optimize their operations, reduce their carbon footprint, and enhance their customer engagement.

Seek external support: SMEs should seek external support from government programs, industry associations, and sustainability experts to enhance their knowledge and capabilities in sustainability and innovation.

By following these recommendations, SMEs can adopt innovative practices that enhance their sustainability, improve their competitiveness, and contribute to their long-term success.

References

Abou-Shouk, M. A., Lim, K. H., & Megahed, F. M. (2021). "Digital innovation in small and medium-sized enterprises (SMEs): A systematic literature review", *Journal of Business Research, 135*, 594–606.

Acosta, A.S., Crespo,A.H., & Agudo,J.C. (2018). "Effect of market orientation, network capability and entrepreneurial orientation on international performance of small and medium enterprises (SMEs)." *International Business Review, 27*(6), 1128–1140. https://doi.org/10.1016/j.ibusrev.2018.04.004.

Adomako, S., & Opoku, R. A. (2018). "The impact of customer feedback on customer relationship management in small and medium enterprises", *Journal of Small Business and Enterprise Development, 25*(3), 401–420.

Al-Ma'aitah, A. (2016). "Small and Medium Enterprises and Technological Innovation: A Review of the Literature", *International Journal of Business and Management, 11*(4), 288–299.

Alniacik, U., & Alniacik, E. (2012). "The effects of customer orientation and entrepreneurial orientation on innovativeness and performance of SMEs", *Journal of Global Strategic Management, 10*(2), 72–81.

Andersson, S. (2014). "Innovative SMEs and Growth in a Long-Term Perspective." *Journal of Small Business Management, 52*(2), 225–241.

Ndesaulwa, A. P. & Kikula, J. (2016). "The Impact of Innovation on Performance of Small and Medium Enterprises (SMEs) in Tanzania: A Review of Empirical Evidence", *Journal of Business and Management Sciences, 4*(1), 1–6.

Ayadi, M., & Amara, N. (2016). "Environmental management practices and their impact on firm performance in small and medium-sized enterprises." *Journal of Cleaner Production, 135*, 1247–1255.

Bessant, J., & Tsekouras, G. (2001). "Developing innovation capability in organisations: a dynamic capabilities approach", *International Journal of Innovation Management, 5*(3), 377–400.

Birley, S., & Westhead, P. (1994). "A Taxonomy of Business Start-up Reasons and their Impact on Firm Growth and Size." *Journal of Business Venturing, 9*(1), 7–31.

Blackburn, R. (2012). "Segmenting the SME Market and Implications for Service Provision: A Literature Review." 10.13140/RG.2.2.18121.57443.

Blackburn, R., & Schaper, M. (2012). "Government Support for Small Business Innovation: The Australian Experience." *Journal of Small Business Management, 50*(2), 152.

Chen, C.-J., Lee, Y.-D., & Wu, W.-T. (2019). "The impact of innovation capabilities on SMEs' innovation performance: Evidence from the semiconductor industry in Taiwan", *Journal of Business Research, 98*, 54–64.

Chesbrough, H. (2006). "Open innovation: A new paradigm for understanding industrial innovation", In H. Chesbrough, W. Vanhaverbeke, & J. West (Eds.), *Open innovation: Researching a new paradigm*, 1–12.

Dasgupta, M. (2021). "Sustainable innovation initiatives by small and medium enterprises: a systematic literature review." *Journal of Small Business & Entrepreneurship, 35*(4), 550–573. DOI: 10.1080/08276331.2021.1898177.

Martins, A., Branco, M. C., Melo, P.N. & Machado, C. (2018). "Sustainability in Small and Medium-Sized Enterprises: A Systematic Literature Review and Future Research Agenda," *Sustainability, 14*(11), 6493. https://doi.org/10.3390/su14116493

Adam, N. A. & Alarifi, G. (2021). "Innovation practices for survival of small and medium enterprises (SMEs) in the COVID-19 times: the role of external support", *Journal of Innovation and Entrepreneurship volume*, *10*, 15 (2021). https://doi.org/10.1186/s13731-021-00156-6

Rao, P., Verma, S., Rao, A.A. & Joshi, R. (2022), "A conceptual framework for identifying sustainable business practices of small and medium enterprises", *Benchmarking: An International Journal*, ahead-of-print, https://doi.org/10.1108/BIJ-11-2021-0699

De Sá, L. V., Ferreira, J. J., & Silva, R. M. (2016). "The role of innovation in enhancing SMEs' competitiveness", *Journal of Technology Management & Innovation*, 11(4), 48–56.

Pereira, R. & Franco, M. (2021). "Cooperation between universities and SMEs: A systematic literature review", Industry and Higher Education, 36(1), https://doi.org/10.1177/0950422221995114.

Demeter, K., & Matyusz, Z. (2019). "Cost Reduction Potential in SMEs through Collaborative Supply Chain Management." Sustainability, 11(2), 366.

DeTienne, D. R., & Chandler, G. N. (2004). "Opportunity Identification and Its Role in the Entrepreneurial Classroom: A Pedagogical Approach and Empirical Test". *Academy of Management Learning & Education*, *3*(3), 242–257.

Dorian O. & Mora S. (2019). "Sustainable Development Challenges and Risks of Industry 4.0: A literature review", *Global IoT Summit (GIoTS)*, 1–6.

González-López, M., Rodríguez-Ariza, L., & Arjona-Fuentes, J. M. (2019). "Factors influencing innovation management in SMEs", *Journal of Business Research*, 99, 365–373.

Elbanna, S., & Child, J. (2017). "The internationalization of new and small firms: A resource-based view", *Journal of World Business*, 52(1), 46–62.

García-Villaverde, P. M., Sánchez-Hernández, M. I., & Madariaga-Pérez, M. (2017). "Trust and commitment in SMEs' customer relationships: A conceptual framework", *Journal of Business Research*, *76*, 1–6.

Gliem, J. A., & Hsuan, J. (2017). "An exploratory study of factors that contribute to new market opportunity identification", *Journal of Small Business Strategy*, *27*(2), 55–68.

OECD (2022). "Building Financial Resilience to Climate Impacts: A Framework for Governments to Manage the Risks of Losses and Damages", OECD Publishing, Paris, https://doi.org/10.1787/9e2e1412-en.

Hervani, A.A., Helms, M.M. & Sarkis, J. (2005), "Performance measurement for green supply chain management", Benchmarking: An International Journal, Vol. 12 No. 4, pp. 330–353. https://doi.org/10.1108/14635770510609015

Hilke, E. & Jacke, B. B. (2009). "Corporate sustainability and innovation in SMEs: Evidence of themes and activities in practice", *Business Strategy and the Environment*, *19*, 417–435.

Homburg, C., Jozić, D., & Kuehnl, C. (2017). "Customer experience management: Toward implementing an evolving marketing concept", *Journal of the Academy of Marketing Science*, *45*(3), 377–401.

Howells, J., Roper, S., & Wang, M. (2017). "Absorptive capacity and open innovation in small firms", *International Small Business Journal*, *35(*3), 306–326.

Hsu, C. L., & Tsou, H. T. (2018). "The effect of social media interaction on customer relationship management", *International Journal of Information Management*, *39*, 221–226.

Hu, M. C., & Mathews, J. A. (2008). "National innovation capacity and the global division of labour: theory and evidence." *Industry and Innovation*, *15*(3), 269–294.

Jiang, L., Wang, X., Li, H., & Chen, Y. (2020). "Service quality and customer loyalty in small and medium-sized enterprises: The role of customer relationship management", *International Journal of Hospitality Management*, *86*, 102414.

Kafouros, M. I., Buckley, P. J., Sharp, J. A., & Wang, C. (2008). "The role of internationalization in explaining innovation performance", *Technovation*, 28(1–2), 63–74.

Khanna, V. & Sharma, R. (2017). "Customer Switching Behavior in Retail Banking in India", International Journal of Applied Business and Economic Research (SCOPUS), Volume: No.15 (2017) Issue No.:9 (May 2017) Pages: 427–441.

Dasgupta, M. (2023) "Sustainable innovation initiatives by small and medium enterprises: a systematic literature review", *Journal of Small Business & Entrepreneurship*, *35*(4), 550–573, DOI: 10.1080/08276331.2021.1898177

Lindholm-Dahlstrand, Å., & Jacobsson, S. (2003). "Innovation and entrepreneurship in small and medium-sized enterprises: the influence of entrepreneurial attitudes, external relationships and learning orientation." *International Journal of Entrepreneurial Behaviour & Research*, 9(4), 160–175.

Lindelof, P. & Lofsten, H. (2005). "Academic versus corporate new technology-based firms in Swedish science parks: an analysis of performance, business networks and financing." *International Journal of Technology Management*, 31(3–4), 334–357. https://doi.org/10.1504/IJTM.2005.006638

Aslam, S. Elmagrhi, M. H., Rehman, R. U. & Ntim, C. G. (2021). "Environmental management practices and financial performance using data envelopment analysis in Japan: The mediating role of environmental performance", *Business Strategy and the Environment*, *30*(4), 1655–1673.

Mahajan, V. & Sharma, R. (2017). "Future of Depository with Introduction of Payment Bank- A Game Changer to Capital Market", International Journal of Applied Business and Economic Research (SCOPUS), Volume: No.15 (2017) Issue No.:9 (May 2017) Pages: 343–356.

Das, M., Rangarajan, K. & Dutta, G. (2020). "Corporate sustainability in small and medium-sized enterprises: a literature analysis and road ahead", *Journal of Indian Business Research*, Vol. 12 No. 2, 271–300.

Majid, S., Zhang, X., Khaskheli, M.B., Hong, F., King, P.J.H., & Shamsi, I.H. (2023). "Eco-Efficiency, Environmental and Sustainable Innovation in Recycling Energy and Their Effect on Business Performance: Evidence from European SMEs." *Sustainability*, *15*, 9465. https://doi.org/10.3390/su15129465

Mazzarol, T., & Reboud, S. (2017). "The Driving Forces of Technological Innovation in SMEs: An Investigation of the Australian Wine Industry", *Journal of Small Business Management*, 55(S1), 106–123.

Mehta, K., Sharma, R., & Vyas, V. (2019). "Efficiency and ranking of sustainability index of India using DEA-TOPSIS", *Journal of Indian Business Research*, *11*(2), 179–199. https://doi.org/10.1108/JIBR-02-2018-0057.

Mehta, K., Sharma, R., Vyas, V. & Kuckreja, J.S. (2022). "Exit strategy decision by venture capital firms in India using fuzzy AHP", *Journal of Entrepreneurship in Emerging Economies*, *14*(4), 643–669. https://doi.org/10.1108/JEEE-05-2020-0146

Mehta K., Sharma R., & Chugh, A. (2017). "Management of Forex Risk Exposure: A Study of SMEs and Unlisted Non-Financial Firms in India", *International Journal of Applied Business and Economic Research*, *15*(9), 43–54.

Mehta K. & Sharma R. (2017), "Contrarian and Momentum investment strategies: Evidence from Indian Stock Market", *International Journal of Applied Business and Economic Research*, *15*(9), 107–118.

Mehta, K., Sharma, R., Vyas, V. & Kuckreja, J.S. (2022). "Exit strategy decision by venture capital firms in India using fuzzy AHP", *Journal of Entrepreneurship in Emerging Economies*, 14(4), 643–669. https://doi.org/10.1108/JEEE-05-2020-0146

Naldi, L., Nardqvist, M., Sjoberg, K. & Wiklund, J. (2015). "Entrepreneurial orientation, risk-taking, and performance in family firms." *Family Business Review*, *28*(3), 266–284.

Ndubisi, N. O., & Wah, C. K. (2015). "An empirical study of the effects of customer relationship management on customer satisfaction and loyalty in Malaysian SMEs", *Journal of Small Business Management*, *53*(4), 919–926.

O'Cass, A., & Ngo, L. V. (2011). "Balancing internal and external factors of SME innovation and performance." *Journal of Small Business Management*, *49*(1), 55–80.

Klewitz, J. & Hansen, E.G. (2014). "Sustainability-oriented innovation of SMEs: a systematic review", *Journal of Cleaner Production*, *65*, 57–75, https://doi.org/10.1016/j.jclepro.2013.07.017.

Pan, Y., & Chen, Y. (2019). "Customer relationship management for small and medium-sized enterprises: a review." *International Journal of Information Management*, *44*, 110–123.

Parry, G. et al. (2017). "Innovation, Cost Savings and Enhanced Sustainability in SMEs: The Case of Environmental Management Accounting." *Sustainability Accounting, Management and Policy Journal, 8* (2), 137–163.

Phan, D. H. B., et al. (2019). "Barriers and drivers of renewable energy adoption in SMEs: evidence from Vietnam." *Journal of Cleaner Production*, 235, 1234–1246.

Paredes-Frigolett, H., Rivera-Camino, J., & Garces-Ayerbe, C. (2020). "Intellectual property and innovation in SMEs: A systematic literature review", *Journal of Business Research*, 113, 246–257.

Piatkowski, M., & Gupta, K. (2015). "Innovation in SMEs: A review of the literature", *Journal of Innovation Management*, 3(4), 18–43.

Rehman, A., & Khan, A. (2014). "Drivers of Innovation in Small and Medium-Sized Enterprises: A Review", *Journal of Small Business Management*, 52(4), 471–491.

Sánchez, A., Popescu, D., Iulia, C., Ciocârlan-Chitucea, A., & Popescu, D. (2011). "How to Improve Small and Medium-Sized Enterprises Profitability by Practicing an Efficient Human Resources Management." *Theoretical and Applied Economics, 01*(554).

Sánchez, J. A. M., & Lago, A. (2018). "Knowledge Management and Innovation in SMEs: A Systematic Review of the Literature", *Journal of Knowledge Management*, 22(1), 60–83.

Kotsios, P. (2023). "Business resilience skills for SMEs", *Journal of Innovation and Entrepreneurship, 12*, 37 (2023). https://doi.org/10.1186/s13731-023-00304-0

Sanzo, M. J., Santos-Vijande, M. L., & Álvarez-González, L. I. (2017). "Market orientation and new market opportunities", *Journal of Business Research, 75*, 33–41.

Saunila, M., & Ukko, J. (2015). "Collaboration and innovation performance in small and medium-sized enterprises: Empirical evidence in Finland", *Technology Analysis & Strategic Managemen*t, 27(5), 518.

Sharma, R., Mehta, K. & Goel, A. (2022). "Non-linear relationship between board size and performance of Indian companies", *Journal of Management and Governance,* https://doi.org/10.1007/s10997-022-09651-8

Sharma, S., Singh, G., & Aiyub A.S. (2020). "Use of Social Networking Sites by SMEs to Engage With Their Customers: A Developing Country Perspective." *Journal of Internet Commerce, 19*(1), 62–81. DOI: 10.1080/15332861.2019.1695180

Schlegelmilch, B. B., & Bohm, S. (2018). "Digitalization as a Cost Reduction Driver in Small and Medium-Sized Enterprises: Insights from a German Survey." *Journal of Business Research*, 89, 388–396.

Seville, E., Brunsdon, D., Dantas, A. & Masurier, J. L. (2015). "Organisational resilience: researching the reality of New Zealand SMEs", *Journal of Business Continuity & Emergency Planning*, 9(2), 112–125.

Vanhaverbeke, W., Roijakkers, N., & Hagedoorn, J. (2018). "Creating new markets with new technologies", *Research Policy*, 47(10), 1760–1773.

Vyas, V., Mehta, K. & Sharma, R. (2020). "Investigating socially responsible investing behaviour of Indian investors using structural equation modelling", *Journal of Sustainable Finance & Investment*, 1–23 DOI: 10.1080/20430795.2020.1790958

Zahra, S. & George, G. (2002). International entrepreneurship: Research contributions and future directions". In M. Hitt, R. D. Ireland, M. Camp and D. L. Sexton (eds.) Strategic entrepreneurship: Entrepreneurial strategies for wealth creation. New York: Blackwell, pp: 255–288.

Zawislak, P. A., Alves, H., & de Oliveira, M. P. V. (2019). "Business model innovation and new market opportunities: Exploring the influence of external and internal factors", *Technological Forecasting and Social Change*, 146, 168–179.

Zighan, S., Abuhussein, T., Al-Zu'bi, Z. and Dwaikat, N.Y. (2023). "A qualitative exploration of factors driving sustainable innovation in small and medium-sized enterprises in Jordan", *Journal of Enterprising Communities: People and Places in the Global Economy*.Ahead of print no.

Zott, C., & Amit, R. (2018). "Business model innovation: Creating value in times of change", *International Journal of Innovation Management*, 22(06), 1–17.

Anshul Jain

15 Effect of Government Policies on SME Innovation and Entrepreneurship

Abstract: Small and Medium Endeavours (SMEs) assume a critical part in the monetary turn of events and development, setting out work open doors and adding to advancement and business. Policies to encourage the growth of small and medium-sized enterprises (SMEs) have been developed by governments that are aware of their significance to their economies. This chapter looks at the impact of government strategies on SME development and business. Grants, subsidies, and tax breaks are some of the government policies designed to encourage SME innovation and entrepreneurship. These policies aim to give small and medium-sized businesses (SMEs) the money they need to grow and innovate. However, several factors influence these policies' ability to encourage SME innovation and entrepreneurship. One of the elements that influence the adequacy of government approaches to SME advancement and business venture is the size of the SMEs. Due to their larger size and easier access to resources, large SMEs are more likely to benefit from government policies. On the other hand, smaller SMEs may not have access to the same resources and may struggle to compete with larger SMEs. The nature of the industry is another factor that affects how well government policies for SME innovation and entrepreneurship work. For example, it may be more difficult for small and medium-sized businesses (SMEs) to compete with larger businesses because some industries may require more significant investments in R&D. Also, enterprises that are overwhelmed by giant firms might be less helpful for SME development and business venture. The efficacy of government policies regarding SME innovation and entrepreneurship is also significantly influenced by the regulatory environment. Excessively complicated guidelines can ruin the capacity of SMEs to advance and contend with more prominent firms. On the other hand, SMEs may be able to access the resources they require to innovate and expand in a regulatory environment that is favourable. Moreover, admittance to support is essential for SME development and business. SMBs can significantly benefit from government policies that make it easier to get financing. However, a variety of factors, including the SME's size and industry, determine whether financing is available.

Keywords: Government regulations, Public policy, Small and medium-sized enterprises (SMEs), Innovation, Entrepreneurship, Economic development, Tax incentives, Access to finance, Technology adoption, Intellectual property rights

Anshul Jain, Jagran lake city University, Bhopal, India

https://doi.org/10.1515/9783111170022-015

Introduction

Small and medium-sized businesses, or SMEs, are crucial to economic expansion and development. They assume a pivotal part in setting out work open doors, stimulating development, and advancing business (Mehta et al., 2017). As a result, small and medium-sized businesses (SMEs) are critically important, and governments worldwide have developed policies to encourage their growth (Mehta & Sharma, 2016). Tax incentives, grants, subsidies, and access to financing are among the policies developed by governments to support SMEs. These policies aim to give small and medium-sized businesses (SMEs) the money they need to grow and innovate. But be that as it may, the adequacy of these arrangements in advancing SME advancement and business ventures relies upon different variables. This chapter investigates how government policies affect entrepreneurship and innovation in small and medium-sized enterprises. This chapter has investigated the variables that influence the viability of government approaches, including the size of the SMEs, the idea of the business, the administrative climate, and admittance to funding. A review of previous studies on the effects of government policies on SME innovation and entrepreneurship is the first part of the chapter. Next, the various kinds of government policies, their intended outcomes, and the factors that influence their effectiveness are examined in the literature review. The studies conducted in past have examined different dimensions related to the capital market conditions, role of board structure and other sustainability related aspects affecting the performance of a firm and other strategic decision of the businesses (Sharma et al., 2020; Mahajan & Sharma, 2017; Mehta et al., 2022). Additionally, the literature review identifies areas for additional research and gaps in the existing literature. The next section of the chapter looks at the factors that affect how well government policies for SME innovation and entrepreneurship work. The size of the SMEs, the nature of the industry, the regulatory environment, and access to financing all play a role in determining whether government policies are effective. The chapter also talks about how these things work together and affect how well government policies work. Then, case studies of nations with policies to encourage SME innovation and entrepreneurship are presented. The case studies demonstrate the various government policies, their intended outcomes, and their effectiveness. In addition, the case studies shed light on the elements that affect the efficacy of government policies and offer suggestions for creating policies that encourage SME innovation and entrepreneurship. The chapter wraps up with a summary of the most important findings and suggestions for policymakers. The chapter stresses the significance of developing policies that consider the nature of the industry, the size of small and medium-sized businesses, the regulatory environment, and access to financing. The chapter additionally features the requirement for additional exploration to grasp the viability of government strategies more readily on SME development and business venture.

Policies Developed by Governments to Support Small and Medium-Sized Businesses (SMEs)

Throughout the world, governments have developed policies to provide SMEs with the resources they need to innovate and expand. These strategies incorporate duty impetuses, sponsorships, awards, and admittance to support. These policies give small and medium-sized businesses (SMEs) the financial support they need to innovate and expand.

Charge Impetuses: State-run administrations can offer expense-motivating forces to SMEs to lessen their taxation rate. Tax breaks, tax credits, and exemptions are all examples of tax incentives. Small and medium-sized businesses (SMEs) can get the resources they need to grow and innovate by taking advantage of tax breaks.

Subsidies: State-run administrations can give endowments to SMEs to help their turn of events. Grants and low-interest loans are two examples of subsidies. In addition, small and medium-sized businesses (SMEs) may be able to obtain the resources they require through sponsorships to expand their operations and make R&D investments.

Grants: SME development can be aided by grants from governments. Grants can help start new businesses or finance research and development projects.

Financing Availability: Small and medium-sized businesses (SMEs) can access financing to help them grow. Admittance to funding can be given through government-upheld credits, advance certifications, or value support. Admittance to funding can furnish SMEs with the vital assets to advance and develop.

Literature Review

In recent years, the Indian government has implemented various policies to encourage innovation and entrepreneurship in small and medium-sized businesses (SMEs). This literature review aims to investigate how these policies affect entrepreneurship and innovation among SME owners in India. The Start-up India program is one of India's primary government initiatives to encourage entrepreneurship and innovation among small and medium-sized enterprises. This program, launched in 2016, provides start-ups with various incentives and support, including tax breaks, funding, and mentorship. Over 50,000 new businesses had signed up for the program as of 2021, demonstrating its success in encouraging entrepreneurship in India. The Make in India program is another important government policy encouraging SME innovation and entrepreneurship. This program began in 2014 and aims to encourage domestic manufacturing and attract foreign investment. However, the program offers a scope of impetuses, including tax reductions, sponsorships, and simpler admittance to funding. While the program has effectively drawn in unfamiliar speculation, its effect on

SME advancement and business is unclear. The Indian government has also implemented several policies to encourage innovation in particular industries in addition to these programs. For instance, the 2015-launched Digital India program aims to encourage the use of technology in various fields, including agriculture, education, and healthcare. To encourage innovation in these industries, the program provides a variety of incentives and assistance. Additionally, the Public Biotechnology Improvement Procedure, sent off in 2015, expects to advance development in biotechnology by offering financing and backing to new companies and SMEs in this area.

According to studies, India's SME innovation and entrepreneurship can be significantly impacted by government policies. For instance, a survey conducted in 2018 by Agarwal and Shukla found that the Start-up India program had a beneficial effect on innovation and the creation of new businesses in India. Similarly, Kamath and Paul's study from 2019 found that the Make in India program helped small and medium-sized enterprises (SMEs) in the manufacturing sector. However, some obstacles in India prevent SME innovation and entrepreneurship from being promoted. The inability to obtain financing is one of the most significant obstacles. Even though start-ups can get funding and support from government programs like the Start-up India program, many small and medium-sized businesses (SMEs) still can't get financing. As a result, they may be unable to make R&D investments or adopt new technologies.

Another test is the absence of a framework and backing for development. Even though government programs like the Digital India program offer incentives and support for innovation, more infrastructure investment and assistance for small and medium-sized enterprises (SMEs) to adopt new technologies and innovate are still required. Government policies have significantly impacted SME innovation and entrepreneurship in India. Start-up India and Make in India programs have successfully promoted innovation and entrepreneurship, and sector-specific policies have fostered innovation in particular industries. However, promoting SME innovation and entrepreneurship in India is also difficult due to a lack of infrastructure and financing. To further encourage SME innovation and entrepreneurship in India, it will be essential to address these obstacles.

The Literature on the Effects of Government Policies on SME Innovation and Entrepreneurship. There is a wide range of research on the subject. A few examinations propose that administration strategies can advance SME development and business venture. However, different examinations recommend that administration strategies may not be compelling in advancing SME advancement and business ventures.

Czarnitzki and Delanote's (2015) research also found that government policies can encourage innovation in SMEs. According to the study, SMEs that receive subsidies from the government for research and development exhibit higher levels of innovation than SMEs that do not. However, some studies suggest that government policies may not be able to encourage innovation and entrepreneurship among small and medium-sized businesses. For example, according to a study conducted by Audretsch, Bonte, and Mahagaonkar (2012), government policies may be ineffective at encouraging entrepreneurship and innovation in SMEs. The investigation discovered that SMEs in nations with better government approaches don't have more elevated development and business venture levels than in countries with less ideal government arrangements. Even the increasing exposure SMEs for international markets confirmed the impact of international regulatory framework on the performance of SMEs (Mehta et al., 2017; Agarwal & Shukla, 2018).

Factors Influencing the Effectiveness of Government Policies

1. Size of the SMEs: The size of the SMEs may affect how healthy government policies work. Some approaches may work better for smaller businesses than for larger ones. For instance, while subsidies may be more effective for larger companies, tax incentives may be more beneficial to smaller businesses.
2. The nature of the business: The nature of the industry may also impact the efficacy of government policies. Policies encouraging research and development may be more effective in specific sectors with higher requirements than others. Similarly, policies that make it easier for businesses to access financing may be more successful in specific sectors than in others.
3. Administrative Climate: The efficacy of government policies may also be affected by the regulatory environment. Policies may not be as effective in sectors like healthcare and energy with high regulatory barriers. Policies that reduce regulatory obstacles may be more effective at encouraging innovation and entrepreneurship in these sectors.
4. Admittance to Supporting: Admittance to funding is an essential variable influencing the viability of government strategies. Strategies that give SMEs admittance with financing might be more successful in advancing advancement and business ventures. However, policies that address this issue may be more effective because funding availability may be restricted in some nations.
5. The Structure of Government Programs: The plan of government strategies may likewise influence their viability. Poorly designed policies may not be able to encourage entrepreneurship and innovation. Moreover, small, and medium-sized businesses (SMEs) may be less likely to apply for policies if, for instance, they must submit a large amount of documentation or must wait a long time for their turn.

Indian Government Policies for Supporting SMEs

Small and medium-sized businesses (SMEs) can benefit significantly from government policies encouraging innovation and entrepreneurship. Tax breaks, access to financing, subsidies for research and development, training programs, and business incubators are all examples of these policies. Coming up next are probably the most widely recognized arrangements that state-run administrations execute to help SMEs:

1. Rewards for taxes: Governments frequently support SMEs by implementing tax incentives. These impetuses can take different structures, including tax breaks, derivations, and exceptions. In addition, charge motivators can lessen the monetary weight on SMEs and let loose assets that can be utilized for advancement and business ventures.
2. Admittance to Supporting: The availability of financing is a crucial factor in the expansion and development of SMEs. Low-interest loans, equity financing, or guarantees are all ways in which governments can help SMEs. Small and medium-sized businesses (SMEs) may be able to hire more workers, expand their operations, and invest in R&D with this assistance.
3. Subsidies for Research and Development: Subsidies for research and development (R&D) are policies that give small and medium-sized businesses (SMEs) money to do R&D. Research, and development endowments can assist SMEs with growing new items and administrations, work on existing ones, and upgrade their seriousness on the lookout.
4. Preparing Projects: Policies that offer SMEs opportunities for training and development are known as training programs. These programs can help small and medium-sized businesses adopt new technologies, increase their market knowledge, and improve their management and operational skills.
5. Business Start-Ups: Business incubators provide SMEs with office space, shared services, and mentoring assistance. Small and medium-sized businesses (SMEs) can benefit from incubators' ability to provide them with a supportive setting for innovation and entrepreneurship and assist them in overcoming the initial difficulties associated with starting a business.

The size of the SMEs, the nature of the industry, the regulatory environment, access to financing, and the design of these policies all have an impact on their efficacy. Therefore, governments must consider these aspects when formulating policies to assist SMEs. Coming up next are a few prescribed procedures for creating compelling strategies:

1. Discussions with SMEs: When developing policies to support SMEs, governments must consult with them. This can assist in ensuring that policies are effective in fostering innovation and entrepreneurship and are tailored to SMEs' requirements.
2. Assessment of Policies: Legislatures must routinely assess their strategies' adequacy. This can assist in determining where policies need to be enhanced and whether or not they are achieving their intended goals.
3. Cooperation with Private Sector Organisations: For SMEs to be supported, governments need to work with the private sector. Small and medium-sized businesses (SMEs) may access financing, mentorship, and other resources to aid their development.

4. Flexibility: Policies need to be able to change with the market and be flexible. This can assist small and medium-sized businesses in adapting to market shifts and seize new opportunities.

Government policies can significantly impact SME innovation and entrepreneurship. Consider these essential points:

Access to funding - Small and medium-sized enterprises (SMEs) need financing to grow and invest in innovation. Concerning SMEs' access to funding, here are some important considerations:

Options for conventional financing: Traditional sources of financing, such as bank loans and credit lines, are available to SMEs. However, these options may be challenging to obtain for new or small businesses with poor credit.

Other options for financing: Crowdfunding, peer-to-peer lending, and factoring are becoming increasingly popular with small and medium-sized businesses. Small and medium-sized businesses (SMEs) can get funding through these options without needing collateral or a good credit history.

Government initiatives: Numerous government programs provide funding specifically for SMEs. These programs may offer grants, loans, or tax incentives to encourage SME innovation and growth.

Angel investors and venture capitalists: Angel investors and venture capitalists provide SMEs with funding in exchange for equity. These financial backers regularly search for high-development potential and might be more ready to put resources into less secure tasks (Platform, 2017).

Accelerators and incubators: Hatcheries and gas pedals give SMEs subsidizing, mentorship, and assets to help them develop and succeed. These programs may provide access to networks of investors and industry experts and frequently concentrate on technologies or industries.

SME innovation and expansion depend on having access to funding. Small and medium-sized businesses (SMEs) can obtain the financing they require to invest in innovation and expand their operations by looking into traditional and alternative financing options, locating government funding programs, collaborating with venture capital firms and angel investors, and participating in incubators and accelerators.

Regulations and Bureaucracy

SME innovation and entrepreneurship can be significantly hampered by regulations and bureaucracy. Here are a few central issues to consider:

Compliance costs: Guidelines can be excessive for SMEs to conform to, especially for more modest organizations with restricted assets. The cost of hiring regulatory experts, carrying out studies and assessments, and purchasing the necessary equipment are all examples of compliance costs.

Bureaucracy: SMEs may find it more challenging to navigate the regulatory landscape, and the innovation process may be slowed down as a result of bureaucracy. Permits, licenses, and certifications can be complicated and take a long time to obtain.

Inflexibility: It's possible that regulations won't change as technology or market conditions change. Due to this, small and medium-sized businesses (SMEs) may find it challenging to adapt to shifting circumstances.

Uncertainty: Regulations may be unclear about how they apply to circumstances and open to interpretation. This can make SMEs vulnerable and may deter them from putting resources into development.

Regulations on a global scale: Small and medium-sized businesses (SMEs) may be subject to different regulatory regimes in various markets, making international regulations particularly challenging. Compliance costs and complexity may rise as a result.

Regulations and bureaucracy can have a negative impact on entrepreneurship and innovation in small and medium-sized enterprises (SMEs). Streamlining regulations and providing clear guidelines, lowering compliance costs, and assisting small and medium-sized businesses (SMEs) in navigating the regulatory landscape are examples. Governments can assist in the promotion of innovation and the expansion of small and medium-sized enterprises (SMEs) by establishing a regulatory environment that is more favourable.

Intellectual Property Protection

Licensed innovation assurance is essential for SMEs to safeguard their inventive thoughts and advancements. Here are a few central issues to consider:

Patents: Licenses give lawful security to developments and provide the patent holder with the selective right to fabricate, use, and sell the innovation for a specific timeframe. Patents can help small and medium-sized businesses safeguard their cutting-edge technologies, processes, and goods.

Trademarks: Branding elements like logos, names, and slogans are protected by trademarks. By registering a brand, you can stop other companies from using branding elements similar to yours and could confuse customers in the market.

Copyrights: Software, books, and other original works of authorship are all protected by copyrights. Copyrights can help small and medium-sized businesses safeguard their creative works and prevent others from using or reproducing them without permission.

Secrets de trade: Formulas, procedures, and customer lists are examples of confidential information that provide a competitive advantage. SMEs can safeguard trade secrets by utilising nondisclosure agreements and other legal safeguards.
Security on a global scale: It's essential for small and medium-sized businesses (SMEs) to be aware of the various intellectual property laws in each nation. Global assurance can be acquired through licenses, brand names, and different means.

Intellectual property protection is essential for SMEs to safeguard their cutting-edge concepts and technologies. Small and medium-sized businesses (SMEs) can prevent others from using their intellectual property without permission by acquiring copyrights, trademarks, patents, and other legal protections. Small and medium-sized businesses (SMEs) can also benefit from government assistance navigating the intellectual property landscape and protecting their innovations.

Education and Training

Innovation and entrepreneurship in SME sectors require formal education and training. Here are a few central issues to consider:
Enhancement of skills: SMEs need representatives with the right abilities to advance and develop their organizations. Instruction and preparing projects can assist representatives with fostering the capabilities they need to work with innovations, promote new items, and oversee business activities.
Education in entrepreneurialism: Business venture schooling can assist people with fostering the abilities they need to begin and maintain a fruitful business. This might include classes on marketing, finance, business planning, and other essential business skills.
Accelerators and incubators: Early-stage SMEs receive assistance and resources from incubators and accelerators. They might provide mentoring, opportunities for networking, funding, and entry to facilities and equipment.
Aid from the government: Education and training programs for SMEs can be supported by governments. This could include money for schools, grants for small and medium-sized businesses to take part in training programs, or tax breaks for companies that invest in employee education and training.
Continuous learning: For SMEs to remain competitive in a business environment that is rapidly changing, lifelong learning is essential. Employees should be encouraged throughout their careers to keep learning and improving their skills.

For SME innovation and entrepreneurship, education and training are essential. Small and medium-sized enterprises (SMEs) can cultivate the talent they require to innovate and expand their businesses by investing in skill development, entrepreneurship education, incubators and accelerators, and lifelong learning. In addition, States can uphold SME schooling and preparing programs through subsidizing, awards, and duty motivators, assisting with establishing a stronger climate for SME development.

Tax Policies

SME innovation and entrepreneurship can be significantly impacted by tax policies. Here are a few central issues to consider:

Charge impetuses: SMBs may be motivated to invest in growth and innovation by tax incentives. For instance, research and development (R&D) tax breaks can help pay for new processes or products. In addition, charge derivations for capital speculations can urge SMEs to put resources into new hardware or offices.

Tax compliance: For small and medium-sized businesses (SMEs), tax compliance can be time-consuming and costly, mainly if they operate in multiple jurisdictions (Sharma & Sharma, 2023). If supported and guided, SMBs may feel less pressure to comply with tax laws.

Charge rates: SMBs may be discouraged from investing in growth and innovation by high tax rates. SMEs may be able to keep more of their earnings and reinvest them in their businesses thanks to lower tax rates.

Taxation on a global scale: International tax regulations may be complicated for SMEs that operate in multiple nations. Governments can provide support and resources to assist SMEs in navigating these regulations and lowering compliance costs.

Stability in tax policy: For SMEs to plan, tax policies need to be consistent and predictable. Small and medium-sized businesses (SMEs) may be discouraged from long-term investments if tax policies are frequently modified.

SME innovation and entrepreneurship can be significantly impacted by tax policies. Governments can create a more favourable environment for SME growth by simplifying tax regulations, lowering tax rates, supporting international taxation, providing tax incentives for innovation and development, and ensuring the stability of tax policy.

Government Procurement

Small and medium-sized businesses (SMEs) can benefit from government procurement because it can help them innovate and expand. Here are a few central issues to consider:

Reserved programs: Small and medium-sized businesses (SMEs) can receive priority in some government contracts. This can help small and medium-sized businesses compete for government contracts and give them a steady source of income.

Procedures for purchasing: SMBs can be more competitive for government contracts with simplified procurement procedures. Small and medium-sized businesses (SMEs) can benefit from government assistance navigating procurement procedures and requirements.
Advancement acquirement: SME innovation can be encouraged by procurement by governments. Governments, for instance, can impose procurement standards that enable small and medium-sized businesses (SMEs) to develop novel processes or products.
Terms of payment: Payment terms that are favourable to SMEs can be established by governments. With longer payment terms, SMEs can manage their cash flow and reduce financial risk.
Transparency: Government procurement should be open and fair to guarantee that SMEs have equal opportunities to compete for contracts. States can give clear rules and guidelines to obtain and guarantee that the acquisition interaction is fair and impartial.

Government acquisition can be a significant wellspring of business for SMEs and can uphold their advancement and development. Governments can make it easier for small and medium-sized enterprises (SMEs) to compete for government contracts by implementing set-aside programs, streamlining procurement procedures, encouraging innovative procurement, establishing favourable payment terms, and ensuring transparency and fairness. This can assist SMEs with developing their organizations and adding to the economy.

Case Studies

Case Study 1: Singapore's Innovation-Driven Economy

With a thriving startup ecosystem and a strong emphasis on research and development (R&D), Singapore has established itself as a global centre for innovation and entrepreneurship. Through a variety of programs and policies, the government has helped this ecosystem in significant ways.

One of the necessary arrangements that have helped Singapore's advancement-driven economy is the foundation of the Organization for Science, Innovation, and Exploration (ASTAR) in 1991. ASTAR is a statutory board that encourages research and development in various fields, including engineering, information and communications technology, and biomedical sciences. It aids researchers and entrepreneurs in creating innovative goods and services by providing funding, infrastructure, and technical assistance.

The Startup SG initiative is another policy that has supported entrepreneurship in Singapore. This initiative consists of several programs that provide startups at various stages of development with opportunities for networking, mentoring, and funding. Startup SG Equity, on the other hand, offers co-investment funding for early-stage startups, and Startup SG Founder provides up to S$30,000 in financing to first-time entrepreneurs.

Singapore has emerged as a leading destination for investors and startups because of these policies. Singapore is ranked first in the world for innovation input, which includes factors like human capital and research, and second for innovation output, which provides indicators like knowledge and technology outputs, according to the Global Innovation Index 2020.

Case Study 2: Rwanda's ICT-Led Development

Rwanda has taken huge steps in advancing ICT-drove improvement lately, with the public authority assuming an essential part in driving this change. The nation has utilized innovation to drive economic development and work on friendly results, like medical care and training.

One of the key strategies that have assisted Rwanda with turning into a forerunner in ICT is the foundation of the Rwanda Improvement Board (RDB) in 2008. The RDB is a single source for services like investment promotion, business registration, and licensing. It has made it easier for entrepreneurs to start and expand their businesses in Rwanda by streamlining the process.

Establishing the Rwanda Coding Academy is another policy that has aided ICT-driven development in Rwanda. Talented high school graduates receive free instruction in coding and other ICT-related skills at this academy. It has opened new opportunities for entrepreneurship and technological innovation and contributed to the country's growth of a skilled workforce.

With a thriving technology sector and a rapidly expanding economy, Rwanda has emerged as a leader in ICT-led development due to these policies. As a result, Rwanda's GDP grew by an average of 8% annually between 2010 and 2019, making it one of the world's fastest-growing economies, according to the World Bank.

Case Study 3: Sweden's Social Safety Net

With a wide range of services and benefits for its citizens, Sweden's social safety net is regarded as one of the world's best. Moreover, because it provides a safety net for people who take risks and start new businesses, this safety net has helped the country's innovation and entrepreneurship thrive.

The progressive taxation system is one of the key policies that has supported entrepreneurship in Sweden. The nation has an exceptionally moderate duty framework, with higher workers paying more of their pay in charges. This system contributes to redistributing wealth and funds social services and other public goods that encourage innovation and entrepreneurship.

The availability of affordable healthcare and childcare services is another policy that has contributed to the encouragement of entrepreneurship in Sweden. Because these services are heavily subsidized by the government, it is easier for entrepreneurs to start and expand their businesses without worrying about paying for childcare or healthcare.

Furthermore, Sweden has a liberal parental leave arrangement, which permits guardians to get some much-needed rest work to focus on their kids. This approach has assisted with advancing orientation equity and has urged more ladies to enter the labour force, setting out new open doors for business ventures and development.

Additionally, the Swedish government offers grants and low-interest loans to entrepreneurs as forms of financial assistance. The Swedish Development Organization (Vinnova) gives subsidizing and backing to research and advancement, while ALMI, an administration-claimed funding organization, provides funding and support to new companies and independent ventures.

Sweden's social safety net fosters innovation and entrepreneurship, allowing individuals to take chances and realize their goals without fear of poverty. Consequently, Sweden has emerged as a pioneer in innovation, with a flourishing startup ecosystem and a workforce of highly skilled individuals.

Case Study 4: Japan's Abenomics Policy

Abenomics is a bunch of financial strategies presented in Japan in 2012 by State leader Shinzo Abe. The Japanese economy, which had been stagnant for years, was to be revived, and problems like deflation, a shrinking workforce, and a large national debt were to be addressed by Abenomics.

Monetary policy, which included the Bank of Japan's aggressive program of quantitative easing, was one of Abenomics' most essential components. The goal of this policy was to boost lending and investment, reduce interest rates, and increase the money supply.

Fiscal policy, which increased government spending on social programs and infrastructure, was another critical aspect of Abenomics. This spending was planned to invigorate financial development and make occupations.

In addition, structural changes were included in Abenomics to make the Japanese economy more adaptable and competitive. Deregulation, tax incentives for business investment, and encouraging female labour force participation were among these reforms.

In general, the Abenomics policy significantly impacted the Japanese economy, which experienced increased growth and inflation in the years that followed its implementation. The country's startup ecosystem also benefited from the policy, which resulted in increased investment and support for entrepreneurship.

The introduction of the "Startup Visa" program in 2018, which made it possible for entrepreneurs from other countries to start businesses in Japan, is one illustration of this. The program's benefits included office space, fast-track visas, and assistance from government agencies.

The introduction of the J-Startup program in 2018 is yet another illustration of how Abenomics has affected entrepreneurship. Fintech, healthcare, and mobility startups in Japan were this program's primary focus, providing funding and assistance to these businesses.

Regardless of these positive turns of events, a few pundits contend that Abenomics didn't go far enough in resolving primary issues in the Japanese economy, for example, the maturing populace and unbending work market. Nonetheless, the policy was a significant effort by the Japanese government to support entrepreneurship and revive the economy.

Case Study 5: Israel's Innovation Ecosystem

Israel has earned the "Startup Nation" moniker due to its highly successful innovation ecosystem. The following are some significant contributing factors to this success:

Aid from the government: Innovation and entrepreneurship have been significantly supported by the Israeli government. It has given subsidizing to innovative work, as well as duty motivators for organizations that put resources into Research and development.

Military assistance: Military help is necessary for Israel, and numerous Israelis get top-notch specialized preparation during their administration. As a result, there is now a large pool of workers with advanced technical skills.

Societal norms: Innovation, taking chances, and entrepreneurship are highly valued in Israeli culture. In some other cultures, failure is not as stigmatized as it is, which encourages innovation and experimentation.

Innovative instruction: There are numerous programs in Israel's robust educational system that emphasize innovation and entrepreneurship. This includes entrepreneurship courses offered by universities and incubators and accelerators that provide startup founders with mentoring and training.

Capacity availability: Venture capitalists and angel investors willing to invest in cutting-edge startups are well-established in Israel. Venture capital funds and international investors are also available to Israeli businesses.

Networking and collaboration: Startups and established businesses collaborate and share resources and knowledge in the Israeli innovation ecosystem. There are likewise areas of strength for gas pedals, incubators, and cooperating spaces that give chances to systems administration and joint effort.

Israel's innovation ecosystem has been thriving because of all these factors, which have resulted in numerous innovative startups and biotech, cyber security, and artificial intelligence technologies.

Conclusion

Government policies can play a crucial role in supporting SME innovation and entrepreneurship. The government has taken several initiatives in India to promote entrepreneurship and support SMEs. For example, the introduction of the Startup India campaign in 2016 has been a significant step towards creating a favourable ecosystem for startups, including tax exemptions, funding support, and more accessible compliance procedures.

Nonetheless, despite these endeavours, there are still moves that should be tended to, for example, the absence of admittance to back, restricted accessibility of gifted HR, and administrative obstacles. To support small and medium-sized businesses (SMEs) and encourage entrepreneurship in the nation, the government must address these issues and implement efficient policies.

In addition, it is essential to remember that the legal framework, cultural norms, and social capital all play a role in determining whether government policies are successful. Thus, policymakers must adopt a comprehensive strategy and consider all essential elements to establish a strong climate for SMEs and businesses.

The Indian government's endeavours to help SME advancement and business ventures are praiseworthy. However, there is still a long way to go, and policymakers must continue to focus on creating a favourable environment for small and medium-sized businesses (SMEs) to thrive, including addressing the sector's challenges and implementing effective policies. Through this, India can release the capability of its businesspeople and SMEs, making position, advancing economic development, and adding to the nation's turn of events.

References

Acs, Z. J., & Audretsch, D. B. (2010). *Innovation and small firms*, Cambridge, MA: MIT Press.

Acs, Z. J., & Szerb, L. (2007). "Entrepreneurship, economic growth and public policy", *Small Business Economics*, *28*(2–3), 109–122.

Acs, Z. J., & Audretsch, D. B. (2003). "Government policy toward entrepreneurship", CESifo DICE Report, 1 (3), 19–25.

Agarwal, S., & Shukla, A. (2018). "Assessing the impact of Start-up India on start–up creation and innovation in India", *International Journal of Innovation Management*, *22*(02), 1–19.
Audretsch, D. B., & Keilbach, M. (2007). "Entrepreneurship capital and economic performance", *Regional Studies*, *41*(6), 857–871.
Audretsch, D. B., & Keilbach, M. C. (2007). "The theory of knowledge spillover entrepreneurship", *Journal of Management Studies*, *44*(7), 1242–1254.
Audretsch, D. B., & Thurik, A. R. (2001). "What's new about the new economy? Sources of growth in the managed and entrepreneurial economies", *Industrial and Corporate Change*, *10*(1), 267–315.
Audretsch, D. B., Bonte, W., & Mahagaonkar, P. (2012). "Financial signaling by innovative nascent ventures: the relevance of patents and prototypes." *Research Policy*, *41*, 1407–1421.
Beck, T., Demirgüç–Kunt, A., & Levine, R. (2003). "Law and finance: Why does legal origin matter?", *Journal of comparative economics*, *31*(4), 653–675.
Carayannis, E. G., & Rakhmatullin, R. (2014). "The quadruple innovation helix and intelligent specialisation strategies for sustainable and inclusive growth in Europe and beyond", *Journal of the Knowledge Economy*, *5*(2), 212–239.
Crescenzi, R., & Gagliardi, L. (2018). "The innovative performance of firms in heterogeneous environments: The interplay between external knowledge and internal absorptive capacities", *Research Policy*, *47*(4), 782–795.
Czarnitzki, D. & Delanote, J. (2015). R&D policies for young SMEs: Input and output effects. *Small Business Economics*. *45*. 10.1007/s11187-015-9661-1.
Decker, R. A., & Haltiwanger, J. (2018). "The Role of Entrepreneurship in US job creation and Economic Dynamism", *Journal of Economic Perspectives*, *32*(3), 3–24.
Díaz-García, M. C., & Jiménez–Moreno, J. (2010). "Entrepreneurial intention: The role of gender", *International Entrepreneurship and Management Journal*, *6*(3), 261–283.
European Commission. (2016). "SME Definition", Retrieved from https://ec.europa.eu/growth/smes/business-friendly-environment/sme-definition_en
European Commission. (2018). "The 2018 SME Performance Review", Brussels: Author.
Fagerberg, J., Fosaas, M., & Sapprasert, K. (2012). "Innovation: Exploring the knowledge base", *Research Policy*, *41*(7), 1132–1153.
Global Entrepreneurship Monitor. (2019). "Global Entrepreneurship Monitor 2018/2019 Global Report", Retrieved from https://www.gemconsortium.org/report/50632
Hall, B. H., & Lerner, J. (2010). "The financing of R&D and innovation". In B. H. Hall & N. Rosenberg (Eds.), *Handbook of the Economics of Innovation*, Vol. 1 (pp. 609–639). Amsterdam: Elsevier.
Henrekson, M., & Sanandaji, T. (2018). "The interaction between entrepreneurship and institutions", *Journal of Institutional Economics*, *14*(3), 471–498.
Innovation Policy Platform. (2017). "Innovation Policy Database", Paris: OECD and World Bank Group.
Johnson, S., McMillan, J., & Woodruff, C. (2002). "Property rights and finance", *American Economic Review*, *92*(5), 1335–1356.
Kautonen, T., Tornikoski, E. T., & Kibler, E. (2011). "Entrepreneurial intentions in the third age: The impact of perceived age norms", *Small Business Economics*, *37*(2), 219–234.
Kenney, M., & Patton, D. (2019). "Reconsidering the Bayh–Dole Act and the current university innovation system", *Research Policy*, *48*(3), 773–783.
Kirzner, I. M. (2015). "Entrepreneurial discovery and the competitive market process: An Austrian approach", *Small Business Economics*, *44*(1), 17–29.
Kamath, G. B., & Paul, J. (2019). "Make in India: A boon to the SMEs in the Indian manufacturing sector", *Journal of Small Business & Entrepreneurship Development*, *7*(1), 44–58.
Klapper, L. F., & Love, I. (2011). "The impact of business environment reforms on new firm registration", *World Bank Policy Research Working Paper* No. 5832.

Koellinger, P., Minniti, M., & Schade, C. (2007). "I think I can, I think I can": Overconfidence and entrepreneurial behavior. *Journal of Economic Psychology*, *28*(4), 502–527.

Lee, J. W., & Lee, Y. J. (2019). "The effect of government policy support on SMEs' innovation and export", *Sustainability*, *11*(14), 3887.

Mahajan, V. and Sharma, R. (2017). "Future of Depository with Introduction of Payment Bank– A Game Changer to Capital Market", *International Journal of Applied Business and Economic Research*, *15*(9), 343–356.

Mehta K. and Sharma R. and Chugh, A. (2017). "Management of Forex Risk Exposure: A Study of SMEs and Unlisted Non-Financial Firms in India", *International Journal of Applied Business and Economic Research*, *15*(9), 43–54.

Mehta, K., & Sharma, R. (2016). "SMEs and corporate social responsibility: Indian perception", *SCMS Journal of Indian Management*, *13*(3), 58–67.

Mehta, K., Sharma, R., Vyas, V. and Kuckreja, J.S. (2022). "Exit strategy decision by venture capital firms in India using fuzzy AHP", *Journal of Entrepreneurship in Emerging Economies*, 14(4), 643–669. https://doi.org/10.1108/JEEE-05-2020-0146

Muñoz, P., & Dimov, D. (2015). "The call of the whole in understanding the development of sustainable ventures", *Journal of Business Venturing*, *30*(4), 632–654.

OECD. (2017). *OECD Science, Technology and Industry Scoreboard 2017*, Paris: Author.

Organisation for Economic Cooperation and Development (OECD). (2019). "Boosting Productivity and Inclusive Growth in Latin America", Retrieved from https://www.oecd.org/dev/boosting-productivity-and-inclusive-growth-in-latin-america-9789264311912-en.htm

Piva, E., Santarelli, E., & Vivarelli, M. (2019). "The determinants of young firms' innovative activity: Empirical evidence from Europe", *Small Business Economics*, *53*(1), 41–58.

Schumpeter, J. A. (1934). *The Theory of Economic Development: An Inquiry into Profits, Capital, Credit, Interest, and the Business Cycle*, Cambridge, MA: Harvard University Press.

Shane, S., & Venkataraman, S. (2000). "The promise of entrepreneurship as a field of research", *Academy of Management Review*, *25*(1), 217–226.

Sharma, A. & Sharma, R. (2023). Exploring Tax Decision Factors: A Perspective from North Indian Tax Practitioners. Journal of Tax Reform, 8(3), 285–297. https://doi.org/10.15826/jtr.2022.8.3.122

Sharma, R., Mehta, K. & Goel, A. (2022). "Non-linear relationship between board size and performance of Indian companies", *Journal of Management and Governance*, https://doi.org/10.1007/s10997-022-09651-8

Sharma, R., Mehta, K., & Vyas, V. (2020). "Responsible Investing: A Study on Non–Economic Goals and Investors' Characteristics", *Applied Finance Letters*, *9(SI)*, 63–78. https://doi.org/10.24135/afl.v9i2.245

Small Business Administration. (2019). *Small Business Innovation Research (SBIR) and Small Business Technology Transfer (STTR) Programs*, Washington, DC: Author.

United Nations Conference on Trade and Development (UNCTAD). (2019). "Policy Framework for Digital Entrepreneurship", Retrieved from https://unctad.org/system/files/official-document/diae2019d3_en.pdf

United Nations Conference on Trade and Development. (2019). *The Least Developed Countries Report 2019*, Geneva: Author.

World Bank. (2021). "Enterprise Surveys", Retrieved from https://www.enterprisesurveys.org/en/

World Bank. (2019). *Doing Business 2020: Comparing business regulation in 190 economies*, World Bank Publications.

Ali Albouti and K. D. Balaji

16 A Study on Various Aspects of SMEs' Orientation for Corporate Social Responsibility

Abstract: Today, being responsible and sustainable is essential to conducting business internationally. However, small and medium-sized firms (SMEs) have received less attention from academics and policymakers than huge multinational corporations. Recent studies have highlighted the significance of learning for SMEs to engage in corporate social responsibility (CSR), but there is still a lack of knowledge regarding how SMEs learning orientation affects their CSR as well as how development affects SMEs internationalization and performance. From a practical standpoint, it is particularly crucial to shed light on these dynamics because, in the majority of nations, SMEs account for a sizable portion of enterprises in terms of both number and employment. The current study makes a contribution by demonstrating how CSR affects various performance kinds in SMEs and how SMEs learning orientation affects their CSR. By shedding light on the causes and effects of CSR for SMEs, the study adds to the body of knowledge on responsibility, sustainability, and SME internationalization. The author explored a number of CSR-related subjects in this chapter, including need, problems and challenges, ideas, obligations to employees, and the environment. And the main headlines discussed the thorough investigation of CSR for SMEs and the introduction of several social concerns and SMEs-related policies. This chapter also includes several case studies from India for reference.

Keywords: Corporate Social Responsibility (CSR), Small and Medium Enterprises (SMEs), CSR orientation, CSR implementation, Sustainability, Social responsibility, Business practices, Environmental sustainability

Introduction

Corporate social responsibility, or CSR, is a relatively new issue that affects the business world, and an increasing number of businesses are starting to understand how important it is to have CSR. However, it is a significant issue for businesses because they must use corporate social responsibility to create a sustainable social environment and development. In addition, CSR gives them a chance to gain a competitive and comparative advantage over rival businesses. In today's world, where competi-

Ali Albouti, K. D. Balaji, Faculty of Management, SRM University

https://doi.org/10.1515/9783111170022-016

tion is unavoidable and maintaining a competitive edge is essential to a company's existence, businessmen must employ all available means to do so.

Corporate social responsibility (CSR) is the idea that businesses should think about how their actions affect society and the environment in addition to their primary objective of making a profit. Small and medium-sized businesses (SMEs) are becoming increasingly aware of the value of integrating CSR into their corporate goals. CSR can be viewed in the context of SMEs as a way to benefit both the company and society. It entails considering how corporate activities will affect society, the economy, and the environment and deliberately attempting to advance these causes. Small and medium-sized enterprises (SMEs) can approach CSR by concentrating on corporate moral conduct, environmental sustainability, worker well-being, community involvement, and philanthropy. These initiatives can potentially improve the environment and society, the SME's market standing and competitiveness. Due to their limited resources, SMEs may find it difficult to implement CSR practices, but doing so may also open up opportunities for innovation and market distinction. Adopting a CSR perspective can also assist SMEs in attracting and retaining clients, staff members, and investors who are becoming increasingly concerned about how enterprises affect society and the environment. By integrating CSR into their business strategies, SMEs can benefit from long-term value creation for all stakeholders, including the firm itself, society, and the environment.

Corporate social responsibility, however, is typically associated with large corporations and multinationals. Small and medium-sized enterprises (SMEs) are frequently forgotten when CSR is debated among academia, the media, and the broader civil society. Due to their high profile and greater ability to draw media attention, big profit companies are more concerned with their reputation and image than smaller ones. Being exposed to public opinion causes people to continually work to preserve their relationships with customers and other important stakeholders and engage in CRS. Apart from that, their size, profits, and resources enable businesses to invest more in corporate social responsibility. Without question, CSR is vital for small and medium-sized businesses as well, and they can implement CRS practices in various unique ways. Small businesses can participate in CRS for a variety of reasons, and several instances support the value of CRS and the enormous benefits it can provide even to small businesses. It has nothing to do with size. Corporate social responsibility (CSR) should apply to large and small businesses because every company has stakeholders and social impacts. Sustainability and governance issues in big corporates are investigated by researchers with more intensity (Sharma et al., 2022; Vyas et al. 2023). The relationship between small and medium-sized businesses and corporate social responsibility is thoroughly discussed in this essay. First, certain definitions of fundamental terminology, like CRS and Small and Medium Enterprises (SMEs), are mentioned. The significance of CRS implementation for SMEs is then discussed, and finally, the advantages of CRS practice in terms of competition are mentioned. Examples of European SMEs with CRS practises make up a sizable portion of the following analysis, which is concluded at the end.

Definition

The term "corporate social responsibility" is crucial to start the examination of the topic concerning some definitions, particularly the CRS definition. CSR is defined in a variety of ways. The fundamental tenet of corporate social responsibility, or responsible entrepreneurship, is the obligation that firms have to support the long-term progress of their communities. In its most basic form, corporate social responsibility (CSR) refers to a company's duty to society or, more precisely, its stakeholders—those impacted by its policies and practices. These responsibilities relate to acting morally or responsibly. According to the widely accepted definition from the EU, CSR is "a concept whereby companies integrate social and environmental concerns in their business operations and their interaction with stakeholders voluntarily and goes beyond what the law requires." In order to meet societal objectives, businesses must choose to go above and beyond the bare minimum of legal requirements and obligations resulting from collective agreements. In other words, it entails achieving financial success while also managing the expectations of others, including customers, vendors, and the surrounding neighbourhood.

Furthermore, it entails making a beneficial impact on society and controlling the environmental effects of the business. Social and environmental concerns must be considered in order for economies to succeed. Applying this principle is advantageous for society but can also directly benefit each organization and ensure its long-term competitiveness. Companies focus on CSR implementation because of this.

Corporate Social Responsibility (CSR) is a business approach companies follow to make a social impact and focus beyond profits. Its main purpose is to enhance the company's image, earn customer loyalty and generate more sales. It also benefits society and the environment as businesses work for the collective good.

SMEs in General

According to figures from the World Bank Group, SMEs made up over 50% of all jobs worldwide and approximately 90% of all enterprises in 2012. Their proportion in Europe, there are even more businesses overall. Supplying two-thirds of the private sector jobs and attaining nearly 99 per cent. It's also interesting to note that nine out of ten SMEs in Europe have fewer than ten employees or are "micro" SMEs. So why do we claim that they are so crucial to the economy? The entrepreneurial spirit and abilities are cultivated and used in SMEs, which explains why they are vital to economic growth (Mehta et al., 2017). MSMEs have a big impact on the overall business ecosystem (Mehta et al., 2019; 2022). Start-ups and new enterprises, often small or micro businesses, are common in many countries (Mehta et al., 2022a). Moreover, they serve as a hybrid of R&D facilities and incubators for new ideas. But this is but a portion of what they have done. Contrary to the prevalent belief, corporate social responsibility is primarily the responsibility of large firms and is too expensive for SMEs. It seems that SMEs have a lot more expertise in this area. They do this by implementing CSR principles in their daily routines constantly and naturally.

Small business practises missions, and, therefore, the individual employees are heavily influenced by the personal and ethical standards of owners and managers. Because they can easily relate to the immediate and indirect benefits of their job for the firm and the broader community in which the SME operates, the personnel frequently also strongly believe in the moral principles regulating a small company's business. More and more individuals nowadays worry about how their actions affect the environment, society, the economy, etc. Young people are increasingly looking for careers in organizations that perform ethically and sustainably. The consumer behaviour and capital market operations can further affect the growth pattern of firms (Khanna & Sharma, 2017: Mahajan & Sharma, 2017).

Another significant characteristic of SMEs is that they frequently meet the highly unique demands of an area or community. Because the social and environmental concerns they deal with are local, the positive influence on the community and the region is bigger and more palpable when combined with the ethical conduct of the business, making their CSR practices more practical and result oriented.

Some issues that SMEs want to address can be out of their price range. However, in certain situations, SMEs could work together and pool their resources, expertise, and efforts to accomplish the desired impact. The EU prioritizes the development of networks for SMEs to exchange and discuss their best practices, and the Commission allocates funds to the cause by fostering such a culture of sharing. As a result, SMEs help today's knowledge-based economy continue to grow, lower the costs of some problems, and ultimately produce better solutions. This leads to three further ideas that are currently highly well-liked. Especially interaction, openness, and successful communication. Because fewer people can coordinate within and between small businesses, they are frequently accomplished instinctively and informally, making their internal operations more efficient and long-lasting. The variety of information and skills SME employees acquire can also be very advantageous to them. Employees in small businesses frequently go beyond the scope of their official job titles and continually take on new tasks and responsibilities. Companies frequently spend money on employee training, which aids in human capital growth. Even though SMEs perform responsibly in their ways, many individuals are still unaware of this. This is because documenting and publicizing these efforts is too expensive for small businesses, and some of their CSR operations are only known to a select few.

Furthermore, as it is generally understood, the term "corporate social responsibility" may not be the most appropriate when discussing SMEs. Their business practises may also be called "responsible entrepreneurship"—a concept that EU institutions attempt to popularize. And this is exactly what they are—opportunities that businesspeople take advantage of to foster healthy competition, new employment prospects, and the development of their staff members' knowledge and abilities. And a more dynamic economy.

Need for the Study

Corporate Social Responsibility (CSR) is the term used to describe how businesses behave ethically and socially responsibly towards their stakeholders and the general public. Small and medium-sized businesses (SMEs) must implement CSR practices, even though CSR is typically linked with larger organizations.

Here are some reasons why CSR is important for SMEs:

- **Enhanced reputation**: Adopting CSR practices can improve an SME's standing with its clients, partners, staff members, and the general public. This may boost customer loyalty and trust, ultimately aiding in the company's expansion.
- SMEs implementing CSR practices are better positioned to compete in the market since they are viewed as more ethical and responsible than their rivals. This might assist SMEs in standing out from the competition and luring in new clients.
- **Better risk management**: SMEs can identify and manage risks associated with social and environmental issues, such as climate change, labour practices, and supply chain management, by adopting CSR practices. This can assist SMEs in avoiding legal obligations and reputational harm.
- **Improved access to capital:** As strong CSR practises indicate sound management and low risk, many investors and lenders are increasingly looking for companies with these practices. Therefore, SMEs who implement CSR practices may have easier access to financing.
- **Social benefit**: Finally, implementing CSR practices can benefit society by fostering moral and sustainable corporate practices. This can support the company's long-term viability and help create stronger communities.

In conclusion, CSR is critical for SMEs because it may boost their reputation, increase their competitiveness, improve risk management, improve access to funding, and positively impact society. According to a survey of 500 SMEs in India conducted by the India SME Forum, 60% of respondents said they participate in CSR activities. The most popular CSR activities are supporting education and skill development, promoting environmental sustainability, and fostering community development. By implementing CSR strategies, SMEs can show their dedication to moral and ethical business conduct and construct a more durable and robust company over time.

Issues and challenges regarding CSR in SMEs

There are several issues regarding Corporate Social Responsibility (CSR) in Small and Medium Enterprises (SMEs) that need to be addressed:

- **Lack of resources**: SMEs frequently lack the financial and personnel resources necessary to engage in CSR activities. They might not have the resources and knowledge to conduct ethical and sustainable business practices.
- **Limited knowledge:** Many SMEs might not be aware of the value of CSR practices or the advantages they may provide. They might not have access to training, advice, or knowledge on how to use CSR practices.
- **Limited communication and interaction with stakeholders**: SMEs may struggle to maintain relationships with their customers, employees, suppliers, and local communities. This may limit the impact of CSR practices and lead to a lack of awareness of their expectations and demands.
- **Limited access to financing**: Because CSR projects may be viewed as high-risk ventures, SMEs may have trouble getting funding for them. They may find it challenging to finance their sustainability programmes or make investments in ethical supply chains.
- **Limited regulatory framework:** It's possible that CSR practices in SMEs are not subject to adequate regulatory frameworks or norms. Due to the lack of defined criteria or incentives, it may be challenging for SMEs to embrace CSR practices.
- **Limited scalability**: Due to a lack of resources and knowledge, SMEs may have trouble expanding their CSR practices as they expand. Due to this, it may be challenging for them to continue their sustainable business practices and control their impact as they grow.

By addressing these problems, small and medium-sized enterprises (SMEs) can engage in sustainable and ethical business practices and assist in creating a more ethical and sustainable business sector. This can be accomplished by laws and programmes that assist SMEs in implementing CSR practices, such as access to financing, public awareness campaigns, and legal frameworks that reward ethical company conduct. Additionally, SMEs can overcome difficulties when implementing and expanding their sustainability initiatives by developing their competence and knowledge in CSR practices.

Review of Literature

In an article published in 2013, it discussed incentive elements for small and medium-sized businesses (SMEs) to engage in corporate social responsibility (CSR) practises are investigated empirically in this research. Data from SMEs in Rajasthan were gathered using a standardized questionnaire, yielding 132 useful responses. Using AMOS 19, confirmatory factor analysis was performed on the data to check for model fit and scale item unidimensionality. Four underlying dimensions in the CSR motivation of SME managers were revealed by confirmatory factor analysis. Themes such as "Customer Propositions," "Stakeholder Value," "Founder Characteristics and Business Values," and "Business Motives" are expressed in four motivational dimensions that were discovered. The survey found that, in acknowledgement of their social responsibilities and commercial goals, SMEs are both willing and able to contribute significantly to support mostly local events and organizations (Roy et al., 2013; Mehta & Sharma, 2016). A study in 2021 conducted surveys which identified thirteen factors as significant obstacles preventing Indian SMEs from engaging in CSR. According to the ISM model, the key factors preventing Indian SMEs from engaging in an active and meaningful CSR engagement are their lack of information and expertise about CSR and their concentration on tactical rather than strategic needs. In addition, their insufficient employee involvement requirements, the limited necessity for CSR engagement, and lesser perceived CSR advantages limit their CSR engagement. Finally, due to less intense societal and governmental pressure, Indian SMEs do not recognize the necessity for CSR engagement (Dixit et al., 2021),

Even though SMEs are socially accountable to their many stakeholders, CSR is not a component of their strategy; rather, it is more of an ad hoc and self-driven approach. They identify CSR with a religious attitude rather than with business imperatives. The concept of CSR among them is still philanthropic and non-institutionalized due to the limitations they confront regarding the resources and personnel that may be used for CSR initiatives (Jain et al., 2016). A very small percentage of SMEs actively participate in CSR projects. The cause can be linked to a lack of funding, a lack of government backing (in the form of incentives and programmes), a lack of significant effects on the company's reputation, and a general lack of awareness in society. Furthermore, the respondent SMEs' opinion of the effects of applying CSR practises was most strongly influenced by their "good relations with stakeholders." The findings also showed no connection between an organization's performance and CSR initiatives (Gupta et al., 2012).

It was discovered that SMEs still engage in informal CSR practises and that partnerships and environment-related CSR are essential for this efficacy. The study's variables will assist SMEs in developing a formal CSR strategy and address the demands of business and society in the twenty-first century (Dawar and Singh, 2022).

In 2019, a research paper explained the idea of CSR in MSMEs and how it is implemented. It examines the boundaries of investments, their significance for MSMEs, and their different dimensions. Finally, it outlines the difficulties MSMEs have regarding CSR and offers solutions (Basariya and Al Kake, 2019).

In their findings, Doshmanli et al. (2018) showed a significantly favourable association between the growth of SMEs and all four elements of economic, legal, ethical, and discretionary social responsibility.

An attempt to assess the state of CSR in India and focused on identifying and analyzing the problems and obstacles that CSR initiatives in India must overcome was conducted by (Kumar et al., 2019).

Research Methodology

In this research study, the following research methodologies were implemented based on the objectives:

- **Literature review:** To comprehend the present state of research and pinpoint knowledge gaps, a thorough assessment of the literature on CSR in SMEs has been conducted.
- **Case Studies:** To determine the best practices and methods other SMEs can adopt, in-depth case studies of effective CSR practices in SMEs were done. The case studies contained various CSR practices, such as environmental sustainability, social responsibility, and ethical governance, and can be chosen based on the sector, size, and location.
- **Policy Analysis:** To determine their efficacy and pinpoint any areas needing improvement, policies and efforts of governments, non-governmental organizations, and industry associations that support CSR practises in SMEs were examined.
- **Cross-case analysis**: To find patterns, themes, and connections across several SMEs and circumstances, a cross-case analysis of the data gathered using the techniques above was carried out. This can aid in gaining a thorough understanding of the causes, difficulties, and advantages of CSR practises in SMEs and guide the creation of programmes and policies that encourage their participation in CSR practices.

Research Problems

Despite the growing significance of corporate social responsibility (CSR) for small and medium-sized businesses (SMEs), little is known about the reasons behind, obstacles to, and advantages of implementing CSR practices in the context of SMEs. For example, only 22% of SMEs in India, according to research by the Federation of Indian Chambers of Commerce and Industry (FICCI), have official CSR policies in place. Furthermore, while there is a sizable body of research on CSR in big businesses, there is considerably less information on how CSR is used in SMEs and how it impacts their performance, competitiveness, and reputation. According to a report by the Indian Institute of Management Bangalore's Centre for Corporate Governance and Citizenship, SMEs in India have trouble implementing CSR practices because of a lack of funding, awareness and understanding, and the difficulty in determining the effects of CSR initiatives. As a result, the research problem is to examine the reasons for adopting CSR practices in SMEs and the difficulties and rewards of doing so and to comprehend how CSR impacts business outcomes and stakeholder relationships. Specifically, the research can focus on the following questions:

- What drives SMEs to adopt CSR practices, and how are they different from those of big businesses?
- What are SMEs' biggest obstacles to implementing CSR practices, and how do they overcome them?
- How do the advantages of CSR for SMEs compare to those of major firms regarding business success, competitiveness, and reputation?
- How do SMEs inform their stakeholders about their CSR initiatives, and how do these communications impact their relationships with those stakeholders and how they view the company?
- How effective are government policies at supporting sustainable and moral business practises, and what role do they play in promoting CSR practises in SMEs?

Objectives of the Research

From the extensive literature review, the following objectives were framed:

- To comprehend the driving forces behind SMEs' adoption of CSR practices: This goal tries to pinpoint the factors that lead SMEs to adopt CSR strategies, such as moral considerations, stakeholder pressure, or business advantages.
- To investigate the difficulties SMEs have applying CSR principles: This goal identifies the challenges SMEs have while implementing CSR practices, such as a lack of resources, knowledge, or awareness.
- To evaluate the positive effects of CSR practises for SMEs, such as better reputation, staff motivation, customer loyalty, or access to financing, this purpose attempts to measure the advantages of CSR practises for SMEs.
- To evaluate how CSR affects stakeholders in SMEs: This goal intends to examine how CSR practises SMEs' interactions with their stakeholders, such as clients, staff members, suppliers, or local communities.
- To determine the best CSR practises in SMEs: This purpose seeks to draw attention to the effective tactics and methods that SMEs employ to put CSR practises into practice, such as collaborations, innovation, or communication.
- To investigate how government funding and policies contribute to CSR promotion in SMEs: This objective examines how well public policies and initiatives, including tax incentives, certification programmes, or awareness campaigns, encourage SMEs to engage in CSR activities.

By achieving these goals, studying CSR in SMEs can help us better understand the obstacles and opportunities presented by adopting sustainable and responsible business practices by small and medium-sized enterprises. Additionally, it can shed light on the possible advantages and drawbacks of CSR for SMEs and help shape the laws and programmes that encourage their participation in CSR practices.

Importance of CSR in SMEs

Small and medium-sized enterprises (SMEs) and other firms should prioritize corporate social responsibility (CSR). Business stakeholders, such as employees, clients, suppliers, and the public, are called stakeholders in corporate social responsibility, or CSR.

The following are some arguments in favour of CSR for SMEs:

- First, building a reputation and a brand is important for SMEs because they frequently compete in highly intense markets. Therefore, SMEs can improve their reputation and develop a favourable brand image by participating in CSR initiatives. This can result in more devoted customers and higher sales.
- Talent attraction and retention: SMEs frequently struggle to find and keep talented staff. SMEs can attract job applicants looking for employers who share their values and are dedicated to positively influencing society by exhibiting a commitment to CSR.
- Developing stronger connections with stakeholders: SMEs rely largely on their connections with stakeholders, such as clients, suppliers, and the neighbourhood. SMEs can develop trust with their stakeholders and strengthen these connections by participating in CSR activities.
- Cost savings: CSR initiatives can also aid SMEs in making long-term financial savings. Implementing waste reduction techniques, for instance, can lower the expenses associated with garbage disposal while reducing energy consumption and utility expenditures.
- Social impact: SMEs have a rare chance to positively influence their regional communities. Small and medium-sized businesses (SMEs) can promote social concerns by participating in CSR initiatives, such as funding neighbourhood events, local charities, or jobs for underrepresented groups.

In general, CSR is crucial for SMEs since it may aid in cost savings, the development of a favourable brand image, attracting and retaining talent, strengthening stakeholder relationships, and creating positive societal effects.

Benefits

When SMEs conduct themselves ethically and responsibly, they significantly increase employee retention. In the first place, staff members are more likely to want to be associated with a trustworthy and effective business. Additionally, when a company has a small staff, more informal ties are more likely to develop, resulting in a truly cohesive team that communicates well. This increases worker loyalty and increases motivation to work for the organization. The corporation can no longer benefit from the growing experience of its employees, which also makes investing in employee development more rational.

Additionally, trustworthy businesses steadily gain their customers' loyalty. People tend to be illogical, and choosing a specific service provider or product frequently relies heavily on the emotional connections the customer develops with the business. And on the flip side, the growing number of socially and ecologically conscious individuals who we stated would enjoy working for a responsible company are also customers. Reduced prices for resources like paper, water, and power are one advantage a business could have if it adheres to ethical, environmental norms. Supporting students and educational institutions is another CSR activity SMEs should engage in because this goes beyond merely providing cash assistance. But also exchanging expertise and experience. One very modest Bulgarian business could serve as an illustration. Its primary business is creating business simulations, training, team-building exercises, and consulting for other companies. Its name is in your hands. This company offers training and expert assistance to the organization's members in close collaboration with AIESEC Bulgaria, the largest student-run organization in the world. They participate in practically all AIESEC conferences in Bulgaria and, where necessary, invite members to some of their events. This collaboration benefits AIFSEC members greatly, but it also benefits the company by allowing it to connect with many energetic young students who have experience working at student organizations. AIESEC alumni who have already demonstrated professionalism and interpersonal abilities make up almost half of IN YOUR HAND's staff.

Another intriguing situation involves Triodos Bank, a former Dutch bank. The bank has conditions for the companies it lends money, and one of its key target markets is ethical and responsible small enterprises. Their lending strategy is focused on supporting the growth and innovations in sustainable industries, and they fund initiatives that can benefit society, culture, or the environment. Their criteria also consider the potential adverse effects of projects on people and the environment. As a result, every small firm with ethical and sustainable business plans can obtain financing from the bank, which has offices in the Netherlands, Belgium, Spain, the United Kingdom, and Germany. It's also interesting to note that Triodos Bank had a start-up share capital of only 540 000 Euro when it was founded in 1980, making it a very tiny lending facility, especially compared to its rivals' average size. However, because of its effective and responsible operations, it has grown into a significant and highly profitable financial organization.

Concepts of CSR and Their Realization in Small and Medium Enterprises

CSR is a very broad field, as was already mentioned, and every firm approaches it differently. However, the four main fields of environment, employees, market, and society are the foundation of the most prevalent CSR principles. They encompass most of the firm's steps to contribute to an ethically sound business. These four CSR areas will be explained, along with their key traits and exemplary use in small and medium-sized European businesses. Refer to Table 16.1 for information regarding CSR spending by manufacturing companies in India and Figure 16.1 has depicted the sector-wise prescribed CSR spendings in INR.

Table 16.1: CSR Spending by the Manufacturing Companies in India.

Industry	CSR Expenditures to be Incurred as per Companies Act 2013	Amount spent on CSR Activities during the year	% Of CSR Spent	No. of Companies
Food and Agro-based	4,801.80	4,748.80	98.90	79
Chemical& Chemical Products	21,864.00	19,800.80	90.56	191
Construction Material	2,859.00	3,136.50	109.71	52
Consumer Goods	2,914.40	2,804.90	96.24	48
Diversified Sector	1,296.10	1,416.40	109.28	23
Machinery	2,362.20	1,644.90	69.63	87
Metal & Metal product	4,674.10	5,587.50	119.54	71
Textile	1,466.80	1,280.00	88.47	71
Transport Equipment	8,206.40	7,447.90	90.76	82
Misc. Manufacturing	498.10	210.90	42.34	31
All Manufacturing Companies	50,922.90	48,078.60	94.41	735

Source Computed from the Data Compiled from CMIE Prowess Data

Role and Growth of CSR in SMEs

The topic of corporate social responsibility (CSR) is significant and has received a lot of attention recently. It alludes to corporations' obligation to society in addition to their financial and legal responsibilities. CSR encompasses a variety of endeavours, including altruism, environmental sustainability, and moral business conduct. The

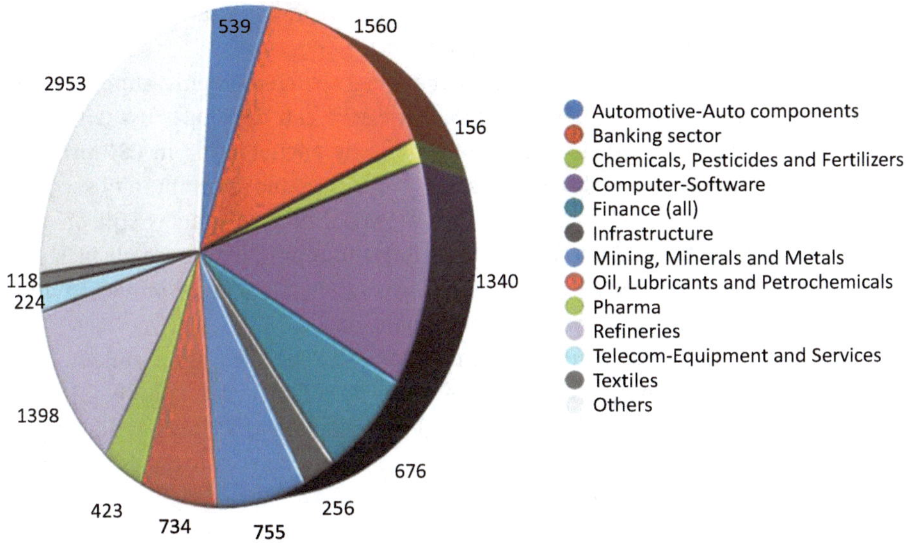

Figure 16.1: Sector-Wise Estimated Prescribed CSR (in INR Cr).

function and development of CSR in Small and Medium-Sized Enterprises (SMEs) will be covered in this essay.

- The global economy depends heavily on SMEs. They contribute to local economic growth, make up a sizable share of enterprises, and offer employment possibilities. However, SMEs frequently encounter several difficulties, including scarce resources, a lack of access to funding, and fierce competition. It is challenging for SMEs to prioritize CSR projects because of these issues.
- Despite these difficulties, CSR has grown in significance for SMEs. This results from several things, such as rising social and environmental consciousness, shifting consumer and stakeholder expectations, and possible CSR advantages for sustainable corporate success.
- Constructing trust and reputation is one of the main functions of CSR in SMEs. Small businesses frequently rely on client loyalty and word-of-mouth recommendations to stay in business. Therefore, SMEs can develop a favourable brand image and improve their reputation by showcasing a commitment to CSR, which can result in more devoted customers and improved sales.
- CSR may also assist SMEs in finding and keeping skilled personnel. Younger generations of workers are increasingly interested in working for organizations that share their beliefs and are dedicated to improving society. SMEs may attract these workers and stand out from rivals by participating in CSR projects.
- The promotion of sustainable business practices is another function of CSR in SMEs. Small businesses frequently have a big effect on the environment since they might not have the money to adopt sustainable practices. However, SMEs

may lessen their environmental impact and support the international fight to prevent climate change by prioritizing CSR projects.
- Relationships between SMEs and their stakeholders, such as clients, suppliers, and the neighbourhood, might benefit from CSR. SMEs can develop trust with their stakeholders and strengthen these connections by participating in CSR projects. This may result in higher sales, better supplier ties, and more community support.
- Despite the growing significance of CSR in SMEs, many obstacles still prevent many small enterprises from putting CSR efforts into practice. These obstacles include a lack of knowledge and comprehension of CSR, a lack of resources, and the idea that CSR is not crucial for economic expansion.
- Governments, non-governmental organizations (NGOs), and other stakeholders are increasingly helping SMEs undertake CSR efforts to overcome these obstacles. For instance, while NGOs offer training and coaching to assist SMEs in developing CSR strategies, some governments support and give resources to SMEs to execute sustainable business practices.

In conclusion, CSR is an important idea for SMEs since it may support the development of trust and reputation, talent recruitment and retention, the promotion of sustainable business practices, and improved stakeholder connections. While SMEs could encounter several obstacles when adopting CSR activities, increased support for and understanding of CSR can help to get beyond

These obstacles support the expansion and sustainability of small businesses worldwide.

CSR Towards SMEs

The term "corporate social responsibility" (CSR) towards SMEs refers to larger firms' obligation towards the smaller companies they work with. This includes vendors, business associates, and even rivals. Here are some examples of how larger businesses can show CSR to SMEs.
- Fair and ethical business practises: Larger firms should ensure they deal fairly and ethically with SMEs. This entails showing them respect, paying them on time, and giving them chances for professional advancement.
- Support for small firms: Large organizations can show CSR towards SMEs by supporting local enterprises. This can involve cooperating with them on community development projects, giving them access to finance and resources, and procuring goods and services from nearby SMEs.
- Mentorship and coaching: To assist SMEs in expanding and developing their enterprises, larger organizations might offer them mentorship and coaching. This can entail exchanging best practices, giving opportunities for training and growth, and giving guidance and assistance.

- Sustainable purchase: Using sustainable procurement strategies, larger firms can show their CSR commitment to SMEs. One way to do this is to purchase goods and services from SMEs that value sustainability and social responsibility.
- Community involvement: Through community development projects, larger firms can interact with the neighbourhood and assist SMEs. This can involve supporting neighbourhood SMEs to promote economic development, sponsoring neighbourhood events, and providing grants and funds for neighbourhood projects.

Overall, larger firms must show CSR towards SMEs since it can help to forge lasting bonds, encourage regional economic growth, and promote the expansion and sustainability of the greater community. Figure 16.2 has shown the four elements of CSR.

Figure 16.2: Four Elements of CSR.

Environment Oriented CSR

Today, hardly any subject is as well-known as global warming. All around the planet, the "greenhouse effect" causes unpredictability in the weather to the melting of the polar ice caps, which will lead to greater sea levels, floods, and many other calamities (see Figure 16.3 to understand various actions taken by organization for environment sustainability).

However, the general people know this critical situation and care about the earth's future, not just green political parties. Compared to 50 years ago, people now pay more attention to a company's environmental practices. Customers choose goods and services from sustainable sources over those at competitive prices and high quality without hurting their surroundings. To maintain their competitiveness in the market, corporations are under pressure from the demand side to operate sustainably.

The cornerstone of the firm policy should be the utilization of input from sustainable sources and their sufficient use. On the one hand, it serves the goal of preserving the environment. On the other side, the most efficient use of resources will reduce the company's variable costs and, as a result, a competitive advantage over businesses that utilize their inputs less effectively. This goes along with a decrease in waste production since, in some industries, a certain level of waste cannot be avoided. In these situations, the company must keep the number of waste products to a minimum and try to recycle them. When recycling is not an option, waste must be disposed of properly.

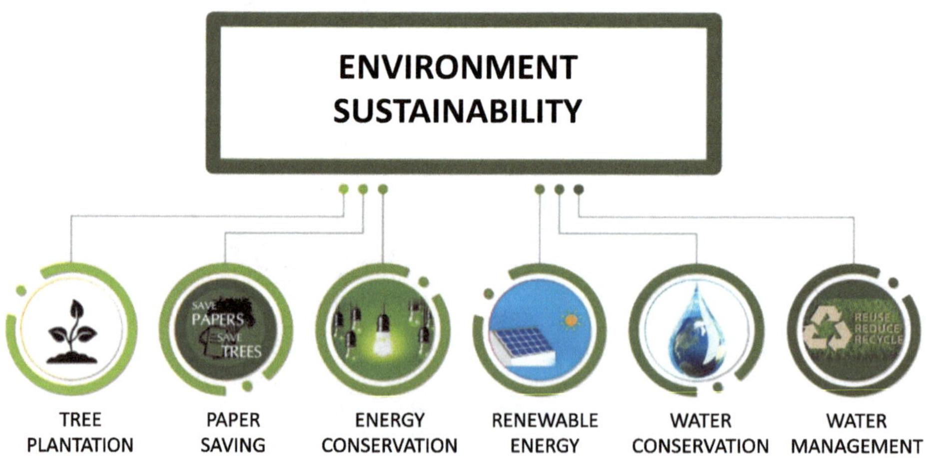

Figure 16.3: Actions for Environment Sustainability.

The responsibility to inform others about current difficulties or problems is another significant leverage point for ethical behaviour towards the environment. In these times of globalization, businesses from all over the world work together. It is becoming more difficult to manage material flows; there are more options for transportation, and maintaining a supply chain is challenging. However, more than just a single link in the chain has to participate in environmental conservation. To make sure the company develops sustainably. Environmental issues must be discussed, and protective measures must be set up throughout the supply chain.

The London-based, medium-sized British business "Wood and Beyond" sells hardwood goods. The supplier is chosen by the business based on whether or not they employ sustainable resources. The company fights against natural exploitation with this strategy. They even received a "red data list," where endangered animals and trees are identified.

Based on this guiding concept, the company has a stellar reputation, which is one of its main competitive advantages when paired with its commitment to great quality.

With 138 people, the Danish company Kvadrat operates in the textile business. In the category of "best national company's 50–500 employees" to work in 2013, they came in at number twenty-one. But Kvadrat offers more than just a great environment to work in. They also hold themselves to high standards for environmental preservation.

The business's primary goal, created in 1968, is to strike a balance between economic considerations, social responsibilities, and environmental issues. The business ensures that the items meet the pertinent EU Ecolabel criteria to achieve this balance.

In addition, Kvadrat continuously lowers its CO2 emissions and minimizes waste generation by analyzing and tracking every stage of manufacturing to identify potential improvements. To make the entire facility greener, they put a CTS device (a building management system) at their headquarters in 2013.

To minimize the influence on the environment throughout the entire supply chain, it also sets tight guidelines for its suppliers. But still ensuring that their items are of a high calibre to satisfy their customers.

Employees Oriented CSR

"A company's greatest asset is its workforce, and your employees are your product."
British businessman and billionaire Richard Branson

Employees are a company's greatest asset, but why?

Depending on the business division, staff costs may account for 70% (industrial sector) or even 90% (comet sector) of total expenses. Most businesses rely on labour, except for a small number of highly automated businesses. In addition, some countries in Europe, like Germany, are experiencing a demographic shift. Therefore, businesses must compete for the best personnel by giving special attention to present and prospective employees.

An ethically proper approach to treating a company's employees can involve, for instance, improving the working environment. Workplace safety measures will satisfy and safeguard employees' health, as well as reduce disease cases and shield against productivity loss. Additionally, sick pay expenses for the company will be decreased.

Another aspect of an ethical attitude towards employees is ensuring a reasonable work-life balance. In addition, excessive working stress can lead to psychological conditions like burnout and additional expenses for the company.

Demanding excessive overtime hours is prohibited by European labour legislation. According to economic studies, a happy employee is more productive than a dissatisfied one, which benefits the organization more. In addition to a healthy work-life balance, more and more employees are looking for opportunities to advance in their careers for a variety of reasons, including better income, increased responsibility, and personal fulfilment. So a business should provide training. Education and other initiatives to educate their workforce and provide equitable opportunities for promotion.

A right to participate in company decisions is something that many employees want in addition to the chance for promotion. Therefore, it is preferable to provide employees with the chance to share their thoughts rather than letting them decide on the company's primary strategic goals. Nowadays, most businesses make choices without consulting the parties affected. However, there are times when "bottom-up" decisions outperform "top-down" judgements. Because those who are directly involved have a better understanding of fractals than the majority of management above. Furthermore, the range of ideas is far wider with this bottom-up method than if only one person made the decision.

Overall, it can be said that failing to treat employees ethically leads to increased costs, less productivity, and if the behaviour is made public, severe reputational damage (for example, for Wal-Mart or Amana).

The 1953-founded German medium-sized company Gebudereinigung GmbH provides free German language instruction to employees with immigrant backgrounds. The company's goal is to integrate outsiders as effectively into society as it can. The fact that there is improved communication between employees and consumers and fewer issues as a result is advantageous to the business itself.

The business generally engages in various CSR activities, not just among its workforces. As a result, it received recognition on multiple occasions, such as in 2009 when it received the "B.A.U.M. Umweltpreis" for its long-standing commitment to ecological standards and holistic cleaning practises, or in 2002 for its outstanding efforts to integrate foreign nationals into German society.

Market-Oriented CSR

This CSR idea focuses on generating extra (social) value for customers, suppliers, and business partners. By involving every participant in the supply chain, a new CSR value emerges: a sense of community. As time passes, it becomes more and more crucial to implement this idea. Because in many fields, it is the only way to set yourself apart from the competition (see Figure 16.4).

The methods to provide high value are demonstrated in the heels that follow.

Increasing product quality and safety is one approach to pursuing this aim. Therefore, each link in the supply chain benefits in some way: producers and suppliers can be proud of better products and exploit this in a positive PR campaign, and buyers can justify spending more money.

Businesses increase the dependability of their products for their customers by providing free and voluntary services. For this reason, the business' CSR initiative continues without incurring additional expenses.

Fair pricing is a crucial component of a market-oriented CSR. This is somewhat of the bottom because, with reasonable and decent prices, the supply chain relationships and the values that have previously developed remain strong. However, it goes beyond just fair rates. Transferring the funds on schedule is crucial because businesses, especially smaller ones, have limited liquidity.

The idea of contracting with local partners in terms of communication and working on joint (local) initiatives is closely tied to the environmental notion. In addition, this emphasizes the local image and ensures the backing of local cities and politicians, both crucial for economic success.

A business can lay the groundwork for future regional business collaborations and maximize value creation by focusing on the local market.

It is simpler to create standards of behaviour and output throughout the entire supply chain with such a corporate alliance.

You can use the Finnish company "Eko-Expert-" as a concrete example. By using a unique method, they are reusing outdated building isolation material. As a result, customers benefit from significant financial savings and a competitive edge in addition to the environmental benefit.

Indeed, this idea has a serious drawback for the companies that make isolation material. However, over the long term, "Expert" adds considerably more value.

The German manufacturer of kitchen facilities "Die Möbelmacher GmbH" is an even better example. For their primarily regional clients, they organize cooking demonstrations and classes. Clients have the opportunity to test all the various kitchen recommendations during these visits and learn about the principles and fundamental concepts underlying the items.

Society Oriented CSR

Both the population and the society are ageing. The daily stress that working people experience is significantly impacted by both facts. Businesses have the chance to reduce this strain by leveraging their social effect. Although an SME's influence is modest, you should not undervalue their collective or local impact.

By employing disabled people, an SME indirectly "takes care" of them for a while and relieves a lot of pressure at another location. This is referred to as "social integration". But It's not just about relieving strain; it's also about fostering a sense of inclusion

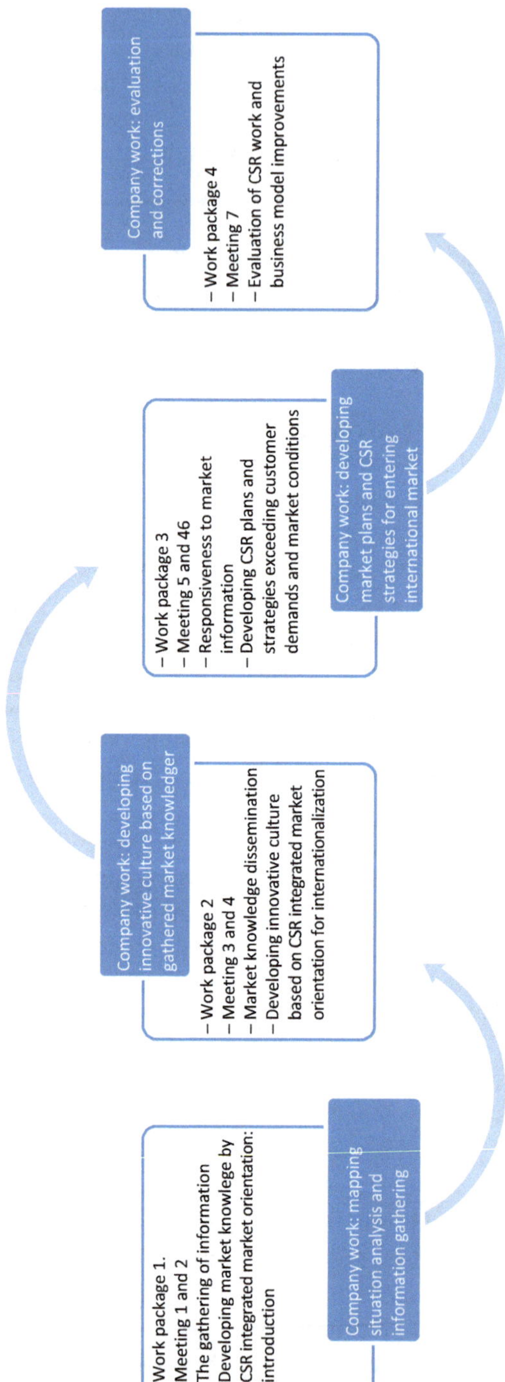

Figure 16.4: Market Oriented CSR.

and social acceptance for persons with disabilities. Yes, this applies to everyone, not just people with disabilities. There is a chance for "Social Integration" with former inmates- Addicts, etc. A corporation can restore many people's confidence in this way. When we talk about people with disabilities, it is important to note that they frequently require unique infrastructure systems, such as entrances, bigger letters, or customized pathways. An SME can begin enhancing local infrastructure because they are fully aware of where assistance is required.

It is not required for a company to address an issue on its own. But, of course, a firm can donate money or in-kind services to a local organization like hospitals, schools, etc.

However, even an SME can expand outside of its immediate region. For example, the business might assist international organizations or poor nations. Because SMEs frequently have far deeper relationships with their overseas suppliers, they can usually identify the unique needs for assistance in the supplier's afflicted region. As mentioned, one can support society by making monetary or in-kind donations. However, the narrative is not over yet. More and more businesses offer employee programmes. Where a small portion of a company's employees has the opportunity to learn new skills by working with, for example, people with disabilities, this generates a whole new "win-win" value and can be extremely beneficial to society (see Figure 16.5).

Figure 16.5: CSR Activities.

The Norwegian SME "Stormberg AS" serves as a useful illustration. A wholesaler hired more than 25% of people with disabilities and about 30% of ex-offenders, school dropouts, and others who would struggle to reintegrate into society independently.

The Polish PR-Consulting firm "Toolbox Creative Communications" is another excellent example. They decided to provide their work for free to any social organizations working to enhance relations between Jews and Poles. Only two effects are completely new clientele and more informed individuals.

Comprehensive

As the name suggests, a comprehensive CSR concept addresses every aspect of the business. Along with market satisfaction and employee care, it's also important to guarantee a sustainable environment for future generations and the greatest possible benefit to society.

For example, Ketchum Pleon is a BBDO Worldwide subsidiary based in Germany. Ketchum operates in the communication sector and has 330 employees dispersed across seven locations in Germany. Düsseldorf serves as the primary office.

The business is actively involved in CSR. Along with supporting 95 children in Tanzania, India, and other developing nations, Ketchum participates in annual celebrations of International Women's Day and International Day of the Girl. International Literacy Day and Movember. Through yearly improvements to local travel policies and practises, the company enterprises are also committed to managing local facilities with a very high level of energy efficiency and preventing greenhouse gases. As well as that. By maintaining close ties with numerous colleges and high schools, Ketchum shows that they care about its current and future employees by ensuring that they receive the training they need and that graduates have higher chances of finding jobs.

Disadvantages of CSR

Since the 1960s, when the idea of CSR was first made public, several discussions and papers have been written on the topic. It is quite challenging to define a notion or even a theory. Since there are numerous definitions of CSR, as stated in the theoretical section, there may be numerous definitions of its advantages and disadvantages.

The same is true of the arguments favouring and against using CSR techniques. In a nutshell, the issues are in allocating the time and resources required to achieve CSR standards, no matter what they may be.

Even while the CSR approach may have a distinctly good overall impact on society, certain articles, writers, and businesses maintain that CSR is not the best strategy for businesses of all sizes and, therefore, the free market.

Profit Maximization

Theoretically, the free-market company environment and CSR practises do not mix well. Additionally, in a capitalist society, the role of business is to maximize profits and improve economic efficiency rather than to serve the public good. Only by meeting shareholder expectations can firms hope to reduce expenses and increase income.

Their current duty is to balance the demands of CSR and other stakeholder groups and the financial expectations of business owners. What is a cost rise for large corporations may be fatal for struggling SMEs. Speaking of shareholders, they may have wildly different expectations. Investing in businesses that uphold high standards of honesty makes some shareholders happy, while it might not make others.

Competitiveness

The argument of competitive disadvantage and profit maximization are very similar. Due to increased opportunity costs for CSR, the modern economy has grown so complicated that entire businesses may become uncompetitive. However, some businesses find investing resources or money in CSR initiatives difficult.

1. **Social Issues are the Concern of the Government.**

The following argument has been emphasized numerous times, mostly by businesspeople and economists. Riley contends that in free-market systems, businesses only exist to maximize profits. Therefore, government and NGOs should only be concerned with social responsibility, aside from. According to Milton Friedman, businesses already make a significant contribution to society by paying taxes to their governments.

CSR Policies on SMEs

Policies governing CSR (Corporate Social Responsibility) for SMEs (Small and Medium-sized Enterprises) might differ by nation, sector, and firm size. When implementing CSR policies for SMEs, there are some general principles and practices that can be taken into account. These consist of the following.

- Raising SME knowledge of the advantages of CSR and educating and training them on how to execute CSR policies can be important first steps in advancing ethical business practices.
- CSR policies specifically tailored to SMEs' requirements and available resources can be crucial to ensuring their viability and effectiveness. Depending on the nature of the organization and its stakeholders, this may entail giving particular CSR areas, like social or environmental challenges, priority.
- Collaboration and Partnerships: Collaboration and partnerships between SMEs and larger businesses, non-profit organizations, or industry associations can aid in the sharing of resources and information and present chances for SMEs to put complete CSR policies into practice.
- Financial Assistance: By giving financial assistance or incentives to SMEs that invest in CSR activities, it is possible to reduce the expenses of implementing CSR policies.

- Transparency and Accountability: SMEs may foster trust with stakeholders and show their dedication to ethical business practises by being honest and accountable about their CSR policies and practises.

CSR (Corporate Social Responsibility) policies for SMEs (Small and Medium-sized Enterprises) can include promoting collaboration and partnerships, providing financial support or incentives, encouraging transparency and accountability, and tailoring policies to fit the particular needs of SMEs. These regulations seek to encourage ethical business conduct and develop an industry that is more environmentally and socially conscious.

Business Case for CSR by SMEs

Although CSR is not a quick fix for corporate success, it is a long-term investment that pays off. In industrialized countries, CSR has benefited businesses in several ways, including employee retention and recruitment, staff development and motivation, consumer loyalty, reduced energy costs, and, most crucially, visibility that would not have been possible otherwise. CSR can grow to be an increasingly important source of innovation in the knowledge economy that India wishes to become. It makes information exchange and access easier. Enterprises can better benefit from these benefits by handling CSR strategically and consciously. Continuous improvement is at the heart of CSR, which should be understood as emerging from the contemporary concept of business excellence.

CSR initiatives can support SMEs in various ways to increase their competitiveness in a developing nation like India. A suggested list might include the following:

- Attracting and keeping consumers and business clients (pressures and opportunities in the supply chain), particularly because SMEs must constantly look for new markets and sources of income.
- Maintaining a permit to operate from the neighbourhood to be a good neighbour.
- Strengthening linkages to the community, particularly where infrastructure and/or human development are lacking.
- Meeting fresh needs and specifications from investors, insurers, and banks. The effectiveness of this as a driver for SMEs to participate in CSR heavily depends on how seriously the financial community regards the risks and possibilities that CSR-related issues represent.
- Finding and keeping motivated, dedicated workers, especially in light of how quickly the market and technology are evolving and the increased demand for adaptable, engaged workers. Good working conditions, which are attained by ethical corporate conduct and a participatory management approach, typically have a good impact on employee morale and increase job satisfaction and loyalty to the company. CSR may become a crucial differentiator for businesses as competition to entice the best, highly qualified individuals increases.

- Staff development and training. For instance, employees or managers of a business can develop new skills and competencies through volunteer work in the neighbourhood, which can also lead to knowledge transfer and access to fresh information that is advantageous to the business.
- Public perception and standing among internal and external stakeholders.
- Through the media, education, and the activities of stakeholders, businesses may change people's ideas of their position in society—which is not only about making money.
- Possibilities for networking.
- The need for new sources of creativity and innovation in business, product/market innovation, differentiation, and competitive advantage.

Some of these concerns are more likely than others to boost competitiveness, and not all of them will be applicable to all SMEs. Many mention enhanced reputation and higher employee morale. Among the most crucial factors are: Instead of always using the same formula, the business case needs to be built around the specific characteristics of each SME. The potential business case may be impacted by the exact type of the firm and the environment it works in. An SME hasn't always been motivated to participate in CSR by the business case. SMEs should be responsive to values-based motives while promoting CSR.

When considering potential competitive benefits from CSR, it seems especially important to concentrate on the following areas: cost savings from environmental measures; opportunities from addressing societal issues with innovative products or services; increasing the appeal of a product or service to public authorities or large company clients; attracting, retaining, and motivating staff by providing a good and stimulating working environment; enhancing image, loyalty, and trust amongst internal stakeholders. In addition, joint action with other businesses (and stakeholders) in the same sector, area, or cluster may result in further competitive advantages.

Findings

From an in-depth literature review analysis, the following findings were found to be prevalent in the CSR of SMEs:
- SMEs may find it difficult to execute sustainable and ethical business practices since they frequently lack the personnel and financial resources needed to participate in CSR activities.
- There is a need for awareness-raising efforts and capacity-building programmes because many SMEs may not understand the significance of CSR practices or the potential benefits that they can provide.

- The effectiveness of CSR practises in SMEs depends on effective stakeholder involvement since it can ensure that stakeholders' needs and expectations are recognized and satisfied.
- For SMEs looking to implement CSR practices, access to money can be a major obstacle. Many SMEs struggle to secure funding for their sustainability projects.
- Scalability is a problem for many SMEs as they try to expand while keeping their sustainable practices and impact management.
- Regulatory frameworks and standards might be crucial to encourage and support CSR practices in SMEs.
- SMEs may not have the requisite resources or knowledge to effectively measure and report the impact of CSR practices.

These results show the necessity for various measures to encourage and support ethical and sustainable business practices in the SME sector, as well as the significance of resolving the difficulties SMEs have in implementing CSR practices.

Suggestions

Based on the findings related to Corporate Social Responsibility (CSR) in Small and Medium Enterprises (SMEs), here are some suggestions for addressing the challenges:

- Access to resources: To assist SMEs in implementing ethical and sustainable business practises, governments, NGOs, and other stakeholders can give them access to finance and other resources like technical assistance and training.
- Raising awareness: SMEs can be encouraged to learn more about the value of CSR practices, their potential rewards, and the various ways they can be put into practice.
- Engagement with stakeholders: SMEs should be encouraged to interact with their stakeholders, such as clients, staff members, suppliers, and local communities, in order to better understand their goals and wants and create CSR strategies that satisfy them.
- Access to financing: Governments and other interested parties might provide financing programmes for SMEs implementing CSR strategies. Offering loans, grants, and other forms of financial assistance are examples.
- Scalability: Scalable and flexible CSR can be designed and implemented by SMEs, and they can be encouraged to create long-term sustainability policies that can be modified as their companies expand.
- Regulations and standards: Governments can develop regulations and standards that encourage and promote CSR practices in SMEs. They can also offer direction and support to SMEs to ensure they comply with current regulations and standards.

- Measurement and reporting: Besides encouraging SMEs to share their knowledge and best practices with other SMEs, governments and other stakeholders can give SMEs the tools and guidelines they need to measure and report the effectiveness of their CSR practices.

Implications of the Study

- Access to resources: Studies can be done to determine the particular resources SMEs need to apply CSR practices and to look into efficient ways to give them access. This may involve examining the effects of various forms of assistance, such as instruction, technical support, and financial support, on the adoption and accomplishment of CSR practices in SMEs.
- Raising awareness: Research can be done to determine the best channels and messaging for reaching SMEs and evaluate the success of various programmes for raising awareness of CSR practices in SMEs. This may also entail looking at how peer-to-peer networks and partnerships help SMEs promote CSR practices.
- Stakeholder engagement: Research can be done to examine efficient methods for interacting with various stakeholder groups, such as clients, employees, suppliers, and local communities, as well as to pinpoint the elements that make stakeholder engagement in CSR practices among SMEs successful.
- Access to financing: Studies can be undertaken to determine how different financing mechanisms affect the adoption and success of CSR practises in SMEs and to pinpoint the best methods for financing such businesses. This may also entail looking into how public-private partnerships help finance CSR projects for SMEs.
- Scalability: Research can be done to examine practical methods for developing and putting into practice CSR practises that are scalable and flexible, as well as to determine the elements that lead to successful scalability in SMEs. This may also entail looking into how innovation and technology may help SMEs adopt scalable CSR practices.
- Regulatory frameworks and standards: Research can be done to determine the best strategies for encouraging and assisting CSR practices among SMEs and evaluate the influence that regulatory frameworks and standards have on the adoption and success of CSR practices in SMEs. This may also entail looking into how networks and industry associations support CSR practices among SMEs.
- Measurement and reporting: Research can be done to examine practical methods for gauging and disclosing the effects of CSR initiatives in SMEs as well as to pinpoint the elements that make for effective measurement and reporting. This may also entail looking into how certification and labelling programmes help SMEs promote accountability and transparency in their CSR practices.

Conclusion

As a result, researching corporate social responsibility (CSR) in small and medium-sized firms (SMEs) can aid in our understanding of the reasons for, obstacles to, and advantages of implementing CSR practices in the setting of small businesses. Understanding the motivations behind SMEs' participation in CSR practises, examining the difficulties they encounter in doing so, evaluating the advantages of CSR for SMEs, analyzing the impact of CSR on SMEs' stakeholders, identifying the best practises of CSR in SMEs, and examining the role of government policies and support in fostering CSR in SMEs can all be included in such a study's objectives.

The Corporate Social Responsibility Voluntary Guidelines, the Corporate Social Responsibility National Voluntary Guidelines, and the Swachh Bharat Abhiyaan (Clean India Mission) are just a few measures the Indian government has made to encourage CSR practises among SMEs. By fulfilling these goals, we may gain a deeper understanding of the sustainable and ethical business practices that SMEs can embrace and the possible advantages and dangers of doing so. This information can guide the creation of policies and programmes that motivate and assist SMEs in engaging in CSR activities, ultimately assisting in the growth of a more sustainable and ethical business sector. In general, researching CSR in SMEs can aid in the development of a better, more ethical, and sustainably run corporate environment.

The Five Case Studies from India

1. The Sports Goods Foundation of India (SGFI), headquartered in Jalandhar, coordinates activities to end child labour in the sports goods sector and support youth education. In addition to setting up tuition centres for underprivileged kids, SGFI also conducts school health check-up programmes.
2. S. Kumar's Agri-Business Corporation, situated in Hyderabad, aims to bring about change through innovative, sustainable, and environmentally friendly green activities. The company's CSR foundation, GUESS (Green Universe Environmental Services Society), was created due to its unwavering dedication to fostering sustainable livelihoods and environmental protection in rural and remote places.
3. Ahmedabad-based Shashwat Systems created the Shashwat Foundation. Its CEO actively promotes women-owned businesses throughout Gujarat and works tirelessly to mentor, coach, and train the state's many young and aspiring female entrepreneurs. She consistently identifies promising young women business owners, mentors them as they travel the road to success, and guides them along the way.
4. Sohrab Enterprises, situated in Malerkotla (Ludhiana, Punjab), manages the HARF charity trust. Education (Sohrab Public School), a primary health centre, a widow stipend programme, and an orphan girl marriage assistance unit are all

included under the trust. "Service to mankind, national integrity, and communal harmony" are the company's three core values. The Group's many socially conscious projects are purposefully and carefully created to support this credo.

5. Motif India InfoTech, situated in Ahmedabad, engages the public in raising money for charitable organizations as part of its CSR. Motif gives NGOs a platform, mobilizes funding for them, and raises awareness of those who best perform socially responsible services. Every year, Motif hosts the Motif Charity Walk, an activity that raises money for worthy causes and increases public awareness of them.

References

Ahmad, N. H., Ramayah, T., Halim, H. A., & Rahman, S. A. (Eds.). (2017). "*Handbook of research on small and medium enterprises in developing countries*", IGI Global.

Basariya, S. R., & Al Kake, M. F. (2019). "Corporate social responsibility in micro, small, and medium industries", *International Journal of Control and Automation, 12*(5), 238–243.

Bikefe, G., Umaru, Z., Araga, S., Faize, M., Ekanem, E., & Daniel, A. (2020). "Corporate social responsibility (CSR) by small and medium Enterprises (SMEs). A systematic review".

Blackburn, R., De Clercq, D., & Heinonen, J. (Eds.). (2017). "*The SAGE handbook of small business and entrepreneurship*", Sage.

Corporate Social Responsibility and Employee Wellbeing – Spectrum.Life https://www.spectrum.life/blog/corporate-social-responsibility-and-employee-wellbeing/

Dawar, G., & Singh, S. (2022). "How can small and medium enterprises effectively implement corporate social responsibility?: An Indian perspective", *Global Business Review, 23*(3), 756–784.

Dixit, S. K., & Priya, S. S. (2021). "Barriers to corporate social responsibility: An Indian SME perspective", *International Journal of Emerging Markets* (ahead-of–print).

Doshmanli, M., Salamzadeh, Y., & Salamzadeh, A. (2018). "Development of SMEs in an emerging economy: Does corporate social responsibility matter?", *International Journal of Management and Enterprise Development, 17*(2), 168–191.Environment Protection – Spark Minda Foundation

Gupta, S., Sukhmani, & Kalra, N. (2012). "Impact of corporate social responsibility on SMEs in India", *Asia-Pacific Journal of Management Research and Innovation, 8*(2), 133–143. https://sparkminda.com/csrminda/environment-protection/https://www.geeksforgeeks.org/social-responsibilities-of-a-business-meaning-need-and–types/

Jain, P., Vyas, V., & Chalasani, D. P. S. (2016). "Corporate social responsibility and financial performance in SMEs: A structural equation modelling approach", *Global Business Review, 17*(3), 630–653.

Katamba, D. (2012). "*Principles of corporate social responsibility (CSR): A guide for students and practising managers in developing and emerging countries*", Strategic Book Publishing.

Khanna, V. & Sharma, R. (2017). "Customer Switching Behavior in Retail Banking in India", *International Journal of Applied Business and Economic Research, 15*(9), 427–441.

Kumar, N. (2019). "Corporate Social Responsibility: An analysis of impact and challenges in India", *International Journal of Social Sciences Management and Entrepreneurship (IJSSME), 3*(2).

Kumar, R., Saha, R., PC, S., & Dahiya, R. (2019). "Examining the role of external factors in influencing green behavior among young Indian consumers." *Young Consumers, 20*(4), 380–398.

Mahajan, V. & Sharma, R. (2017). "Future of Depository with Introduction of Payment Bank– A Game Changer to Capital Market", *International Journal of Applied Business and Economic Research, 15*(9), 343–356.

Mehta, K., Sharma, R. & Chugh, A. (2017). "Management of Forex Risk Exposure: A Study of SMEs and Unlisted Non–Financial Firms in India", *International Journal of Applied Business and Economic Research, 15*(9), 43–54.

Mehta, K., & Sharma, R. (2016). "SMEs and corporate social responsibility: Indian perception", *SCMS Journal of Indian Management, 13*(3), 58–67.

Mehta, K., Sharma, R., Vyas, V. (2019) "Efficiency and ranking of sustainability index of India using DEA-TOPSIS", *Journal of Indian Business Research, 11*(2), pp. 179–199. https://doi.org/10.1108/JIBR-02-2018-0057.

Mehta, K., Sharma, R., Vyas, V. (2022a). "A quantile regression approach to study the impact of aluminium prices on the manufacturing sector of India during the COVID era", *Materials Today: Proceedings, 65* (8), 3506–3511, https://doi.org/10.1016/j.matpr.2022.06.087.

Mehta, K., Sharma, R., Vyas, V. and Kuckreja, J.S. (2022b). "Exit strategy decision by venture capital firms in India using fuzzy AHP", *Journal of Entrepreneurship in Emerging Economies, 14*(4), 643–669. https://doi.org/10.1108/JEEE-05-2020-0146

Okpara, J. O., & Idowu, S. O. (Eds.). (2013). *"Corporate social responsibility: Challenges, opportunities and strategies for 21st-century leaders"*, Springer Science & Business Media.

Osuji, O. K., Ngwu, F. N., & Jamali, D. (2019). "Introduction to Corporate Social Responsibility in Developing and Emerging Markets: Institutions, Actors and Sustainable Development", *Corporate Social Responsibility in Developing and Emerging Markets: Institutions, Actors and Sustainable Development, 1.*

Popal, P. (2019). *"Small to medium-sized enterprises and corporate social responsibility: The role of international networks"*, Routledge.

Rahman, H., & Ramos, I. (2012). "Open innovation in SMEs of developing and transitional economies. In *Strategic and pragmatic e-business: Implications for future business practices* (pp. 377–395)", IGI Global.

Ray, S., & Raju, S. S. (Eds.). (2014). *"Implementing corporate social responsibility: Indian perspectives"*, Springer Science & Business Media.

Roy, A., Vyas, V., & Jain, P. (2013). "SMEs motivation: corporate social responsibility", *SCMS Journal of Indian Management, 10*(1), 11.

Spence, L. J., Frynas, J. G., Muthuri, J. N., & Navare, J. (Eds.). (2018). *"Research handbook on small business social responsibility: Global perspectives"*, Edward Elgar Publishing.

Sundström, A., Hyder, A. S., & Chowdhury, E. H. (2020). "Market–oriented CSR implementation in SMEs with sustainable innovations: an action research approach", *Baltic Journal of Management, 15*(5), 775–795.

Tench, R., Jones, B., & Sun, W. (Eds.). (2018). *"The critical state of corporate social responsibility in Europe"*, Emerald Group Publishing.

Vyas, V., Mehta, K., Sharma, R. (2023). "The nexus between toxic-air pollution, health expenditure, and economic growth: An empirical study using ARDL", *International Review of Economics and Finance, 84*, 154–166 https://doi.org/10.1016/j.iref.2022.11.017.

Priya Sachdeva and Archan Mitra

17 SME and Environmental Sustenance: Digital Marketing in SMEs via Data-Driven Strategies

Abstract: This study explores how Small and Medium Enterprises (SMEs) might combine data-driven marketing tactics with environmental sustainability. There is a noteworthy void at the junction of these topics despite the substantial literature on each of them separately. This study explores the importance and potential of digital marketing and data-driven tactics in SMEs, the difficulties and opportunities in integrating environmental sustainability in SMEs, and the potential advantages of combining these techniques through a thorough literature analysis. According to the study, while SMEs must overcome obstacles to use data and digital technologies for environmental sustainability, they also stand to earn a lot of advantages, such as increased competitiveness, better customer involvement, and a reduced environmental footprint. The findings add to the ongoing conversation on sustainable business practises and provide useful insights for SMEs wanting to navigate the digital landscape effectively. The convergence of data-driven digital marketing and environmental sustainability is suggested to represent an interesting horizon for SME research and practise, and this study underscores the need for more research in this field.

Keywords: Small and Medium Enterprises (SMEs), Digital marketing, Data-driven strategies, Environmental sustainability, Sustainable business practices

Introduction

Small and medium-sized firms (SMEs) account for a sizeable portion of all businesses worldwide and are essential to stimulating economic growth, creating job opportunities, and fostering regional expansion (OECD, 2020). Small and medium-sized enterprises' (SMEs') business practises have a big impact on the larger socioeconomic and ecological setting, especially in terms of environmental sustainability. This is a result of SMEs having a significant economic impact (Gadenne, Kennedy, & McKeiver, 2009). The importance of integrating environmental sustainability into the operational strategies of small and medium-sized businesses (SMEs) has grown.

Nowadays, businesses of all sizes are encouraged, if not required, to understand and reduce their ecological footprints as a crucial component of their strategic and

Priya Sachdeva, Amity School of Communication, Amity University, Noida, India
Archan Mitra, School of Media Studies, Presidency University, Bangalore, India

https://doi.org/10.1515/9783111170022-017

operational decisions (Revell & Rutherfoord, 2003). A number of variables, including as statutory requirements, customer preferences, and the moral duty to address the detrimental effects of commercial operations on the environment, have contributed to the development of sustainable business practises (Schaper, 2002a). Despite the incentive to do so, small and medium-sized businesses (SMEs) have unique challenges when implementing sustainable practises. According to Gadenne et al. (2009), these difficulties are caused by a variety of limitations, such as scarce resources, inadequate knowledge, and institutional hurdles.

The commercial environment, particularly in the area of marketing, has undergone tremendous change as a result of the development of digital technology. Digital marketing, according to Kumar and Rajan (2012), is the use of digital technology, mostly on the Internet, to advertise goods or services. Small and medium-sized businesses (SMEs) have been able to improve their competitive edge through process optimization, client reach expansion, and business process improvement thanks to this strategy. Enterprises now have more options than ever to customize their marketing efforts, optimize their use of resources, and make well-informed decisions thanks to the introduction of data-driven strategies in the field of digital marketing (Wedel & Kannan, 2016).

Notable is the possibility for small and medium-sized businesses (SMEs) to advance their environmental sustainability goals through the use of data-driven digital marketing techniques. The environmental benefits of digital marketing over traditional marketing channels, such as less paper use and carbon emissions, have long been recognized (Sarkar & Costa, 2008). As a result, 4.0 has tremendous potential to improve resource efficiency and sustainably generate commercial value across all social, economic, and environmental spheres (Mehta et al., 2019). Additionally, small and medium-sized firms (SMEs) can improve resource allocation, reduce inefficiencies, and create environmentally friendly business decisions by having the ability to collect, examine, and interpret significant amounts of data (Erevelles, Fukawa, & Swayne, 2016).

The ecological sustainability of small and medium-sized businesses (SMEs) and the potential role of data-driven digital marketing tactics in achieving this goal are the two research fields that come together in this study. Although each of these fields has been the subject of much investigation on its own, there is little literature connecting them. By examining how small and medium-sized businesses (SMEs) can use data-driven digital marketing techniques to enhance their environmental performance and significantly advance the larger sustainability goals, the current study seeks to fill the aforementioned research gap.

Research Objectives

Based on the focus of the literature review, the following research objectives can be derived:
- To analyze the current role of digital marketing in SMEs
- To explore the interplay between SMEs and environmental sustainability
- To investigate the potential of data-driven digital marketing strategies in promoting environmental sustainability in SMEs

Literature Review

A comprehensive review of literature was conducted in accordance with the PRISMA guidelines (Moher, Liberati, Tetzlaff, & Altman, 2009) to synthesize information from diverse scholarly databases. A thorough search was conducted using particular keywords such "SMEs," "digital marketing," "data-driven strategies," and "environmental sustainability" in the databases Google Scholar, Scopus, and EBSCOhost. Excluding redundant and unnecessary papers was the main goal of the initial scan, which resulted in a final selection of 34 pertinent publications for further analysis.

In order to increase their market reach and competitive advantage, small and medium-sized firms (SMEs) must now include data-driven strategies and digital marketing into their business models (Kumar & Rajan, 2012). Academic experts including Chaffey and Ellis-Chadwick (2019), Wedel and Kannan (2016), and have stressed the need of implementing these methods in order to increase revenue, customer engagement, and operational efficiency. The importance of Small and Medium-sized Enterprises (SMEs) in fostering environmental sustainability is also growing at the same time. Gadenne et al. (2009), Revell and Rutherfoord (2003), and Schaper (2002b) have all looked at the possibility of small and medium-sized firms (SMEs) having a beneficial influence on environmental sustainability. However, these studies have shown that SMEs usually face challenges like limited resources and a lack of expertise in this field.

An important turning point for the future of SME operations is the convergence of digital marketing and environmental sustainability inside small and medium-sized firms (SMEs). In their scholarly publications, Sarkar and Costa (2008) as well as Erevelles, Fukawa, and Swayne (2016) examined how digital marketing might help businesses reduce their environmental impact and promote sustainable business decisions. The results of this systematic research point to a promising area of opportunity where data-driven tactics, digital marketing, and environmental sustainability converge, which may result in a number of advantages. However, it emphasizes the need for more research to clarify the practical issues, challenges, and prospects in this area.

Theoretical Framework

Data Driven Decision Making for SMEs

Data-driven decision-making, as defined by Provost and Fawcett (2013), is the process of making choices based on data analysis rather than merely on intuition. A marketer has the choice to choose advertisements based on instinct and personal experience or by looking at facts related to how different adverts were received by customers. The definitions of business intelligence and marketing intelligence reflect their contribution to decision-making facilitation. Popovi et al. (2012) claim that intelligence systems are essential in supplying businesses with high-quality information that is essential for their decision-making processes. Decision-makers have the benefit of quick information access, effective analysis, and correct information presentation thanks to intelligence systems. Due to the adoption of intelligent systems, small and medium-sized businesses (SMEs) are capable of making informed judgements and carrying out suitable activities. According to Popovi et al. (2012), the ability to think creatively, plan strategically, make correct predictions, and solve problems effectively is what is meant by innovation. The outcomes shown in Figure 17.1 show the beneficial effects of combining marketing intelligence with data-driven decision-making techniques on the development of activities that result in value creation. The study also reveals the moderating role of the asset orchestration capability and the intermediary role of the search and selection capacity. A SME's ability to search and select can shed light on the relationship between the use of marketing intelligence and data-driven decision-making, as marketing intelligence provides decision-makers and marketers with pertinent and superior information that enhances their decision-making abilities. Addi-

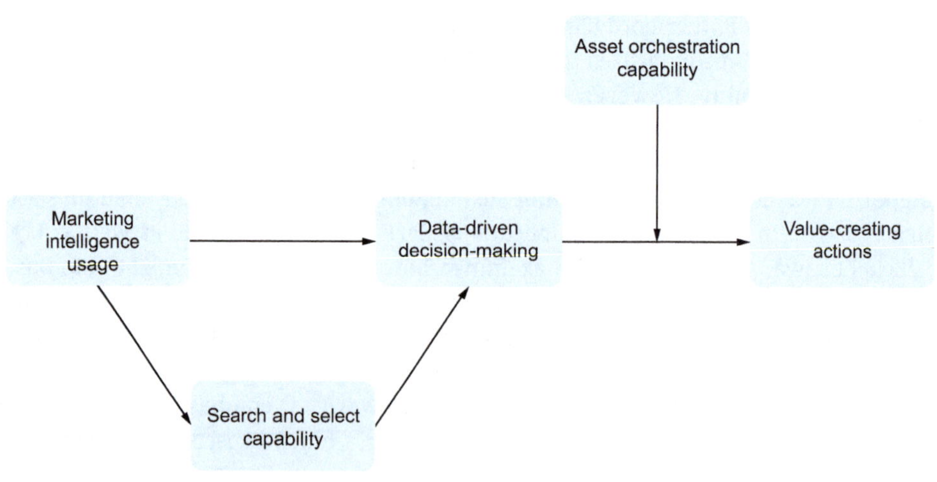

Figure 17.1: Theoretical Framework.

tionally, the ability to orchestrate assets has a positive effect on the relationship between data-driven decision-making and actions that produce value. SMEs' efficient asset orchestration, based on judgements drawn from their marketing intelligence platform, makes it easier to carry out value-creating operations (Boekelder, 2018).

The abundance of data that marketing managers and other people in positions of power must deal with nowadays has made data-driven decision-making a crucial component of small and medium-sized businesses. This suggests that choices are justified by facts, not by feelings or anecdotes, but by empirical data. Despite the use of marketing intelligence in decision-making, the activities that follow may not always result in value generation. The results of this study show that small and medium-sized businesses (SMEs) must have the ability to put these decisions into practise by efficiently managing their resources. According to some researchers, a subject matter expert's (SME) managerial practises for executing change determine their capacity to orchestrate assets. As a result, it is crucial for marketing managers and other important decision-makers to take the proper actions after making their choices. Small and medium-sized businesses' (SMEs) capacity to respond to market changes is essential to their success, with the speed at which they make campaign alterations being a deciding factor. Small and medium-sized businesses (SMEs) that are agile in adjusting to new circumstances are more likely to succeed in an era of fast change. According to Huang et al. (2014), the ability to adapt is a crucial skill that affects a firm's capacity to succeed in changing environments. Small and medium-sized businesses (SMEs) must therefore be flexible and have the ability to change their operational plans. Additionally, there is a chance that costs will go up since marketing activities need to be changed. The findings suggest that, if they can efficiently coordinate their resources, small and medium-sized businesses (SMEs) can successfully implement decisions obtained from their marketing intelligence systems and complete actions that produce value. On the basis of the findings of this inquiry, the theoretical framework is ad-

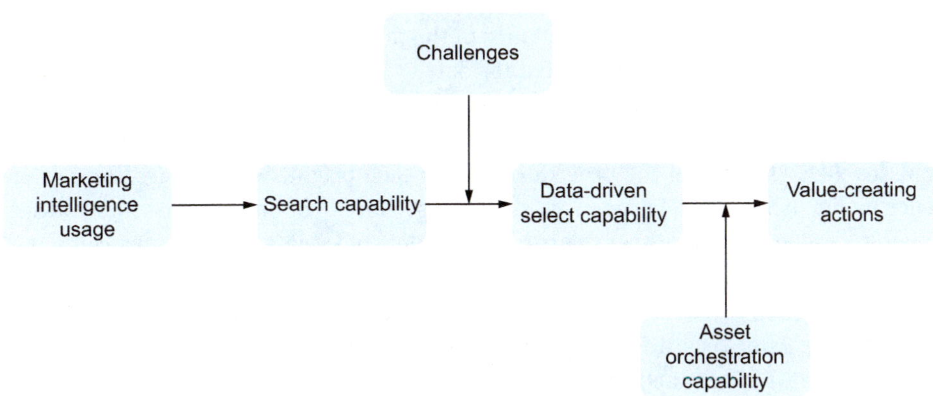

Figure 17.2: New Theoretical Framework.

justed. As a result, a unique framework is suggested, building on the findings of the interviews and surveys that were done. The aforementioned model, created by (Boekelder, 2018), is shown in Figure 17.2.

Data-Driven Decision Support for Manufacturing SMEs

Manufacturing SMEs use more IT systems to automatically collect data. Data is kept in databases and file servers in the heterogeneous IT landscape, but it is not integrated or used for decision support. It promotes data-driven decision support in SMEs, particularly in manufacturing project management. Researchers have examined various fields of research related to the manufacturing sector (Mehta et al., 2022). SimCast is a four-step method model to help firms understand the benefits of data analytics, visual analytics, and big data to better manage their projects as depicted in Figure 17.3.

Phase 1—Pre-project: The pre-project, dubbed Quickcheck, must specify participant expectations and clarify next stages. Since this phase's costs aren't value-added, SMEs often view it as lost time. "The later changes to a product (or project) become necessary, the more expensive it becomes," firms disregard.

Interviews assess firm data availability and use. Recording data availability, data provision, data processing, and IT infrastructure at the moment of analysis is the focus. The interview will also reveal how the organization plans project durations, notably logistical processes, and how much historical project data is used to anticipate future project durations. Comparing firm data to data requirements aids this conclusion. This phase encompasses the company's data utilization, processing, and visualization goals.

Phase 2: Process Analysis and Mapping: The process model should present and describe production and logistics value-adding operations (Pfeffer, M., 2014). After that, a top-down analysis and acceptance of the processes are done. After BPMN documentation, each process is inspected for data creation, sources, and infrastructure.

Reuse defines a reference model. It is a suitable pattern for the class of technical or business data to be modelled (Koch, 2011). Value-adding procedures are categorized for this. Before applying the procedure model, each production area creates a reference model. Ishikawa diagrams first show cause-and-effect linkages. Assembly, disassembly, and production areas record estimation parameters for each production phase. All estimating parameters schedule the production area. The categorization lets you compare production areas and detect probable links that affect process duration already. After recording the process, compare it to the reference process and describe the value-adding activities to create the specification sheet in step three.

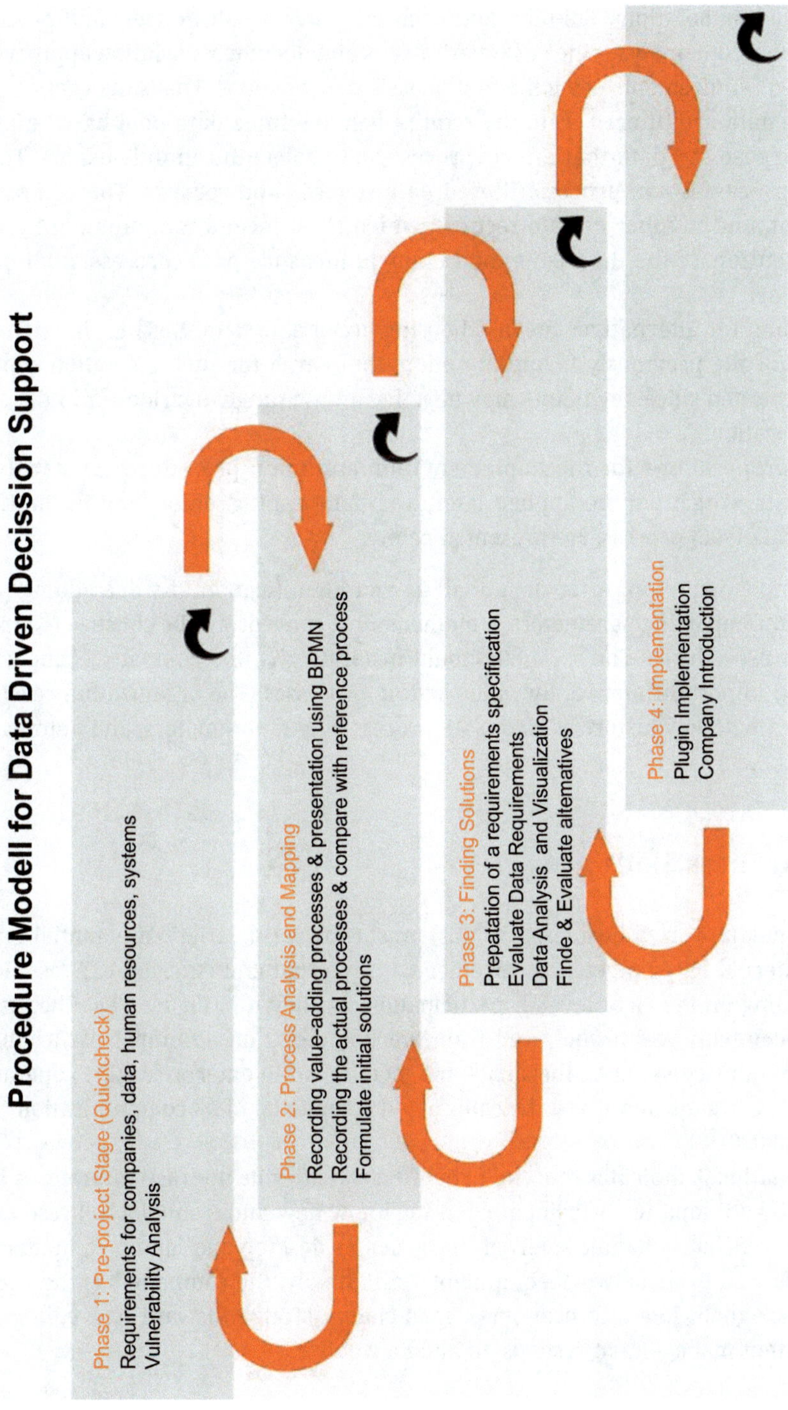

Figure 17.3: Procedure Model for Data Driven Decision Support.

Phase 3: Finding Solutions: Solution approaches involve a holistic view and processing. The consultant analyses the customer's needs and documents solution approaches and detailed requirements using the first phase's specifications. That's the goal.

Usable data are filtered from the requirements-defined data pool based on the inquiry purpose. All data that affects process and project duration is usable. Thus, all target processes can process filtered data sources and records. The completeness, extent, and number of data records, which must meet a minimum, are given special attention. If the data isn't good enough, measure or record essential data from the start.

Searching for alternatives means choosing acceptable data. Despite the high acceptability of the previously favoured option, the search for such a solution should not be discounted since key points may have been unwittingly overlooked in the earlier consideration.

Basic preparations for the implementation and main procedures of statistical data analysis, which will be applied later, and data mining, embedded in the KDD (Fayyad et al., 1996) process, are presented below.

Phase 4: Implementation: After data analysis and identification of value-adding process duration impacting parameters, a mathematical concept will be constructed from calculation procedures. The solution should instantly give the company influencing criteria and important metrics for value-adding processes. The organization receives a dashboard with key historical data, SME process length parameters, and automated suggestions.

SME e-Business Skills

Small and medium-sized businesses (SMEs) must consider a variety of potential internal and external ICT competences together with internal and external ICT resources when deciding on the right level of participation, as shown in Figure 17.4. The placement of a company within the given framework depends on a number of variables, such as the industry in which the small- and medium-sized enterprise (SME) operates, the size of the organization, and the calibre and complexity of its communication (Depaoli et al., 2020).

Combination A indicates that the firm often classifies its interaction levels as low or medium. Additionally, the company has the know-how and technological resources required to efficiently handle internal gear, such as desktop and laptop computers, a few servers, and basic network equipment. Additionally, the company has the necessary software tools, like web browsers, email clients, straightforward web editors, or simple content management systems, to build a website.

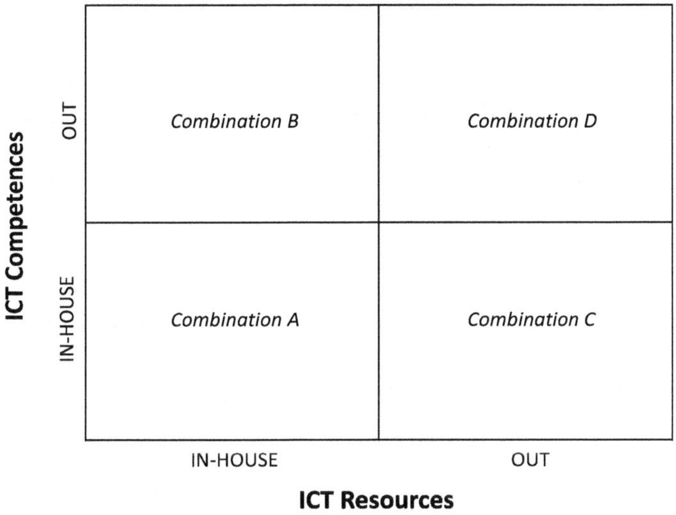

Figure 17.4: SME e-Business Skills.

Combination B, marked as medium or high interaction levels, combines internal technology with external expertise, such as a technology consultant, to make it easier to use specific software for support needs. Engaging with professional service providers is one method for gaining the specialized skills required for fundamental customer engagement activities.

Combination C stands out for its moderate to high degrees of engagement, which are driven by internal capabilities and outside technology like an application service provider (ASP). To satisfy client needs, this entails putting in place high-performance infrastructure and systems to manage heavy traffic loads on online portals. To effectively manage relationships with the supplier, a particular level of internal skills must be possessed.

A significant and thorough degree of interaction defines Combination D. The suggested remedy entails outsourcing, which entails transferring technical capabilities to a third party provider. This is often the solution chosen for supply chain management systems.

Advisory services, whether publicly funded or not, may serve as a means to reduce the risk of small and medium-sized enterprises succumbing to the current state of the information and communication technology (ICT) market. According to these permutations, small and medium-sized enterprises (SMEs) must possess proficient managerial skills and a certain level of comprehension regarding the current state of the ICT market to effectively select optimal e-commerce solutions that cater to their requirements.

Interaction-Based e-Business Development Model

The nonlinear development model shown in Figure 17.5 is meant to help business owners understand the several levels of interactions and the internal and external actors involved in the planning and execution of e-business. The efficiency enhancements that AI makes possible can also benefit alternative energy sources. Businesses are already using this technology to determine the daily availability of energy-generating facilities like wind turbines, hydroelectric plants, biomass plants, and others (Sharma et al., 2021). The management of SME's can use digital technologies to determine the levels of contact that are now possible as well as those that could profit from the application of specific digital solutions. The model's capacity to incorporate the interactions carried out by the organization gives it a distinct benefit in the context of SMEs (Depaoli et al., 2020).

Three essential ideas, including the integration of interaction, the fusion of technology and organization, and the redefining of e-business, have been used to develop the model.

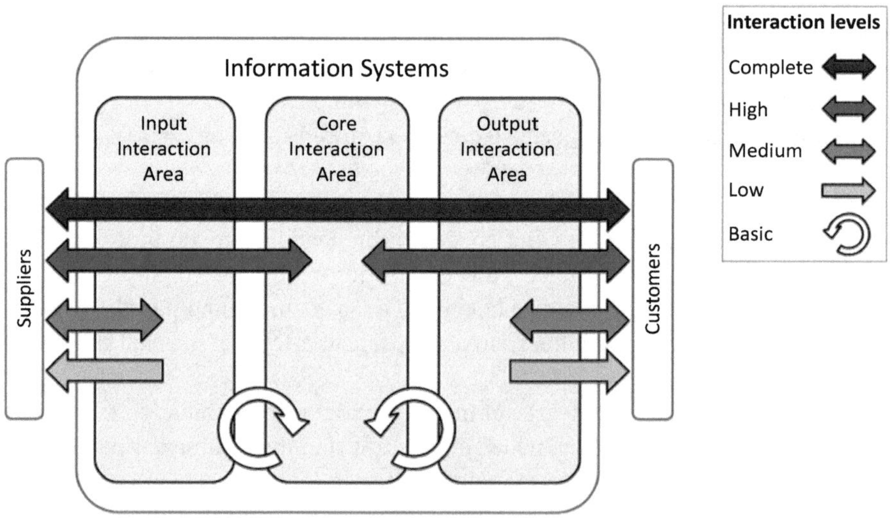

Figure 17.5: Interaction Based e-Business Model.

The concept of integrating interaction pertains to the integration of digital and non-digital modes of interaction employed by individuals, teams, and organizational units to facilitate internal and external communication in the pursuit of the firm's business goals. The relevance of interaction in organization theory is evident as it employs diverse approaches to elucidate the matter of coordination and integration.

Digital Marketing and Data-Driven Strategies in SMEs

The use of data-driven tactics and digital marketing is expanding inside the Small and Medium Enterprises (SMEs) business models. These businesses are always adapting their strategies to fit with changing customer needs and technical advancements in response to the dynamic digital world. The practise of using digital technology, with a particular concentration on the Internet, in order to promote goods and services is referred to as "digital marketing" (Kumar & Rajan, 2012). Small and medium-sized businesses (SMEs) can now take use of a wide variety of digital marketing channels thanks to the rise of social media, search engines, and mobile technologies.

The importance of digital marketing in enhancing the competitiveness and market reach of small and medium-sized firms (SMEs) has been proven in the literature. Digital marketing offers a cost-effective way for small and medium-sized businesses (SMEs) to compete in the market and broaden their audience reach, claim Chaffey and Ellis-Chadwick (2019). By employing digital technologies, small and medium-sized businesses (SMEs) have the opportunity to grow their client base beyond regional boundaries. They are now able to interact with clients on a global scale because to this. Instantaneous and direct engagement with clients is made possible by digital marketing, which can help build relationships and increase customer satisfaction and loyalty (Kumar & Rajan, 2012). Additionally, by using digital marketing, small and medium-sized businesses (SMEs) may compete on an even playing field with their larger competitors. Digital marketing platforms like social media and email marketing can be accessed with minimum costs, in contrast to traditional marketing channels that generally need considerable financial inputs. Small and medium-sized businesses (SMEs) can build their brand and communicate their value proposition without spending a lot of money on marketing, claim Chaffey and Ellis-Chadwick (2019).

Digital marketing requires the use of data-driven methods, which involve using data analytics to guide decision-making. The aforementioned techniques are predicated on the idea that data may provide essential insights into customer behaviour, market trends, and business performance provided it is properly studied and analysed. Wedel and Kannan (2016) assert that the use of data-driven techniques can enhance several aspects of digital marketing, such as customer segmentation, targeting, performance measurement, and optimization.

The adoption of data-driven strategies is connected with a number of benefits for small and medium-sized businesses (SMEs). First of all, it lets businesses to tailor their marketing campaigns by sending tailored messages and promotions to certain customers. According to Wedel and Kannan (2016), the use of data analytics to enable personalization has the potential to significantly boost consumer engagement and raise conversion rates. Additionally, putting data-driven techniques into practise can help small and medium-sized businesses make the most of their resources. According to Rojas-Méndez, Meyer, and Chapa (2020), organizations may efficiently allocate resources by identifying the marketing activities that produce the highest return on investment.

Data-driven approaches have the significant benefit of promoting well-informed decision-making. Due to their limited resources and the volatile nature of the market, small and medium-sized businesses (SMEs) commonly deal with unpredictability. Data analytics can reduce uncertainty and speed up decision-making by delivering accurate and timely insights. This strategy can support continual learning and improvement, allowing organizations to successfully adapt to changing conditions and thrive, claim Rojas-Méndez et al. (2020). For small and medium-sized businesses (SMEs), the use of data-driven strategies and digital marketing offers enormous possibilities. These elements may boost competitiveness, broaden market penetration, maximize operational effectiveness, and encourage reasoned decision-making. Small and medium-sized businesses (SMEs) must adopt these approaches and continually improve their knowledge and skills in order to be competitive in the market given the rapidly changing digital environment.

SMEs and Environmental Sustainability

Small and Medium-sized Enterprises (SMEs) are not exempt from the need for enterprises to take into account the issue of environmental sustainability. Because they make up a sizeable portion of the global economy, small and medium-sized businesses (SMEs) have the potential to significantly contribute to both the creation and the mitigation of environmental effects. Small and medium-sized businesses (SMEs) must think about their ecological impact and work to implement sustainable business practises given the worsening environmental problems and growing public interest about sustainability. Due to their massive ecological footprints and prominent public presence, multinational firms have historically been the focus of scholarly research on corporate sustainability. Due to the significant number of SMEs and their combined impact, experts have recognized the importance of environmental sustainability in the small and medium-sized firm (SME) sector (Schaper, 2002a). Small and medium-sized businesses (SMEs) may have small environmental footprints, but their combined impact is significant.

The contribution of small and medium-sized businesses (SMEs) to promoting environmental sustainability has been thoroughly analysed by Schaper (2002). The author contends that SMEs can contribute significantly through a variety of channels to the improvement of environmental sustainability. Small and medium-sized businesses (SMEs) can reduce the amount of waste they produce, use less energy, and promote recycling practises throughout their operations. Additionally, small and medium-sized businesses (SMEs) usually have close relationships to the communities in which they operate, providing a chance to encourage the adoption of environmentally friendly practises within those communities. Despite the potential advantages, many small and medium-sized businesses face challenges when seeking to integrate environmental sustainability practises into their daily operations. Small and medium-sized businesses (SMEs) commonly experience resource constraints, such as financial, human, and technological limitations, which limit their capacity to deploy resources towards sustainability objectives (Gadenne et al., 2009). Additionally, small and medium-sized businesses (SMEs) may lack awareness of the environmental effects of their operations and the potential benefits of adopting sustainable techniques. People may be discouraged from adopting sustainable practises if they view environmental regulation as a burden.

Small and medium-sized businesses (SMEs) can be encouraged to embrace environmentally sustainable practises by a number of variables, though. According to Revell and Rutherfoord's 2003 theory, the relevant drivers can be categorized as being either regulated, market-based, or ethical. Regulational pressures like environmental laws and regulations may inspire small and medium-sized businesses (SMEs) to improve their environmental performance. Customers' preferences for sustainable goods and services and the potential for cost savings through resource efficiency are examples of market-based variables. Contrarily, ethical incentives come from the personal beliefs that the owners and executives of a corporation have. Additionally, implementing environmental sustainability practises has the potential to benefit small and medium-sized businesses (SMEs) in a variety of ways. The adoption of sustainable practises can have positive financial effects, enhanced customer relationships, and improved business image in addition to reducing environmental harm. The application of energy efficiency techniques can lower operational expenses, according to Schaper's (2002b) research. Additionally, incorporating eco-friendly product designs may appeal to customers who place a high value on environmental sustainability. In conclusion, despite the challenges they face implementing sustainable practises, small and medium-sized businesses can still gain a lot by embracing environmental sustainability. Due to their combined impact on the environment, Small and Medium-Sized Enterprises (SMEs) must have environmental awareness and expertise. The active participation of policymakers, researchers, and business support agencies is responsible for the development of sustainable business practises among SMEs. These organizations are in charge of giving SMEs the information, resources, and incentives they need to successfully pursue sustainability.

Integrating Data-Driven Digital Marketing and Environmental Sustainability

As knowledge of environmental sustainability and digital marketing increases, so does awareness of the potential for synergistic interactions between these two fields. Small and medium-sized businesses (SMEs) have the dual challenge of increasing environmental sustainability while still preserving competitiveness in the digital economy, making the current issue particularly important to them. The combination of environmental sustainability and data-driven digital marketing might offer small and medium-sized businesses (SMEs) a fresh strategy to deal with the aforementioned difficulties. Data-driven digital marketing is being used more frequently today than ever before, giving firms a strong tool to improve consumer interaction, optimize resource allocation, and strengthen decision-making processes (Wedel & Kannan, 2016). According to Schaper (2002a), the need for environmental sustainability has become a critical economic imperative due to legislative requirements, consumer expectations, and moral considerations. The question focuses on how these two areas might converge.

Through the optimal use of resources, data-driven digital marketing has the potential to advance environmental sustainability. Digital marketing systems can gather enormous amounts of data, giving small and medium-sized businesses (SMEs) a thorough insight of consumer behaviour and market preferences. Small and medium-sized businesses (SMEs) can improve their marketing efforts by using this data, ensuring that their resources are allocated to the most productive activities. According to Erevelles, Fukawa, and Swayne (2016), the upshot of this approach may lead to less garbage being produced, less energy being used, and ultimately less of an influence on the environment. Additionally, the use of digital marketing can help to promote sustainable consumption. Small and medium-sized businesses (SMEs) can tailor their marketing communications to emphasize the ecological benefits of their services by using data analysis to get insight into the preferences and habits of consumers. This could lead to a shift in customer attitudes and actions in favour of more ecologically friendly products. According to a study by Sarkar and Costa (2008), businesses can use digital marketing tools to promote environmentally friendly items and encourage consumers to make eco-friendly purchases.

Utilising data-driven marketing strategies has the potential to improve transparency, which is essential for advancing environmental sustainability. By employing digital technologies, small and medium-sized businesses (SMEs) have the opportunity to tell different stakeholders, including clients, investors, and regulators, about their environmental performance. The aforementioned action has the potential to encourage trust, accountability, and continual improvement of environmental performance, claim Erevelles et al. (2016). However, there are some difficulties in combining data-driven digital marketing with environmental sustainability. Small and medium-sized firms (SMEs) usually struggle to utilize data and digital technologies because of a lack of resources and knowledge, according to Gadenne et al. (2009). Additionally, there could be tensions between commercial and environmental aims, which would call for a prudent approach to administration and equilibrium.

The potential benefits of this combination are remarkable, though. Environmental sustainability and data-driven digital marketing can be combined to increase environmental sustainability and the competitiveness of small and medium-sized businesses (SMEs). This approach aligns with the growing emphasis on sustainable corporate behaviour and the digital economy, positioning small and medium-sized firms (SMEs) for success in the modern day. In conclusion, the combination of ecological sustainability with data-centric digital marketing offers a favourable area for future research and application. Small and medium-sized businesses (SMEs) are faced with potential opportunities to bring fresh ideas, boost worth, and contribute to the betterment of society as the knowledge base in these fields grows.

Findings and Discussion

A number of conclusions are drawn from the systematic review of the literature and synthesis of the subjects covered. They can be grouped into three primary components that correlate to the earlier stated study aims.

The Function and Potential of Data-Driven Strategies and Digital Marketing in SMEs

According to the research, digital marketing and data-driven strategies have a large potential to improve SMEs' operational efficiency and competitiveness (Chaffey & Ellis-Chadwick, 2019; Kumar & Rajan, 2012; Wedel & Kannan, 2016). Due to the cost-effective platform that digital marketing offers SMEs, they can compete with larger companies while having more limited resources. Additionally, data-driven strategies give SMEs insightful knowledge of market trends and consumer behaviour, boosting resource optimization, decision-making, and customer engagement (Rojas-Méndez, Meyer, & Chapa, 2020).

Opportunities and Challenges in SMEs' Integration of Environmental Sustainability

The literature review emphasized both the significance of SMEs in promoting environmental sustainability and the difficulties they encounter in doing so (Gadenne, Kennedy, & McKeiver, 2009; Schaper, 2002a). Despite the potential benefits, SMEs sometimes lack the funding and knowledge needed to support sustainability projects. However, regulatory requirements, commercial demand, and ethical considerations push them in the direction of environmental sustainability (Revell & Rutherfoord, 2003). Additionally, environmental sustainability can provide a number of advantages, including cost savings, greater customer relations, and improved brand recognition for businesses (Schaper, 2002b).

Integrating Environmental Sustainability With Data-Driven Digital Marketing

A promising possibility for SMEs is the combination of data-driven digital marketing and environmental sustainability. Reduced waste, lower energy use, and smaller environmental footprints can all be attributed to data-driven strategies' efficient resource utilization (Erevelles, Fukawa, & Swayne, 2016). Additionally, SMEs can promote sustainable consumption and improve transparency about their environmental performance by using digital marketing tools. Despite the difficulties, this integration can have a positive impact on SMEs' competitiveness and overall sustainability (Erevelles et al., 2016; Sarkar & Costa, 2008).

The results support the existence of a research void at the nexus of environmental sustainability in SMEs, data-driven marketing, and digital marketing. This gap offers SMEs the chance to innovate, add value to their operations, and improve the environment all at the same time. As a result, this research helps to close the knowledge gap while providing useful recommendations for SMEs trying to navigate the digital world sustainably.

Conclusion

This study's goal was to look into how ecological sustainability, data-driven marketing strategies, and small and medium enterprises (SMEs) can all coexist. Each of the aforementioned topics has received a wealth of insights from the literature review when taken separately. However, it has also brought to light a significant gap in the literature where these topics overlap. The findings of this study demonstrate how effectively data-driven marketing strategies and small- and medium-sized enterprises' (SMEs') competitiveness may be increased. It is clear that small and medium-sized businesses (SMEs), despite facing challenges in integrating sustainable practises into their daily operations, have a substantial impact on environmental sustainability. The study's most important finding relates to the enormous potential for combining ecological sustainability and data-centric digital marketing. The adoption of a synergistic strategy enables small and medium-sized businesses (SMEs) to maximize the use of data, improving resource management efficiency, promoting sustainable consumption habits, increasing transparency, and generally improving environmental performance. In spite of the challenges, incorporating these approaches can give small and medium-sized businesses a competitive advantage and make a substantial contribution to the advancement of sustainability.

This study delivers fresh opportunities for upcoming scholarly exploration through the examination of this comparatively untouched topic and provides realistic viewpoints for small and medium-sized businesses. The study of strategies for successfully integrating ecological sustainability with data-driven digital marketing within small and medium-sized businesses (SMEs) will be a major area of focus in the emerging field of sustainable business practises. In conclusion, Small and Medium Enterprises (SMEs) play a varied and dynamic function in the modern business landscape that goes beyond traditional economic issues. The current study shows that small and medium-sized businesses (SMEs) have a significant edge when using data-driven strategies and digital marketing to achieve both economic success and ecological sustainability. Small and medium-sized businesses (SMEs) must use creative, adaptable, and responsible methods to successfully navigate the digital and environmental frontiers.

References

Boekelder, S. (2018). "*The impact of marketing intelligence on SMEs* (Master's thesis)", University of Twente).

Chaffey, D., & Ellis-Chadwick, F. (2019). "Digital marketing", Pearson UK.

Depaoli, P., Za, S., & Scornavacca, E. (2020). "A model for digital development of SMEs: an interaction-based approach", *Journal of Small Business and Enterprise Development*, *27*(7), 1049–1068.

Emmanouilidis, C., Taisch, M., Kiritsis, D. (2012). "Advances in Production Managemnt Systems – Competitive Manufacturing for Innovative Products and Services", IFIP WG 5.7 International Conference, APMS 2012 Rhodes Greece, September 24–26, 2012, Revised Selected Papers, Part I, Springer Heidelberg, 2012.

Erevelles, S., Fukawa, N., & Swayne, L. (2016). "Big Data consumer analytics and the transformation of marketing", *Journal of Business Research*, *69*(2), 897–904.

Fayyad, U., Piatetsky-Shapiro, G., Smyth, P. (1996). "From Data Mining to Knowledge Discovery in Databases, American Association for Artificial Intelligence", in: AI Magazine, Vol. 17, No. 3, S. 41, 1996

Gadenne, D., Kennedy, J., & McKeiver, C. (2009). "An empirical study of environmental awareness and practices in SMEs", *Journal of Business Ethics*, *84*(1), 45–63.

Gudehus, T. (1993): Logistik – Grundlagen, Strategien, Anwendungen, 3., neu bearbeitete Auflage, Springer-Verlag Berlin Heidelberg 2004 und 2005, in: Baumgarten, H., Prozessanalyse logistischer Abläufe, Fabrik 43, Jahrgang 6, 1993

Huang, P. Y., Pan, S. L., & Ouyang, T. H. (2014). "Developing information processing capability for operational agility: implications from a Chinese manufacturer", *European Journal of Information Systems*, *23*(4), 462–480.

Koch, S. (2011): Einführung in das Management von Geschäftsprozessen – Six Sigma, Kaizen und TQM, 1. Auflage, Springer-Verlag Berlin Heidelberg, 2011

Kumar, V., & Rajan, B. (2012). "Social coupons as a marketing strategy: a multifaceted perspective", *Journal of the Academy of Marketing Science*, *40*(1), 120–136.

Mehta, K., Sharma, R., & Vyas, V. (2019). "Efficiency and ranking of sustainability index of India using DEA-TOPSIS", *Journal of Indian Business Research*, *11*(2), 179–199. https://doi.org/10.1108/JIBR-02-2018-0057.

Mehta, K., Sharma, R., & Vyas, V. (2022). "A quantile regression approach to study the impact of aluminium prices on the manufacturing sector of India during the COVID era", *Materials Today: Proceedings*, *65*(8), 3506–3511, ISSN 2214-7853, https://doi.org/10.1016/j.matpr.2022.06.087.

Moher, D., Liberati, A., Tetzlaff, J., & Altman, D. G. (2009). "Preferred reporting items for systematic reviews and meta-analyses: the PRISMA statement", *PLoS Med*, *6*(7), e1000097.

OECD (2020). "Small and Medium Enterprises (SMEs)", Retrieved from: https://www.oecd.org/cfe/smes/

Pfeffer, M. (2014): Bewertung von Wertströmen, Kosten-Nutzen-Betrachtung von Optimierungsszenarien, Springer Fachmedien, Wiesbaden, 2014

Popovič, A., Hackney, R., Coelho, P. S., & Jaklič, J. (2012). "Towards business intelligence systems success: Effects of maturity and culture on analytical decision making", *Decision Support Systems*, *54*(1), 729–739.

Provost, F., & Fawcett, T. (2013). "Data science and its relationship to big data and data-driven decision making", *Big data*, *1*(1), 51–59.

Queckbörner, S. (o. J.): Was ist Data Mining?, Technische Universität Kaiserslautern, o. J.

Revell, A., & Rutherfoord, R. (2003). "UK environmental policy and the small firm: broadening the focus", *Business Strategy and the Environment*, *12*(1), 26–35.

Sarkar, A. N., & Costa, A. I. A. (2008). "Dynamics of open innovation in the food industry", *Trends in Food Science & Technology*, *19*(11), 574–580.

Schaper, M. (2002). "Small firms and environmental management: predictors of green purchasing in Western Australian pharmacies", *International Small Business Journal*, *20*(3), 235–251.

Schaper, M. (2002). "The essence of ecological sustainability in SMEs in Australia", *Greener Management International*, *2002*(38), 89–99.

Sharma, A. & Sharma, R. (2022). "Exploring Tax Decision Factors: A Perspective from North Indian Tax Practitioners", *Journal of Tax Reform*, *8*(3): 285–297. https://doi.org/10.15826/jtr.2022.8.3.122

Sharma, R., Mehta, K. & Sharma, O. (2021). "Exploring Deep Learning to Determine the Optimal Environment for Stock Prediction Analysis", *2021 International Conference on Computational Performance Evaluation, ComPE* 2021, 148–152.

Sharma, R., Reynolds, P., Scheepers, R., Seddon, P. B., & Shanks, G. G. (2010). "Business Analytics and Competitive Advantage: A Review and a Research Agenda", In DSS (pp. 187–198).

Wedel, M., & Kannan, P. K. (2016). "Marketing analytics for data-rich environments", *Journal of Marketing*, *80*(6), 97–121.

Wikum, E. (o.J.): Making Analytics work through practical project management. Online: http://analytics-magazine.org/making-analytics-work-through-practical-project-management/

List of Contributors

Shivani Bajaj is Assistant Professor in Marketing and Finance at Maharishi Markandeshwar (deemed to be) University, Mullana, Ambala. She is a graduation and postgraduation Gold Medallist and has a multifarious experience in teaching and research. She obtained her MBA from GLA University, Mathura, India. Her areas of expertise are finance, marketing and research.

M. Chithra Balamurugan, is Assistant professor of Human Resource Management at GSB. As an academician for nine years, her past workplaces include VJIM (Hyderabad) and Veltech (Chennai). As a corporate trainer, she has conducted personality development sessions in various corporate companies and educational institutions. MRF, Nokia and Loyola top her clientele list. Her areas of expertise include stress management, communication skills and interpersonal skills. She is a Masterclass IELTS trainer. She did her postgraduation in Management from Pondicherry Central University with HR as her area of specialization. She completed her M.Phil. from Alagappa University and earned a doctorate from Hyderabad Central University in green human resource management. She has presented her research work at conferences and workshops and has also published in national and international journals.

Vyomkesh Bhatt is currently Assistant Professor in Department of Management Studies, G L Bajaj Institute of Technology and Management, Greater Noida. He has completed his master's and bachelor's degrees with honours in finance and is currently pursuing his Ph.D. in the banking domain.

Vinita Choudhary has a Ph.D. in finance (October 2020) and an M.Sc. (Mathematics), MBA (Finance/IT) with a qualitative experience of 4+ years in the education field. Currently she is Assistant Professor in the School of Management and Commerce. Since 2011 she has taught many courses to undergraduate and postgraduate students of business administration programmes at reputed management colleges. She teaches financial and mathematical subjects including financial management business mathematics, business statistics, operation research to BBA, B.Com, MBA students. She has participated in various national and international workshops, seminars, conferences, and faculty development programmes.

Archana Goel is Assistant Professor at Chitkara Business School. She has M.Com, B.Ed., and Ph.D. degrees and has 12 years of corporate and academic experience. Her Ph.D. is in corporate governance. Her research areas include corporate governance, mergers and acquisitions, financial reporting, etc. She is specialized in teaching accounts, statistics, research methodology and finance courses. She has around 20 papers published in national and international journals of repute and has attended several conferences at the national and international level.

Prayag Gokhale is Head of the Department of MBA at KLE Technological University (Dr. M S Sheshgiri College of Engg. and Tech., Belgaum). He has experience in the area of teaching management subjects for over a decade, and is currently Associate Professor and Placement officer at KLE DR. MSSCET, Belgaum. He has completed his Ph.D. from VTU, Belgaum in the area of behavioural finance which deals with understanding the behaviour of investors in the Indian context. He has also completed more than 20 certification courses from national and international universities in the areas of data science and analytics. He has conducted a number of workshops on MS Excel, MS Access, and statistical tools and software. He has nine international publications in reputed journals to his credit and has also presented eight papers at international and national conferences.

Anshul Jain is an accomplished professional with a diverse background and a passion for making a positive impact in various domains. Holding a B.Tech and M.Tech degree in addition to expertise in Mass Communication MAJMC, he brings a unique blend of technical knowledge and communication skills to his

https://doi.org/10.1515/9783111170022-018

work. As the State Head, he has demonstrated exceptional leadership abilities, effectively managing and leading teams to achieve organizational goals. His strategic vision and ability to navigate complex challenges have earned him respect and recognition in his position. Furthermore, as a Life Skills Trainer, Anshul equips individuals with essential life skills that are instrumental in navigating both personal and professional challenges. His training programmes focus on enhancing self-confidence, communication, and problem-solving abilities.

Neha Kamboj is Assistant Professor in the School of Management, IILM University, Gurugram. She has more than nine years of academic experience and has chaired two conferences and filed six patents. She is also the reviewer of various Scopus indexed journals. Since 2013 she has taught many courses to undergraduate (UG) and postgraduate (PG) students of business administration programmes at reputed management institutes. She teaches financial management, corporate accounting, accounting for business, financial reporting and analysis, multinational financial management, capital market, elements of banking and Indian financial system and financial markets to BBA, B.Com, MBA students. She has participated in various national and international workshops, seminars, conferences, faculty development programmes to keep herself updated and well equipped with the latest innovations and changes in the fields of finance and banking.

Praveen M. Kulkarni is Professor at KLS Institute of Management Education and Research, Belagavi. He has published more than 30 papers in various international journals and conferences and has many research grants to his credit. His experience in the field of academics and industry extends over a period of 20 years. His areas of interest include human resource management, leadership, and psychometric testing.

CS Priyanka Mathur is currently Assistant Professor in the area of finance at the Prestige Institute of Management and Research (PIMR), Indore. She has been associated with PIMR Indore since December 2016. She has also worked as a Guest Faculty at the International Institute of Professional Studies (IIPS) at DAVV in the year 2017. She has two years' corporate experience with Radius Corporate Solutions (India) Pvt. Ltd. where she handled work related to international accounting and taxation. She has handled various academic and administrative responsibilities related to student activities, webinars, examinations and admissions. She has been a speaker at various student induction training programmes at the Institute of Company Secretaries of India (ICSI).

Kiran Mehta is Professor of Finance at Chitkara Business School, possessing 20 years of teaching and research experience. She is a distinguished author, having written the book *Financial Services* published by Cengage, and she holds a doctoral degree in the field of Anomalous Behaviour of Stock Prices in India. With her expertise, she guides Ph.D. candidates from both industry and academia and has contributed to the development of study materials for prestigious institutions such as Jamia Millia Islamia, IMT-Ghaziabad, and Gauhati University. Dr. Kiran has a rich academic profile, including organizing international conferences, conducting workshops, delivering expert lectures, and serving as a respected reviewer for renowned journals.

Archan Mitra is Assistant Professor at School of Media Studies (SOMS), at Presidency University, Bangalore. He has edited various publications and authored *Cases for Classroom Media and Entertainment Business*, an IIM textbook. His doctorate at Visva-Bharati Santiniketan, West Bengal was on "Environmental informatics and communication for sustainability". He is also a qualified science communicator and journalist for the Indian Science Communication Society (ISCOS), corporate trainer with Amity Institute of Training and Development, and social media network analyst. He loves environmental communication. He has received the Journalistic Club of Kolkata Medal of Honour and PRSI Kolkata Chapter Certificate of

Merit. He was a World Bank research assistant at IIM Kashipur. He has published papers in Q1 and Q2 journals in research partnership with IIM Kashipur.

Chaman Lal Pal is a research scholar in the Mechanical Engineering department at NIT Raipur, Chhattisgarh. He holds a bachelor's degree in Mechanical Engineering (2010) and a master's degree in Hydropower Engineering (2013). With six years of teaching experience, his expertise lies in the fields of thermal comfort, building physics, and thermal engineering. Chaman Lal Pal's research interests revolve around these areas, where he actively explores innovative concepts and contributes to the advancement of knowledge.

Bhavesh Parmar, is presently Assistant Professor (Research Methodology) at National Forensic Sciences University, Gandhinagar, Gujarat. He obtained his Ph.D. in Management (2015) from Sardar Patel University (India). He has obtained M.Phil. and MBA degrees from HNGU, Patan (India). He teaches MBA programmes since 2008 in the areas of research methodology and marketing. He has contributed his research to peer reviewed journals, book chapters, monographs, national and international conferences. His teaching, research and consultancy interests are in the areas of marketing, marketing research, celebrity endorsement and event management. He is also a member of the editorial board and on the reviewer board of national and international journals.

Priya Rana is Research Scholar in the finance field at Lovely Professional University (LPU) and is also Assistant Professor at Sanatan Dharma College, Ambala Cantt. She has a bachelor's degree in Commerce (B.com) and a master's in Commerce (M.com) from Kurukshetra University, Kurukshetra. She also obtained a degree in Bachelor of Education from Kurukshetra University, Kurukshetra. She successfully completed the UGC NET (National Eligibility Test) in Commerce in the year 2017. Her research interests include impact investment, socially responsible investment and behavioural finance.

K. Lakshminarayana Reddy is currently working at VTU, Department of MBA as faculty in the domain of marketing. Dr. Reddy has published papers in reputed journals and books. He has also guiding Ph.D. students in the domain of management. He has conducted training programmes for industry and management professionals.

Priya Sachdeva is a pioneer in education and presently an Associate Professor at Amity School of Communication, Amity University, Noida, India. She has an MBA degree and was cited by Amity University for PG in Events &Public Relations (topper, gold medallist) in 2010. She has a Ph.D. in Mass Communication and has completed the Advanced Leadership Program from IIM Lucknow and her third postgraduation from Wharton University in 2022. She is a keen researcher, a passionate educationist and has 20+ years of experience in teaching and research. She is an author of five books. She is a Course Committee Member for Introduction of Mass Media in CBSE affiliated schools and received the International Award for Educational Excellence (2021) powered by Medi links India, Council for Brand Business Promotion and Research as one of the top 100 impactful education leaders in 2021. She is a member of ISTD, PRSI and other professional bodies.

Shefali Saluja obtained a Ph.D. in Management (Corporate Governance) from Chitkara University, Punjab, India in 2021 and has 10 years of experience in business management education and expertise in finance and ethics. She has three years of working experience in Ernst & Young Pvt Ltd prior to joining academics. She has published research papers/articles in highly indexed Scopus journals. She is a member of Association of Certified Fraud Examiner (ACFE) and International Association of Academic plus Corporate society (IAAC). She has filed two patents and five copyrights in diverse areas. Shefali has also been invited internationally including to Spain, Taiwan, Germany, Thailand to deliver sessions on fraud investigations. Her interests include voluntary work with NGOs.

Anupam Sharma is Associate Professor in Maharishi Markandeshwar (deemed to be) University, Mullana, Ambala. An MBA graduate with a Ph.D. in Management from Thapar University, Patiala he has over 18 years' experience in academics and research. He has published various research papers in renowned Scopus indexed national and international journals and books. His areas of interest are marketing and general management.

Renuka Sharma has over 20 years of extensive teaching and research experience, and is Professor of Finance at Chitkara Business School. She possesses an impressive publication track record, with more than 70 research papers published in renowned international and national journals. She has also presented her work at prestigious conferences, earning recognition through multiple best paper awards. As an accomplished author, she has contributed to the book *Financial Services*, published by Cengage. Additionally, she has taken on significant responsibilities as the convener of various international conferences, faculty development programmes, and workshops. Widely respected as an expert speaker, she delivers lectures on diverse topics, including technology innovation in financial markets, doing business in India, SPSS in research, case study analysis, and collaborative learning.

Kapil Shrimal is presently working as Associate Professor at National Institute of Securities Markets, Mumbai and has a Ph.D., MBA, NET and SET in finance. He has more than 15 years of experience in academics and the corporate world. His areas of research are financial markets, financial planning, derivatives, etc.

Navpreet Kaur Sidhu, a former banker, has expertise in business banking operations and has worked as a financial analyst in the corporate sector. Currently employed as Assistant Professor at Chitkara Business School, Chitkara University in Punjab, she is pursuing a Ph.D. in finance while holding a master's degree in finance. She has worked on several projects and served as a representative in India and Canada. With a multilingual skillset, she has won several debates and declarations, adding many honours to her name in public speaking. She is a committed member of WICCI (Women's Indian Chamber of Commerce and Industries) and affiliated with an NGO that promotes animal rights. She possess a copyright registration and has written chapters for several publications on technology and finance.

Priyanka Singh's academic achievements and expertise are in the fields of mathematical modelling, fuzzy logic, and regression analysis. With a master's degree in philosophy obtained in 2012 and a Ph.D. completed in 2018, she has demonstrated a strong commitment to education and research. As Assistant Professor at Government Naveen Girls College in Raipur, Chhattisgarh, Dr. Priyanka Singh has accumulated nine years of teaching experience. Her specialization in mathematical modelling leads to her focusing on applying mathematical concepts and techniques to real-world scenarios, aiming to understand and solve complex problems. Her expertise in fuzzy logic indicates her ability to develop and utilize computational models that can handle uncertainty and imprecision.

Ram Singh is a new age innovative educationist working as Professor at MM Institute of Management Maharishi Markandeshwar (deemed to be university) Mullana, Ambala, Haryana. Dr. Singh has a vast teaching and research experience of more than 14 years. Being a researcher, Dr. Singh holds multifarious positions in the field of academics, such as member of the editorial board of various reputed journals in the domain of Accounting, Finance and General Management, reviewer in IGI Global, Inderscience journals, member and chairperson of the Board of Faculty & Board of Study (Commerce & Management), member in Board of Management, etc. He has published nine books, 30 research papers, 30 book chapters, 10 conference proceedings. Apart from this he is a life member of six International zcademic organizations.

Nidhi Solanki is Assistant Professor with 16 years of work experience (six years in academics and 10 years in the corporate world) in reputed top-ranking universities with NAAC A++. He has a master's degree in finance and HR from ICFAI Hyderabad and is a graduate in commerce. Presently he is pursuing a doctoral degree from Bansthali Vidyapeeth Rajasthan and is interested in future roles in teaching, curriculum development, academic research, educational administration, course coordination, student counselling, classroom management, process development, training delivery management, performance management, impact analysis, leadership development, and organizational development.

Basavaraj S. Tigadi is currently working in the administrative section of Visvesvaraya Technological University (VTU), Belagavi, Karnataka. He has completed his MBA (Marketing), M.Com. and Ph.D (Management) degrees. He has more than 17 years of experience in educational organizations. He possesses strong interpersonal skills and communication skills. He has published many research papers in approved national and international journals.

Sonal Trivedi is Assistant Professor in Birla Global University, Orissa, India. She has two authored and two edited books. She has six patents granted and 10 Scopus indexed papers.

About the Editors

Dr. Kiran Mehta is Professor of Finance at Chitkara Business School, possessing 20 years of teaching and research experience. She is a distinguished author, having written the book *Financial Services* published by Cengage, and she holds a doctoral degree in the field of "Anomalous Behavior of Stock Prices in India." With her expertise, she guides Ph.D. candidates from both industry and academia and has contributed to the development of study materials for prestigious institutions such as Jamia Millia Islamia, IMT-Ghaziabad, and Gauhati University. Dr. Kiran has a rich profile, including organizing international conferences, conducting workshops, delivering expert lectures, and serving as a respected reviewer for renowned journals. Her teaching interests span various domains, including financial markets and services, financial management, and investment analysis. Presently, her research endeavors focus on sustainable business and entrepreneurship, cryptocurrency, ethical investments, and women entrepreneurship. Additionally, Dr. Kiran is the founder and director of a research and consultancy firm, further enhancing her contributions to the academic and professional community.

With over 20 years of extensive teaching and research experience, **Dr. Renuka Sharma** is Professor of Finance at Chitkara Business School. Her doctoral work centered around exploring the "Information Efficiency of the Indian Stock Market." She possesses an impressive publication track record, with more than 70 research papers published in renowned international and national journals. Dr. Renuka has also presented her work at prestigious conferences, earning recognition through multiple best paper awards. Currently, she supervises five Ph.D. scholars from both industry and academia. As an accomplished author, Dr. Renuka has contributed to the book *Financial Services*, published by Cengage. Additionally, she has taken on significant responsibilities as the convener of various international conferences, faculty development programs, and workshops. Widely respected as an expert speaker, Dr. Renuka delivers lectures on diverse topics, including technology innovation in financial markets, doing business in India, SPSS in research, case study analysis, collaborative learning, and cyber security. Her knowledge has transcended borders, as she has given expert talks at global learning courses held at BINUS University in Indonesia. Dr. Renuka actively serves as a reviewer for reputable journals and her teaching interests span security analysis & portfolio management, venture capital, financial management and financial modeling, financial services, derivatives, business research methods, and startup financing (VC&PE). Presently, her research concentrates on SMEs and innovation, responsible investment, corporate governance, behavioral biases, risk management, and portfolios.

https://doi.org/10.1515/9783111170022-019

List of Tables

https://doi.org/10.1515/9783111170022-020

List of Figures

https://doi.org/10.1515/9783111170022-021

Index

https://doi.org/10.1515/9783111170022-022